MAKERS
& BREAKERS

Children & Youth
in Postcolonial Africa

MAKERS & BREAKERS

**Children & Youth
in Postcolonial Africa**

Edited by
ALCINDA HONWANA & FILIP DE BOECK

JAMES CURREY
OXFORD

AFRICA WORLD PRESS
TRENTON

CODESRIA
DAKAR

James Currey
www.jamescurrey.com
is an imprint of Boydell & Brewer Ltd
PO Box 9, Woodbridge, Suffolk IP12 3DF, UK
and of Boydell & Brewer Inc.
668 Mt Hope Avenue, Rochester, NY 14620, USA
www.boydellandbrewer.com

Africa World Press
P.O. Box 1892
Trenton, NJ 08607, USA

Codesria
BP 3304, CP 18524, Dakar, Senegal

British Library Cataloguing in Publication Data
Makers & breakers : children & youth in postcolonial Africa
1. Children – Africa 2. Youth – Africa
I. Honwana, Alcinda II. Boeck, Filip De III. Codesria
305.2'3'096

ISBN 978-0-85255-434-0 (James Currey paper)

ISBN 978-2-86978-153-5 (Codesria paper)

Typeset in 10/10.5 pt Bembo by Avocet Typeset, Chilton, Aylesbury, Bucks

Dedication

In memory of
T.K. Biaya
(died 2002)

Contents

List of photographs

ALCINDA HONWANA & FILIP DE BOECK

Preface

The chapters for this volume are substantially revised versions of papers presented at two conferences held in 1999 in Cape Town, South Africa in June (organized by the SSRC Africa Program), and in Leuven, Belgium in November (organized by Alcinda Honwana and Filip De Boeck). Some additional chapters were solicited by the editors. The volume is unique in several ways. First, it stands out in the range of perspectives from which it draws, with most authors encompassing a variety of disciplines in developing their analytical frameworks. Second, it includes scholars from Africa, Europe and North America and thus offers new information and analysis from a variety of positions on the contemporary lives of African youth. At the same time, these perspectives dialogue and debate with each other in ways that integrate the work as a whole.

What is perhaps most exceptional about the work is the light it sheds on a social category that is under-studied and under-theorized in the social sciences, and misunderstood and stereotyped in public discourse. From Columbine High School to the Thai-Myanmar border where, until recently, twelve-year-old twin brothers were leading rebel attacks, the 'problem' of youth is being constructed as one of the great challenges of the twenty-first century. Nowhere is this question more acute than in Africa, where the micro-politics of households intersects with the macro-demography of huge numbers of young people, many of them unemployable in the formal sectors of national economies. This intersection preoccupies villages, government ministries and international organizations. Youth are portrayed as both perpetrators and victims in civil conflict, as leaders and led in movements of political reform and religious renewal, as innovators and dupes in the globalization of culture. None of these images are unique to Africa: indeed, they are global in scope. But by focusing an analytical lens on the lives of contemporary young Africans, the chapters in this volume establish 'youth' as an historically situated and thus mutable social category that allows us to imagine 'youth' beyond the images of the anomic and violent 'nature' of young people, on the one hand, and their purported ignorance and innocence, on the other. In this sense, the African cases presented here, and the theoretical tools used to comprehend them, have a much wider resonance. Indeed, the volume goes a long way in our understanding of young people as a global category and as vital social actors that connect the local to the global.

The volume takes on the themes of the constructed nature of youth (and children) as a social category and the question of youth agency as a way to navigate through the stereotypes of 'victim' and 'perpetrator'. The title 'Makers and Breakers' captures the complex realities of young people's lives: shaping and being shaped by their social world. The chapters are based on detailed field research in many parts of the continent and constitute a set of theoretically informed case studies. Both the dire circumstances and the extraordinary creativity of young Africans are revealed by taking seriously their voices, imaginations and desires. A portrait of youth emerges which encompasses not only a transitional stage on the road to a socially recognized adulthood, but also an identity with its own social and cultural forms. One of the great strengths of the volume is to show how those forms are particular to specific places (localities and nations) while still intersecting with (and troubling) global conceptions of 'youth'. This issue is an 'emergent category,' and we believe that the book has excellent potential to powerfully and critically inform and shape future debates on youth, in Africa and beyond.

We would like to thank the institutions which made this book possible. We gratefully acknowledge the Social Science Research Council (SSRC) in New York for sponsoring its distribution in Africa, and for organizing a brainstorming meeting on youth in Africa in 1999 that generated important discussions that informed the work. Some of the contributors to this volume took part in it, and the opening chapter of the volume came out of this meeting. A special word of thanks goes to Ron Kassimir, Program Director at the SSRC, for all his work and support. Special thanks to the VLIR, the Flemish inter-university Board (Vlaamse Inter-Universitaire Raad), without whose financial support we would not have been able to organize the international conference out of which the idea for the book arose. This conference was jointly organized by the two editors at the University of Leuven, Belgium (in November 1999), and some of the chapters in this book were especially written for that meeting. We would like to extend our thanks to the African Institute/Institut Africain and to its director, Gauthier de Villers, who unhesitatingly made some further funds available for the conference. We also thank Jan Ovesen for the financial contribution provided by the Anthropology Department of the University of Uppsala to the organization of the Leuven conference.

Notes on Contributors

Ibrahim Abdullah is a historian whose work focuses on African colonial and postcolonial history. He has taught in universities in Africa and North America. His most recent book, *Between Democracy and Terror: the Sierra Leone Civil War,* was published by CODESRIA/UNISA, in 2004.

Nicolas Argenti is a research lecturer in the Centre for Child-Focused Anthropological Research (C-FAR), Brunel University, London. He has conducted research on young people's responses to political violence in North West Province, Cameroon (1991-4) and in southern Sri Lanka (1996-8).

Tshikala Biaya holds a Ph.D. in History (1990) from the University of Laval, Quebec and MAs in Ethno-Psychology (1991) from the University of Kisangani and in History and Social Sciences (1983) from the Ecole Normale Supérieure de Kananga. The diversity of his studies gave him distinct resources for studying the complexities of contemporary urban Africa. His most recent work concerned youth and social conflict in Africa studied through a series of posts at and through CODESRIA in Dakar and the OAU in Addis Ababa. Over the past fifteen years he also held fellowships and teaching appointments at Laval, McGill, New York, Montreal and Iowa Universities. He passed away in Dakar in early July 2002, after having been hospitalized for over a month.

Jean Comaroff is Bernard E. and Ellen C. Sunny Distinguished Service Professor of Anthropology at the University of Chicago. Her publications include *Body of Power Spirit of Resistance: the Culture and History of a South African People,* and (with John Comaroff) *Of Revelation and Revolution* (vols. l and ll), *Ethnography and the Historical Imagination,* and several edited volumes. She is currently working on a book about crime and policing in the postcolony.

John Comaroff is Harold H. Swift Distinguished Service Professor of Anthropology and Social Sciences at the University of Chicago and a senior research fellow at the American Bar Foundation. His research has been conducted primarily in southern Africa in the fields of politics, law, historical anthropology, colonialism and postcoloniality. Most recent publications include, with Jean Comaroff, the co-edited volumes *Millennial Capitalism and the Culture of Neoliberalism* and *Civil Society and the Political Imagination in Africa.* They are currently working on crime and policing.

Filip De Boeck is the Chair of the Department of Social and Cultural Anthropology at the Catholic University of Leuven and Director of the Africa Research Center. He has conducted extensive field research in the Democratic Republic of Congo, and published extensively on his research on postcolonial identities, accumulation and expenditure in informal economies, history, memory, death, and popular urban culture. His most recent book is *Kinshasa: Tales of the Invisible City*, a joint project with photographer Marie-Françoise Plissart (Ghent: Ludion, 2004). In 2004, De Boeck co-curated an award-winning exhibition on Kinshasa for the 9th Architecture Biennial in Venice.

Mamadou Diouf is Professor of History and African American and African Studies, and Associate director of the Center of African American and African Studies, University of Michigan, Ann Arbor. He received his PhD from the University of Paris I, Sorbonne. His publications have focused on the areas of political, urban and intellectual history of Senegal and West Africa. His most recent books are: *Histoire du Sénégal* (2001) and *La Construction de l'Etat au Sénégal* (2002) with D. Cruise O'Brien and Momar C. Diop.

Deborah Durham is an Associate Professor of Anthropology at Sweet Briar College in Virginia. She has conducted field research on cultural identity and liberal democracy, and on youth, in Botswana. She is co-editor with Jennifer Cole of the book *Global Ages: Age, Intergenerational Relations, and the Intimate Politics of Globalization*. Among her other publications are articles on asking and agency (*Journal of the Royal Anthropological Institute*), dress and identity (*American Ethnologist*), sentiment, funerals and the public sphere (*Ethnos; Journal of Southern African Studies*), and youth (*Anthropological Quarterly*, forthcoming in *American Ethnologist*), and chapters in various edited volumes on citizenship and cultural identity in Botswana.

Alcinda Honwana is an Anthropologist and Program Director at the Social Science Research Council in New York. She has carried out extensive research in Mozambique on spirit possession and traditional healing, political conflict and the politics of culture, and the impact of political conflict on young people. She has published a book on *Spirit Possession and Modernity in Mozambique*, and several journal articles and book chapters on children, youth, conflict and cultural politics. She has completed a manuscript on *Child Soldiers in Africa* to be published by University of Pennsylvania Press.

Pamela Reynolds is a Professor of Anthropology at the Johns Hopkins University, Baltimore. Her research and publications focus on the Ethnography of Childhood and she has published books and several articles on child labour among the Tonga of the Zambezi Valley, healers' conceptions of childhood in Zimbabwe, and young political activists who fought for democracy in South Africa. Professor Reynolds has recently established a Centre for the Ethnography of Children and Youth at Johns Hopkins University.

Brad Weiss is Associate Professor of Anthropology at the College of William & Mary, Williamsburg, and is currently a Burkhardt Fellow of the American Council of Learned Societies at the National Humanities Center. He is the author of two books on the social and cultural history of Northwest Tanzania, the editor of *Producing African Futures: Ritual and Politics in a Neoliberal Age*, and he is completing a book on popular culture in urban Tanzania.

Mats Utas is research fellow at the Department of Cultural Anthropology and Ethnology, Uppsala University, Sweden, and postdoctoral research fellow at the Department of Sociology, Fourah Bay College, Sierra Leone. He defended his PhD thesis, 'Sweet Battlefields: Youth and the Liberian Civil War' in June 2003. His current research deals with marginalized youth in urban Sierra Leone, and he has published a chapter on the reintegration of young combatants in the Liberian Civil War in *No Peace, No War* edited by Paul Richards (Oxford: James Currey, 2004).

Introduction

FILIP DE BOECK & ALCINDA HONWANA
Children & Youth in Africa
Agency, Identity & Place

In Africa, young people constitute the majority of the population and are at the centre of societal interactions and transformations. Yet children and youth are often placed at the margins of the public sphere and major political, socio-economic, and cultural processes. The challenging situation on the continent today makes young people particularly vulnerable. Many have little or no access to education, employment and livelihoods, healthcare and basic nutrition. Over the past two decades, political conflict, armed violence, and the HIV/AIDS pandemic created a crisis of unprecedented proportions for younger generations of Africans. Within this stressful environment, how do young people organize and make sense of their daily lives? How do they negotiate their private and public roles and envision their futures?

This book addresses the dynamics of both local and transnational forces that are affecting African young people today. It examines children and youth as plural and heterogeneous categories, with varied and multifaceted experiences and expectations. In addition to interrogating the meanings of childhood and youth in particular social contexts, the contributors to this volume look at young people as a window to understanding broader socio-political and economic transformations in Africa and explore the ways in which these processes of change shape and are being shaped by the young. Despite all the difficulties they face, young people in Africa are actively participating in social, economic, and political developments and, in the process, constructing their own identities. They are often viewed simultaneously as creative and destructive forces. Indeed, youth have been at the forefront of major social transformations, whether in politics, economics, religion, popular culture or community building. Young people often shape and express political aspirations in surprising ways. They are at the frontier of the reconfiguration of geographies of exclusion and inclusion and the categories of public and private. As Diouf notes in his postscript to this volume, young people in Africa have the capacity to fracture public space, and re-invent or even bypass it, in the same way they shattered the nationalist projects of the post-independence state. In economic terms, children and youth are major players in new informal economies and processes of globalization, as well as in the delineation of alternative local forms of modernity. As Christian fundamentalism and other religious movements flourish all over Africa south of the Sahara, young people are at the forefront of movements that embody the expectations and promises of millennial capitalist ideals. Creative and innovative forms of popular culture – theatre, arts, music and dance – are often the exclusive domain of the young as they create, re-invent, and domesticate global trends into local forms. Finally, in terms of community building, children and youth are important actors in redefining and restructuring existing models of kinship and moral matrices of reciprocity and solidarity. More than anyone else, they are the ones who undergo, express, and provide answers to the crisis of existing communitarian models, structures of authority, gerontocracy, and gender relations. Children and youth are the focal point of the many changes that characterize the contemporary African scene, afloat between crisis and renewal.

This book analyzes how young Africans today experience the ruptures and breaches in their lives brought about by historical processes of colonization and decolonization, the state of civil war, and the mechanisms of global capitalism. How do they integrate disruption and fragmentation into their own lives? What collective fantasy spaces do children and youth claim for themselves? How is their social imagination constructed (Durham, 2000), and how does this inform us about their outlook on life, their understanding, interpretation, and formulation of the worlds in which they live? In what ways do their social positions differ from those young people held in the past? How do they relate to tradition? Which are the social 'theatres' in which moments, points, and places of renewed identity formation and reintegrating rites of passage are being shaped?

The voices, views and visions of young people themselves still wait to be heard and considered. We know remarkably little about them. Children and youth, in Africa as elsewhere, have often remained our 'silent others', our voiceless *enfants terribles* (Caputo, 1995; Gottlieb, 2000; Hirschfeld, 1999, 2002). They are often constructed from the outside and from above as a 'problem' or a 'lost generation' (Cruise O'Brien, 1996) in 'crisis' (Everatt and Sisulu, 1992). Ethnographies of childhood and youth often revert to a traditional, 'pre-postmodernist' anthropological approach, speaking for people who are unable to reach influential audiences themselves. As Reynolds (in this volume) remarks, children have rarely been listened to, and when their voices are not silenced, their talk is never unconstrained. Children's voices reach a broader platform only in rare, and sometimes tragic, cases, but even then these subaltern voices are often immediately recuperated, transformed, and inserted into different narratives and agendas set by other interest groups. However, despite these exclusions, many young people in Africa have demonstrated tremendous creativity in making a living for themselves in a climate of social instability and endemic conflict. This book seeks to illuminate this capacity for creativity, which even adverse conditions have not stifled.

The chapters in this collection offer different views into the lives of young people in such diverse places as Angola, Botswana, Cameroon, the Democratic Republic of Congo, Ethiopia, Liberia, Mozambique, Senegal, Sierra Leone, South Africa, Tanzania, Uganda, and Zimbabwe. These studies ground our understanding of issues concerning children and youth, identity and agency, locality and globalization theoretically, ethnographically, and historically, from the past to the postcolony and beyond.

Children, Youth, and Society

The fundamental paradox this volume addresses is: how can we understand children and youth in various African contexts as both *makers* and *breakers* of society, while they are simultaneously being *made* and *broken* by that society? How can we situate their lives in the present, grasp the meanings revealed in their shaping of a future, and ground both in an understanding of the past? None of these aspects of young people's lives can be adequately understood if examined in isolation. This ensemble of influences reflects the full complexity of the interaction between the child, the family, the society, and the world. A myriad of factors make childhood and youth highly heterogeneous categories in terms of gender, class, race, ethnicity, and political position, as well as age. These categories intersect in multiple, often unexpected, ways and interact on different planes simultaneously. As 'makers' of society, children and youth contribute to the structures, norms, rituals, and directions of society while also being shaped by them. They make themselves, through inventive forms of self-realization and an ingenious politics of identity (De Boeck, 1999a; Biaya in this volume), and they make society by acting as a political force, as sources of resistance and resilience, and as ritual or even supernatural agents and generators of morality and healing through masquerade and play (Argenti, 2001; Cartry, 1978; Drucker-Brown, 1999; Gottlieb, 2000; Goldman, 1998). On the other hand, they appear as 'breakers' in various ways: as risk factors for themselves through suicide, drug use, alcohol, and unsafe sex; by breaking societal norms, conventions, and rules; sometimes by breaking limbs and lives (as in the wars described by Abdullah, Utas, and Honwana in this volume); and sometimes by breaking the chains of oppression, as the role of young people in fighting South African apartheid so powerfully illustrated. Young people constantly shake and shape society but are also shaped and shaken by it. Finally, children and youth are pushed, pulled, and coerced into various actions by encompassing structures and processes over which they have little or no control: kin, family, community, education, media, technology, the state and its decay, war, religion, tradition and the weight of the past, and the rules of the global market. In the process they are frequently broken, put at risk, and destroyed by unemployment, exploitation, war, famine, rape, physical mutilation, poverty, homelessness, lack of access to education and medical facilities, and HIV/AIDS (Dawes and Honwana, 1996; Honwana, 1997; Scheper-Hughes and Sargent, 1998).

Children and youth are extremely difficult to grasp and pin down analytically. They are at once an 'emerging influence' and 'submerged by power' (Coulter, 1998). They may be targets, students, servants, orphans, street children, combatants, healers, onlookers, political activists, entrepreneurs, artists, or witches, and they often occupy more than one position at once.

Disregarding this multiplicity in the positions of young people, children and youth have been routinely portrayed as innocent and vulnerable, in need of adult protection. As Honwana points out (in this volume), children and youth are often perceived through opposition to adulthood and as 'people in the process of becoming rather than being'. This view predominates in international law on children's rights (Ennew, 2002). The need to establish global standards of child protection led to the universalization of a specific definition of childhood. Several international agreements define a child as anyone below the age of eighteen (UN Geneva Conventions; UN Convention on the Rights of the Child; The African Charter of Rights of the Child). Here, children and youth appear as pre-social and passive recipients of experience. They are portrayed as dependent, immature, and incapable of assuming responsibility, properly confined to the protection of home and school (Thomas, 2000). This concept developed among the middle class in Europe and North America and has been universalized in such a way that youngsters who do not follow this path are considered either to be at risk or to pose a risk to society. Children who are 'out of place' (Connolly and Ennew, 1996), who do not readily fit within Western cultural fantasies of children as innocent and vulnerable, are quickly perceived as demonic, discontented and disorderly and are often feared and punished as a consequence. Parents who do not follow normative Western child-rearing practices are immediately seen as irresponsible (Levine, et al., 1994).

As Bourdieu reminds us, youth is 'just a word' (Bourdieu, 1993). In this book, we understand childhood and youth to be historically situated social and cultural constructions (Ariès, 1962; James and Prout, 1990). The concept 'youth' is, to adopt Durham's phrase, a 'social shifter': it is a relational concept situated in a dynamic context, a social landscape of power, knowledge, rights, and cultural notions of agency and personhood. According to Durham, 'to imagine youth, and to imagine the concept relationally, is to imagine the grounds and forces of sociality' (Durham, 2000:116). Definitions and notions of children and youth cannot, therefore, be simply based on biology or chronological age. They do not denote a fixed group or demographic cohort (Aguillar, 1997; Kurimoto and Simonse, 1998). Such social and cultural variables as gender, religion, class, responsibilities, expectations, race, and ethnicity play important parts in defining who are regarded or consider themselves as children or youth – and the ways young persons are perceived do not necessarily coincide with their self–definitions. The process of transition between childhood and youth and the period when youth ends and adulthood begins are not the same everywhere; they vary across and within societies and cultures over time. The contributors to this volume focus on young people not simply as proto-adults or future beings but rather as beings-in-the-present and as social actors with an identity of their own (Boyden, 1990; Boyden and Gibbs, 1997; Dawes and Donald, 1994; Göncü, 1999; Honwana, 1999a, 1999b; James, 1993; Reynolds, 1996).

In Africa, very few children and young people enjoy the luxury of being taken care of by their parents or the state until they reach the age of eighteen. Many are expected to work and assume social responsibilities at an early age (Reynolds, 1990). They participate actively in productive tasks, paid labour, household chores, and taking care of younger siblings (Riesman, 1992). Children and youth learn by participating in social and economic processes. This participation takes place in postcolonial conditions that tend, in the formal political and economical domain, to marginalize them and to offer few opportunities. It is part of the African doxa to see young people as strong and resilient; they are often portrayed as survivors who actively grow on their own even under difficult conditions (Gibbs, 1994; Honwana, 1998; Reynolds, 1996). In these societal constellations, children and youth are synonymous with wealth because of the contribution they make to the productive work of the family. They are also valued as a source of future security. Children remain significant in kin-based societies where social health and well-being, as well as status and success, continue to depend not only on wealth in things but also on wealth in people.

Young people constantly cross the frontier between childhood and adulthood. As they actively create and recreate their roles in the face of changing conditions, they blur that social divide. For example, many children and young people are drawn into wars and less structured forms of politically motivated violence, acting as soldiers, spies, bodyguards, and commandos. Child soldiers in Sierra Leone, Uganda, the two Congos, Angola, Mozambique, Liberia, Sudan and Ethiopia provide striking examples of this assumption of roles once reserved for adults (Abdullah, Honwana, and Utas, all in this volume; Abdullah and Bangura, 1997; Bazenguissa-Ganga, 1999; Dodge and Raundalen, 1987, 1991; Furley, 1995; Honwana, 1998, 1999a, 1999b; Peters and Richards, 1998; Richards, 1995; Straker et al., 1992; Utas, 2003; Cohn and Goodwin-Gill, 1994; Machel, 1996; Marten, 2002; Scheper-Hughes and Sargent, 1998; Suarez-Orozco, 1987). Across the continent, the HIV/Aids pandemic has left many orphans to fend for themselves and assume such adult responsibilities as running households and communities (de Waal and Argenti, 2002).

The Study of Children and Youth in Africa

Many earlier analyses of young people in relation to socialization, education, and development portrayed children and youth as objects of adult activity. These studies often focused on the institutional systems in which youth are implicated. More recent work on young people has been concerned with their role in shaping social, political, and economic processes.

In Africa, young people have only recently become an important subject of social inquiry. The last decade has witnessed a proliferation of studies focusing on youth and politics (Bayart et al., 1992; Toulabor, 1995; Mbembe, 1985, 1987; Toungara 1995; Diouf, 1996; Kakwenzire, 1996; Argenti, 1998), particularly their role in the resistance against apartheid in South Africa (Bundy, 1987; Hyslop, 1988; Johnson, 1989; Carter, 1991; Naidoo, 1992; Straker et al., 1992; Seekings, 1993; Reynolds, 1995; Ndebele, 1995; Badat, 1997; Marks, 2001). Young people's direct participation in armed conflict and their postwar rehabilitation also caught the attention of social scientists (Obikeze and Mere, 1985; Dodge and Raunaden, 1987; Boothby et al., 1992; Furley, 1995; Richards, 1995, 1996; Honwana, 1999a). Other early work on children and youth in Africa ranged from a general overview of their evolution and social role (D'Almeida-Topor et al., 1992) to their participation in economic development and the labour market (Ly, 1988; Reynolds, 1990), religious movements and rituals of possession (Last, 1991; Sharp, 1990, 1995; Tayob, 1995), gangs and criminal activities (La Hausse, 1990), and student movements and other associations (Hyslop, 1990; Ojo, 1995). In 1996, Mamadou Diouf examined social movements led by young people that shook the Senegalese political scene in the late 1980s and early 1990s. He argued that, through political demonstrations which were often violent, the youth challenged tradition and authoritarianism and redefined new spaces and forms of citizenship. In the same year, Ali El-Kenz's article on youth and violence illuminated the economic challenges faced by young people on the continent by analyzing cases studies from Senegal and Algeria. He demonstrated that the strong demographic growth that took place in Africa during the last few decades, combined with severe economic crisis, marginalized young people and drove them into cycles of violence, whether spontaneous or organized, official or manipulated. These two studies stimulated major discussions within the continent on the situation and roles of youth in African societies today. In 1997, CODESRIA's journal, *African Development*, published a special issue on youth, violence, and the collapse of the state in Sierra Leone. This collection examined the social origins of the civil war and the development of a 'rebellious/lumpen youth culture' (Abdullah and Bangura, 1997). The contributors looked at youth from a position of marginality, highlighting their status as underclass, subalterns, and 'lumpens', and argued that alienated youths were central to the war and continued political violence in Sierra Leone. This special issue, which followed previous work on the roles played by young people in West African civil wars (Reno, 1993, 1995; Kaplan, 1994; Ellis, 1995; Richards, 1995, 1997), was widely discussed, generating important debates about the dynamics of youth cultures, identity, marginality, citizenship and agency.

Studies of youth outside the continent have also analyzed the production of 'youth culture' by young people themselves (Amit-Talai and Wulff, 1995; Pilkington 1994; Ross and Rose, 1994; Skelton and Valentine, 1998). Emphasis is often placed on young people's capacity for rebellion, opposition, resistance and counter-hegemony, and their sub-culture is frequently described as liminal, caught between childhood and adulthood in a category of natural opposition and Turnerian anti-structure. This tendency toward the politicization of the category of 'youth' flows in part from the influence of studies of working-class youth subcultures, which originated in the Centre for Contemporary Cultural Studies at the University of Birmingham in the UK. This strand of research was strongly characterized by a Marxist or Gramscian perspective (Gilroy, 1987; Hall and Jefferson, 1976; Hebdige, 1979; McRobbie and Nava, 1984; Willis, 1977; for an overview of CCCS research on youth, see Valentine et al., 1998.) Yet the shift from a European to an African context matters. As Max Gluckman (1954, 1960) pointed out, a society can actually be strengthened by ritualized rebellion and conflict because they allow the tensions inherent in systems of domination to be expressed and released in ways that enable the system to continue functioning.

In Africa, until recently, forces of rebellion emanating from children and youth, as from other subaltern groups such as women, were structurally embedded in social dynamics whereby ritualized moments of anti-structure channelled these counter-currents and strengthened the social equilibrium through a pleiad of rites of passage and other rituals of initiation or age-grade associations (Richards, 1956; Turner, 1967). In Africa, the counter-hegemonic reversal of roles and behaviour associated in the West with adolescence and teenage counter-culture were liberated, socially channelled, and ritually embedded within the overall social system. In this way, rather than threatening society, forces emanating from liminal moments and spaces reinforced and replenished the societal whole. In this respect, one could even say that a social category of 'youth' or 'adolescent' did not exist in the African context until recently. The question which then arises is whether the recent emergence of 'youth' – with its multiple subcultures expressed in terms of dress, music, specific modes of violence, and the emergence of new co-operative units such as gangs and '*écuries*' (small-scale economic or religious collaborative groups) which have replaced more traditional kin-based, ethnic, and multigenerational associations – is linked to a more general societal crisis in which the processual transformations from boy to man and from girl to woman have lost their taken-for-granted status and social significance. When and how have young people become a 'problem' or a 'lost generation' in the African scene? When and how have conflict, social tension, and rebellion become signs of a crisis of youth (Richards, 1995) rather than that age-group's normal condition, expressed and ordered to reinforce the societal order? What does it mean when disempowered youths force their way to the centre of society and when their subaltern grammar of protest becomes the leading one? (Abdullah in this volume). In order to understand these transformations, we need to reassess the conflict analysis model propagated by Gluckman and the Manchester school (Jabri, 1996). We must move beyond Gluckman's processual framework to a more action-oriented analysis of young people's individual strategies and aspirations while simultaneously placing individual actors in a broader, diachronic social context.

Various chapters in this book link youth to politics, resistance, contestation, and counter-hegemonic practices, in articulation with a more global scene (Argenti, Abdullah, Durham). If youth is commonly perceived in the process of becoming rather than being, then young people are in a perfect position to navigate and control the new geographies and chronologies of globalization. As Harvey has pointed out in his germinal work on *The Condition of Postmodernity*, globalizing forces are played out in accelerating and intensifying rounds of space/time compression. Time becomes spatialized, annihilating place as the site of being (Harvey, 1989, 2000). When the Comaroffs (in this volume) describe young people's use of the internet as a new form of transnational activism which transforms local places of youth expression into a global cyberspace, they refer precisely to youths' ability to tap into globalizing spatial politics as a newly found source of power. But the majority of Africa's young people are still excluded from participation in this new transnational form of empowerment. For many young people in Africa, the possibilities of becoming seem constantly curtailed by cultural, political, and economic constraints that work hegemonically to pin them down to localized place and imprison them in a precarious and fragile state of being (Henderson, 1999; Jewsiewicki and Letourneau, 1998).

Globalization, Pain, and Agency

In August 1999, the frozen bodies of Yaguine Koita and Fodé Tounkara, two fourteen-year-old boys from Conakry, Guinea, were discovered hidden in the landing gear of a Sabena aircraft at the Brussels international airport. On one of the bodies was found a letter addressed to Europe's political leadership, addressing an eloquent plea to the powerful for a better life and a more hopeful future for Africa's youth. Here is an extract from their letter:

> Gentlemen, members and leaders of Europe, we appeal to your solidarity and kindness to help Africa. Please help us, we are suffering enormously in Africa, we have problems, and some weaknesses with regard to children's rights ... we have war, disease, lack of food, etc. ... in Guinea we have many schools but a big absence of education and training. Therefore, if you see that we are sacrificing ourselves, and expose our own lives it is because we are suffering a lot in Africa, and we need your support to fight poverty and end war in Africa. Nevertheless, we want to study and we ask you to help us study so that we can live like you but in Africa. Finally, we beg you to accept our apologies for taking the liberty to address you this letter, because you are eminent personalities, which we ought to respect.

The tragic story of Yaguine and Fodé makes one read with different eyes Wole Soyinka's poem, 'The Children of This Land' (Soyinka, 2000):

> The children of this land are old.
> Their eyes are fixed on maps in place of land.
> Their feet must learn to follow
> Distant contours traced by alien minds.
> Their present sense has faded into past.

A year after their tragic death, Yaguine and Fodé had become 'symbols for all the youth in the country', said Thierno Diallo, editor-in-chief of *Le Lynx*, a local weekly in Conakry. In Belgium, a memorial banner with the whole text of the boys' message was put up against the wall of a house in the middle of Brussels, near a government building that houses asylum seekers from all over the globe. The Togolese novelist and playwright Kangni Alem devoted a play, *Atterrissage*, to the two boys (Kangni Alem, 2002). Their letter continues to be debated (Ferguson, 2002).

Confronted with young Africa knocking loudly at the doors of 'Fortress Europe', the West must reflect on its own strategies of inclusion and exclusion. We must understand the hopes and dreams, the despair and tears of those whom Europe pushes to the periphery. The increasing participation in global and diasporic movements in the West made African children and youth important subjects of social inquiry (Ly, 1988). The deaths of the two boys from Guinea, as well as the sad fate of many young diasporic Africans in the West, all unfortunate members of the new 'alien-nation' (Comaroff and Comaroff, 1999), echo the dilemmas and struggles that children and youth face on the African continent. Why are these young Africans so powerfully attracted to the West? What is their vision of a good life? What is their cultural politics, and in what geographies, ecologies, and subjectivities is it located and imagined?

The chapters in this collection work through experiences of marginalization, dislocation, violence, disenfranchisement, and pain, but they are also about desire, hope, and the powerful longing to create or to take part, as active participants, in other spaces of empowerment. Agency, in these contexts, is always painful; yet, as Weiss argues, pain can also produce agency.

But where is the 'lieu identitaire', the 'geography' in which African youth's agency is situated? (Collignon and Diouf, 2001; Letourneau, 1997; Skelton and Valentine, 1998; Stephens, 1995; Wyn and White, 1997). Often, as in Yaguine and Fodé's case, an imagined topos or the Idea of the West is situated elsewhere, effectively placed beyond the reach of most young people within Africa, but creatively re-invented, captured, and domesticated by them both in and outside Africa. Significantly, Yaguine and Fodé mention that they want to 'live like you (Europeans) but in Africa'. This revealing phrase expresses the deep tension between the mimetic and the impulse to transplant this elsewhere into home.

In his chapter on barbershops in Arusha, Tanzania, Weiss illustrates how the iconic global world that is staged around these shops is not only mediated by the West's imperative gaze but also authored by young people themselves. Similarly, the *sapeurs* of Brazzaville and Kinshasa claim and 'tame' the West through their appropriation of what they ironically call *bilamba mabe*, 'bad clothes', or French, Italian, and Japanese designer fashions. Through a political economy of elegance, they refashion the West in their own terms (De Boeck, 1999a; Friedman, 1994; Gandoulou, 1989; Gondola, 1999; Yoka, 1991).

On the one hand, then, the dreams, stories, and imaginaries of the diasporic experience of the West clearly illustrate that young people in Africa are not merely passive victims of the societal crisis that pervades the worlds in which they grow up. Rather, it illustrates the fact that they are searching for their own ways out of a life that they feel to be without a future. Such a perspective on young people's economies of desire in relation to the West continues, however, to lock African youth into the dynamics of the mimetic, into discourses of loss and absence, and into the displacement and dislocation of local desires. As Seremetakis has rightly pointed out, 'The discourse on loss, which offers no alternatives, empties the neo-colonial site of all internal content, leaving it an empty and receptive shell for external cultural colonization. Thus the ideologies of loss and crisis in the neo-colonial periphery are an integral part of the political logic of mimetic modernization' (Seremetakis, 1994: ix; De Boeck, 1999b). By this logic, the Western cultural model of childhood and youth, with its music, tastes and fashions, its politics of style, patterns of consumption, management of free time, and opportunities and obligations, appears as the globalized norm, while the African site becomes characterized by poverty, war and violence, offering very slim opportunities to children and youth. Of course, the same forms of exclusion occur within the First World as well. Chin's recent study of consumer habits among black young people in New Haven, Connecticut, acknowledges the profound constraints under which poor and working-class youth struggle to survive in a wealthy society still shaped by class and racial discrimination (Chin, 2001).

Without denying these constraints on youth within the West itself or downplaying more global dynamics that shape youth in contemporary Africa, this book situates itself primarily at the local African level. From this site, most contributors analyze the dialectical linkages between the global flow and the local geographies and imaginaries of youth culture. The book also aims to bring African children and youth out of the diaspora, as a spatial reality and as a state of mind, by stressing the role of young people as active participants in broader social, political and economic fields within Africa itself. Their practices go well beyond imitating, possessing, and refashioning the West. As Argenti's discussion of a Cameroonian dance group by the name of 'Mondial' illustrates, the exogenous becomes a source of power which is sometimes political and highly threatening. Weiss argues that youth's cultural practice is not about 'the "local" expression of a "global" set of forces and institutions, it is, on the contrary, about the connection and simultaneous presence of specific times, places, and persons, with encompassing powers, images and relations'. These partial connections are always multidirectional. We focus on the co-presence of local and global social practices and imaginaries that shape youth but are also shaped by them, in various, often self-invented, spaces and practices of resistance, negation and opposition, but also of collaboration, negotiation and invention. Here the young appear as agents in and of themselves, in their own diverse and often highly specific cultural production.

Beyond the Postcolonial: Marginalization and Agency

Youth in the West, inhabiting a diverse but important general category from which emanates a potential counter-hegemonic force and a politics 'from below', have moved into the centre of mainstream cultural, economic and political domains, determining the outlook of our consumer culture (Gunter and Furnham, 1998) and influencing political agendas. It may be argued that in Africa, with a few significant exceptions, this is not the situation. The majority of young people in postcolonial Africa, although they are at least as heterogeneous as their Western counterparts, are generally much more marginalized, and often, though not always, they have a much less promising political and economic role to play, locally but also translocally and globally.

In recent years, a number of scholars have debated the marginalization and exclusion of youth from political and social roles in Africa. African youth, while unable to produce and control space more generally, often manage to author identities and make themselves heard and seen in localized urban niches such as the church, the army or war band, and the school. However, a growing number of children and youth in contemporary Africa are excluded from education, healthcare, salaried jobs, and even access to an adult status, given their financial incapacity to construct a house, formally marry and raise children in turn (De Boeck in this volume). The concept of youth becomes more flexible as students are unable to complete their education; in some cases, both father and son are students, as often happens both within the continent and in the African diaspora where the 'eternal student' has become an established social terminus.

Increasingly, whole groups of young people no longer fit in any of the common sites of youth self-realization. More often than not, these youngsters seem literally 'out of place'. Many were involuntarily dislocated, including homeless street children (De Boeck and Biaya in this volume), young diamond diggers and *garimpeiros*, refugee children, war or AIDS orphans, and other 'children of tribulation' (Reynolds, 1990; see also Barrett, 1998a, 1998b; Bazenguissa and MacGaffey, 1995; Bruyère, 2001; Hérault and Adesanmi, 1997; Kilbride et al., 2000; Marguerat and Poitou, 1994; Noy et al., 2001; Utas et al., n.d.; Wong, 1999). Given the inherent ambiguities surrounding such children and youth throughout Africa, responses towards them have been highly ambivalent. Despite the deeply rooted moral and cultural matrix that defines children in terms of intrinsic wealth and as a social good, they are increasingly viewed as troublesome and potentially dangerous. In Central Africa today, as De Boeck shows, children have become a source of evil in the collective social imaginary. In Congo, religious television channels run weekly shows where child-witches are identified during public mass meetings, and the persecution of witch-children in the streets of Congo's towns and villages is becoming common. This unprecedented demonization of children bespeaks a deeply rooted sense of social crisis.

Despite the contributors' shared focus on agency, the essays in this volume take into account the realities of marginalization and exclusion that are daily experienced by children and young people in Africa today. The chapters propose multiple reasons for this marginalization, addressing the historical trajectory and contemporary complexity of these issues. They also explore the ambiguities of the agency of young people, for example in relation to the experience of pain (Reynolds and Weiss), play and work (Durham and Argenti), and political, religious, and social violence (Utas, Honwana, De Boeck, Abdullah and Biaya). Contributors variously label children's agency as 'anomalous' (Comaroff and Comaroff), a 'victim's agency' (Utas), or as an agency of the weak and, following de Certeau's distinction, as tactical rather than strategic (Honwana). Throughout the chapters, children and youth appear as 'a sign of contradiction', as Janus-faced mutants (De Boeck, 2000), as liminal and interstitial subjects (Honwana), and as hybrids (Comaroff and Comaroff). Their identities, practices, and lived worlds seem constructed in and around an 'uneasy' (Honwana) or even 'illicit' co-habitation (Weiss) of complementary opposites; their agency often arises out of the way in which they are capable of crossing and recontextualizing the boundaries between seemingly contradictory elements. Juvenile agency is activated in the uncharted territories between the ludic and the lethal (Honwana), between the first world of the living and the 'second world' of the dead (De Boeck), between play and work (Durham), between affliction and affection, between pain and pleasure, and between the vulnerable and the violent. The identities and histories being generated in the cultural youth spaces throughout Africa are ambivalent, contextual, negotiable, polysemic and 'heterodox' (Biaya). Yet their margins and borders are not fluid or illusory. On the contrary, both geographically and conceptually, young people's worlds are clearly bounded.

As Hannerz has recently remarked, 'the point is rather that borders are not absolute barriers, but that they become significant social, cultural, political, economic and legal facts in the way they are crossed' (Hannerz, 1999: 326). Producing, maintaining and crossing the borders between geographic locations as well as between conceptual worlds is a process that generates powerful resources, economically as well as politically and culturally. Young people's ability to mediate, positively or negatively, between the manifold oppositions, ruptures and contradictions that seem to characterize African worlds today unfolds in a double dynamic: the perceived marginality and liminality of youth places them squarely in the centre and generates tremendous power. Many of the essays in this volume address the nature of that power, interrogating the ambivalent and often contradictory messages sent to us by African children and youth. These chapters analyze young people's capacity to mediate the contradictions in the socio-cultural frontiers which they tend to occupy. These frontiers are also borderlands between past and present, local and global, near and far, 'tradition' and 'modernity'. The power of the young derives from these spaces of confrontation, mutation and movement in which different cultural itineraries meet and mix. Relegated to non-places and resorting to borderlands, young people, as bearers and producers of these mutant messages, constantly remake their composite identity and lived world and redeploy long-standing local moralities in the intersection with more global forces in new and often surprising ways.

Young people exercise their creative power discursively but also in and through their own bodies, setting in motion a process of self-realization and promotion of social status through consumption and expenditure, appearance, and fashion. This process is a matter of 'self-making', of capturing and 'fixing' the non-steady state of selfhood and identity in different cultural situations (Battaglia, 1995). Many of these chapters address the corporeal dimensions of juvenile vocabularies of self-making. Dance, in particular, enables youth to break through the grasp and control of the postcolonial state and its accompanying ideology of colonialist modernity, with its characteristic politics of disciplining and domesticating people, space, time, labour, and relations of production and consumption along the lines of Western models. Juvenile bodies appear as subversive sites and frontiers of re-territorialization of official cultural and political grammars, as in Argenti's description of the Mondial dance group. Ultimately, these bodies illustrate how far African youth at the forefront and on the margins of mainstream socio-cultural production have moved beyond the standard frames, possibilities, restrictions, and contradictions of colonial and postcolonial models, leading the way into the new and as yet uncharted territory of the post-postcolony (Biaya).

For more and more young people, both colonial and postcolonial frameworks no longer function as a seamark for their own orientation. These models have even lost their appeal as negative beacons triggering resistance against the old orders. For these young people the existing frames of reference, which are mapping power relations onto the world in sometimes contested but nevertheless clearly circumscribed and clear-cut ways between the centre and the periphery, the former metropole and the postcolony, the haves and the have-nots, the past and the present, have lost all epistemic power. To many young people in contemporary Africa, from Free Town to Kinshasa and Addis Ababa, the order through which the postcolonial world has existed seems to have become entirely devoid of meaning. What is more, it has become incomprehensible, even unknown, and totally irrelevant to young people's own understanding of the lives they lead. These older modes, frames, and aesthetics of living in, and giving order and meaning to, local and more global worlds seem to be replaced, to varying degrees, by alternative forms of sociality and being-in-the-world, opening up a space in which few of the former rules apply and which, in consequence, onlookers experience as shockingly violent, frighteningly chaotic, and bewilderingly exotic. At this juncture, local youth frontiers in Africa seem to converge in a transnational move beyond the qualities of the postcolonial world. These youth move in worlds governed by rules, norms, ethics and moralities that seem to have broken quite radically with all kinds of pasts, with the neo-colonial dictates of the mimetic but also with the ambiguities of the multi-layered palimpsestual meanings that the postcolonial context generates. These youth environments may be hybrid in actual make-up and composition, but they deny, or have become totally unaware of, the conventions of their own hybrid historicity; or they knowingly reject it, in a radical denial of the palimpsestual overdrive with which late postcoloniality confronts them on a daily basis. Their world makes a continuous attempt not at being chaotic and exotic but at achieving self-explanatory clarity and simplification, to serve as an antidote to the incomprehensible and cruel injustices of the world they are condemned to live in. Looked at from the outside, the worlds of these young people are often shockingly self-referential, their horizons astonishingly limited, and their lives self-contained, despite the global *bricolage* that gives form to the local contents of these youth universes (Behrend, 2002; Biaya, 2000; Hansen, 2000; Remes, 1999). But, lived from within, this limitation is experienced as a necessary attempt at self-protection. One has to reach deep inside and tap into one's own sources of strength in order to be able to create meaning and transparency amid the opacity of a fragmented world.

The 'Diversity of Voices'

This book is divided into four parts. The first part locates children and youth in the context of global transactions. In their chapter, Jean Comaroff and John Comaroff examine the predicament of youth in the global world by pointing to global youth cultures of desire, self-expression, and representation. They argue that, while these juvenile cultures become increasingly global in their reach, they take different forms in different locations as processes of domestication re-contextualize and reshape them to address local concerns. Thus, the young tend to 'occupy the innovative and uncharted frontiers along which the global meets the local', and where the tensions and contradictions of modernity confront their daily lives.

Following on from this global analysis, the second part is concerned with agency and pain. Honwana and Utas contribute powerfully terrifying accounts of young people's involvement in violence and war. Drawing from her research in Angola and Mozambique, Honwana examines young people's experiences and the context of their involvement in armed conflict by looking at the processes of their recruitment and initiation into cultures of violence and terror. She presents an analysis of the child/soldier paradox and discusses the interstitial position of child combatants. Child-soldiers are located in an interstitial space, a twilight zone which embodies the contradictions and ambiguities of being simultaneously children and soldiers, victims and perpetrators. Honwana argues that child-soldiers constitute a heterogeneous group and cannot be viewed as simply empty vessels into which violence is poured. They exercise an agency of their own, a 'tactical agency' that helps them cope and try to maximize the immediate circumstances of the military environment in which they operate.

In the same vein, Utas's study of young women in the Liberian civil war emphasizes that their participation transcends 'victim dynamics', as these young women constantly oscillate between the positions of victim and perpetrator. He discusses the experiences of girls in the Liberian war, drawing on the stories of three women to show the intricate realities of their lives. He argues against the simplistic view that women are merely victimized in situations of war, and through his research findings he suggests the need to rethink the inimical oppositions of victim/perpetrator, civilian/soldier, and propose new and more complex understandings of gender configurations and life experiences in war contexts.

In the sequence of these accounts of violence and suffering, Reynolds' and Weiss's essays focus on the question of pain. Reynolds' examination of the ways in which children experience, recognize, and express pain shows us that the hurts of young people are shaped and given expression, or hidden and silenced, by their context and cultural matrix. The chapter focuses on the suffering experienced by children and youth in contexts of political conflict, ranging from the fight against apartheid and a community's stand against the forces of the state in South Africa to the tensions experienced by a community in the aftermath of a war of liberation in Zimbabwe. Reynolds argues that pain is not just 'pain' as universally defined, and that locally generated social meanings can alter the meaning of children's pain and suffering. These local meanings of pain need to be considered if their suffering is to be addressed.

Weiss's study of young people in Arusha's barbershops in Tanzania analyzes pain as a mode of social consciousness and examines how marginality and subjugation from global processes of consumption are experienced and expressed as pain. He looks at how the world of hip hop and gangsta rap becomes central to Arusha's youth culture, and discusses the paradox embedded in the fantasies of popular culture and the subjectivities of the youth who participate in it. As he points out, young men in Arusha 'perceive themselves to be marginal to, and so *subjugated* by, the global order of signs and values they intensely desire; and yet, this subjugation is experienced as 'pain' which can greatly contribute to the subjective sense of *connection* to that world-wide community'. Pain, he argues, is the existential condition of marginality through which young people can act upon their subjugation to transform it.

Even in conditions of great deprivation, young people's lives are not just about pain and suffering; they are also about play. The third section of the book emphasizes the ludic side of their lives, especially dance and performance. Argenti discusses two masquerade groups: Mondial, a new group of young male maskers; and Baate, the name given to a host of recent female masking groups in the kingdom of Oku in the Cameroonian grassfields. The Oku palace authorities banned certain performances by these two groups, which occupy a subaltern position in the models of place, identity and authority constructed by the palace elite in their quest for modernist forms of rule. By analyzing the reasons for this ban, Argenti demonstrates how young people and women, through their masked performances, subvert elite discourses of power and 'tradition' and how, through the bodily subversion displayed in their dances, they question established boundaries while creating new ones.

Durham's essay examines the ambiguous relationship between play and work among Herero youth in Botswana and the ways in which notions of play and work are perceived and enacted. She argues that, although the Herero Youth Association and its core business, singing, are interpreted as 'just play' by most Herero, such activities directly or indirectly promote a Herero ethnic revival and projects to benefit the whole community, subtly intruding upon and reconfiguring local topographies of social power and local political discourses and practices. Thus 'play' is a source for creative and imaginative change through which youth redefine spaces and logics of sociability and the public sphere at the intersection between community and state. At the same time, it is a label that enables the established powers to redefine these activities as 'not serious', thereby engineering the means for containment and control of the agency and potential power of local youth.

The last section of the volume examines the transformative capacity of children and youth by focusing on their postcolonial experiences as urban citizens. Taking three murders which occurred in Freetown between 1967 and 1973 as the starting point for his study of youth cultures in Sierra Leone's capital, Abdullah demonstrates how the socially constructed borders between working-class and middle-class youth started to collapse under the strain of political repression and the appearance of new 'imagined youth communities'. These emerged around new forms of urban youth leisure, the *odelay* masking societies, as well as new urban spaces, neighbourhood meeting points or *pote*. Abdullah analyzes how different groups of youth were gradually fused into a new hybrid category constructed around common ideals. The emergence of this new category of youth inaugurated a conversion of the political landscape which was rooted in violence. His underlying argument revolves around the role of subaltern youth cultures in the creation of alternative political power-scapes in Sierra Leone and postcolonial Africa.

De Boeck's essay explores the phenomenon of witchcraft accusations against children in Kinshasa. As a result of these widespread accusations, thousands of children end up in the street. Child-witches have become an integral part of daily life in the Congolese capital, against a background of mounting Christian fundamentalism and a radical religious transfiguration of public space in the city. De Boeck offers an analysis of the underlying reasons for this phenomenon, which is unprecedented in its scale. He points to the destructurations and transformations of existing patterns of kinship in the urban context and links these to profound shifts occurring in relations of gift, reciprocity and exchange. His analysis shows how the growing epistemological breach between reality (the first world) and its double (the second world) creates the conditions for the overt invasion of the space of the living by the spirits of the dead.

Biaya's comparative analysis of urban youth in Dakar, Addis Ababa, and Kinshasa points out the heterodoxy of young people's lives in the continent today and the creative ways in which they attempt to move beyond the meanings and frontiers of the postcolonial world. Biaya argues that the violent cultures of the street which develop throughout Africa consecrate the young person as political actor. By adopting a cultural aesthetics that introduces a radical rupture with the existing logics of the postcolonial reality, these youngsters mix and blend bodily images, attitudes and practices that appear as globalized and through which new figures of disobedience are generated. Introducing an epistemological breach within the diverse urban worlds in which they develop, these youth street cultures mark both the emergence of radically new forms of sociality and the permanence of institutional violence.

The book ends with an Afterword by Mamadou Diouf which sketches the trajectories and the predicament of African youth and highlights the contributions this volume makes in broadening our understandings of the situation of youth in Africa today. In his own words: 'In the diversity of voices this collection makes heard and in the readings it proposes, the authors challenge us regarding the various imaginaries at work on the African continent.' 'This volume,' he continues, 'takes on the task of decrypting these significations and indicates the new fields of work to be opened and new objects for study.'

References

Abdullah, I. & Y. Bangura (eds). 1997. *Lumpen Youth Culture and Political Violence: The Sierra Leone Civil War*, Special Issue of *African Development* 23: 3–4.

Aguillar, M. (ed.). 1997. *The Politics of Age and Gerontocracy in Africa*. Trenton, NJ: Africa World Press.

Amit-Talai, V. & H. Wulff (eds), 1995. *Youth Cultures: A Cross-cultural Perspective*. London: Routledge.

Argenti, N. 1998. 'Air Youth: Performance, Violence and the State in Cameroon,' *Journal of the Royal Anthropological Institute* 4 (4): 753–81.

— 2001. '*Kesum-body* and the Places of the Gods: The Politics of Children's Masking and Second-world Realities in Oku (Cameroon),' *Journal of the Royal Anthropological Institute* 7 (1): 67–94.

Ariès, P. 1962. *Centuries of Childhood*. New York: Vintage Press.

Badat, S. 1997. *Black Student Politics, Higher Education and Apartheid: from SASO to SANSCO, 1968–1990*. Pretoria: Human Sciences Research Council.

Barrett, M. 1998a. *The Conditions for Repatriation of Angolan Refugees in Meheba Settlement: A Report from a Minor Field Study in Zambia*, Department of Cultural Anthropology and Ethnology, Uppsala University.

— 1998b. *Tuvosena, 'Let's Go Everybody': Identity and Ambition among Angolan Refugees in Zambia*, Working Papers in Cultural Anthropology No. 8, Department of Cultural Anthropology and Ethnology, Uppsala University.

Battaglia, D. 1995. 'Problematising the Self: A Thematic Introduction,' in *Rhetorics of Self-Making*, ed. D. Battaglia. Berkeley, CA: University of California Press.

Bayart, J. F., A. Mbembe & C. Toulabor. 1992. *Le Politique par le bas en Afrique Noire: Contributions à une problematique de la démocracie*. Paris: Karthala.

Bazenguissa-Ganga, Remy. 1996. 'Milices politiques et bandes armées à Brazzaville: Enquête sur la violence politique et sociale des jeunes déclassés,' *Les Etudes du CERI* (Centre d'Etudes et de Recherches Internationales) No. 13. Paris: CERI.

Bazenguissa-Ganga, Remy. 1999. 'The Spread of Political Violence in Congo-Brazzaville,' *African Affairs* 98 (386): 37–54.

Bazenguissa-Ganga, Remy & J. MacGaffey. 1995. 'Vivre et briller à Paris: Des jeunes Congolais et Zaïrois en marge de la légalité économique,' *Politique Africaine* 57: 124–33.

Behrend, H. 2002. '"I am Like a Movie Star in My Street": Photographic Self-Creation in Postcolonial Kenya,' in *Postcolonial Subjectivities in Africa*, ed. Richard Werbner. London: Zed Books.

Biaya, T. K. 2000. 'Hair Statements in Urban Africa: The Beauty, the Mystic and the Madam,' in *The Art of African Fashion*, ed. Els van der Plas and Marlous Willmsen. Trenton, NJ: Africa World Press.

Boothby, Neil, Peter Upton & Abubacar Sultan. 1992. 'Boy Soldiers of Mozambique,' in *Refugee Children*. Refugee Studies Programme, Oxford, March.

Bourdieu, P. 1993. 'Youth is just a Word,' in P. Bourdieu, *Sociology in Question*. London: Sage.

Boyden, J. 1990. 'Childhood and the Policy Makers: A Comparative Perspective on the Globalization of Childhood,' in *Constructing and Reconstructing Childhood: Contemporary Issues in the Sociological Study of Childhood*, ed. A. James & A. Prout. London and Washington, DC: Falmer Press.

Boyden, J. & S. Gibbs. 1997. *Children and War: Understanding Psychological Distress in Cambodia*. Geneva: UN.

Bruyère, J. M. 2001. *L'envers du jour. Mondes réels et imaginaires des enfants errants de Dakar*. Paris: Editions Léo Scheer.

Bundy, Colin. 1987. 'Street Sociology and Pavement Politics: Aspects of Youth and Student Resistance in Cape Town, 1985,' *Journal of Southern African Studies* 13: 303–30.

Caputo, V. 1995. 'Anthropology's Silent "Others": A Consideration of Some Conceptual and Methodological Issues for the Study of Youth and Children's Cultures,' in *Youth Cultures: A Cross-cultural Perspective*, ed. V. Amit-Talai & H. Wulff. London: Routledge.

Carter, Charles. 1991. '"We are the Progressives": Alexandra Youth Congress Activists and the Freedom Charter, 1983–1985,' *Journal of Southern African Studies* 17 (2).

Cartry, C. 1978. 'Jeux d'enfants Gourmantché,' in *Systèmes de signes: Textes réunis en hommage à Germaine Dieterlen*. Paris: Hermann.

Chin, E. 2001. *Purchasing Power. Black Kids and American Consumer Culture*. Minneapolis, MN and London: University of Minnesota Press.

Cohn, I & G. S. Goodwin-Gill, 1994. *Child Soldiers: The Role of Children in Armed Conflicts*. Oxford: Clarendon Press.

Collignon, R. & M. Diouf (eds), 2001. *Les Jeunes, hantise de l'espâce public dans les sociétés du Sud?* Special issue of *Autrepart*, 18.

Comaroff, J. & J. Comaroff, 1999. 'Alien-Nation: Zombies, Immigrants, and Millennial Capitalism,' *CODESRIA Bulletin* 3–4: 17–28.

Connolly, M. & J. Ennew (eds), 1996. 'Children Out of Place,' *Childhood* 3 (2).

Coulter, C. 1998. 'Youth after War: Emerging Influence or Submerged by Power'. Unpublished project proposal, Dept. of Anthropology, University of Uppsala.

Cruise O'Brien, D. 1996. 'Youth Identity and State Decay in West Africa,' in *Postcolonial Identities in Africa*, ed. R. Werbner & T. Ranger. London: Zed Books.

D'Almeida-Topor, H., C. Coquery-Vidrovitch, O. Goerg & F. Guitard (eds). 1992a. *Les jeunes en Afrique, Tome I: Evolution et rôle*. Paris: L'Harmattan.

— 1992b. *Les jeunes en Afrique, Tome II: La politique et la ville*. Paris: L'Harmattan.

Dawes, A. & D. Donald. 1994. *Childhood and Adversity: Psychological Perspectives from South African Research*. Cape Town: David Philip.

Dawes, A. & A. Honwana. 1996. 'Children, Culture and Mental Health: Interventions in Conditions of War.' Paper presented at conference on Children, War and Prosecution, Maputo, 1–4 December.

De Boeck, F. 1999a. 'Domesticating Diamonds and Dollars: Identity, Expenditure and Sharing in Southwestern Zaire (1984–1997),' in *Globalization and Identity: Dialectics of Flow and Closure*, ed. B. Meyer & P. Geschiere. Oxford: Blackwell.

— 1999b. 'Dogs Breaking Their Leash: Globalization and Shifting Gender Categories in the Diamond Traffic between Angola and D. R. Congo (1984–1997),' in *Changements au féminin en Afrique Noire, Anthropologie et Littérature*, ed. D. De Lame & C. Zabus, *Vol. 1. Anthropologie*. Tervuren/Paris: Musée Royale de l'Afrique Centrale/L'Harmattan.

— 2000. 'Borderland Breccia: The Mutant Hero and the Historical Imagination of a Central-African Diamond Frontier,' *Journal of Colonialism and Colonial History* 1 (2) (electronic journal).

de Waal, Alex & Nicolas Argenti (eds). 2002. *Young Africa: Realising the Rights of Children and Youth.* Trenton, NJ: Africa World Press.

Diouf, Mamadou. 1996. 'Urban Youth and Senegalese Politics: Dakar 1988–1994,' *Public Culture* 8 (2): 225–50.

Dodge, C. P. & M. Raundalen (eds). 1987. *War, Violence, and Children in Uganda*. Oslo: Norwegian University Press.

Dodge, C. P. & M. Raundalen, 1991. *Reaching Children in War: Sudan, Uganda and Mozambique*. Uppsala: Sigma Forlag.

Donald, David, Andrew Dawes & Johann Louw (eds). 2000. *Addressing Childhood Adversity: Psychological Perspectives from South African Research*. Cape Town: David Philip Publishers.

Drucker-Brown, S. 1999. 'The Grandchildren's Play at the Mamprusi King's Funeral: Ritual Rebellion Revisited in Northern Ghana,' *Journal of the Royal Anthropological Institute* 5 (2): 181–92.

Durham, D. 2000. 'Youth and the Social Imagination in Africa,' *Anthropological Quarterly* 73 (3): 113–20.

Ellis, S. 1995. 'Liberia 1989–1994: A Study of Ethnic and Spiritual Violence,' *African Affairs* 94 (375).

El-Kenz, A. 1996. 'Youth and Violence,' in *Africa Now: People, Policies, Institutions*, ed. S. Ellis. The Hague/London/Portsmouth, NH: DGIS/James Currey/Heinemann.

Ennew, J. 2002. 'Future Generations and Global Standards: Children's Rights at the Start of the Millennium,' in *Exotic No More: Anthropology on the Front Lines*, ed. J. MacClancy. Chicago and London: University of Chicago Press.

Everatt, D. & E. Sisulu (eds). 1992. *Black Youth in Crisis Facing the Future.* Johannesburg: Ravan Press.

Ferguson, J. 2002. 'Of Mimicry and Membership: Africans and the "New World Society"', *Cultural Anthropology* 17 (4): 551–69.

Friedman, J. 1994. 'The Political Economy of Elegance: An African Cult of Beauty,' in *Consumption and Identity*, ed. J. Friedman. Chur, Switzerland: Harwood.

Furley, O. 1995. 'Child Soldiers in Africa,' in *Conflict in Africa*, ed. O. Furley. London: Tauris Academic Press.

Gandoulou, J. D. 1989. *Au coeur de la sape: Moeurs et aventures des Congolais à Paris*. Paris: L'Harmattan.

Gibbs, S. 1994. 'Post-War Reconstruction in Mozambique: Reframing Children's Experience of War and Healing,' *Disasters* 18 (3): 268–300.

Gilroy, P. 1987. *'There Ain't No Black in the Union Jack': The Cultural Politics of Race and Nation*. London: Hutchinson.

Gluckman, M. 1954. *Rituals of Rebellion in South-East Africa*. Manchester: Manchester University Press.

— 1960. *Order and Rebellion in Tribal Africa*. Glencoe, IL: Free Press.

Goldman, L. R. 1998. *Child's Play: Myth, Mimesis and Make-Believe*. Oxford and New York: Berg.

Göncü, A. (ed.). 1999. *Children's Engagement in the World: Sociocultural Perspectives*. Cambridge: Cambridge University Press.

Gondola, D. 1999. 'La sape des *mikilistes*: Théâtre de l'artifice et représentation onirique,' *Cahiers d'Etudes Africaines* 39 (1), 153: 13–47.

Gottlieb, A. 2000. '"Where Have All the Babies Gone"? Toward an Anthropology of Infants and Their Caretakers,' *Anthropological Quarterly* 73 (3): 121–32.

Gunter, B. & A. Furnham. 1998. *Children as Consumers: A Psychological Analysis of the Young People's Market*. London: Routledge.

Hall, S. & T. Jefferson (eds). 1976. *Resistance through Rituals*. London: Hutchinson.

Hannerz, U. 1999. 'Epilogue: On Some Reports from a Free Space,' in *Globalization and Identity: Dialectics of Flow and Closure*, ed. B. Meyer & P. Geschiere. Oxford: Blackwell.

Hansen, K. Tranberg. 2000. 'Gender and Difference: Youth, Bodies and Clothing in Zambia,' in *Gender, Agency and Change*, ed. Victoria Ana Goddard. London and New York: Routledge

Harvey, D. 1989. *The Condition of Postmodernity: An Enquiry into the Origins of Cultural Change*. Oxford: Blackwell.

— 2000. 'Cosmopolitanism and the Banality of Geographic Evils,' *Public Culture* 12 (2): 529–64.

Hebdige, D. 1979. *Subculture: The Meaning of Style*. London and New York: Methuen.

Henderson, P. C. 1999. 'Living with Fragility: Children in New Crossroads,' doctoral dissertation, Dept. of Social Anthropology, University of Cape Town.

Hérault, G. & P. Adesanmi (eds). 1997. *Youth, Street Culture and Urban Violence*. Ibadan: IFRA.

Hirschfeld, L. A. 1999. 'L'enfant terrible: Anthropology and its Aversion to Children,' *Etnofoor* 12 (1): 5–26.
— 2002. 'Why Don't Anthropologists Like Children?' *American Anthropologist* 104 (2): 611–27.
Honwana, A. 1997. *Sealing the Past, Facing the Future: Trauma Healing in Mozambique, Accord No. 3.* London: Coalition Resources (Special Issue on the Mozambican Peace Process).
— 1998. 'Okusiakala Ondalo Yokalye, Let's Light a New Fire: Local Knowledge in the Post-War Reintegration of War-affected Children in Angola,' Consultancy Report for Christian Children's Fund.
— 1999a. 'Negotiating Post-War Identities: Child Soldiers in Mozambique and Angola,' *CODESRIA Bulletin* 1 & 2: 4–13.
— 1999b. 'Untold War Stories: Young Women and War in Mozambique,' paper presented at the Leuven Conference on Children and Youth as Emerging Social Categories in Africa, November.
— 2001. 'Children of War: Local Understandings of War and War Trauma in Mozambique and Angola,' in *Civilians in War*, ed. Simon Chesterman. Boulder, CO: Lynne Rienner.
Human Rights Watch. 1994. *Easy Prey: Children and War in Liberia.* London: Human Rights Watch Children's Project.
Hyslop, Jonathan. 1988. 'School Student Movements and State Education Policy: 1972–1987,' in *Popular Struggles in South Africa*, ed. William Cobbett & Robin Cohen. London: James Currey.
— 1990. 'Schools, Unemployment and Youth: Origins and Significance of School and Youth Movements,' in *Education: From Poverty to Liberty*, ed. B. Nasson & J. Samuels. Cape Town: Credo Press.
Jabri, V. 1996. *Discourses on Violence: Conflict Analysis Reconsidered.* Manchester: Manchester University Press.
James, A. 1993. *Childhood Identities: Self and Social Relationships in the Experience of Childhood.* Edinburgh: Edinburgh University Press.
James, A. & A. Prout (eds). 1990. *Constructing and Reconstructing Childhood: Contemporary Issues in the Sociological Study of Childhood.* London and Washington, DC: Falmer Press.
Jewsiewicki, B. & J. Letourneau (eds). 1998, *Les jeunes à l'ère de la mondialisation: Quête identitaire et conscience historique.* Quebec: Septentrion.
Johnson, Shaun. 1989. '"The Soldiers of Luthuli": Youth in the Politics of Resistance in South Africa,' in *South Africa: No Turning Back*, ed. Shaun Johnson. Bloomington, IN: Indiana University Press.
Kakwenzire, Joan. 1996. 'Preconditions for Demarginalizing Women and Youth in Ugandan Politics,' in *Love and the Struggle for Democracy in East Africa*, ed. Joseph Oloka-Onyango, Kivutha Kibwana & Chris Maina Peters. Nairobi: Claripress.
Kangni Alem. 2002. *Atterrissage.* Libreville: Editions Ndzé.
Kaplan, R. 1994. 'The Coming Anarchy' *Atlantic Monthly* 273 (2).
Kilbride, P., C. Suda & E. Njeru. 2000. *Street Children in Kenya: Voices of Children in Search of a Childhood.* Westport, CT and London: Bergin & Garvey.
Kurimoto, E. & S. Simonse. 1998. *Conflict, Age & Power in North East Africa.* Oxford: James Currey.
La Hausse, P. 1990. 'The Cows of Nongoloza: Youth, Crime and Amalaita Gangs in Durban, 1900–1930,' *Journal of Southern African Studies* 16 (1).
Last, Murray. 1991. 'Adolescents in a Muslim City: The Cultural Context of Danger and Risk,' *Kano Studies*, special issue.
Letourneau, J. (ed.). 1997. *Le lieu identitaire de la jeunesse d'aujourd'hui, Etudes de cas.* Paris: L'Harmattan.
Levine, R. A., S. Dixon, S. Levine, et al. 1994. *Child Care and Culture: Lessons from Africa.* Cambridge: Cambridge University Press.
Ly, B. 1988. 'The Present Situation of Youth in Africa,' in *Perspectives on Contemporary Youth*, ed. J. Kuczynski, S. N. Eisenstadt, B. Ly, and L. Sarkar. Tokyo: United Nations University.
Machel, G. 1996. *Impact of Armed Conflict on Children*, Report to the Secretary General of the United Nations, August 26.
Marguerat, Y. & D. Poitou (eds). 1994. *A l'écoute des enfants de la rue en Afrique Noire.* Paris: Fayard.
Marks, M. 2001. *Young Warriors: Youth Politics, Identity and Violence in South Africa.* Johannesburg: Witswatersrand University Press.
Marten, J. 2002. *Children and War.* New York and London: New York University Press.
Mbembe, Achille. 1985. *Les jeunes et l'ordre politique en Afrique.* Paris: L'Harmattan.
—1987. *Afrique Indocile.* Paris: L'Harmattan.
McRobbie, A. & M. Nava (eds). 1984. *Gender and Generation.* London: Methuen.
Naidoo, Kumi. 1992. 'The Politics of Youth Resistance in the 1980s: The Dilemmas of a Differentiated Durban,' *Journal of Southern African Studies* 18 (1).
Ndebele, Njabulo. 1995. 'Recovering Childhood: Children in South African National Reconstruction,' in *Children and the Politics of Culture*, ed. Sharon Stephens. Princeton, NJ: Princeton University Press.
Noy, F., K. Mlenzi & F. Wa Simbeye. 2001. *Avoir 20 ans à Dar Es-Salaam.* Paris: Editions Charles Léopold Mayer.
Obikeze, Dan S. & Ada A. Mere. 1985. *Children and the Nigerian Civil War: A Study of the Rehabilitation Programme for War Displaced Children.* Nsukka: University of Nsukka Press.
Ojo, J .D. 1995. *Students' Unrest in Nigerian Universities.* Ibadan: IFRA and Spectrum Books.

Peters, K & P. Richards. 1998. 'Jeunes combattants parlant de la guerre et de la paix en Sierra Leone,' *Cahiers d'Etudes Africaines* 150–52: 581–617.

Pilkington, H. 1994. *Russia's Youth and its Culture: A Nation's Constructors and Constructed*. London: Routledge.

Remes, P. 1999. 'Global Popular Musics and Changing Awareness of Urban Tanzanian Youth,' *Yearbook for Traditional Music* 31: 1–26.

Reno, W. 1993. 'Foreign Firms and the Financing of Charles Taylor,' *Liberian Studies* 18 (2): 00–00.

—— 1995. *Corruption and State Politics in Sierra Leone*. Cambridge: Cambridge University Press.

Reynolds, Pamela. 1990. 'Children of Tribulation: The Need to Heal and the Means to Heal War Trauma,' *Africa* 60 (1): 1–38.

—— 1991. *Dance Civet Cat: Child Labour in the Zambezi Valley*. Athens, OH: Ohio University Press.

—— 1995. 'Youth and the Politics of Culture in South Africa', in *Children and the Politics of Culture*, ed. S. Stephens, Princeton, NJ: Princeton University Press.

—— 1996. *Traditional Healers and Childhood in Zimbabwe*. Athens, OH: Ohio University Press.

—— 1998. 'Activism, Politics and the Punishment of Children,' in *Childhood Abused: Protecting Children Against Torture, Cruel, Inhuman and Degrading Treatment and Punishment*, ed. Geraldine Van Bueren. Aldershot: Ashgate

Richards, A. 1988 (1956). *Chisungu: A Girl's Initiation Ceremony among the Bemba of Zambia*. London: Routledge.

Richards, P. 1995. 'Rebellion in Liberia and Sierra Leone: A Crisis of Youth?' in *Conflict in Africa*, ed. O. Furley. London: Taurus Academic Press.

—— 1996. *Fighting for the Rain Forest: War, Youth and Resources in Sierra Leone*, Oxford/Portsmouth, NH: James Currey/Heinemann.

Riesman, P. 1992. *First Find Yourself a Good Mother. The Construction of Self in Two African Communities*. New Brunswick, NJ: Rutgers University Press.

Ross, A. & T. Rose (eds). 1994. *Microphone Fiends: Youth Music and Youth Culture*. New York and London: Routledge.

Scheper-Hughes, N. & C. Sargent (eds). 1998. *Small Wars: The Cultural Politics of Childhood*. Berkeley, CA: University of California Press.

Seekings, Jeremy. 1993. *Heroes or Villains? Youth Politics in the 1980s*. Johannesburg: Ravan Press.

Seremetakis, C. N. 1994. *The Senses Still: Perception and Memory as Material Culture in Modernity*. Chicago and London: University of Chicago Press.

Sharp, Lesley. 1990. 'Possessed and Dispossessed Youth: Spirit Possession of Children in Northwest Madagascar,' *Culture, Medicine and Psychiatry* 14: 339–64.

—— 1995. 'Playboy Princely Spirits of Madagascar: Possession as Youthful Commentary and Social Critique,' *Anthropological Quarterly* 68 (2): 75–88.

Skelton, T. & G. Valentine (eds). 1998. *Cool Places: Geographies of Youth Cultures*. London: Routledge.

Soyinka, W. 2000. 'The Children of This Land,' *Michigan Quarterly Review* 39 (2): 376 (Special Issue, *Secret Spaces of Childhood*).

Ssewakiryanga, Richard. 1999. "New Kids on the Blocks': African-American Music and Uganda Youth,' *CODESRIA Bulletin* 1 & 2.

Stephens, S. (ed.). 1995. *Children and the Politics of Culture*. Princeton, NJ: Princeton University Press.

Straker, G. et al. 1992. *Faces in the Revolution: The Psychological Effects of Violence on Township Youth in South Africa*. Cape Town: David Philip.

Suarez-Orozco, M. M. 1987. 'The Treatment of Children in the Dirty War Ideology, State Terrorism, and the Abuse of Children in Argentina,' in *Child Survival*, ed. Nancy Scheper Hughes. Dordrecht: Kluwer.

Tayob, Abdulkader. 1995. *Islamic Resurgence in South Africa: The Muslim Youth Movement*. Cape Town: University of Cape Town Press.

Thomas, N. 2000. *Children, Family and the State: Decisionmaking and Child Participation*. Basingstoke: Macmillan

Toulabor, Comi M. 1995. 'Jeunes, violence et democratization au Togo,' *Afrique Contemporaine* 180: 106–25.

Toungara, Jeanne Maddox. 1995. 'Generational Tensions in the Parti Democratique de Cote d'Ivoire', *African Studies Review* 38 (2): 11–38.

Turner, V. 1967. *The Forest of Symbols: Aspects of Ndembu Ritual*. Ithaca, NY and London: Cornell University Press.

Utas, M. 2003. *Sweet Battlefields: Youth and the Liberian Civil War*. Uppsala: Institute for Cultural Anthropology and Ethnology.

Utas, M., M. W. Gbessagee & C. Kiawu. n.d. 'Youth Social Reintegration in Sinoe Country, Liberia. Qualitative Assessment Report,' Belgian Red Cross/Liberian National Red Cross Society Report.

Valentine, G., T. Skelton & D. Chambers. 1998. 'Cool Places: An Introduction to Youth and Youth Cultures,' in *Cool Places: Geographies of Youth Cultures*, ed. T. Skelton & G. Valentine. London and New York: Routledge.

Willis, P. 1977. *Learning to Labour: How Working Class Kids Get Working Class Jobs*. Westmead: Saxon House.

Wong, L. (ed.). 1999. *Shootback: Photos by Kids from the Nairobi Slums*. London: Booth-Clibborn Editions.

Wyn, J. & R. White. 1997. *Rethinking Youth*. London: Sage.

Yoka Lye Mudaba, A. 1991. 'Système de la mode à Kinshasa: culte du para'tre,' in *La ville africaine et ses urgences vitales*, ed. Mashin Maringa. Kinshasa: Facultés Catholiques de Kinshasa.

I   Children & Youth in a Global Era

1   JEAN COMAROFF & JOHN COMAROFF
Reflections on Youth
from the Past to the Postcolony

Prolegomenon
... philosophy does not concern itself with children.
It leaves them to pedagogy, where they're not in very good hands.
Philosophy has forgotten about children.
(Bernhard Schlink, *The Reader*, p.141)

There has long been a tendency in the public discourse of the West to speak of youth as a transhistorical, transcultural category. As if it has existed everywhere and at all times in much the same way. This is in spite of the fact that anthropologists and historians have insisted, for almost as long, that the cultural meanings and social attributes ascribed to 'youth' have varied a great deal across time and space; recall Malinowski and Margaret Mead, not to mention Philippe Ariès. It is also an anthropological truism that the way in which young people are perceived, named, and represented betrays a lot about the social and political constitution of a society. Thus it is that, in nineteenth-century Britain, down-class juveniles were referred to as 'nomads'; their terrains, the internal colonies of the industrial metropole, were called 'Jungles,' even 'Africas' (Hebdige, 1988:20). Similarly, in late twentieth-century North America and South Africa (Seekings, 1993:xii, citing David Everatt), white pre-adults are typically termed 'teenagers', while their black counterparts are 'youth'; adolescents with attitude, so to speak. In this manner, language racializes and demonizes difference without explicitly marking it. 'Words,' Joseph Conrad (1957:11) once said, are 'the great foes of reality'. But they also open a window onto its secrets.

   Far from constituting a universal category – a social status generated by the abstract sociological principle of generation – youth, as we speak of them here, are the historical offspring of modernity; modernity, that is, as the *ideological formation* which arose during the Age of Revolution, 1789-1848 (cf. Hobsbawm, 1962), and was honed in the fraught dialectics of empire; modernity as an ideological formation which naturalized its own telos in a model of human development (Lukose, 2000) that casts 'youth' as both the essential precondition and the indefinite postponement of maturity.[1] Industrial capitalist society has been more or less unique in making childhood into a site of self-conscious cultural reproduction, releasing its young from the workplace so that they might

---

[1] Constructs like 'racial adolescence', deployed by civilizing missions abroad to measure the (lack of) 'progress' of colonized peoples towards 'modernity', demonstrate the ideological uses of this form of developmentalism; see W.C. Willoughby (1923:239) for a South African instance.

enter the rarified world of education, the latter being the space in which the nation-state seeks to husband its potential, in which it invests its human capital, in which, says Foucault (1976:81), it 'hides its dreams'. Yet juveniles are also the creatures of our nightmares, of our social impossibilities and our existential angst.

It is in this latter sense that, for Hebdige (1988:17), youth enter modernist narratives only when they stand for trouble. But the matter is more ambiguous than this suggests. Trouble, Butler (1990:vii) insists, need not merely be cast in the negative. It can also imply the productive unsettling of dominant epistemic regimes under the heat of desire, frustration or anger. Youth, in other words, are complex signifiers, the stuff of mythic extremes (Blanch, 1980:103), simultaneously idealizations and monstrosities, pathologies and panaceas. This has been true for a very long time. Witness the ambivalent appearance of the young in Dickensian London, on the one hand as orphans and artful dodgers, yet also as the bearers of Great Expectations. Or the discordant images of juvenile activists in late twentieth-century Africa: contrast, for example, the preternatural child soldiers of Mozambique or Sierra Leone, the very epitome of civil disintegration (Honwana, 1999), with the heroic 'young lions' of South Africa, who were the harbingers of democracy and the end of *apartheid*. Such contrasts are likely to persist: in Brazil, homeless children have come to symbolize *both* the collective shame of the nation-state and its future resurrection through proper planning and legal intervention (Veloso, n.d.).

In short, 'youth' stand for many things at once: for the terrors of the present, the errors of the past, the prospect of a future. For old hopes and new frontiers (see De Boeck in this volume). In all of these tropic guises, of course, they are figures of a popular imagination far removed from more nuanced social realities.[2] This is crucial to keep in mind as we interrogate the place of young people in the late twentieth-century nation-state – especially those neoliberal nation-states currently in difficulty – in Africa and elsewhere.

Generation Trouble

The meaning of globalization, at least as an analytic concept, might still be in dispute in some circles. But few would deny that one global feature of the contemporary world – from Chicago to Cape Town, Calcutta to Caracas – is a sense of crisis surrounding the predicament of juveniles. Although it is always locally mediated and modulated, that predicament appears to arise out of the workings of neoliberal capitalism and the changing planetary order of which it is part. It takes many forms, patently. But it seems everywhere to be founded on a counterpoint, a doubling, a contradiction perhaps. On the one hand is the much remarked exclusion of the young from national economies, especially from their shrinking, metamorphosing productive sectors. As the frenzied expansion of the free market runs up against the demise of the welfare state, a process that manifests itself in an ever widening gulf between rich and poor, the commonwealth of all but a few sovereign polities has been drastically eroded. In the upshot, most are unable to sustain previous levels of social services and benefits, to afford the cost of infrastructural reproduction, or to underwrite a labour market in which there is regular or secure

---

[2] Apart from all else, 'youth' are always only a fraction of those not yet adult: that fraction whose anomalous agency asserts itself in honour or breach of communal order. Often they are the mutant citizens of the modern nation, purveyors of its violent undersides. This is a point to which we shall return.

employment in any abundance. Even in advanced industrial societies, the modernist dream of infinite progress – a narrative according to which each generation does better than its predecessor – is constantly mocked; mocked, by conditions that disenfranchise many people,[3] disproportionately the young and unskilled of the inner city and the countryside, from full waged citizenship in the nation-state.[4] This, despite the claims by some that the current generation of mainstream American 'kids' is more compliant, less cynical than those who came before them (Howe and Strauss, 2000). To be sure, patterns of polarization and exclusion, among youth and across the age spectrum at large, are ever more palpable in these neoliberal times.

On the other hand is the recent rise of assertive, global youth cultures of desire, self-expression, representation; also, in some places, of potent, if unconventional, forms of politicization to go along with them. In the cyberspace age, juveniles have an enhanced capacity to communicate in, and act effectively on, the world at large. Generation has become a concrete, quotidian principle of social mobilization, inflecting other dimensions of difference, notably, race, gender, ethnicity and class.[5] Transnational youth activism, and the mutually comprehensible signifying practices on which it is based, are facilitated by planetary flows – of currencies, people, value – across old sovereign boundaries (see Venkatesh n.d.[a]:6; Appadurai 1990). The young have taken to the internet and to the streets in growing numbers as post-Fordist economics recasts relations between capital and labour, profoundly altering global geographies of production. More of this below.

In the late twentieth century, in sum, youth have gained unprecedented autonomy as a social category *an und für sich*, both in and for themselves. This is in spite, or perhaps because, of their relative marginalization from the normative world of work and wages. In many Western contexts they, along with other disenfranchised persons,[6] add up to an incoherent counter-nation with its own illegal economies of ways and means, its own spaces of production and recreation, its own parodic patriotisms. Elsewhere (1999b), we use the term 'alien-nation' to describe the phenomenon; in like vein, Zizek (1997:127f) treats these disenfranchised persons as the 'symptoms' of late-capitalist universalism, whose imminent logic ensures that their equivalent deprivations never find unified voice in some 'rainbow coalition, notwithstanding progressivist liberal hopes and expectations'. As this suggests, youth embody the sharpening contradictions of the contemporary world in especially acute form. Take South Africa, for example. Here, in the *apartheid* years, the juvenile black counter-nation had a palpable opponent in the racist state. With

---

[3] This theme was sounded repeatedly by proponents of Ralph Nader's Green Party in the 2000 US elections. Michael Moore, radical film-maker and anti-corporate activist, described Nader as the champion of 'young people, who feel disenfranchised and dispossessed by mainstream American politics' (special election report, *848*, National Public Radio, 6 November 2000).

[4] While it might be argued that, constitutionally, citizenship in liberal democracies has never included a right to work, the provision of unemployment benefits, workers' compensation, and pensions to the nationals of welfare states has implied entitlement to an income. Such benefits are widely under threat in this neoliberal age, but the obligation to sustain the highest possible levels of employment continues to be one of the taken-for-granted expectations of government everywhere, notwithstanding the ferocious realpolitik of market competition. In this essay, we use the notion of 'waged citizenship' to imply social and moral membership in the national commonweal.

[5] This is not to imply that youth forms a 'homogeneous, sociological category of people which thinks, organizes and acts' in coherent ways (Seekings, 1993:xiv); but the same may be said of 'working class politics' (*pace* Seekings, *loc.cit.*). Youth, like the working class, is a politically constructed category; both are rooted in their relationship to the means of production and consumption. Increasingly, moreover, they are entailed in each other (see Corrigan and Frith, 1976; Comaroff and Comaroff, 2000a).

[6] Most notably, immigrant workers and non-autochthonous minorities; see Comaroff and Comaroff (2000b).

the demise of the *ancien regime*, the dispossessed won the right to enter the workplace as 'free' individuals. But, in a tragic irony, this occurred just as the global impact of neoliberal capitalism began to kick in. Now large-scale privatization, the loss of blue-collar employment, and the erosion of working-class identities vitiate the prospects of building an inclusive social democracy. Young people of colour, would-be citizens of the 'new' millennial order, must find their place in a society whose hard-won nationhood is already subverted by forces that compromise the territorial sovereignty of its political economy.

But we are running ahead of ourselves. In order to push our understanding of the contemporary predicament of youth beyond the merely superficial, to explore further the doubling – the ambiguous threat and promise – inherent in its formation, it is necessary to dig a little deeper into the modernist archaeology of the category. For it is here that we are likely to find the source of contemporary generation troubles, or, at least, our apprehension of them.

A Brief History of Youth

Foucault (1976:80) may or may not have been correct in claiming that modern Western society is unique in accentuating the gulf between children and adults. But we *do* appear to have romanticized and commodified that space, making it a site wherein immature carelessness confronts full-grown desire, wherein an irrepressible sense of invincibility seems to drive precocious power. Of course, the nation-states of Europe were not alone in marking out 'youth' as a life-phase whose liminal force could be tapped for the collective good. Age-based societies in Africa mobilized premarital warriorhood to this end as well; indeed, those who languish between corporeal and social maturity, debarred from marrying or establishing families, have become the footsoldiers of adult hegemony in many places. Youth, from this perspective, are everywhere a *potential* category of exclusion and exploitation, a source of surplus value.

It is arguable that twentieth-century European polities, with their technologies of mass production, communication, and coercion, have been singularly well positioned to idealize and utilize the physical and imaginative resources of the young. Yet one of the hallmarks of the present moment, of the age of globalization and postcoloniality, has been a diminishing of the capacity of governments – if not of the market forces they foster – to control adolescent bodies, energies, or intentions. From the spread of global youth cultures and environmental politics to the sprouting of urban gangs, soccer armies, and neoNazi cadres, the nation-state plays host to forces that it can no longer adequately rein in. Often, moreover, the more radical of these forces name themselves – Hip Hop Nation, Gay Nation – in ways that both mimic and mock it, all the better to trouble its sovereignty. Thus the phalanxes of football supporters in the new Europe savage people and property, assault police, and transgress boundaries at home and abroad – all in the name of national pride (Buford, 1993). Likewise, the rise of libertarian militias, whose youthful troops declare war on established government in the name of purer forms of patriotism, albeit often at the behest of more cynical, less visible father figures.

How has this come to be? Whatever its resemblance to comparable usages in other periods and places, the Euroconstruction of 'youth,' we repeat, is the outworking of a specific set of social conditions; its evolution, still ongoing, bespeaks a submerged history of modernity and its imperial underbelly. While those covered by the term have long had their deviant identity thrust upon them (see below) – and, since World War II, sold to them – they have increasingly made it their own. A brute *deus ex machina* propels this unfolding story: the complex relationship between capital and the nation-state. Industrial capitalist economies were capricious in the ways in which, Janus-faced, they both begat and undermined equalities of citizenship and entitlement; and their post-industrial counterparts have cumulatively subverted national sovereignty and the substantive rights of subjects. The sanguine expectations that once framed bourgeois cultures of progress and their civilizing missions abroad – ideals that vouchsafed the young a future under the sign of 'development' – are, as we have already said, sorely compromised by the growing inequalities wrought in the name of neoliberal capitalism. Postmodernity is often characterized as modernism bereft of its hopeful, utopian thrust.

Concomitantly, the new age of globalism might be seen as one in which the world-wide fabrication of desire, of the promise of infinite possibility, meets the impossibilities occasioned by widening disparities of wealth, itself a corollary of the devolution and decommissioning of economies of manufacture. In the face of all this, many youthful entrepreneurs, having been raised in advanced commodity cultures, find their own ways and means. Sometimes these involve the supply of hitherto unimagined 'services,' sometimes the recommissioning of the detritus of consumer society, sometimes the resale of purloined property of the state, sometimes the short-circuiting of existing networks of exchange. For a burgeoning number, they entail entry into the lower reaches of the transnational trade in drugs, and/or into a netherworld in which the deployment of violence becomes a routine mode of production and redistribution – often in a manner that replicates the practices of international business. And visibly corrodes the authority of the state. But more of this in due course.

If, to return to the earlier moment, it was the rise of industrial capitalism that first created the conditions for the emergence of a semi-autonomous category of 'youth,' it was in the exploding cities of modern Europe that this category first took on a manifest sociological reality. Hebdige (1988;19f; see above) has argued that the young first showed their insolent face, across modern Britain, in the 'delinquent' crowds that gathered in manufacturing towns, where the offspring of the rising working-class were often left to survive, and to create their own social worlds, independent of paternal or patrician control (Blanch, 1980; Gillis, 1974; Jones, 1984). Observers were particularly disturbed by children and adolescents in urban slums, by the 'wandering tribes' or 'young Arabs' who inhabited the internal colonies at the heart of London and Manchester (Mayhew, 1851:277f). These were the artful dodgers of the Dickensian inner city, to whom we alluded above, the mutant citizens of its alien-nation. They inspired a civilizing crusade, prompting the founding of Ragged Schools and Reformatories, and, in due course, a compulsory system of state education – also a pedagogic mission to 'the dark places' of the earth. One might note, with the hindsight of history (Willis, 1977), not least South African history, that state education would not so much eradicate the alien-nation as reproduce it by different means. The South African Broadcasting Corporation, in collaboration with the Department of Education, recently commissioned a team of the country's most gifted young film-makers to make a docudrama on *postapartheid* schooling.[7] They painted a chilling portrait of endemic frustration and routine violence, prompting widespread and anguished national debate.

Youth as a sign of contradiction, as the figuration of mythic bipolarity, is enshrined in

[7] *Yizo Yizo*, a thirteen-part series, broadcast on SATV3 in 1998. It was created and written by Mtutuzeli Matshoba and Angus Gibson, and directed by Angus Gibson and Teboho Mahlatsi.

the foundations of the modern collective imaginary. In the abstract, the term congeals pure, utopic potential. In everyday reality, however, 'youth' is a collective noun that has all too often indexed a faceless mass of persons who were underclass, unruly, male, challengingly out of place – and, at once physically powerful and morally immature, always liable to seize the initiative from their elders and betters. They personify the failure of moral reproduction, the dangerous obverse of capitalist optimism, the limits of a meliorist, bourgeois social vision. The tensions embodied in this pre-adult population, exacerbated where differences of race or creed colour those of generation, have peaked in periods of economic slump. For, as surplus citizens, youth are not born. They are made by historical circumstances. And rarely as they like.

But if these young people have embodied the threat of civil disorder, they can also be harnessed for state projects of organized violence, in particular, for mobilization as soldiers. Often, those not yet deemed ready to live as full citizens of the nation-state have been called upon to die for it. (Remember, in this respect, the Africans who served the colonial powers in both world wars; see, for example, Bent, 1952.) This is the flip side of the story of youth and modernity: adolescence as the infantry of adult statecraft, as the ever more reluctant blood and bone of national aspiration. At the core of the making of 'modern' youth, then, has been the role of the state in naturalizing, exploiting, and narrating the relationship between juveniles and violence, a relationship all too neatly eclipsed in the disciplinary logic of peacetime discourses about adolescent deviance.

And so it is that the association of juveniles with the threat of precocious, uncontained physicality – sexual, reproductive, combative – has haunted popular and scholarly perceptions alike in the twentieth century. In the 1920s, a rapidly professionalizing sociology (first in America, then in Europe) depicted 'youth' as a disruptive masculine force in the city, as purveyors of violent crime and ready recruits to the barbarities of life in gangs. Functionalist sociology turned historical contradiction into social pathology, and took these youth to be its epitome. They were tribal, feral beings who hunt in packs, anti-citizens, an affront to bourgeois family values and social order. Delinquent, downclass, male, and violent, they were also increasingly black. Nor is this true only in the northern and western hemispheres. Recent South African history is another instance. In the final years of struggle against *apartheid*, the category of 'youth' expanded to include diverse classes of freedom fighters: students, workers, even criminals. In this story, it is true, not all young blacks are youth. But all youth are black. Also overwhelmingly, if not exclusively, male. And if some people never become 'youth,' others seem unable to outgrow the label, even in middle age (see Buford, 1993; Seekings, 1993:11). Shades here again of Mannheim's foundational insight, recalled by Bundy (1987:304) in the African context, that generation is a social, not a chronological, category. It is also a political one – with deep material roots.

The Rise of Global 'Youth Culture'

The rise of neoliberal capitalism on a planetary scale has further complicated the modernist construction of youth. Often associated with the events of 1989, this epochal transformation was heralded by the thoroughgoing shifts in global power, economy, and modes of communication set in motion in the wake of World War II, shifts that would reshape the structure of international capital and intensify its workings. As we shall see, those shifts would not merely reconstruct colonial relations, national economies and international markets in goods, services and signs. They would also globalize the division of labour, remake human subjects, alter the relationship between production and consumption, and reform identities and citizenships across the world. While in no sense homogenizing, this process involved novel forms of space-time compression, as well as the reformulation of boundaries and localities everywhere. It also ushered in a new moment in the history of youth; to be sure, as we noted earlier, an electronically mediated 'youth culture' was one of its earliest, most expansive cultural expressions, providing a lexicon for the ever more explicit assertion of juveniles across the globe as agents in and of themselves.

It is significant, in this respect, that the USA – 'the only victor' of the Great War (Fussell, 1975:317) – emerged as *the* major economic and cultural force on the international scene after 1945. For here, where postwar affluence and pronatalism combined to usher in a fresh phase of expansionist capitalism, the 'teenager' became the new model consumer-citizen, the term itself an invention of the marketing industry (Cook, 1998). Equipped with disposable wealth to spend on commodities and 'leisure' (Cohn, 1969; Hebdige, 1988:30), this was the first generation set loose to craft itself in large part through consumption. Capitalists for the first time saw youth as a market with its own infinitely cultivable needs. 'Fawning like mad' (Cohn, 1969:15), they manufactured the means – clothes, music, magazines, dances – for creating age-based collectivities with unprecedented self-awareness, visibility, and translocal potential.

The capacity of the languages of youth culture to mark emergent identities and consciousness was shown when the 'rebels without a cause' of the 1950s became rebels with causes aplenty, from the romance of white hippy flower power to militant Black Panther antiracism. And while the naive self-absorption of lifestyle politics and rock resistance might have been evident from its roots in Haight Ashbury, the mass protests against the Vietnam War demonstrated that a self-conscious youth counter-culture could engage mainstream politics. Artful dodgers became draft dodgers, and the right of states to commandeer the means of violence, especially in the bodies and purposes of youth, was seriously challenged. Neither was this a purely parochial struggle; that much was attested by simultaneous upheavals among restive students in many parts of the world. The historical significance of these youth uprisings remains an open question. But one thing about them is clear: youth activism was a precursor of new sorts of social movements, movements born of the creative refiguring of local means and ends in the light of global, media-driven identities, ideologies, and vocabularies. The sounds of the 1960s, perhaps the true Age of Youth, traversed a multicentred, electronically unified planet, fuelled by transnational commercial interests. Amidst a rapidly proliferating flow of signs and values (Appadurai, 1990; Hannerz, 1989), youth culture began to construct an 'elsewhere' – a universe-wide, alienated age-grade – that gave pre-adults the language for an identity apart from the 'soiled and compromised parent culture' (Hebdige, 1988:30).

This age-grade, purely a figurative community, of course, was inherently tenuous and virtual. Its imagining could seldom fully transcend the limitations imposed by the commodity-dependence of mass cultural forms. As actors-through-consumption, teenagers bought – literally – into mainstream interests at the same time as they contested them. In so doing, they typified the predicament of would-be subversives in advanced capitalist contexts, of those who struggle to seize control of commodified signs and practices, thus to use them in ways that do more than merely reaffirm the *status quo*. Located far from sites of primary production, theirs is often a politics of style. Its iconoclasm is effected on camera-ready bodies, or, more recently, along digital frontiers where hackers

and 'cyberpunks' protest freedoms lost as computer technology becomes ever more subject to corporate control (Coleman, n.d.). To the critically minded, like Hebdige
(1988:35), their exertions appear ambiguous, as 'neither affirmation nor refusal'. Their
iconoclastic play with mainstream commodity forms often signals subversion – as in the
case of Punk and Rap – and may discomfort the guardians of property and propriety.
But it must always struggle to remain ahead of encroaching market forces, forces that
threaten to neutralize its effects by reducing its creativity to bland consumer goods.

Beyond the Politics of Metaphor

Still, we mistake the possibilities of the moment if we see youth culture simply as a 'politics of metaphor' (Hebdige, 1988). It is a mistake that flows from focusing more on the
products of that culture, on its disembodied images and texts, than on their situated production and use. The potential of its signs and objects to be (re)deployed, to be 'cut and
mix[ed]', has made them easily available for the fashioning of a wide variety of identities and projects; identities and projects whose sometimes subversive strain, itself often
acted out rather than spoken out, underlies the ambivalences endemic to the late twentieth-century representation of the young, *sui generis*. Also, perhaps to the political spirit
of the age writ large. For the productive aspect of 'youth culture' has expanded as juveniles have come to participate on a global scale in shaping their own markets, both legal
and illegal, as their signifying practices have connived with those species of post-Fordist
capital that owe little loyalty to local establishments or economies. Youth have been integral to the opening up of new economic spaces of unprecedented profitability – the fertile Silicon Valleys, where young 'nerds,' eschewing academic credentials and professional
regulation, have become multimillionaires, the childlike insouciance that typifies this
field, in image if not in terms of real control, being legible in the bespectacled boyish-
ness of an aging Bill Gates.

The libertarian possibilities of electronic technologies that simultaneously privatize
and globalize the means of communication are intrinsic to the effects of capitalism in its
neoliberal guise, and have generated new openings for juvenile adventurers, ostensibly
unfettered by a gerontocratic establishment. This is captured in the equivocal figure of
the 'hacker,' an under-age outlaw bent on maintaining the freedom of the information
highway, and redeeming his (more rarely her) creative potential from the grasp of evil
corporations and imperious governments (Coleman, n.d.). A string of American movies
(like *Hackers*, *Wargames*, and *Johnny Mnemonic*) rehearse popular nightmares of electronic
whizkids breaking into top security enclaves and threatening to hold the state and its
guardians to ransom. Recent reports in the US media, interestingly, tell of teenage e-
traders amassing huge fortunes in their bedrooms while putatively doing their 'home-
work'.

But suburban cyberbrats are hardly unique in their capacity to mine the potential of
new economic frontiers. Every bit as inspired and ingenious have been the ventures of
less advantaged young people from the inner cities, from postcolonial and postrevolu-
tionary societies, and from other terrors incognita, who seek to make good the promise
of world-wide laissez-faire. Here, too, liberalization has created room for youthful entrepreneurs to manoeuvre beyond the confines of modernist modes of production, polity,
legitimacy. Take the burgeoning 'bush economies' of Cameroon and Chad, where 'mar-

ket boys' cross borders, change passports, trade currencies, and traffic in high-risk cargo like guns and drugs; in so doing, they invent fresh ways of getting rich on the margins of global markets (Roitman, n.d.). Or consider the ferociously escalating teenage diamond trade – another amalgam of danger, desire, and deregulation – that provisions armies in West and Central Africa, setting up innovative configurations of libertarian commerce, violence, and profit (De Boeck, 1999). Or observe the young Mouride men from Senegal who have taken to translocal enterprise with such energy that they talk of New York as 'a suburb of Dakar'; their remittances finance major reconstruction of urban neighbourhoods at home, transform local power relations and, concomitantly, highlight the dwindling capacity of the nation-state to sustain its infrastructure (Mamadou Diouf, pers. comm.; Buggenhagen n.d). These fluid economies are usually not altogether free of gerontocratic control, of course. Nor do they supplant all formal political and economic arrangements, with which they have complex and multiple interconnections. But they do circumscribe and relativize them in significant ways, thereby challenging their exclusive sovereignty.

In sum, youth culture, in an epoch of liberalization, has shown itself uniquely able to link locales across transnational space; also to motivate the kinds of material practices that, in turn, have redrawn the maps of high modernism. Contemporaneity is its essence. In this, it echoes present-day pop, whose fast moving 'sampling' distends the normative by juxtaposing sounds in startlingly labile ways, not least when it cannibalizes ethnomusics from across the planet. Small wonder that our nightmare adolescent – wearing absurdly expensive sports shoes, headphones blaring gangsta rap, beeper tied to a global underground economy – is a synthesis of street child and corporate mogul.

A qualification here. The marginalization of young people, at least in its present-day form, may be a very general structural consequence of the rise of neoliberal capitalism. And 'youth culture' may be increasingly global in its reach. But this does not mean that the predicament of juveniles, or the manner of its experience, is everywhere the same, everywhere homogenized. Neither in its social nor in its cultural dimensions is this the case. It takes highly specific forms, and has very different material implications, in Los Angeles and Dakar, London and Delhi. Hip hop, Air Jordans, and Manchester United colours may animate youthful imaginations almost everywhere, often serving as a poignant measure of the distance between dream and fulfilment, between desire and impossibility, between centres of great wealth and peripheries of crushing poverty. But these signs are always domesticated to some degree. Otherwise they would have very little density of meaning. Appropriated and recontextualized, they are translated into hybrid languages capable of addressing local concerns. Thus it is that rap music is inflected in one way on the Cape Flats, another on the streets of Bombay or Havana. Writes Richard Ssewakiryanga (1999:26):

> Today in Uganda, rap music is not only received in its American form, but repackaged by borrowing from some of the traditional folklore to fill in the incomprehension … suffered by the audience listening to the poetics of American rappers.

Imported images, he notes, quickly penetrate local repertoires of humour, irony, anger. At the same time, these media remain points of intersection, points of connection between here and elsewhere, between sameness and difference, between received identities and a global imaginary.

Partly as a result of all this, youth tend everywhere to occupy the innovative, uncharted borderlands in which the global meets the local; this often being audible in the elaboration of creolized argots – like Street Setswana and Kwaito in South Africa – that give voice to imaginative worlds very different from those of the parental generation.[8] These frontiers are also sites of tension, particularly for young people who confront the contradictions of modernity as they try to make good on the millennial promise of democracy and the free market in the newly liberalized states of Africa and Eastern Europe. In the late twentieth century, we have suggested, the image of youth-as-trouble has gained an advanced capitalist twist as impatient adolescents try to 'take the waiting out of wanting,' thus to lessen the gulf between hope and fulfilment. In the process they have felt their power, power born of a growing willingness and ability to turn to the use of force, to garner illicit wealth, to hold polite society to ransom. Bill Buford (1993:264f) has said that it is only in moments of concerted violence that riotous British soccer fans experience a real sense of community, a point others have extended to gangland wars in US cities, to witchburning in the northerly provinces of South Africa, and to cognate social practices elsewhere. Is it surprising, then, that so many juveniles see themselves as ironic, mutant citizens of alien-nations, finding scant reflection of themselves in the rites and rhetoric, the provisions and entitlements, of a liberal democratic civic order?

Endnote

> It was the ANC manifesto that proclaimed
> 'jobs for all at a living wage'
> Where are the promised youth brigades?
> Where are the jobs? Where is the living wage?
> Now is the time. (Shaheed Mohamed, *Cape Times*, 29 July 1999)

Elsewhere (2000a) we explore the (onto)logic of neoliberal capitalism, or 'millennial capitalism,' as we refer to it, thus to index not merely its epochal rise at the end of the century, but also the fact that it has become invested with an almost magical, salvific capacity to yield wealth without work, money without manufacture. There we seek to show that structural transformations in the material, moral, and signal relationship of production to consumption have altered the very essence of labour and social reproduction; also the essence of – and mutual bleeding into each other – of class, race, gender, and generation.[9] In the final analysis, it is this epochal history, this analytic *ur*-narrative, that holds the key to any understanding of the present and future predicament of youth, even of its unfolding construction as a category *an und für sich*. Here we have sought to lay out, somewhat cavalierly, bits and pieces of the genealogy, of that *ur*-narrative.

In so doing, we have sought to complicate current talk, at least in populist discourses, of 'the crisis of youth', talk that portrays the predicament of the younger generation in

---

[8] For an excellent study of Street Setswana in the North West Province of South Africa, see Cook (1999).

[9] Age and generation, as the Marxist anthropology of precapitalist societies has long pointed out, may coalesce in self-reproducing structures of exploitation. In many of these societies, youthful cadres provided the labour power, and hence surplus value, for their elders. The parallel with neoliberal capitalism is obvious. Increasingly, 'youth' and 'underclass', both ever more racinated and ethnicized, run together; note, here, Abdullah's (1998) suggestive use of the term 'lumpen youth culture.'

monochromatically bleak terms.[10] As if all were entropy, all catastrophe, all impossibility in this Age of Futilitarianism, this age in which rampant self-interest meets rampant pessimism (Comaroff and Comaroff, 1999a). It is not that these terms are inaccurate. Nor that deep concern is unwarranted. On the contrary. The metamorphosis of the global economy *is* marginalizing many people before they grow to full maturity, excluding them from the prospect of regular employment, treating them increasingly as adults before the law when they transgress the bounds of the normative, demonizing them as they turn to crime in the absence of any other means of livelihood. The young of today, it seems, are more than ever enfranchised as consumers – welcomed into the marketplace in the immediate interests of corporate capital – often then to be excluded from the benefits of mainstream economic participation, political acknowledgement, and civic responsibility (see Venkatesh, n.d.[b]).

But this is only a part of the story.

For one thing, as we have said, the attribution to unruly youth of the standardized nightmares of polite society – not unlike the witch in precolonial and colonial Africa (Wilson, 1951) – goes back to the genesis of industrial capitalism and its bourgeois sensibilities. It is on the back of those situated in the liminal space between childhood innocence and adult responsibility that modernist sociomoral anxieties have tended to be borne. For another thing, it is crucial, if we are to make any real sense of the contemporary predicament of youth, of its neomodern construction as a category in and for itself, that we stress its intrinsic bipolarity, its doubling. Youth is not *only* a signifier of exclusion, of impossibility, of emasculation, denigration, and futility. Nor, by all accounts, is it experienced as such. While they may not, for the most part, have captured the mainstream – and may, indeed, constitute an infinitely exploitable market, an inexhaustible reservoir of consumers, an eternal fount of surplus value to be extracted – the young remain a constant source of creativity, ingenuity, possibility, empowerment, a source of alternative, yet-to-be-imagined futures.

[10] No less problematic are statements of unqualified optimism about a new and undifferentiated 'millennial generation' in the US, bereft of the cynicism and rebelliousness of their parents (Howe and Strauss, 2000)

References

Abdullah, Ibrahim. 1998. 'Bush Path to Destruction: The Origin and Character of the Revolutionary United Front/Sierra Leone,' *The Journal of Modern African Studies*, 36(2):203-35.

Appadurai, Arjun. 1990. 'Disjuncture and Difference in the Global Cultural Economy,' *Public Culture*, 2(2):1-24.

Bent, Alan R. 1952. *Ten Thousand Men of Africa: The Story of the Bechuanaland Pioneers and Gunners, 1941-1946*. London: HMSO.

Blanch, Michael. 1980. 'Imperialism, Nationalism and Organised Youth,' in *Working Class Culture: Studies in History and Theory*, ed. J. Clark, C. Critcher and R. Johnson. New York: St Martin's Press.

Buford, Bill. 1993. *Among the Thugs*. New York: Vintage Departures.

Buggenhagen, Beth Ann. n.d. 'Profits and Prophets: Gendered Notions of Wealth and Value in Senegalese Murid Households'. Ms.

Bundy, Colin. 1987. 'Street Sociology and Pavement Politics: Aspects of Youth and Student Resistance in Cape Town, 1985,' *Journal of Southern African Studies*, 13:303-30.

Butler, Judith. 1990. *Gender Trouble: Feminism and the Subversion of Identity*, New York: Routledge.

Cohen, Phil. 1981. 'Policing the Working-Class City,' in *Crime and Society: Readings in History and Theory*. ed. M. Fitzgerald, G. McLennan, and J. Pawson. London: Routledge & Kegan Paul.

Cohn, Nik. 1969. *Rock from the Beginning*. New York: Stein and Day.

Coleman, Enid Gabriella. n.d. 'The Politics of Survival and Prestige: Hacker Ideology and the Global Production of an Operating System', M.A. thesis, Department of Anthropology, University of Chicago.

Comaroff, Jean & John L. Comaroff. 1999a. 'Occult Economies and the Violence of Abstraction: Notes from the South African Postcolony,' *American Ethnologist* 26(3):279-301.
— 1999b. 'Alien-nation: Zombies, Immigrants and Millennial Capitalism,' *CODESRIA Bulletin*, 3/4.
— 2000a. 'Millennial Capitalism: First Thoughts on a Second Coming,' in *Millennial Capitalism and the Culture of Neoliberalism*, ed. J.L. Comaroff and J. Comaroff, Special Edition of *Public Culture*, 12(2):291-343.
— 2000b. 'Naturing the Nation: Aliens, Apocalypse and the Postcolonial State,' *Hagar: International Social Science Review*, 1(1):7-40.
Conrad, Joseph. 1957[1911]. *Under Western Eyes*. Harmondsworth: Penguin.
Cook, Daniel. 1998. 'The Commoditization of Childhood: Personhood, the Children's Wear Industry and the Moral Discourses of Consumption, 1917-1967,' Ph.D. dissertation, University of Chicago.
Cook, Susan. 1999. 'Street Setswana: Evidence for the Double Bind of Class and Ethnicity in the New South Africa,' Ph.D. dissertation, Yale University.
Corrigan, Paul and Simon Frith. 1976. 'The Politics of Youth Culture,' in *Resistance Through Rituals: Youth Subcultures in Post-War Britain*. ed. S. Hall & T. Jefferson. London: Hutchinson.
De Boeck, Filip. 1999. 'Borderland Breccia: The Historical Imagination of a Central African Frontier,' Paper read to a conference on 'The Black West: Reinventing History, Reinterpreting Media', San Diego, April. Also published as 'La frontière diamantifère angolaise et son héros mutant', in *Matière à Politique: Le pouvoir, les corps et les choses*. ed. Jean-François Bayart & Jean-Pierre Warnier. Paris: Karthala, 2004.
Foucault, Michel. 1976. *Mental Illness and Psychology*, translated by Alan Sheridan, New York: Harper Colophon Books.
Fussell, Paul. 1975. *The Great War and Modern Memory*. New York: Oxford University Press.
Gillis, John R. 1974. *Youth and History: Tradition and Change in European Age Relations, 1770-Present*. New York: Academic Press.
Hannerz, Ulf. 1989. 'Notes on the Global Ecumene,' *Public Culture* 1(2): 66–75.
Hebdige, Dick. 1988. *Hiding in the Light: On Images and Things*. London: Routledge.
Hobsbawm, Eric J. 1962. *The Age of Revolution, 1789-1848*. New York: New American Library [Mentor Book].
Holland, Heidi. 1989. *The Struggle: A History of the African National Congress*. New York: G. Braziller.
Honwana, Alcinda. 1999. 'Negotiating Post-War Indentities: Child Soldiers in Mozambique and Angola,' *CODESRIA Bulletin*, 1/2:4-13.
Howe, Neil & William Strauss. 2000. *Millennials Rising: The Next Great Generation*. New York: Vintage Books.
Jones, Gareth Stedman. 1984[1971]. *Outcast London: A Study in the Relationship between Classes in Victorian Society*. New York: Pantheon Books.
Lodge, Tom. 1983. *Black Politics in South Africa Since 1945*. London: Longman.
Lukose, Ritty. 2000. 'Learning Modernity: Youth Culture in Kerala, South India,' Ph.D. dissertation, University of Chicago.
Marx, Karl. 1967. *Capital: A Critique of Political Economy*, Vol. I. New York: International Publishers.
Mayhew, Henry. 1851. *London Labour and the London Poor: A Cyclopaedia of the Condition of Those that Will Work, Those that Cannot Work, and Those that Will not Work*. Vol. I. London: G. Woodfall.
Meli, Francis. 1989. *A History of the ANC: South Africa Belongs to US*, Bloomington, IN/London: Indiana University Press/James Currey.
Roitman, Janet. n.d., 'Youth and Livelihood in the Chad Basin', Ms.
Schlink, Bernhard. 1998[1995]. *The Reader*, translated by Carol Brown Janeway. New York: Vintage Books.
Seekings, Jeremy. 1993. *Heroes or Villains? Youth Politics in the 1980s*. Johannesburg: Ravan Press.
Ssewakiryanga, Richard. 1999. '"New Kids on the Blocks": African-American Music and Uganda Youth,' *CODESRIA Bulletin*, 1–2.
Veloso, Leticia Medeiros. 1998. 'Children are the Future of the Nation: Law, the State, and the Making of Tomorrow's Citizens in Brazil,' Doctoral Research Proposal, University of Chicago.
Venkatesh, Sudhir. n.d.[a]. 'Robert Taylor, The Problem of Order, and the General Crisis of Governability,' Dissertation outline, Department of Sociology, University of Chicago.
— n.d.[b]. 'Understanding Exclusion and Creating Value: African Youth in a Global Age,' Conference statement, Ms.
Walshe, Peter. 1971. *The Rise of African Nationalism in South Africa: The African National Congress, 1912-1952*. Berkeley & Los Angeles: University of California Press.
Willis, Paul. 1977. *Learning to Labor: How Working Class Kids Get Working Class Jobs*. New York: Columbia University Press.
Willoughby, William. C. 1923. *Race Problems in the New Africa: A Study of the Relation of Bantu and Briton in those Parts of Africa under British Rule*. Oxford: Clarendon Press.
Wilson, Monica. 1951. 'Witch Beliefs and the Social Structure,' *American Journal of Sociology* 56:307-13.
Zizek, Slavoj. 1997. *The Plague of Fantasies*. London: Verso.

II The Pain of Agency
The Agency of Pain

2

ALCINDA HONWANA
Innocent & Guilty
Child-Soldiers as Interstitial & Tactical Agents

> My first military assignment was to attack a village and steal cattle ... we burnt down that village ... and with my gun I killed the ammunition chief ... I am very sad about my story ... but I had no choice. (Fernando, only 9 at the time he entered the military)

At the age of 10, Marula was kidnapped by Renamo insurgents, during a rebel attack on his village in Gaza province, southern Mozambique. Marula, his father, his younger sister and other villagers, who were also kidnapped, walked for three days, carrying military equipment and items looted from the village, before reaching the Renamo camp. The family was separated at the camp. While the father was sent to the men's ward, and the sister to the women's sector, Marula was ordered to join a group of young boys. A few weeks later Marula started military training. He was not allowed to see his father and sister, but they managed to arrange secret meetings on a few occasions. It was during one of these secret encounters that they agreed to try and run away. The attempted escape went wrong and they were caught. Marula was ordered to kill his own father. And so he did. Following this, his first killing, Marula grew into a fierce Renamo combatant and was active for more than seven years. He does not even remember how many people he tortured, how many he killed; how many villages he burnt; and how many food convoys and shops he looted. After the war, he returned to his village where his paternal uncle (the only close relative who survived the war) refused to welcome him home. The uncle could not forgive Marula for killing his brother, the boy's own father. Eventually, through the skilful intervention of his uncle's wife, Marula came to stay in the house despite his uncle's disapproval. Victim, or perpetrator? Innocent, or guilty? Child, or soldier? What can we make of Marula and his disturbing story?

In the past decade or so the issue of child participation in political conflict has captured the attention of the world. Images of young people carrying guns and ammunition flash across our television screens. Children's involvement in armed conflict is not a recent phenomenon or one that is unique to our times. Historically young people have been at the forefront of political conflict in many parts of the world. However, the magnitude of the problem today is such that this issue has gained new dimensions. Specialists in war studies and other analysts have pointed out the new character of most contemporary civil wars, which make defenceless civilians – especially children – particularly vulnerable (Gersony, 1988; Vines, 1991; Finnegan, 1992; Minter, 1994; Clapham, 1998; Reno, 1998; Kaldor, 1999; Ignatieff, 1999; Berdal and Malone, 2000). These 'new' wars reflect in many respects a 'total societal crisis'. Young civilian populations are frequently abducted and forced to join the military. These young combatants are often transformed into merciless killers committing the most horrendous war atrocities. In this regard, concepts of childhood, children's rights and children's agency also need to be re-thought, re-considered.

Why do images and tales of child-soldiers shock us so? Reports of children taking human lives are increasingly infiltrating public awareness, both from conflict zones as well as from non-conflict contexts, such as the murder of three-year-old James Bulger by two ten-year olds in the UK in 1993, the Michigan killings by a six-year-old, and the 1999 Columbine school shootings in the United States. The idea of children killing and waging war defies established and accepted norms and values with regard to the categories of childhood and adulthood. As pointed out in the Introduction to this volume (Honwana and De Boeck), in modern society childhood is often associated with vulnerability, innocence, and dependence upon adult guidance and nurture. Soldiers, on the other hand, are associated with strength, aggression, responsibility, and the maturity of adulthood. Children are to be defended. Soldiers defend. Children are to be protected. A soldier's mandate is to protect. Therefore, the combination of the two words *child* and *soldier* creates a paradox as these children of war find themselves in an interstitial space between these two conditions. They are still children, but they are no longer innocent; they perform adult tasks, but they are not yet adults. The possession of guns and a licence to kill places them outside of childhood. But at the same time such attributes do not constitute full-scale incorporation into adulthood, given, among other things, their age and physical immaturity. Therefore, they are located in a twilight zone, a blurred intermediary space, in which these two 'worlds rub against each other in – sometimes uneasy – intimacy' (De Boeck, 1999). Moreover, these children's lives also constitute a twilight experience, as their behaviour and actions are those of quasi-child or crypto-adult (Jenks, 1996). In this twilight space and twilight experience, one finds embodied the entanglements – the displacements, the overlaps and the mimesis – of this juxtaposition. These interstices provide the terrain for the emergence of new strategies of selfhood and identity (Bhabha, 1994).

It is this ambiguous terrain in the child-soldier's everyday life actions that will be examined in this chapter. The idea is to go beyond the clear-cut demarcations between child and adult, or between *innocence* and *guilt*, and examine the intricate ways in which the condition of child-soldier cuts across these established borders. By their very nature, child-soldiers find themselves in a liminal position which breaks down established dichotomies between civilian and soldier, victim and perpetrator, initiate and initiated, protected and protector, maker and breaker. With these multiple interstitial positions, child-soldiers epitomize the idea of transience, belonging simultaneously to several states of being with multifaceted identities. In this way, they occupy a world of their own. Their lives are situated somewhere between a world of 'make-believe' – a child's world of play and games, of pretence (of children playing with guns) – and reality – where the ludic becomes shockingly lethal, and the game turns out to be deadly. Here the ludic is transformed into the grotesque and the macabre (Bakhtin, 1984).

Within this interstitial space, child-soldiers are not devoid of agency. On the contrary, these young soldiers are agents in their own right, but this agency is of a specific type. Drawing from de Certeau's (1984) distinction between 'strategies' and 'tactics', I argue that child-soldiers display what I call a 'tactical agency', one that is devised to cope with and maximize the concrete, immediate circumstances of the military environment in which they have to operate. They are not in a position of power, they may not be fully conscious of the ultimate goals of their actions, and may not expect any long-term gains or benefits from it – which would, in de Certeau's terms, make their actions 'strategic'. Nonetheless, they are fully conscious of the immediate returns, and act within certain constraints, to seize opportunities that are available to them. Their actions, however, are likely to have both beneficial and deleterious long-term consequences.

The ethnographic settings for this study are the Angolan provinces of Luanda, Moxico, Bie, Huambo and Uige. I conducted research there in1997 and 1998[1] during the peaceful period between the Lusaka Accords of 1994 and UNITA's return to war in October 1998.[2] While this constitutes the main source of field material for the chapter, I shall also make use of materials collected in the course of similar research undertaken in Mozambique in 1995 and 1999. The study tries to convey young people's experiences of war and the context of their involvement in political violence. First, it analyzes the child/soldier paradox by developing further some ideas about this interstitial positionality of young combatants. Here, preconceived ideas of childhood versus soldiering are deconstructed as one looks at how society reinforces such dichotomies. Secondly, it examines the impact of political violence on young people, many of whom are simultaneously victims and active participants in the war, by looking at the processes of their recruitment and initiation into a culture of violence and terror. Finally, the chapter explores the borderland (Argenti, in this volume), identity and location of the young soldiers. It analyzes their lives within the confines of their military activity: their fears, sorrows, pains and joys. It ends with a discussion of the actions and the agency of the young combatants by emphasizing their interstitial subjectivity and tactical agency in the context of political violence.

The Interstitial: An Uneasy Co-habitation

> M'appelle Birahima. J'aurais pu etre un gosse comme les autres … un sale gosse ni meilleur ni pire que tous les sales gosses du monde … j'ai tué pas mal des gens avec mon kalachnikov. C'est facile. On appuie et ça fait tralala. Je ne sais pas si je me suis amusé. Je sais que j'ai eu beaucoup de mal parce que beaucoup de mes copains enfant-soldats sont morts. (Ahmadou Kourouma, 2000)[3]

The binary *child-soldier* produces an oxymoron. How can an innocent child become a soldier? Here a clarification is necessary. Although, for lack of a better word, I have been using the term soldier, what I mean is a specific type of combatant (not the 'regular' sol-

[1] My research in Angola was carried out while I was working as a consultant for the Christian Children's Fund (CCF) in Angola. I worked with a team of Angolan researchers who helped me collect the information for the project. The material presented in this chapter results also from interviews conducted by other team members.

[2] The postcolonial conflict in Angola started in 1975, when the three nationalist movements of the MPLA (Movimento Nacional de Libertacao de Angola), UNITA (Uniao Nacional para a Independencia Total de Angola) and FNLA (Frente Nacional de Libertacao de Angola) fought each other for control over the country. The MPLA emerged victorious and proclaimed Angola's independence in November 1975. In the subsequent years, while the FNLA faded in importance, UNITA reconstituted itself as anti-Marxist and pro-Western to continue its anti-government insurgency. The war rages on to this day, and was only briefly interrupted by the short-lived peace accords of Bicesse from May 1991 to October 1992, and Lusaka from November 1994 to October 1998.

[3] Quote from Amadou Kourouma's novel *Allah n'est pas Obligé*, that I translated as follows: 'My name is Birahima. I could have been a boy like any other … . A dirty boy, neither better nor worse, than all the other dirty boys of the world … . With my Kalachnikov, I killed lots of people. It is easy. You press and it goes tralala. I am not sure that I enjoyed it. I know that I suffered a lot because many of my fellow child-soldiers have died.'

dier). I am referring to the type of fighter that fills the ranks of some guerrilla-rebel groups in postcolonial wars: an inadequately trained and outfitted individual, who, frequently, without mercy, harasses, loots, and kills defenceless civilians indiscriminately. In southern Mozambique, for example, they were known as *matsanga*[4], a term which was generalized to mean bandit, outlaw, criminal and the like. It is this type of combatant into which most child-soldiers are transformed. The ambiguity inherent in this child-fighter will be discussed after I have examined some socially constructed ideas attached to the notions of childhood and adulthood (especially soldiering) which inform this paradoxical, uneasy and illicit cohabitation (Mbembe, 1992; Weiss, in this volume).

Contemporary studies of childhood are increasingly committed to the idea that childhood constitutes a social artifact rather than a natural biological state. Childhood as a social category constitutes a relatively recent concept. Ariès (1962) locates the genesis of the modern concept of childhood in the eighteenth century, together with bourgeois notions of family, home, privacy and individuality (Stephens, 1995). As childhood and adulthood became increasingly differentiated, each sphere elaborated its own symbolic world. In modern Western society, the major tenet of contemporary understandings of childhood is the assumption that children evolve through established phases of development (Boyden and Gibbs, 1997), and that childhood stands in opposition to adulthood. By this conception, child development is generally taken to be a natural and universal phase of human existence, one shaped more by biological and psychological considerations than by social factors (Freeman, 1993). In international humanitarian law, children often appear as pre-social and passive recipients of experience who need to be segregated from the harsh realities of the adult world, and to be protected from social danger (Ariès, 1962) until they reach the age of 18 (Honwana, in press). Thus, childhood appears as a transitional stage (Jenks, 1996), and its temporal dimension is robbed of immediate status (Caputo, 1995), as children are seen as something in the 'process of becoming rather than being' (James, 1993). Children are perceived to know less than adults, as opposed to knowing something else that has to do with their particular situation and surroundings (Amit-Talai and Wulff, 1995). So, children need nurture and enlightenment, and are seen to be immature and incapable of assuming responsibilities. In this sense, childhood should constitute a carefree, secure and happy phase of human existence (Summerville, 1982; Boyden, 1990). Although this notion of childhood is often generalized and even 'universalized', it derives from a Western and middle-class view of childhood that is not unquestionably shared around the globe.

In many social contexts, the notion of childhood differs dramatically from that outlined above. Unlike middle-class children whose parents and families are in a position to support them until they are able to sustain themselves – in many cases till well over the age of 18 – many children in other parts of the world are exposed to work and social responsibilities at an early age. They participate actively in productive activities, in household chores, and in the care of younger children. In Angola and Mozambique, as in many other contexts, children are often portrayed as strong, as survivors who grow in difficult

---

[4] *Matsanga* is what the RENAMO soldiers were called in southern Mozambique. The term derives from the name of RENAMO's first president and military leader Andre Matsangaissa. He was a former FRELIMO combatant who later joined the opposition. Andre Matsangaissa died in combat in 1989 (see Vines, 1991). *Matsangas* were associated with violence and terror and indiscriminate killings. Although government soldiers were also reported to behave in a similar fashion, this was considered to be more of an exception than the rule. RENAMO used terror as a matter of policy and strategy (see Gersony, 1988; Vines, 1991; Finnegan, 1992; Minter, 1994).

conditions (Honwana, 1998). Being a child in this particular context seems to have little to do with age (although people sometimes refer to age limits) but is essentially linked to social roles, expectations and responsibilities. Among the Chokwe, in Moxico, children are identified through roles; they are even named according to what they do or are supposed to do. For example, *tchitutas* is the name attributed to girls and boys around the age of 5 to 7, whose role is to fetch water and tobacco for the elders, or take messages to neighbours. Similarly, *kambumbu* are children around 7 to 13 years of age who start participating more actively in household chores (especially girls) and helping parents in the field, or with fishing and hunting. Then there are the *Mukwenge wa lunga* (boys) and the *mwana pwo* (girls) who, around the age of 13 have to pass the rites of initiation. In Mozambique, young girls become wives as early as 13 or 14 years of age, and become mothers soon after that. As such, they are introduced to the roles and responsibilities of married life and motherhood. In such a societal context, emphasis is placed on roles rather than on age. As an elderly Angolan, 75-year-old Sonama, pointed out:

> In the past there wasn't this thing of saying that this person is 18 years of age or 10 years of age and, therefore, must do this and that. The elders in the family identified the passing of time through the seasons: the time to plant the maize; the time of the harvest, etc. And in this way children just grew freely, and parents would know what tasks to assign to them depending on the way they were growing. Some children grow faster than others, both mentally and physically.

These examples show the different ways in which childhood can be understood. As James and Prout have pointed out, looking at childhood not as a universal category but as a social and historical construct means that 'the institution of childhood provides an interpretative frame for understanding the early years of human life. In these terms, it is biological immaturity rather than childhood which is a universal and natural feature of human groups' (1990:3). As a social construct, societies understand childhood to be dissimilar from adulthood, and they devise processes to articulate this transition, which might take place in different ways and at different stages in diverse social and cultural settings. The transition is often seen as a process rather than a single event. It is often composed of a series of gradual transformations, or initiations. The initiatory dimensions do not necessarily take place at the same time. For example, in describing the rites of passage from childhood into adulthood, Grimes (2000) identifies several ritualized moments. The *rites of childhood* which follow from birth and precede entry into adolescence; the *adolescent initiations* which articulate the transition from childhood into adolescence; and the *adult initiations* that negotiate an exit from adolescence and entry into adulthood.

However, these divisions are not cast in stone since they may vary cross-culturally and over time. Like childhood, notions of youth, adolescence and teenage are also social constructs: what defines youth? Is it age, biology, social roles, social expectations and responsibilities? Or is it a combination of all or some of these factors? For example, in some social settings an unmarried 45-year-old, who does not have a job and lives at his parents' home, can be considered to be still in a state of 'prolonged youth' because he or she does not take part in the roles and responsibilities associated with adulthood. One can reach manhood or womanhood without necessarily becoming an adult. The notion of adulthood here is primarily understood in terms of social roles and responsibilities. In fact, among the Chokwe, initiation processes involve both a physical and a social dimension. The former focuses on the definition of adult masculinity and feminity on an immediate physical level through the biological changes in the body-self, and the latter effects an introduction into the roles and responsibilities of social adult personhood. The *mukaand* circumcision rituals transform boys into men by defining adolescent masculinity in terms of hunting capacities and sexual prowess. But it is in the *muiingoony* ritual complex, which takes place after circumcision, that the transition into the roles and responsibilities of adult manhood is articulated (see Bastin, 1984; De Boeck, 1991). For the transition to be properly established, society has to prepare young people to assume these new roles. The ritualized moments of the initiation constitute symbolic enactments of the transition. The initiation is gradual and processual; it starts at home at a tender age and continues well beyond ritual performance.

Warfare and soldiering, on the other hand, are, in many societies, generally perceived as activities for the initiated. In many societies, the transition into adulthood (even more so, into manhood) is effected through military service. It is not by chance that the age of conscription in many countries is 18. Thus, military service, being a soldier, and fighting wars are perceived to be an introduction into 'grown-up' pursuits that distinctly mark the boundary between protectors and protected. Soldiers in regular armies are generally seen as the defenders of the nation and its people and, as such, they are associated with stamina, strength, aggression, responsibility, manhood and adulthood. The transition from civilian into soldier constitutes a carefully designed process of re-configuring identities (Roberts, 1994; Cock, 1991). Military conscripts are often subjected to a training regimen that encourages and praises competitiveness, insensitivity, dominance, and aggression. Soldiers are products of socialization whereby their bodily condition is enhanced to epitomize physical power and strength. Soldiers are taught to manipulate arms, be ready for military combat, and kill. The military institution thus becomes a locus for the creation of a specific notion of masculinity. Cock notes that notions of masculinity constitute powerful tools in the making of men into soldiers. She sees a direct connection between masculinity and militarism, and remarks that 'the army is an institutional sphere for the cultivation of masculinity; war provides the social space for its validation' (1991:58). Women generally occupy marginal positions because military discourse and ideology are heavily drawn from definitions of masculinity and femininity that cast women as weak and place them in traditional feminine roles (Cock, 1991). Even though in Angola and Mozambique girls were also abducted to participate in the war (Honwana, 1999b), it was essentially boys who were subjected to military training[5] and, thus, authorized to kill. Although the conditions under which the taking of human life is considered acceptable vary from culture to culture, killing is generally seen as an extreme measure reserved for highly circumscribed circumstances. When licenced, the responsibility for killing lies with initiated individuals – persons whose military training prepares them emotionally for the consequences of such an act.

In Mozambique and Angola the fact that the majority of the children who participate in these wars were abducted, many at a very tender age, before they had attained manhood, means that they did not have the time to be socially prepared to assume these roles. Many people interviewed mentioned that, beyond the massive killings and material destruction, the war has created a crisis in moral values. There is no longer respect

---

[5] There are a few cases in which girls were trained to be soldiers. However, the majority were forced to become 'wives' of soldiers and commanders, to cook and clean the camps, to search for water, firewood and the like. Despite not having military training, many girls were called into performing military tasks such as guarding the camps when men were absent, and accompanying men on looting missions (for more on young women and war in Mozambique see Honwana, 1999b).

for rules and norms, for adults and for the elderly: 'Children these days do not listen to the adults';[6] 'there is no notion of good and bad among young people';[7] 'with the war, initiation ceased to be performed'.[8] Given that the war is regarded as a very serious affair, it is believed that soldiers need to be well prepared (trained) for such a tremendous task. Being well prepared to fight a war is understood to go beyond physical strength and mastery of military weapons, and to include a sense of responsibility, of right and wrong, of good and bad war practices (some sort of war ethics) – something that is acquired through a 'social' initiation. Such an initiation is supposed to have started at home and been continued throughout the initiation process, well before they reached military service. Previously, as some Mozambicans and Angolans stated, that knowledge was provided to young men growing up into manhood and adulthood. They were initiated to become valuable members of society, 'but today things are upside down, nothing works normally anymore, it is complete chaos'.[9] As asserted by some elderly people in Mozambique and Angola, the absence of these initiation ritual practices creates a relapse in the process of maturing into an adult person. However, besides the family and the 'traditional' initiation rites, institutions such as the school, the church and children's and youth associations play a role in the initiation into adult roles. But these institutions have been seriously disrupted by the war. It is therefore within an environment of societal chaos that young people have to make sense of their own world, and their own transition into adulthood. In this process many youngsters construct their own imaginary spaces and symbolic worlds, with the means available to them. War and political violence are some of them.

As stated above, the fact that children are capable of violence clearly falls outside entrenched modernist formulations of childhood. Children who behave violently – who rape, murder and kill – pose a conundrum because they dismantle the idea of the romantic innocence and vulnerability of childhood. What makes the connection between children and violence particularly disconcerting is precisely the fact that the 'imagery of childhood and that of violent criminality are iconologically irreconcilable' (Jenks, 1996:125). A child killing indiscriminately, a child killing his/her own parents and raiding his/her own village turns the world 'upside down', upsetting social norms and codes. It is not by chance that this has become one of the most important contemporary issues confronting the international community.

Indisputably, in the past decade, the issue of child participation in armed conflicts is increasingly moving to the forefront of political, humanitarian and academic agendas. In 1995 the United Nations commissioned the Machel Study on the impact of armed conflict on children, which gave rise to the UN Special Office for Children and Armed Conflict. Many humanitarian organizations have launched programmes to protect children from direct participation in warfare. Studies and publications on the issue have greatly expanded in the past years (Dodge and Raundalen, 1991; Boothby et al., 1992; Goodwin-Gill & Cohn, 1994; Human Rights Watch, 1994; Furley, 1995; Honwana & Pannizo, 1995; Cairns, 1996; Reynolds, 1996; Richards, 1996; Brett & McCallin, 1996; Abdullah & Bangura, 1997; Dawes & Honwana, 1997; Boyden & Gibbs, 1997; Wessells, 1997; Peters & Richards, 1998; Honwana, 1998, 1999a; Bazenguissa-Ganga, 1999). Child participation in war has also been a theme for novels (Kourouma, 2000). The dramatic

---

[6] *Seculo* (means elderly person in Umbundu) Kapata, interviewed by the CCF team in Kuito, 1997.
[7] *Seculo* Afonso mentioned this to me in Kuito in February 1998.
[8] Antonio Sonama, Uige interview conducted by a member of the CCF team.
[9] A *kimbanda* from Kuito whom I interviewed in July 1997.

shift of social roles and responsibilities of children effected in war contexts[10] and in other social spheres (see De Boeck in this volume on child–witches) is intrinsically linked to the breakdown of societal structures and long-standing moral matrices in contexts of extreme social crisis.

The Initiation into Violence: The Construction of a Warlike Persona

> After four months of training they put me to a test. They put a person before me and ordered me to shoot him. I shot him. After the test they considered me good and they gave me a gun.
> (Fernando, 13 years old)

In this section, I examine the immediate reasons and the processes through which children become involved in armed conflicts as soldiers. Although the focus of this chapter is on the ambiguity of their position, it is important to understand how this twilight condition – the encounter between the child and the soldier – is created. In other words, how are the socially established barriers between childhood and soldiering broken down? As I discuss in this section, their interstitial position is achieved through a careful process of 'initiation' into a new culture of terror and violence that starts with recruitment.

Thousands of children have been directly exposed to the war as combatants in Angola.[11] UNITA has been very active in recruiting children into its army. There are also accounts of the use of children as soldiers by the government forces, although to a lesser extent. Children are used to carry weapons and other equipment, in the front lines, in reconnaissance missions, in mining, and in espionage. Due to the fact that they are still in the process of maturation, children are frequently perceived by adults (with differences across societies) as being particularly susceptible to ideological conditioning. The systematic preference for children as soldiers is often based on assumptions that children are easier to control and manipulate; they are easily 'programmed' to feel little fear or revulsion for their actions. Children are also believed (by their abductors and mentors) to possess excessive energy and that, once trained, they can carry out attacks with greater enthusiasm and brutality than adults (Furley, 1995; Human Rights Watch, 1994). Some authors have argued that the use of children as soldiers results from shortage of manpower, as the adult reserve is exhausted due to war, poverty and disease (Brett, 2000). It seems to me that it was not by chance or just because of shortage of manpower that armies of children were created. There seems to have been a concerted and well-

[10] The case of two Thai or Burmese children who were the military and spiritual leaders of the rebel movement (see Seth Mydans, 'Burmese Rebel Chief: More Boy than Warrior', *New York Times*, 10 April 2000 for full story).

[11] It is estimated that around one million children have been directly affected by the war. Statistics estimate that more than 500,000 children have died during the war. Many were kidnapped in military incursions. About 50 per cent of the displaced population are children under 15 years of age. UNICEF statistics pointed out that in 1993 nearly 840,000 children were living in difficult circumstances (Minter, 1994). Thousands of children are unaccompanied, orphaned or separated from their families, and many were dragged into armies and militias, in 1997 it was estimated that about 10,000 child-soldiers would be demobilized by March 1997. Indirectly the war has affected many more children. Malnutrition has increased, due to low food production and displacement. The deterioration of health-care services during the war has resulted in higher infant and child mortality rates. Many children were prevented from attending school, due mainly to displacement and the destruction of schools· The situation of children in the country is therefore appalling. In addition to problems of death and physical trauma, dire poverty, hunger and ongoing social and emotional problems caused by this prolonged exposure to political violence make their situation much worse.

thought-out strategy of using and manipulating children in warfare both in Angola and Mozambique. The creation of child-soldiers does not constitute, in my view, an isolated incident happening here and there. Child-soldiering is part of a warfare strategy that cuts across and is shared across several war zones around the globe.

Drawing from Appadurai's (1991) notion of *ethnoscape*,[12] Nordstrom introduces the idea of 'war-scapes' to describe the interconnectedness between local and global networks in war situations. Such a notion permits us to go beyond the individual expressions of war in particular places, to understand a global culture of war which links these particular war sites to a vast web of 'foreign strategists, arms, supplies, soldiers, mercenaries, power brokers, and development and interest groups ... ' (1997:37). She goes on to say that 'as these many groups interact, local and transnational concerns are enmeshed in the cultural construction of conflict that is continually reconfigured across time and space' (*ibid.*). This is precisely what happens in Angola, where intricate networks of local and global interests play a role in the conflict. In this process of interactions, information about war tricks and new technologies are transmitted from one war to another through soldiers, military advisers, and mercenaries. Media reports and popular war films (Richards, 1996) are also forms of spreading this type of information. In this way, ideas and values about what constitutes 'acceptable' warfare practices are constructed, reconfigured and established.

Many of the children who participated in the war in Angola and Mozambique, were brutally abducted from their families and forced to follow the soldiers into the military camps. The street, the home, and the school constitute some of the sites from which children were commonly kidnapped to join war activity.

> I was walking ... When I was near the railway line, UNITA soldiers came and said, 'Hey boy, come with us, we want you to do some work for us'. It was a lie. They took me to N'gove. And there I did my military training, which lasted only five months due to an attack we suffered from the government troops ... My training should have lasted eight months.[13]

One child recalls that it was during a beautiful moonlight evening that he was abducted by a group of UNITA soldiers at home. His family was sitting outside in the courtyard when

> Suddenly we heard gun shots and we all ran to hide inside the house. The soldiers came into the house and asked everybody to line up outside. Then they told me to go with them. I was taken to a military base and shown how to operate with guns.

He was eleven when this happened.[14] Young girls were also recruited to live and work in military camps. While it was extremely difficult to interview young women in Angola, during my research in Mozambique this was facilitated through my involvement with a local NGO supporting young girls affected by the war (Honwana, 1999b).

> I was taken with my parents from our home ... Renamo soldiers kidnapped us, and took all our cattle. We were taken to the military base. My father, my mother, and I were separated. I suffered a lot while I was there. I am not going to tell you everything that happened to me in the military camp because it was very ugly.[15]

---

[12] Appadurai uses the notion of *ethnoscape* to capture the idea of a transnational *ethnos* which is constructed as people migrate, interact and reconfigure their own histories and identities. In this sense the *ethnos* assumes a 'slippery, non-localized quality'.
[13] Interview conducted in March 1998 by members of the CCF team in Huambo.
[14] An ex-child-soldier from Kunje interviewed by the author in February 1998.
[15] A 17-year-old girl, interviewed.

Traditional leaders, particularly in Angola, were involved in the recruitment of child-soldiers in certain areas of the country. In colonial times, *sobas* (chiefs) had to collect taxes from the population, and now they had to provide UNITA (and in some cases the government army) with young recruits. There are several accounts of their participation in recruitment.

> *Sobas* had to provide UNITA with soldiers from their *sobados* (areas of jurisdiction of the *sobas*), so they would ask the teachers to give them children. I was taken from school straight to the UNITA base where I had military training for three months before starting to go on missions.[16]
>
> They told me to go with them ... Later I managed to escape and returned home. But the UNITA soldiers asked the *soba* to show them my house and, in the evening, they came and took me for the second time[17]

Sobas were not the only members of the community who took part in recruitment. There were cases in which teachers and parents had to give their pupils, sons, and daughters to the *soba*, who then sent them to join the military. As remarked by a young man,

> UNITA asked the *sobas* to give a certain number of boys (periodically). Parents were responsible for encouraging the boys to stay with UNITA, and to return them if they escaped. If the boys escaped and were not returned to the *soba*, the families would suffer[18].

The mother of an ex-child-soldier explained that her son was kidnapped and then sent back by a commander because he was very ill. When the UNITA troops who abducted him found out that he was back home, they blamed it on her and her husband. In her own words:

> They said that I prevented him from joining the military ... I said no, the boy was very ill. My husband is a very religious person ... and the UNITA soldiers harassed him, and he had to let them take our son ... [19]

In these circumstances, parents became unable to protect their own offspring, and had to surrender to political pressures and the power of guns, often manipulated by very young soldiers. Not all child-soldiers were forcibly recruited. There were those who volunteered to join the military, as the following accounts confirm.

> I started military service in 1994. I volunteered to join the government army because we were suffering a lot in my village ... I wanted to defend my province and help my family with the products that I could get from the military ambushes.[20]

> I volunteered, no one forced me. The *soba* only said that he had been instructed by the government to encourage all young people to join the army and fight for their country. I volunteered to avoid being 'rusgado' (picked up in the street) because they could be nasty to you.[21]

[16] I conducted this interview in July 1997 in Viana (near Luanda) at the OIM Transit Centre, where recently demobilized young soldiers were waiting for their relatives to come and take them home.

[17] A 17-year-old from Malange interviwed by the author in February 1998.

[18] Extract from an interview I conducted with Mr Francisco from Malange, February 1998.

[19] Mrs Andrade was interviewed in Malange, February 1998 by the author and Carlinda Monteiro.

[20] Interview conducted in Cambandua – Bie by members of the CCF team in March 1998.

[21] He was 13 years old when he joined the army. Interview conducted by CCF team in Kuito.

The last account raises an interesting connection between voluntary and forced recruitment. Although in some cases young people volunteered for ideological reasons and were aware of the strategic objectives of the war they were waging, the same is not true for all volunteers. Indirect coercive mechanisms were used to persuade young people to enter the military. Intimidation, social pressure, physical protection, possibilities of exercising revenge, and access to food and shelter, security and adventure are some of them. The dividing line between voluntary and forced recruitment can sometimes be very imprecise and ambiguous. Another contributing factor to voluntary participation is boredom when the lack of opportunities in very impoverished rural settings may drive many young people into war (Geffray, 1990; Honwana, 1998, 1999a). Particularly important is the sense of security and power that the possession of a gun seems to provide. As pointed out by one young man, 'no one messes with you when you have a gun ... You can defend yourself.'[22] Sometimes, the inducement to take up arms came from the need to avenge the deaths of family relatives or from the sheer fun and adventure of wearing military gear and carrying an AK47.

There are a variety of actors involved in child recruitment. There seems to be a sort of communal 'complicity' (for lack of a better word) in the process, even if that 'complicity' arises from the fact that parents, teachers and chiefs were all impotent and incapable of doing anything to stop young children from being made to participate in war. Making a child join the military can often be seen as a strategy for protection, both for the child, for the family and, sometimes, for the community (see Utas, in this volume; Furley, 1995; Honwana, in press).

Military training of child recruits involves them in manipulating firearms and in heavy physical exercise that pushes children to high levels of physical exhaustion in order to create mental states conducive to ideological indoctrination (Cock, 1991; Goodwin-Gill & Cohn, 1994). 'A soldier must learn to dehumanise other people and make them into targets, and to cut himself off from his own feelings of caring and connectedness to the community. His survival and competence as a soldier depend on this process' (Roberts, 1983 quoted in Cock, 1991:56). The initiation into violence of many child-soldiers in Angola and Mozambique was often designed to cut off their links with society – family, friends and the community at large. Young recruits who had been forcibly inducted often had to endure long periods of darkness, severe beating and deliberately instilled terror to impress on them that there was no going back. Once under training, discipline was very harsh and the penalty for failed attempts to escape was execution. Intense psychological pressure was placed on them to remould their identities (Honwana, 1998, 1999a). Almost all ex-child soldiers whom I met, and who were former UNITA and RENAMO soldiers, referred to a sort of parade during which they were forced to watch the execution of those who had been found attempting to escape. Sometimes, new child recruits were ordered to kill a colleague who tried to escape.

> Whoever did not want to fight was killed ... They would slice the throat of those who did not want to fight ... I was trained for three days on how to march and run. Then they gave me my weapon and I got used to fighting. The orders were to kill anyone we caught and to bring back anything they had on them.[23]
>
> I saw someone being killed (in the parade), he was my friend and was also a soldier, and one day while he was trying to flee someone denounced him and he was caught. He was imprisoned for a few days ... one day they brought him to the parade; they tied his arms and legs

[22] A 19-year-old ex-child-fighter from Bie, interviewed by members of the CCF team.
[23] Words of a 20-year-old former child-soldier from Malange. I spoke to him in February 1998.

against a post, then blindfolded him and then shot him. The executor then sucked his blood. I felt very sad; it was terrible to witness all that.[24]

Other initiation strategies used to isolate and alienate the recruits were forcing them to eliminate their own relatives (as in Marula's case, mentioned in the introduction to this chapter), and to attack and loot their own towns and villages, precisely to impress on them the impossibility of going back. Children were sometimes given new names and were forbidden to use their birth names, traditional names or nicknames that related to their past experiences at home with family, relatives and friends (see Honwana, 1998, 1999a). *Liamba* (marihuana) and bullet-powder were used to enhance their combative morale and to make them fearless and more courageous in performing horrible deeds. Many youngsters mentioned the *Jura*[25] during which they were forced to sing and dance non-stop the whole night through. The practice was aimed at keeping them busy and making them forget about home and their parents, brothers, sisters and friends. Forgetting, here, constitutes a strategy to disconnect and cut ties with society (Lambek and Antze, 1996). Terror and fear were important instruments in the dehumanization process. These young recruits lived under constant fear of being accused of wrongdoing, of treason, or of attempted escape.

The initiation into violence was a ritualized process that often drew on local ritual practices. For example, in the camps child recruits were made to suck or drink the blood of the people they killed, which was believed to make them fearless and remorseless. Blood-sucking was a common theme in my conversations with former child-soldiers. Many of them would, even without being asked, mention this practice.

> I used to drink the blood of the people I killed ... Today I cannot look at red wine because I feel like killing and sucking blood again.[26]
> I drank blood on the day I finished my military training, in the swearing-in ceremony. We all had to drink 2 spoons of blood each. They told us that this was important to prevent us from being haunted by the spirits of the people we might killl.[27]

Local herbal medicaments were sometimes made available to recruits in order to make them fight fearlessly and to provide them with protection during combats. There were references to healers who helped the soldiers in the camps. Commanders often had recourse to treatments by *kimbandas* (healers) to win battles and protect them from death.

> In order not to be afraid of fighting the war we had to kill a person at the parade ... Those who cried in the evening (after having killed) were treated by the *kimbandas*.[28]

The blood-sucking and *kimbanda* treatments are certainly linked to local 'traditional' ritual forms and healing practices. The sucking of human and animal blood is, in many societies, an integral part of the initiation of healers, diviners, chiefs and other individuals who are called to perform functions that somehow situate them above common mortals (Honwana, 1996). Because UNITA sees itself as a political movement attached to the

[24] An 18-year-old I interviewed in Lombe, Malange in February 1998.
[25] Jura – a form of ritual celebration adopted by UNITA during which young soldiers were forced to sing and dance non-stop throughout the night.
[26] A former young fighter from Malange in an interview conducted by members of the CCF provincial team, June 1997.
[27] Interview conducted by the author in July 1997.
[28] A former young soldier from Malange interviewed by the author in Viana in July 1997.

masses, it appropriates and manipulates a language and set of symbols that resonate deeply with local systems of meaning in order to achieve its own objectives. By accessing these 'traditional' forms, UNITA sees itself as strengthening the alliance with its support base. The MPLA, on the other hand, is portrayed by UNITA as an urban-based, mainly *Creole,* movement marginally linked to the masses.

Together with the hard physical exercise, manipulation of weapons and the imposition of a very strict code of conduct all represented a powerful ritualized initiation into a culture of violence and terror. However, while initiation may have transformed some children into strong and fierce combatants, it does not seem to have brought about their 'social' transition into adults and responsible persons – at least within certain locally shared and accepted parameters. This was clear from the conversations with elderly Angolans and Mozambicans who saw the violent and terrorizing actions employed by many child-soldiers as falling outside what they would consider 'acceptable' responsible adult behaviour, even in times of war.

Postcolonial conflicts do not exhibit the features of the kind of war that shaped the formulation of the Geneva Conventions. They cannot be categorized as warfare which involves confrontation between nations/states, and in which soldiers fight each other on the battlefield. Postcolonial conflicts constitute a different kind of guerrilla war[29] (Ellis, 1976; Reno, 1988; Clapham, 1998; Kaldor, 1999; Ignatieff, 1999). As pointed out by Ignatieff (1999:6), 'war used to be fought by soldiers; it is now fought by irregulars. This may be one reason why postmodern war is so savage, why war crimes and atrocities are now integral to the very prosecution of war.' These new wars are essentially moved by economic, and often, private interests – the 'privatisation of violence' (Berdal and Malone, 2000). They primarily target defenceless civilians, especially children, women and elderly people. In these conflicts, terror becomes a fundamental weapon of war, and anything is apparently permitted. Stories about soldiers cutting off women's breasts and men's genitals, chopping off people's arms, legs, ears and noses, and many other types of atrocities which defy human imagination have become all too familiar in these war settings (Gersony, 1988; Finnegan, 1992). These wars thus constitute a 'total crisis' in people's lives, and they are meant to be precisely that. They may destroy not only people's material possessions but also their moral fibre and sense of dignity. This might partially explain why some parents found themselves in a situation in which they had to give their own children to the military, or traditional leaders and teachers had to become recruiters of young soldiers.

It also raises the issue of the distinction between civilians and soldiers. In contexts like the one described above, many civilians may be forcibly called upon to perform military tasks at any time (see also Utas on women in the Sierra Leonean war in this volume). Many are given arms and forced to fight without proper military training, for the pressures of war do not often allow for formal military preparation. Many of these so-called soldiers – amongst whom we find many children – do not have proper military gear, and

---

[29] In *A Short History of Guerrilla Warfare,* John Ellis (1976) describes guerrilla wars as not simply a military phenomenon but also a political activity which involves popular participation. It is a 'struggle of the weak against superior members and technology'. Normally in these kinds of wars the political programme of the leadership has to mesh with the basic aspirations of the people in order to channel their ability to fight. The people are persuaded to fight rather than being coerced by repressive structures. This was the case of many liberation wars, including the one Angolans fought against Portuguese colonization. Although these postcolonial wars still maintain some of the features of guerrilla warfare in many respects, the relationship with the people is often one of repression and complete disrespect. They abduct people and force them to fight and support their struggle. This seems to be dramatically different from the traditional guerrilla warfare discussed by Ellis.

often have none at all. In different periods of the war, these abducted civilians find themselves being used by both warring factions, depending on which gains control over their village/town. As Cock (1991) points out, in these kinds of civil wars the separation between the 'battlefield' and the 'home front' becomes very blurred. The idea that war compels men to go and fight in order to protect the women, the children, and the elderly who remain passive and secure at home – one of the features of the 'traditional' Western type of warfare – no longer holds. It is a myth. Civilians, and especially women and children, are increasingly incorporated into war activities in ways that defy established conventions about civilian protection in times of war. This is the context of these 'new' wars in which children actively take part.

The Twilight Zone: An Experience and a Space for Manoeuvre

> These 'in between' spaces provide the terrain for elaborating strategies of selfhood – singular and communal – that initiate new signs of identity, and innovative sites of collaboration, and contestation … (Homi Bhabha, 1994).

As mentioned above, child-soldiers constitute an 'in-between' category that moves beyond established borders. And this intermediary position can be depicted within their daily military life. Despite being indoctrinated and instrumentalized during the initiation process, these young men and women somehow manage to develop a world of their own, situated within this ambiguous state of being simultaneously children and soldiers. In the previous section, I brought to the fore their vulnerability, and how they are manipulated, often against their will, into becoming fierce combatants and often merciless killers. In this section, I intend to convey the ways in which these children bring about imaginary spaces for themselves within this context of violence and terror. How do they find space and time to still be children – play children's games, miss their relatives, cry over their pains and sorrows, and the like? How is this twilight position enacted in their everyday lives? I will just let these children's voices be heard. What follows is a collection of extracts from children's narratives about their experiences of war: their feelings, fears, sorrows, sadness, loss, pain, expectations, hopes, and their coping mechanisms. These accounts speak for themselves.

The feelings presented by some of these young soldiers were diverse. They expressed fear of being taken to the battlefield to fight, fear of being killed, fear of their commanders. In many respects this was a relationship built in fear and terror, as any minor wrong move could signify death – both during combat as well as in the camps where they were constantly kept under surveillance.

> During the war I was very scared of going into combat. I thought I was going to die. Before going on missions, I always thought of my parents and asked in silence for them to pray for me. I was particularly scared of the migs (airplanes) that bombarded us … In my quiet time I would always be longing to be at home with my father and my mother. I often remembered the things we did together as a family: for example when we went to work in the fields my father would always come last, my mother in front and myself in the middle. (20-year-old from Angola)
>
> I escaped death twice. The first time was in Caxito when we fell into an ambush and a bullet just missed me. Oh, my god, I was so frightened. The second time was when we were sur-

prised by the enemy. I tried to run, but a bullet hit me. I was rescued by my colleagues, who took me to a safe place. I thought I was going to die, but again I escaped. (20-year-old from Angola)

The war is not good. I will not recommend it to my future child (his girlfriend is pregnant). In the war you have no say. You are always under the orders of the commanders, and they can make you do absolutely anything. I was very frightened when I took part in a 24-hour combat to recapture Mbanza-Congo from the government forces. We were under intense fire for 24 hours. In the end we had to withdraw as our ammunition was finished. That day I thought I was going to die because I was not protected by the *kimbanda*, all the chiefs were well protected. I saw them being treated by the *kimbanda*. (20-year-old from Angola)

Our chiefs were really mean and nasty. We were very scared of them. One day, while we were still doing our military training, we got permission to go bathe in the river, but we stayed there for quite a while because we started playing, swimming and enjoying ourselves. Time just flew. Our instructor came to look for us. He was so furious that he shot my friend, who died on the spot. I feel so sad when I remember all these things. (16-year-old from Angola)

My brother and I were together in the same camp. My brother was caught while trying to escape and was tied to a tree and killed. I was watching, but I had to keep myself from crying because if they had discovered that we were related I could have been killed too. (18-year-old from Angola)

These accounts of fear also involve a great deal of pain – not just physical pain (which no doubt was very common in the camps) but also emotional and psychological pain, the pain of watching a brother and a close friend being shot and killed on the spot (see Reynolds and Weiss in this volume).

One day during a combat in Kibaxe, my friend was shot and died next to me. I managed to take him to the edge of the nearby river. Together with other friends, we buried him. He was my best friend ... In the war nobody could cry, if the commanders saw you crying they would take measures. (18-year-old from Angola)

I was kidnapped with three friends of mine ... while we were in the bush looking for firewood. A group of RENAMO soldiers stopped us, pointed their guns at us, and forced us to go with them. We had to carry their bags and boxes of products ... We walked until our feet got swollen. I lived in the base for three years ... The nights were dreadful because we were there to be used by the soldiers. A soldier per night ... The lucky ones were those who were chosen by an officer who had a hut for them to live in and who protected them as his wives. (18-year-old from Mozambique)

There was a lot of famine in the war. Sometimes, we didn't have any food to eat, and we had to loot the villages. We would get there and attack the village, and grab all the goats, chickens, millet or *fuba* (maize or cassava meal) we could find. The villagers couldn't say or do anything. Those who tried to resist were beaten or even shot. Sometimes, we would tell them to cook a meal for us. The chiefs would sleep with the girls. Many girls cried and shouted, but nobody could do anything to prevent it. (18-year-old from Angola)

I was taken by force by *matsanga* in 1991. My first assignment was to loot the shops. They burnt all the shops after we emptied them. Then they forced us to go with them and carry the loot to the military base. We walked for 3 days ... On our journey to the base the soldiers killed those who got tired of walking and carrying heavy loads ... When we got to the base I was chosen by one of the commanders to be his wife ... In 1992, I gave birth to a baby girl. (22-year-old from Mozambique)

I felt very, very sad when I found out that most of my relatives were killed in an attack on my village, carried out by one of our groups. Those who didn't die disappeared. I didn't feel like fighting with them anymore because UNITA killed my own family ... I was living with this big pain inside my heart, but I couldn't say anything. I just did what I did, because I was forced to do it. I didn't fight because I wanted to. (19-year-old from Angola)

Many of the children had problems living with this pain as well as with the pain they inflicted on others. Some expressed remorse for the atrocities committed, and the impotence to act differently, given the circumstances.

During the war I was very sad because of all the violence and killings we had to do. Now I continue to be sad because some people here in the village say that I was responsible for the people killed in the war because I belonged to UNITA. They despise me. I am afraid of them. (17-year-old from Angola)

When we were on our 'reconnaissance' missions, we often killed the people who came across our path. Many of them didn't do us any harm. I didn't like that, I was very sad to witness and be part of that, but I couldn't say anything because many of my colleagues had smoked *liamba* (marihuana). (19-year-old from Angola)

My first military assignment was to attack a village and steal the cattle … We burnt down that village … and with my gun I killed the ammunition chief … I am very sad about my story … but I had no choice. (17-year-old from Mozambique)

Most of us (those who carried out these attacks) were children. The boys had guns and they smoked marihuana mixed with bullet powder. That is why they were able to be so ruthless and kill so many people. When I think of that I become very depressed. (20-year-old from Angola)

Some of them mentioned that, in their spare time, they often managed to get a chance to just sit and talk to their friends about things that would help to remove them from the environment of war. But their conversations had to be in secret because the military commanders did not like to hear them talking about home and their families.

During the war we had some days of rest, one or two days a week in which we would stay in the camp. We couldn't go far because to go out one had to ask for a '*guia de dispensa*' (authorization) and that was not easy to get. But during that time we tried to meet with our friends and the people from our village or nearby villages who lived in the camp. (20-year-old from Angola)

In the military camps, in our free time, especially at night before going to sleep, we would sit and chat with our friends. Our conversations were about our relatives, and our friends who stayed at home. I often felt *saudade* (missing/longing) for my family, my mom, and my dad, my brothers and sisters. (19-year-old from Angola)

In the war I had my friends Luis, Dino, Nelo, Marino and Nando. When we managed to get time together, we played games like 'pessonha' and soccer. We also talked about our families and our villages. We wondered whether our parents were alive or dead … I was often ill there. I had headaches and diarrhoea. When I was frightened by something my heart would beat very, very fast. (19-year-old from Angola)

We couldn't talk about our homes and our relatives, if they heard us talking about that they immediately thought that we were planning to escape, and would punish us. We used to talk in secret, when it was safe to do so … I once managed to escape together with my friend, but because we didn't know the area very well we ended up in another UNITA camp. We were both severely beaten by the soldiers. (19-year-old from Angola)

When we had a chance, we would play music – somebody had a radio – and dance in our barracks. We couldn't play it too loud, though. The chief of our group was not so bad; sometimes, he allowed us to have a bit of fun. Sometimes, we would also play soccer, but not very often. Life there was not a happy life. (19-year-old from Mozambique)

Abducted child combatants often had to find ways of protecting themselves, and coping with the hardships of war and military life. They often deceived their commanders and chiefs with lies and tricks, or by obscuring the truth. They found several mechanisms to try and beat the system as they grew to know it better.

When I was kidnapped, I gave the soldiers a false name, not my real one. I didn't want them to know my family and make my parents suffer. (19-year-old from Angola)

During the war, one had to pretend to be stupid to be left alone. Those who were smart and spunky were always controlled by the chiefs and given heavy and hard tasks. (17-year-old from Mozambique)

When they asked you to do something really bad and you didn't want to do it, you had to pretend that you didn't understand very well what they wanted, or you had to do it the wrong way, so that they would ask someone else to do it. But that was very risky because if the chief was vicious you could be severely punished for it. It was a gamble. (20-year-old from Angola)

I knew of a group of boys, who found a way of fleeing from the camp late at night. They would go out and loot goods for themselves, and sleep with girls in the nearby villages. They would hide their looted things in the bush. The commanders didn't know they were doing that. If caught, they could be imprisoned or even killed. (17-year-old from Mozambique)

When I was afraid of going to fight I would pretend to be ill ... but sometimes it didn't work. They would insist that you go even if you were really ill. My friend once escaped death. He was ill and the commander let him stay in the camp. The other three who went on the mission died. He escaped because he stayed in the camp. It was his lucky day. (22-year-old from Mozambique)

If the commander told me to go on a mission and kill everyone, sometimes I felt compassion for the people and, if the commander wasn't there, I would let them run home instead of killing them. It was very hard to kill, and then look at all the dead bodies. (17-year-old from Mozambique)

I was working as the security guard of a commander. I had to carry his bags and guard his house. When the commander was drunk and asleep, I would leave him and run to see my friends, and a girl I met there. We liked each other a lot. We had to keep our relationship secret because the big soldiers could take her from me, if they found out that I was seeing her. (19-year-old from Angola)

Many of the young combatants felt that they had lost time in the war and that they gained very little, if anything, from it. They also talked about what they would like to do in the future.

If I could I would have told those who gave orders to start the war to talk amongst themselves and stop the war. Because of the war, I cannot be a truck driver. I needed to have studied, but I lost my time in the war. When I came back, I learned that my father had died. Now I cannot study. I have to work to help my mother and my younger siblings. (20-year-old from Angola)

I want to have a wife and twelve children, but I don't want my children to go to war. There is a lot of suffering in war. (19-year-old from Angola)

I lost my time in the military and now I can't manage to study to learn a profession ... When I think of all this my heart beats and becomes very sore and I am unable to sleep at night. (18-year-old from Angola)

We suffered a lot. The things that they promised us we never saw. No, we don't want to return to war. That is why we were so happy when we were called for demobilization. (17-year-old from Mozambique)

When demobilization came I was happy because I was still young and I wanted to go home and study. (18-year-old from Angola)

Victims, or Agents?

I didn't want to fight, they forced me to fight and kill people ... now I am not well, I act like a crazy person ... the spirits of those I killed in the war are haunting me and making me ill. (Nelito, 19 years old)

Some people here in the village say that I was responsible for the people killed in the war because I belonged to UNITA. They despise me. I am afraid of them. (Ben, 17 years old)

What arises from all of the above is the question of agency. And here we return to Marula's story. Should we consider child combatants to be passive victims, empty vessels into which the capacity for violence has been poured? Or are they active agents, fully culpable and accountable for their actions? There is no easy answer, because the extenuating circumstances and internal emotional states of children vary from case to case. Nevertheless, their actions in the war are complex, and certainly transcend, in my view, the often simplistic and moral analysis that depicts them solely as victims. Certainly they are victims, but they also became more than just victims. The processes in which they became involved transformed them into something else – an oxymoron – that, as I stated in the title of this chapter, brings together this ambiguous association of *innocence* and *guilt*. While they cannot be, on the one hand, considered fully responsible for their actions, they cannot, on the other hand, be completely deprived of agency.

Can these youngsters be considered 'real' agents? Is not power implicit in the notion of agency? Giddens's reformulation of the concept of human agency in his theory of structuration might be helpful here. He considers agency to be the capability of doing something, rather than the intention of doing something. 'Agency concerns events of which an individual is the perpetrator, in the sense that the individual could, at any phase in a given sequence of conduct, have acted differently. Whatever happened would not have happened if that individual had not intervened' (1984:9). For Giddens, the agent is a human being with transformative capacity – with the power to intervene or to refrain from intervention. Agency is intrinsically connected to power. To be able to act otherwise, the individual must be able to exercise some sort of power. The power of the individual can be constrained by a range of circumstances. To 'have no choice' (as many former child-soldiers mentioned) does not mean, in Giddens's terms, the dissolution of agency as such. Giddens conceives power as presuming regularized relations of both autonomy and dependence between actors in contexts of social interaction. All forms of dependence offer some resources whereby those who are subordinated can influence the actions of their superiors. This view of agency and power makes these young combatants agents in their own right, since they can, at certain moments, mobilize resources to change the activities of their superiors. They can, for example, pretend to be ill to avoid certain tasks. They can plan to escape. Or they may not perform their duties properly. This constitutes what Giddens calls the '*dialectic of control*' (1984:16). Despite being agents, the nature of the agency of these children is a complex one, as it disassembles the 'traditional' binary opposition between the *child* and the *adult*.

In trying to make sense of the ambiguous actions of these young soldiers, I turn to de Certeau's (1984) analysis of trajectories, strategies and tactics. In *The Practice of Everyday Life*, de Certeau tries to grasp the complex models of action of 'consumers', a euphemistic term that he uses to identify the dominated, the subalterns (Chatterjee, 1993; Spivak, 1993). He sees consumers' actions as intricate trajectories that are 'indirect' and 'errant', and that obey only their own logic. However, he realizes that to represent these actions as 'trajectories' does not do much justice to them, because although 'trajectory', as a category, suggests movement, it also involves a 'plane projection, a flattening out' which fails to capture the *bricolage* and the intricate meanderings embroiled in these actions. In order to avoid this reduction he suggests a distinction between strategies and tactics. He sees 'strategy' as the calculation or manipulation of relationships or force that becomes possible as soon as a subject of will and power, such as an army, can be isolated from an environment. A strategy 'assumes a place that can be circumscribed as "proper" (propre) and thus serve as the basis for generating relations with an exterior distinct from it (competitors, adversaries)' (1984:xix). A tactic, on the other hand, is a calculated action, which is determined by the absence of the 'proper' (a spatial or institutional locus), and cannot be distinguished as a visible totality. 'The place of a tactic is the space of the other ... it must play on and with a terrain imposed on it ... it is a manoeuvre within the enemy's field of vision ... it operates in isolated actions, blow by blow. It takes advantage of "opportunities" and depends on them ... this gives a tactic more mobility, to be sure, but a mobility that must accept the chance offerings of the moment, and seize on the wing the possibilities that offer themselves at any given moment'(1984:37). As de Certeau puts it very clearly, tactics are the *art of the weak*, who must constantly manipulate events in order to turn them into 'opportunities'. Drawing on Clausewitz's (1976) discussion on deception, he states that 'power is bound by its visibility', while trickery and deception are only possible for the weak. If the forces at the disposition of the strategist are weak, the more will the strategist be able to use deception, and in this way transform the strategy into tactics. Therefore, while strategies are determined by the postulation of a locus of power, tactics are predetermined by the absence of that locus of power.

Following de Certeau's analysis, it is clear that these young combatants exercise what I would call a 'tactical agency'. By 'tactical agency', I mean a specific type of agency that is devised to cope with the concrete, immediate conditions of their lives in order to maximize the circumstances created by their military and violent environment. Their actions, however, come from a position of weakness. They have no power base – the absence of a locus (the *propre*) – and act within the confines of a 'foreign' territory. As de Certeau suggests, tactical actions awaken 'blow by blow' and have the mobility to seize the openings offered at any given moment. As the above testimonies demonstrate, this is precisely how the actions of these children unfold. Somehow, these children managed to create a world of their own within the confines of the environment of political violence and terror in which they had to operate. They created spaces for their conversations about home and their loved ones, even if in secret. They created space for play (soccer games, swimming, and listening to music and dancing) and for laughter. But they also managed to trick and deceive their mentors with a false identity, with escape plans, by pretending to be stupid in order to avoid being deployed in dangerous missions, or by avoiding observing certain rules. Some were fully aware of the acts and atrocities they were committing, and sometimes went well beyond their regular military assignments out of vengeance, greed, immaturity, jealousy, and the like, or in the expectation of being rewarded or positively acknowledged by the commanders. This could also mean having the commander's 'friendship' and protection. Although few would admit to it, some might also have found some thrill in it, and participated enthusiastically in the process. Many of these young soldiers had no prospect of returning home after raiding and burning villages, killing defenceless civilians and looting food convoys. So that was the life they were constrained to live both in the present and for the future. Some of them never had the possibility of forming an idea of life outside the context of war. Their premature recruitment forced them to grow up within this culture of terror and violence. Some were abducted at a very tender age, in some cases as young as 5 or 6 years old. For these children, the military and the war became all they knew of life, and they tried to make the best of it, performing their duties to the best of their abilities. In this sense, these child-soldiers were conscious 'tactical agents' who responded to the demands and pressures of their lives.

By contrast, the exercise of a 'strategic' agency would imply a basis of power – the *'proper'* as de Certeau calls it. It would also require mastery of the larger picture, of the long-term consequences of their actions, in the form of political gain or benefits/profits. That does not seem to be the case for the majority of these child-soldiers. The accounts presented show how some of them see the period spent fighting the war as a waste of time. After years of soldiering and enduring the most adverse conditions of existence, they have nothing: no jobs, no skills, no studies, no homes, no parents, no food or shelter – not even a gun that would make looting possible. They have become completely dispossessed, completely powerless. For example, after demobilization, child combatants under the age of 15 were not accorded the same demobilization package of benefits as regular soldiers because their age precluded them from being defined as soldiers.[30] International conventions (the Geneva Conventions of 1949) did not recognize people aged under 15 as soldiers, thereby leaving children who served in the military in the same situation as many adults without any means of beginning their new lives as civilians.

Navigating Multiple Interstitial Spaces: A Conclusion

This chapter has attempted to convey children's daily experiences of war and political violence. These tales of terror, violence and survival constitute shared experiences that link children war-wide, and which are extended beyond local and regional communities (Nordstrom, 1997). I have argued that armies of child-soldiers do not exist simply because of a shortage of manpower, but that they result from the concerted efforts of both local and global forces. The initiation of young people into violence constitutes a careful process of identity re-configuration aimed at cutting their links with society, and at transforming them into merciless killers. Despite the fact that the majority of them have been forced to enter the military, they are not empty vessels into whom violence is poured. Having started as victims, many of them are converted into perpetrators of the most violent and atrocious deeds. In this transformation process, they also exercise agency of their own – a 'tactical agency', an agency of the weak – which is sporadic, and mobile, and seizes every opportunity that allows them to cope with the constraints imposed upon them.

If tactics constitute these complex actions, which involve calculations and machinations but also some kind of vulnerability – derived from a position of weakness – then, 'tactical agents' are, by definition, also interstitial agents. They become interstitial because they have to produce a myriad of signifying practices, similar to 'wandering lines' (Deligny, in de Certeau, 1984) that only make sense within their own logic – the logic of the 'in-between' which is drawn from the vast possibilities that such a complex condition offers. By virtue of this borderland condition, they are able to be mobile and grab opportunities the moment they arise. Despite being deprived of a locus of power, they are able to navigate within a multiplicity of spaces and states of being: being simultane-

[30] During the process of demobilization in Mozambique this issue gave rise to a mutiny staged by child-soldiers at Renamo's headquarters in Maputo. A group of child-soldiers under 15 years of age waiting to be demobilized in one of the cantonment areas besieged the Renamo leaders claiming the benefits that their colleagues over 15 were getting. They refused to set the Renamo leadership free before their demands were met. The problem was solved by the intervention of humanitarian organizations such as the Red Cross who arranged alternative benefit packages for these child combatants.

ously children and adults, victims and perpetrators, civilians and soldiers, and so forth. Mbembe posits a similar view, when he analyzes the ways in which postcolonial subjects assemble, and make use of, several fluid identities, which need to be 'constantly revised in order to achieve maximum instrumentality and efficacy as and when required' (1992:3). This multitude of identities is what allows these youngsters the possibility to master and manipulate some form of deception and trickery (Clausewitz, 1976) in order to achieve gains, even if small and temporary. In other words, the same logic of the liminal positions that underlines the ritualized initiation into violence is also the one that provides child-soldiers with the opportunities for creating meaning, and signifying practice in the actions of their everyday lives.

References

Abdullah, I. & Y. Bangura (eds). 1997. 'Lumpen Youth Culture and Political Violence: The Sierra Leone Civil War', special Issue of *African Development* 23 (3-4).

Amit-Talai, V. & H. Wulff (eds). 1995. *Youth Cultures: A Cross-Cultural Perspective*. London: Routledge.

Appadurai, A. 1991. 'Global Ethnoscapes: Notes and Queries for a Transnational Anthropology', in *Recapturing Anthropology: Working in the Present*, ed. Richard Fox. Santa Fe: School of American Research Press.

Aries, P. 1962. *Centuries of Childhood*. Harmondsworth: Penguin.

Bakthin, M. 1984. *Rabelais and his World*. (translated by Helene Iswolsky). Bloomington, IN: Indiana University Press.

Bastin, M. 1984. 'Mungonge: Initiation Masculine des Adultes chez les Tshokwe (Angola)', *Baessler Archiv* 32:361-89.

Bazenguissa-Ganga, R. 1999. 'The Spread of Political Violence in Congo-Brazaville'. *African Affairs* 98 (386): 37-54.

Berdal, M. & D. Malone. 2000. *Greed and Grievance: Economic Agendas in Civil War*. Boulder, CO: Lynne Rienner.

Bhabha, H. 1994. *The Location of Culture*. London: Routledge

Boothby, N. Upton, P. & A. Sultan. 1992. 'Boy Soldiers of Mozambique', in *Refugee Children*, Oxford: Refugee Studies Programme, March.

Boyden, J. 1990. 'Childhood and the Policy Makers: A Comparative Perspective on the Globalisation of Childhood', in *Constructing and Reconstructing Childhood: Contemporary Issues in the Sociological Study of Childhood*, ed. A. James, & A. Prout. London and Washington, DC: Falmer Press.

Boyden, J. & S. Gibbs. 1997. *Children and War: Understanding Psychological Distress in Cambodia*. Geneva: UN.

Brett, R. 2000. 'Child Soldiers: Causes, Consequences and International Responses', in *ALT against Child Soldiers in Africa: A Reades*, ed. E. Bennett, V. Gamba and D. van der Merwe, Pretoria: Institute for Security Studies.

Brett, R. & M. McCallin. 1996. *Children the Invisible Soldiers*. Vaxjo: Radda Barnen (Swedish Save the Children).

Cairns, E. 1996. *Children and Political Violence*. Oxford: Blackwell.

Caputo, V. 1995. 'Anthropology's silent "Others": A Consideration of Some Conceptual and Methodological Issues for the Study of Youth and Children's Cultures', in *Youth Cultures: A Cross-Cultural Prespective*, ed. V. Amit-Talai & H. Wulff. London: Routledge.

Certeau, M. de. 1984. *The Practice of Everyday Life* (trans. Steven Rendall). Berkeley, CA: University of California Press.

Chatterjee, P. 1993. *The State and its Fragments: Colonial and Postcolonial Histories*. Princeton, NJ: Princeton University Press.

Clapham, C. (ed.) 1998. *African Guerrillas*. Oxford: James Currey.

Clausewitz, K. von 1976. *On War* (translated by M. Howard & P. Paret). Princeton, NJ: Princeton University Press.

Cock, J. 1991. *Colonels and Cadres: War and Gender in South Africa*. Cape Town: Oxford University Press.

De Boeck, F. 1991. 'Of Bushbucks Without Horns: Male and Female Initiation among the Aluund of Southwest Zaire,' *Journal des Africanistes* 61 (1).

— 1999. 'Borderland Breccia: The Mutant Hero and the Historical Imagination of a Central-African Diamond Frontier'. Paper read at the International Symposium on 'The Black West: Reinventing History, Reinterpreting Media', University of California, San Diego. May. Also published as 'La frontière diamantifère angolaise et son héros mutant', in *Matière à Politique: Le pouvoir, les corps et les choses*, ed. Jean François Bayart & Jean-Pierre Warnier. Paris: Karthala, 2004.

— 1995. 'Bodies of Remembrance: Knowledge, Experience and the Growing of Memory in Luunda Ritual Performance', in *Rites et Ritualisation*, ed. Georges Thinès & Luc de Heusch. Paris: Vrin.

Dawes, A. & A. Honwana. 1996. 'Children Culture and Mental Health: Interventions in Conditions of War'. Paper presented at conference on Children, War and Prosecution, Maputo, 1–4 December.

Dodge, C. & M. Raundalen. 1991. *Reaching Children in War; Sudan, Uganda and Mozambique*. Uppsala: Sigma Forlag.

Ellis, J. 1976. *A Short History of Guerrilla Warfare*. New York: St Martin's Press.

Finnegan, W. 1992. *A Complicated War: The Harrowing for Mozambique*. Berkeley, CA: University of California Press.

Freeman, M. 1993. *The Rights and Wrongs of Children*. London: Francis Pinter Publishers.

Furley, O. 1995. 'Child Soldiers in Africa', in *Conflict in Africa*, ed. O. Furley. London: Tauris Academic Press.

Geffray, C. 1990. *La Cause des Armes au Mozambique: Anthropologie d'une Guerre Civile*. Paris: Credu-Karthala.

Gersony, R. 1988. 'Summary of Mozambican Refugee Accounts of Principally Conflict-related Experience in Mozambique'. Report presented to the Assistant Secretary for African Affairs. Washington, DC: Bureau for Refugee Programs, US State Department, April.

Giddens, A. 1984. *The Constitution of Society*. Cambridge: Polity Press.

Goodwin-Gill, G. & I. Cohn. 1994. *Child Soldiers: The Role of Children in Armed Conflict*. Oxford: Clarendon Press.

Grimes, R. 2000. *Deeply into the Bone; Re-inventing Rites of Passage*. Berkeley, CA: University of California Press.

Honwana, A. 1996. 'Spiritual Agency and Self-Renewal in Southern Mozambique'. Doctoral Thesis in Social Anthropology, University of London (SOAS).

— 1998. 'Okusiakala Ondalo Yokalye, Let's Light a New Fire: Local Knowledge in the Post-War Reintegration of War-affected Children in Angola'. Consultancy Report for CCF Angola.

— 1999a. 'Negotiating Post-War Identities: Child Soldiers in Mozambique and Angola', *CODESRIA Bulletin* 1–2:

— 1999b. 'Untold War Stories: Young Women and War in Mozambique' Paper presented at the Leuven conference on Children and Youth as Emerging Social Categories in Africa, November.

— in press. 'Children of War: Local Understandings of War and War Trauma in Mozambique and Angola', in *Civilians in War*, ed. S. Chesterman. Boulder, CO: Lynne Rienner.

Honwana, A. & E. Pannizo. 1995. 'Evaluation of the Children and War Project in Mozambique'. Research Report for Save the Children US and USAID.

Human Rights Watch, 1994. *Easy Prey: Children and War in Liberia*. London: Human Rights Watch Children's Project.

Ignatieff, M. 1999. *The Warrior's Honor: Ethnic War and the Modern Conscience*. London: Vintage.

James, A. 1993. *Childhood Identities: Self and Social Relationships in the Experience of Childhood*. Edinburgh: Edinburgh University Press.

James, A. & A. Prout (eds). 1990 *Constructing and Reconstructing Childhood: Contemporary Issues in the Sociological Study of Childhood*. London and Washington, DC: Falmer Press.

James, A., C. Jenks, & A. Prout. 1998. *Theorizing Childhood*. New York: Teachers' College Press.

Jenks, C. 1996. *Childhood*. London and New York: Routledge.

Kaldor, M. 1999. *New and Old Wars: Organized Violence in a Global Era*. Cambridge: Polity Press.

Kourouma, A. 2000. *Allah n'est pas Obligé*. Paris: Editions du Seuil.

Lambek, M. & P. Antze (eds). 1996. *Tense Past: Cultural Essays in Trauma and Memory*. New York: Routledge.

Mbembe, A. 1992. ' Provisional Notes on the Postcolony', *Africa* 62 (1): 3-37.

Minter, W. 1994. *Apartheid's Contras: An Inquiry into the Roots of War in Angola and Mozambique*. London; Zed Books.

Nordstrom, C. 1997. *A Different Kind of War Story*. Philadelphia, PA: University of Pennsylvania Press.

Peters, K. & P. Richards. 1998. 'Youths in Sierra Leone: Why We Fight', *Africa* 68 (2):

Pinchbeck, I. & M. Hewitt. 1969. *Children in English Society, Vol. I: From Tudor Times to the Eighteenth Century*. Toronto: University of Toronto Press.

Postman, N. 1994. *The Disappearance of Childhood*. New York: Vintage Books.

Reno, W. 1998. *Warlord Politics and African States*. Boulder, CO: Lynne Rienner.

Reynolds, P. 1996. *Traditional Healers and Childhood in Zimbabwe*. Athens, OH: Ohio University Press.

Richards, P. 1996. *Fighting for the Rain Forest: War, Youth & Resources in Sierra Leone*. Oxford/Portsmouth, NH: James Currey/Heinemann.

Roberts, Barbara, 1984. 'The Death of Machothink: Feminist Research and the Transformation of Peace Studies, *Women's Studies International Forum* 7(4): 195–200.

Spivak, G. 1993. *Outside the Teaching Machine* . London: Routledge.

Stephens, S. (ed). 1995. *Children and the Politics of Culture*. Princeton, NJ: Princeton University Press.

Summerville, J. 1982. *The Rise and Fall of Childhood*. Beverly Hills, CA: Sage.

Vines, A. 1991. *Renamo: Terrorism in Mozambique*. London/Bloomington, IN: Centre for Southern African Studies, University of York/Indiana University Press.

Wessells, M. 1997. 'Child Soldiers', in *Bulletin of the Atomic Scientists*. Chicago, November/December.

3 MATS UTAS
Agency of Victims
Young Women in the Liberian Civil War

In downtown Monrovia a taxi is pulling over to pick up a male passenger. As we are squeezing together (or 'dressing' as Liberians would say) in the back to make room for the newcomer, a woman on the front seat turns to him and bluntly states that he does not respect her. Nothing indicates any relationship between the two. The man – identified by another passenger as a police officer (most possibly indicating that he is a former fighter) – starts to brag about how brave he was during the war. The woman retorts by stating that men were the real cowards during the civil war: 'we were out there when you men were hiding under your beds.' 'Some men don't even dare to pull the trigger; I have seen it myself', she continues and finally ends by saying [boldly] 'please, don't call me a civilian'. The man continues to brag but the woman pretends not to listen any more. The man, now with uncertainty in his voice, says that 'there were only female fighters in Nimba'. She looks at him and signals to the driver that she is getting off, without another word to the man as she leaves the cab. (Monrovia/field-notes)

Introduction

When I started looking for girls in numerous war situations, I found silences and empty spaces, punctuated only sporadically by a handful of researchers focusing on children in general and girls in particular. Their stories account only for the smallest percentage of scholarly and popular work on social and political violence and systems of in/justice. (Nordstrom, 1997b:5)

Too often the girls are considered only as silent victims of (sexual) assault – devoid of agency, moral conscience, economic potential or political awareness ... We need to ask girls to tell their own stories of war, its impact, and potential solutions, rather than assuming the right to speak for them. (Nordstrom, 1997b:36f)

This paper deals with young women's (or girls') lived experiences of the Liberian Civil War.[1] I argue that, if the actions of young women in war were to be categorized as 'victim dynamics', we might in essence rule out not only women, children, refugees and civilians as victims but also most of the fighters who have been the factual vehicles of the Liberian Civil War. There is therefore an evident need to re-operationalize the inimical opposition of victim/perpetrator, civilian/soldier (Keen, 1996, 1999) and to rely on more complex plots of war realities (Maček, 2000; 2001), as well as to establish

---

[1] As the war lasted for seven years, girls grew up and became young women. Consequently, it has not been possible to be consistent in separating a category of girls from one consisting of young women. As such, girls and young women in the text below are interchangeable.

alternative configurations of gender (see Butler, 1990:142ff) in war zones.[2]

The material in this chapter has been collected through intensive participant observation in Monrovia and Ganta (Nimba County) during a one-year research period in 1998. Most of it stems from taped interviews made in Ganta during the second part of my fieldwork.[3] Some additional material was collected during four months of field research in the refugee setting of Danane in the Ivory Coast in 1996. To study a delicate field like women's war experience as a male, and above all a *Qwi plu* (denoting white, or rather civilized, in Mano, the dominant vernacular in the Ganta area), has indeed been a challenge. My experience holds that women rarely speak about these issues to outsiders. Stereotypes of female victimization tend to be consolidated when (even female) social scientists or other researchers carry out interviews with refugees or communities going through a war experience. To circumvent this problem I co-operated with an assistant, a young woman from neighbouring Sierra Leone, who has been through similar scenarios as my informants and whose age matches the target group. Even so, a certain amount of distrust is noticeable in the interviews. This stems mainly from the uncertainty factor of the tape recorder. Active roles in looting, fighting, etc., which are openly discussed in the informal setting, are often omitted or downplayed; consequently, my assistant has often been informed of matters during informal discussions rather than during taped interviews.[4]

A majority of my informants, between the ages of 10 and 18 at the onset of the civil war, were not under parental guidance for most of the civil war, for reasons that are different in each case. Many live in loosely structured youth collectives on which adults have only a peripheral impact. In Monrovia, most of my informants were footloose, and out of touch with the larger society. To a lesser extent this was also the case for my informants in Ganta, who overall were more incorporated in society at large through interaction with neighbours, work places, churches, etc. To enhance the accessibility, I have chosen to base this chapter on the accounts of three key narrators: Bintu, Hawa and Masa.[5] I value these three voices as very representative of young women's war-stories/scenarios. These voices are used here both as accounts for what took place during the war and as sources for a narrative analysis. To make the description 'thicker', I have added the voices of other young women,[6] and of men relating to this subject, as well as personal observations. Though a description of young women's lives in the Liberian war zone, my contribution aims, on a more theoretical level, to take issue with prevailing views on agency and gender stereotypes in war.[7]

[2] It is noted that gender categories are by no means exclusive and that 'cultures do not have a single model of gender or a gender system, but rather a multiplicity of discourses on gender which can vary both contextually and biographically' (Moore, 1994:142).

[3] At this stage of my fieldwork I had just read a draft version of Filip De Boeck's '"Dogs Breaking Their Leash": Globalization and Shifting Gender Categories in the Diamond Traffic between Angola and DR.Congo (1999)'. It inspired me to take a closer look at issues of young women's agency in the civil war.

[4] As noted by Henrietta Moore (1994:141), individuals take up different positions within different discourses, resulting in subject positions that will contradict or be in direct conflict with one other.

[5] The names of the young women have been changed to protect the identity of the informants. The interviews were carried out in English. However, as Liberian English is rather difficult in syntax the quotations have been adapted to a more standard form of English.

[6] In particular, in the section on female combatants I have added material from an additional interview with a female ex-combatant.

[7] People fall in love even during times of war. Due to the focus on agency and young women's tactics in the civil war, issues of love and passion have been largely set aside in this text. Indeed, even if most young women have downplayed such emotions, 'soft' relations still existed. Owing to limitations of space I have also omitted the important topics of religion, morality and issues of tradition, such as the important secret societies and the ever-present issues of witchcraft and sorcery (on the borderline between tradition and modernity).

The Civil War

The Liberian Civil War started when a small group of men led by Prince Johnson entered the eastern town of Butuo on Christmas Eve, 1989. The Libyan-trained, rather ill-equipped, group later became known as the National Patriotic Front of Liberia (NPFL) and within weeks splintered into two NPFL fractions, one led by Charles Taylor, and the other, the Independent National Patriotic Front of Liberia (INPFL), led by Prince Johnson. What initially was seen as a revolution in which the people in Nimba County (Nimbadians), in particular, fought with sticks and cutlasses, was eventually transformed into a war of terror where young people started fighting each other. The violence did not so much serve political ends, but aimed at the protection of one's family, and at accessing sources of power and wealth. Political leaders with their own private interests started making their appearance fighting over the control of mineral-rich areas and logging concessions. Within a few years half a dozen rebel movements had spread terror in the entire country. In this way the NPFL, for instance, that originally claimed to be fighting for the Nimbadians, spread fear throughout the entire Nimba county: NPFL boys looted and molested the very people they were said to be fighting the war for.

After seven years of civil war, between 150,000 and 200,000 people had been killed,[8] 600-700,000 refugees had fled to neighbouring countries, and the majority of the remaining population of 2.2–2.5 million were internally displaced (so-called IDPs).[9] Following peace talks, elections were held in mid-1997. Ironically, in what former US President Jimmy Carter called one of the fairest elections in African history, Charles Taylor and his National Patriotic Party – formed out of the NPFL apparatus – won a landslide victory and thereby accomplished what NPFL combat had failed to do. After the elections Liberians experienced a few years of peace (1997-9) but since late 1999 they have seen the birth and growth of a new rebel movement, Liberians United for Reconciliation and Democracy (LURD) in the north. As of early 2003, yet another rebel movement, Movement for Democracy in Liberia (MODEL), has appeared with its base in the south of the country.

A Middle Road: Appearing as Both Victim and Perpetrator

[W]omen became objective tragedy in wars from which they were excluded. (Virilio, 1989:22)

In her illuminating book *Women and War*, Elshtain argues that people in the Western world 'are heirs of a tradition that assumes an affinity between women and peace' and 'between men and war' (1987:4; see also Rolston, 1989; Aretxaga, 1997). The prototype is that '[m]en fight as avatars of a nation's sanctioned violence' and that '[w]omen work and weep and sometimes protest' within a given framework (Elshtain, 1987:3). In opposition to these simplified images, Elshtain furnishes women with agency in war:

[8] Ellis (1999:312ff) has argued that the death toll was considerably lower. Not surprisingly, statistics from war zones tend to be very approximate.
[9] Readers further interested in the history of the Liberian Civil War have numerous sources to consult. Some of the best would be: Ellis, 1995, 1999; Sesay, 1996; Riley, 1996; Reno, 1996, 1998; Huband, 1998; Atkinson, 1999.

'[W]omen have structured conflicts and collaborations, have crystallized and imploded what successive epochs imagine when the subject at hand is collective violence' (Elshtain, 1987:x).

Another, more recent book on women's activities in war edited by Turshen and Twagiramariya (1998) takes a similar stand. In the introduction, Turshen pronounces that '[t]he enduring wartime picture of "man does, woman is" has depended on the invisibility of women's participation in the war effort, their unacknowledged, behind-the-lines contributions to the prosecution of war, and their hidden complicity in the construction of fighting forces ... [I]t is no longer possible to maintain the innocence of all women.' She further establishes that 'women are also combatants; women resist and fight back; they take sides, spy, and fight among themselves; and even when they don't see active service, they often support war efforts in multiple ways, willingly or unwillingly.' In fact, Turshen's argument for women's agency exposes a rift in feminist studies. Some chapters in the book take a 'traditionalist' stand, arguing that women are stuck within structural confines. On the other hand, there are contributors who contend that women have agency in every situation and use deliberate strategies in the utilization of it.[10] According to a thorough literature study done by DiIorio (1992), the rift is very apparent in the literature on women in war in general.[11] Naturally neither of these divergent theoretical standpoints has to be condemned as false. Individuals might simultaneously be seen as social agents and victims in the structural sense, be it on different levels, as pointed out by the various contributors to a recent book, *Victims, Perpetrators or Actors?* (Moser and Clark, 2001), on gender in armed conflict and political violence.

The discussion of women as victims of war is intimately linked to another victim/perpetrator dichotomy, namely that of fighter and civilian (Maček, 2000:238; 2001). In classic works on war, the dividing line between fighter and civilian was hardly disputed (see, for instance, Clausewitz, [1832] 1993). And even in more recent analyses of scholars like Nordstrom (1997a, b, c) a quite clear-cut line between fighter and civilian prevails. In her otherwise excellent, *A Different Kind of War Story* (1997a), Nordstrom is preoccupied with the civilian population in a way that upholds the opposition between civilian and soldier/rebel, i.e. victim and perpetrator.[12] Among others, Keen (1996, 1999) has questioned the existence of such an opposition. In rich ethnographic accounts, both Aretxaga (1997), and Maček (2000; 2001) have pointed to much more complex realities of war/conflict zones. Women are often believed to live on the fringes of war zones, in camps for internally displaced or as refugees in neighbouring countries (on Liberia see, for instance, Ruiz, 1992; also Malkki, 1995:10ff, 1996), but, as Turshen points out, women and children are only slightly over-represented in refugee populations – since 72 per cent of the African population are either female or under 15 years of age (Turshen and Twagiramariya, 1998:15).

This text elucidates young women's activities in the war zone, and more particularly the ways in which they oscillate between the positions of victims and perpetrators, fight-

---

[10] However, most of the contributions maintain the victim status of women in war (as noted in a review by Sevenzo and Omaar, 1999).

[11] In a study considering historical accounts of women's roles in Africa, Hay (1988) argues that the amount of agency with which authors furnish African women rests heavily upon contemporary trends in the academic world.

[12] Nordstrom's 'War-scapes' are inhabited by military, rebels (or bandits), a few brokers (named jackals) and expatriate businessmen only. In contrast to these evildoers are clearly defined civilians, essentially free of evil. In a personal communication, Nordstrom has acknowledged my criticism and states that this is due to her ethnographic focus and framing rather than a conceptual lack of understanding.

ers and civilians. The agency of any human being is set within certain societal confines. This is not unique to womanhood. Rather, the amount of individual agency or the amount of *victimcy*[13] changes from situation to situation, from one social relation to another – whether you are a man or woman. In war men and women are situated on the same sliding scale between abundant agency and *victimcy*. Even most so-called perpetrators are severely limited in their agency: to survive, civilians are forced to participate in war trade, while fighters are forced by their commanders to participate in atrocities. Likewise, the commanders are forced to command so as to keep their men in place and the enemy terrified. Honwana (1999a; see also Honwana in this volume) has put forward a distinction between 'strategic agency', and 'tactical agency' following de Certeau's (1984) distinction between strategies and tactics. De Certeau 'sees strategies as having long-term consequences or benefits, and tactics as means devised to cope with concrete circumstances, even though those means are likely to have deleterious long-term consequences' (Honwana, 1999a:9). If we follow this distinction, most actors in the Liberian Civil War are limited to 'tactical agency'. Indeed 'tactical agency' can be ascribed to rape victims at the one extreme and female combatants at the other. As the case studies will point out, the same person can be both rape victim and combatant.[14]

Girls in the War Zone[15]

> All that time when the Freedom Fighters (NPFL) were here they could just grab you and force you: saying you are my woman now. (Young woman in Ganta)
> I lived with the soldiers and they did not harm me. (Young woman in Greenville, Sinoe County)
> At that time girls were floating – every fighter was entitled to four or five. (Young ex-combatant in Ganta who fought for INPFL and NPFL)
> The soldiers caught us and put us in the attic [the granary on the farm] and lit fire under us. They also raped us. Even my smaller sister was raped by seven fighters and she later died. She was born in 1984. (Young woman in Sinoe County)

It is difficult to imagine how daily life is experienced in a war zone. Personally, I was caught in the firing-line in Monrovia for a few days in the midst of the war in 1996, and I witnessed some of the horrors of war. Even with such experience, however, it is hard to imagine what it is like to subsist in a war zone for a longer time without being able to pull out. The notion of 'war zone' does not only connote the actual area of combat, but also includes a much larger area into which fighters, war traders and others extend their activities (just as the Liberian war zone includes not only Liberia itself but also the border zones of Guinea, Ivory Coast and large parts of Sierra Leone where Liberian fighters have been active). The struggle of daily life in the war zone was immense for

---

[13] One might say that the most limited form of agency is the ability to depict oneself as a victim, thus reaping the benefits that other people's mercy might give. In my doctoral dissertation (Utas, 2003) I call this form of limited agency *victimcy*. In the presence of foreign humanitarian aid, *victimcy* can at times be a very fruitful mode.

[14] However, as Cynthia Enloe has noted, 'recognizing any woman's agency – her capacity to think and act autonomously – should not lead us to be uncurious about a larger institution's efforts to put that woman's labour and emotions to work for its own patriarchal ends. To reveal a camp follower's and a military commander's simultaneous strategizing is not to argue that they are equals on the field of maneuvers' (Enloe, 2000:39). I thank Chris Coulter for the reference.

[15] Issues of gender relations and ethnographic descriptions of life realms of women and young girls in pre-war Liberia have been discussed elsewhere (Bledsoe, 1976, 1980a, b; Moran, 1988, 1990; Fuest, 1996).

most young women. The war years were a constant battle for protection – under the wing of the right commando. Young women in the war zone had no choice but to cling to a fighter with enough power to protect them. Without such protection, they were running the very real risk of being forced into sexual services, or undergoing rape, forced labour and abduction.[16] Even if protectors were 'big men' – commanders or other key actors – in the rebel armies, they were quite often just hideously young boys. When your protector was out on a mission it would be best to go into hiding. Furthermore, in case the young woman's protector was killed, moved to another location, or simply became unbearable, it was advisable to find another protector beforehand, in order to avoid the risk of going through a rather turbulent period in the time-gap between men. To try to team up with a new man before leaving the old one was a hazardous game that might even endanger the girl's life, if detected by the jealous boyfriend.

Having a relationship with at least one fighter was crucial for the survival of not only the woman herself but her entire family. Looted goods would be delivered by boyfriends returning from the war front and would help to support the family network. Furthermore, it was important for the family to have a 'big man' in the rebel movement so that their estate and property would not be looted and ravaged. It was therefore good to have one of one's sons join the military, or to be related to people with important posts in the rebel movement, but it was even better if one of the daughters was having a relationship with a local commando. My ex-fighter informants described to me how they entered and raided villages in the countryside during the war. Sometimes they caught young girls and women whom they brought along as girlfriends. Sometimes villagers also left behind young girls, or sent them back from their hiding places in the bush, so that they could befriend the fighters and establish a relationship in the hope of protecting their property in this way. This daring move could even make it possible for the relatives to return to the village. Some girls were dumped on the departure of the fighters, but a good many of them were brought along to the front or back to the base. Later these girls might leave or be abandoned somewhere else. Clearly visible all over the war zone was an abundance of displaced young girls with a total lack of social ties in their new settings. In Nimba County, there are still a lot of young Sierra Leonean women around. As the NPFL fought in Sierra Leone, many of the fighters brought girls from the Sierra Leone front line back to Liberia. One of my ex-fighter informants related how one fighter brought back a new girl from the Sierra Leone front every time he went home. Numerous similar accounts report that fighters brought girls back with them to use them as unpaid labour on their farms; my informant used the term 'slave'.

The war has indeed uprooted many people. Many young women left voluntarily, or were forced to leave their families, their towns and villages – their social context. This has made it possible to behave in ways that would not normally be tolerated. To survive, or out of self-interest, many young women teamed up with fighters in looting actions. Sometimes this led to direct participation in the war; sometimes they just stayed in the background. To enlist in the fighting forces was yet another alternative for young girls to protect themselves and their families, and to gain relative independence and power. Statistics from the demobilization in 1997 point to moderate participation by women in the war. Part of the reason could be that only a few of the women who fought in the war were officially enlisted and quite often they did not have their own weapons. Even

---

[16] Rape and sexual abuse in war is a much-discussed topic. On Liberia see Lucas (1997), elsewhere and for theoretic approaches, see Stiglmayer (1994), Card (1996), Littlewood (1997), Omaar & de Waal (1995), as well as sections in numerous monographic accounts of war and violence.

if all factions had their share of women fighters, young women were seldom trained as soldiers.[17] As in the case of Bintu, they often joined their boyfriends to fight. Looting seems to have been a main incentive for participation.

Breaking with accepted social norms has meant that many young women in the post-war era have not returned home but have stayed in whatever setting they found themselves in. In the process of war many young women oscillated between a direct presence in the war zones, residing in displaced camps in Liberia, and taking refuge in neighbouring countries (see Utas, 1997). Camps for the displaced, however, often failed to embrace even the most basic needs. As a consequence, many young women preferred to return to life in the war zone, even if such a life was more hazardous.

Raped, tortured and forced to work

> They would just call you – say, 'come'. When you came they would say, 'I will detain your time today'. That night those girls slept with them. The next morning the girls became the 'wives' of the fighters and then they carried the girls away. (Masa)
>
> Any commando who was ready to see a woman for free would come and rape me – with my sabou [shaved head – as done to prisoners]. I did not have clothes on. They did not even want to know that I was a human being – they did not want to know. (Bintu)
>
> 'Anybody found raping or looting will face a firing squad.' Charles Taylor (in Huband, 1998:77)
> Like one of my friends, they called him 'Disregard', because he killed plenty people. He caught a girl in Ganta parking [car park where shared taxis heading for Ganta leave] when we captured the town of Gbarnga. He caught a girl and asked her to lie down on a table. As she was lying there he took a mortar pestle and cut it into half and nailed her with it. (Young ex-fighter in Ganta)

Women who failed to team up with any of the local 'big men' became the worst victims of war. One of the most dangerous moments for the young women was when the rebels entered an area for the first time and the young women did not have any first-hand experience of how to deal with these men (boys). This is the situation that Masa describes in the first quotation above. The fighters arrive and just make their choice among the village girls, as a way of demonstrating their power.

Hawa was fifteen years old when the war reached her region in southern Liberia. After escaping from a rebel attack on her home town in Grand Gedeh, Hawa and her brother fled north, hiding in the bush, surviving on what they could find in the forest or filch from farms. Eventually the NPFL caught Hawa in the vicinity of Buchanan and she was put into detention, not knowing what would happen to her. She spent two months in jail – a stay marked with physical abuse, rape, mental torture and humiliation until one of the rebel soldiers came to her aid:

> It did not take long time before I started seeing a rebel boy. He just came my way. He said that he wanted me. I said I did not want him, but then I started hearing from other people that he was the commander of the town. That's why I started going with the boy. When I started seeing him I found out that he had a lot of other women. Now when I moved in with the boy I was still facing problems. It was no longer from the rebels but from the other women in the house. The man was having five women and I made it six. I was the youngest of them all.

Even when not in prison, Hawa still faced a lot of problems – mainly deriving from the

[17] The issue of women fighters has been explored in several historic accounts (see for instance, Jones, 1997; Goldman, 1998; Newark & McBride, 1989). Ethnographic accounts of the 'Ferocious Few' (Elshtain, 1987:163-80) are regrettably few (see, for instance, Schalk, 1992, 1994; West, 2000).

other women in the household. As the youngest, and as an 'ethnic outcast' – a Krahn – she naturally had to carry out most of the tasks in the household. And when the boy later died on a patrolling mission she was categorized as belonging to the enemies, and thus blamed for his death.

> The man was not there when we had the last palaver. He had gone on patrol in the Firestone area. That's where the enemy captured and killed him. When the news hit us, saying, 'oh – they kill your husband', then all the other women in the house turned against me. They started making palaver with me. They said, 'but how come this new girl that our husband brought didn't stay long before they captured and killed our husband? That means that the girl killed our husband.' So they set for me. The women called the soldiers that were close to the house to show them the place where I was. I was trying to hide myself. They caught me and arrested me. Once again they carried me back to the soldier barracks. I did not really want to hide myself in the first place but one woman, who did not like my business in the house, was saying she would call the soldiers so they could come and kill me. That's why I hid. So, anyway, the soldier people arrested me and put me back in jail. They said it was because I was a Krahn so I must have been the one who sold out the man.
>
> This time jail was even worse. They used to do bad, bad things to me. They would come in group. They turned me around, put me under the hot sun and then they would start beating me for the whole day. They would also tie me behind the car and drag me around. There were two jails. They kept me in the dark one. That was the place they used to have me. When they were done eating they threw the balance food [the leftovers] for me. When they pee-pee [urinated], they poured the pee-pee water on me. During that time I was sixteen years old.

Yet again another young fighter picked her up and took her with him to Gbarnga and then Ganta. In Ganta she moved between young fighters and even tried to manage life on her own by helping people in their daily housework. Eventually she teamed up with a rebel soldier again. When the boy decided to leave one of his other girlfriends, that girl started to run *bisa* (to gossip) to the high commandos that she was of Krahn origin. So she was taken to the neighbouring town of Saglepie and imprisoned and once again she was severely abused.

> The commandos came for me when my boyfriend was away and they carried me to Saglepie. I spent one month and two weeks there under punishment. They started beating me every morning. They stripped me naked and left me in the sun. They poured [chili]pepper water all over me and let me lie in the sun. I was 'duck-fowled' [elbows tied together at the back – generally called 'tabave'] lying there in the baking sun, my eyes felt like bursting. Sometimes they pointed a gun at me or they would put a knife to my throat pretending to cut it. That's what they were doing to me – kicking me to the left and to the right. Every night different commandos used to come for me. They would carry me to their base and then they would have sex with me. They used to force me, and I knew if I did not agree doing it they would kill me. No, I did not agree, but they used to force me. I did not want to go myself so the people would tie me on the car and then they would drag me there. They tied my hands and were forcing me to have sex with them. I got pregnant from that. When I got pregnant every one of them disowned the belly [implying that no one took the responsibility for the child]. After they disowned the belly God fixed the belly to move [she miscarried].

Hawa's sad story parallels the account of Bintu. Both girls faced extraordinary problems because they slipped out of their own confines and crossed into 'enemy country'. Hawa as a Krahn and Bintu as Mandingo got caught in 'Taylor Land', NPFL territory. In the NPFL's political rhetoric people of Krahn and Mandingo origin were depicted as the main violators of the Liberian people. Bintu left her safe haven in Monrovia and took a risky drive through the heart of NPFL territory to aid her mother who at the time had sought refuge in Guinea.

> [M]y mother wrote me that she was suffering a lot as a refugee in Guinea. I had a [mini]bus and I was making business with it in Monrovia.[18] But I decided to carry this bus to my mother. To get the bus to Guinea I had to pass through Gbarnga [during that time Gbarnga was the headquarters for the NPFL]. It was during the first cease-fire in 1992. February 11 I left from Monrovia to Gbarnga. When I reached Gbarnga I was arrested by Charles Taylor's commandos and raped. They beat me and scraped my hair to *sabou* (skinhead) with a snail shell and then they put me in jail. The man that looted my car was called Johnson.[19] They raped me. I suffered a lot. For eight months I was in jail. They beat me, and raped me, more than more, and I lost everything I had.

In jail Bintu denied that she was Mandingo even under torture and this denial most probably saved her life. In prison she was held with six other girls, all of whom were executed on suspicion of collaborating with enemy groups.

> We were seven and those other girls confessed; they said they were reconnaissance girls and then they killed them right on the spot. They said ULIMO[20] had sent them to come and observe and go tell them how the NPFL fought – how they did things and whatsoever – that's why they were killed.

Eventually the girlfriend of an important NPFL commander, today a minister in the NPP government, felt sympathy for her and backed her by all means. In addition to this, a civilian man, with family relations to another important NPFL commander (Tom King), took an interest in her and advocated her release.

> [A]t that time they were not raping me again because I was in the hand of one person now, Tom King's brother. So they were not raping me again.

Bintu was released from prison after eight months of ordeal. At that time she was pregnant. The baby's father was one of the numerous unknown soldiers that had passed through her prison cell. Even after her release she was not free to leave Gbarnga town and she had to go into hiding when Tom King was out of town.

Joint forces of the NPFL and the RUF (Revolutionary United Front of Sierra Leone) abducted Masa, the third of my key narrators, from her home town in south-eastern Sierra Leone during an attack. One of the NPFL commanders took her back with him to Lofa County in northern Liberia.

> We were hiding in the bush when the rebels were running behind us. So one man captured me and held me by force. He brought me to Liberia here. There we stayed in Lofa. The man that held me in the bush was treating me bad. Every morning he used to beat us. When the people asked him why he was beating the children, the man said, because he was the one who brought us. He was the one that saved our lives so if he wanted to beat us he had the right to do so.

[18] During the war years there was nothing strange in seeing under-age persons driving. Looted cars often ended up in the hands of young fighters – at times also in the hands of their girlfriends. When driving the car through NPFL territory, Bintu most probably caught attention as someone having military connections on the enemy's side.

[19] All names in the text are pseudonyms.

[20] Exiled Krahn and Mandingo people in Sierra Leone formed the United Liberation Movement (ULIMO) as a joint effort to fight the NPFL. ULIMO had just started to infiltrate NPFL territory when Bintu was caught. ULIMO was later split into two (ULIMO-J and ULIMO-K).

The man forced Masa, and two other girls that he also brought from Sierra Leone, to work for him on his farm.[21] Masa was not used to working on a farm and had a hard time adjusting to her new life.

> We were stuck over there. The people told us that we had to make a farm. So I told him that I was not able to make a farm, that I did not do that at home in Sierra Leone. But the man told us that we were forced to make the farm. If we would refuse he would beat us. We were making that farm for a long period of time so I really got tired from it. My body was spoiling now. 'Kro-kro' [rashes that develop into small black scars – word of Sierra Leonean origin] was coming on my body. So I told him: 'this farm business, I'm not able to do it'. So then the man said that if I did not make the farm he would beat me. In fact, the reason why he was beating us every morning, he said, was because we were not able to make the farm. He used to beat us bad, so in the end I complained to his C.O. [Commanding Officer].

In this case Masa was successful in using the existing military structure. The Commanding Officer in the area ordered the man to release her from working on his farm and she managed to move to another family. Eventually she initiated a relationship with one of the boys in the family who was also a soldier. During a peaceful time in 1992 they moved down to Nimba County where she was left once more on a sugarcane farm.

> No, the boy was not fighting now. But I was in that bush – he was in town and I was in the bush suffering. When I was not busy planting sugarcane I was cutting it, or I would cook it. I was always busy and I would not even wear slippers [seen as the ultimate sign of poverty]. His father didn't like me and neither did the other people in the surroundings. So the last time when he told me to go back in the bush again I simply said no 'since me and you come 92 I make my cane, I take the money and give it to you. When you go you can spoil it [waste it on liquor and girls in the town]'. I could be telling him that we must look for money because we had a child. But when I got money he just went and spoilt it.

Towards the end of 1998 she ran away from her man and took refuge with a Sierra Leonean family in Ganta. Apart from lacking money to survive she was suffering most from the fact that she was not able to take the child with her when she ran away from the farm.[22]

These three stories, accounts of severe suffering, are instructive in several ways. Prison experiences, torture and crude coercion are part and parcel of the war experience. But that is only one level of these narratives. As we shall see, it is also possible to discover accounts of personal agendas and agency in the same narratives. There is a clear ambiguity between victimhood and agency.

Boyfriends – bulwark

You mean that you were seeing him only because he was a commando?
  Yes. That was the only way I could be safe. (Hawa)
  But for some women, the military represent security … . women fled villages to seek security next to armed military camps. (Turshen, 1998:15)

Bintu was released from jail after several persons intervened. For her protection she

---

[21] As Meredeth Turshen has pointed out, soldiers entailed in guerrilla warfare often live off the land, thus women are an important agricultural labour force (Turshen, 2001:61).

[22] The yearning for her child was too strong. When I returned to Ganta in early 2000 her Sierra Leonean hosts told me that she had left to visit her child several months earlier and had not yet returned.

teamed up with a high-ranking officer. Her boyfriend was not a fighter himself but she
benefited from the protection that his cousin, who was a commando, provided her with.

> The eyes were on me [the NPFL administration kept her under surveillance]. I had to remain
> in Bong County. I was pregnant when they freed me. The chief of the protocol came and that
> guy Camara also. They talked for me and I was free now. But at that time I was already preg-
> nant. This boy [the boy that helped her out of jail and took care of her] was not a soldier.
> Because of that he could only go around with me if his cousin was in town. The cousin some-
> times came from the bush. His name was Tom King and he was a guerrilla fighter. When Tom
> King came he would be free to take me around in town. The three of us would get in the sol-
> dier car. We would then drive around a little bit and it made me feel a little better. And then
> when Tom King left I would have to hide myself again. If not, other commandos would be
> hunting for me and force me to have sex even though they could see that I was pregnant. They
> would have fucked me on top of that belly again – just because they did not see any other free
> woman. So that was how it was. I did not even dare to go outside if Tom King was not in
> Gbarnga.

Bintu was out of prison now. However, she still had to be very careful. In the lawlessness
of 'Taylor land' she had to play smart – Tom King was her shield, protecting her from all
evil perpetrators. In this case the enemy was dwelling within her confines. As was proven
to her when King left her before the birth of her child:

> So when I gave birth to this baby – it was a boy child – I asked Tom King if he could assist me
> before I could give birth to this baby. Tom King was going to Lofa. They sent him to Lofa again
> to go and fight, and he never had cash to give to me. So he gave me a solar system to sell to
> get cash if I gave birth when he was gone. But one of the generals, named Junior Rambo, came
> and harassed me. He took the solar system from me. So when I gave birth the boy that claimed
> the belly [her boyfriend] never had any money.

After King left, other officers started to harass Bintu. Her civilian boyfriend lacked the
power to protect her from them (when Bintu says that he 'claimed the belly' it means
that he had agreed to be the social father of the child). As King was a fighter, she was
fully aware of the fragile situation. She could not afford to have all her eggs in the same
basket. For that reason she soon started to see another fighter. When King was out of
town, she was in utter need of other protection and support.

> Q: But you told me you were having a relationship with yet another commando when you
> were with Tom King's cousin?
> A: Yes, that was also in Gbarnga and that one too always liked to carry me at the front. But you
> know I was picking chance, I never used to like him too much.

> Q: But how did you manage when you were also seeing the civilian? How were you manag-
> ing to escape and go and meet the fighter?
> A: Because when Tom King was not in town the civilian boy had no power. When Tom King
> was out of town the girl that helped me out of jail [that is the cousin of Bintu's boyfriend – the
> civilian] was the one that covered up for me and gave me the chance to go to the other one.
> Sometimes Tom King used to go for two-three months at the time.

Bintu understood quite correctly the need to master the game, and was therefore prepared when King was killed during a battle in Lofa County. In a related story she
recounts an incident that occurred to another girl who likewise tried to master this hazardous situation.

This story happened once upon a time in one club in Gbarnga. We went to the club and there was this girl who used to go out with one commando. Later she left him because she was very jealous – you hear. This commando used to love around a whole lot so she decided to leave him. And you know, if you told these commandos that you didn't want them – just like when you are fed up with somebody – that meant serious problem. When you retreated from them and they saw you with somebody new, might God bless you that your new boyfriend would have a higher rank than the old one. If your new boyfriend's rank was lower than the old one's then he would definitely go and disturb you. You would be forced to love to [have a relationship/have sex with] him again. So this girl she wanted to act 'qwi' ['civilized' in Liberian English].[23] She left her old boyfriend for a new one.

So we all went out that night – Tom King was in town. You know, when Tom King was in town that was the time I could boil. When we went to the club this girl I am talking about was sitting down there with her new boyfriend. She was two months pregnant for this boyfriend and her new boyfriend had given her money to plait her hair. She had her hair plaited with attachment [synthetic hair]. So her old boyfriend came and met her sitting with the new one. Now this new boyfriend was boasting too much. So it hurt her old boyfriend too much. It wasn't easy; the old boyfriend went and commanded her, saying 'Get your arse out – let's go'. She said 'No I'm not going, you and me are not loving any longer and in fact I'm pregnant with this man's child. So you don't have any right to command me and carry me home.' He replied 'I will command you and carry you home because this man just feels that he is all and all. So for that reason I'm carrying you home.'

A fight broke out in the club – it was not easy that night. They fought until they had rooted up the whole hair of the girl. Her old boyfriend grabbed her one way and the new one another. They tore her skirt open. It was not an easy fight. I myself joined in that night. The boy that I used to sneak out to meet was fighting on the side of the new boyfriend and Tom King was taking the other side. I don't know where the grudge came from. They tore off my own skirt too. It was not an easy thing that night. In the end they had to carry us to the Task Force Office for investigation. I had to explain how I got involved in other people's confusion.

Those were some of the experiences that girls would have if they were having a relationship with a fighter and got tired of their problems. You could not just get rid of them by saying, 'I don't want you'. They wouldn't understand – they would just force you. They could have more than fifty women, but as long as they saw you and their heart would cut for you again they would force you. They would only leave you alone if your new boyfriend had a higher rank than the old one. Then, maybe, they would respect that person but not you – because they would never respect a woman.

This narrative pinpoints some of the difficulties young women were experiencing. Not only did they need a fighter to protect them but also their choice to select this man was very limited. The young woman needed to find someone with a higher rank to be able to leave the old 'boyfriend' without being harassed or forced to hand out sexual favours. A woman who had left a high-ranking officer risked remaining without a man because junior fighters knew the dangers of having an affair with a high ranking officer's ex-girlfriend. Such a woman would thus turn into prey for occasional sexual endeavours by men of any rank and file. Masa recounts another incident that had a fatal outcome.

One man by the name of Johnson killed his own girlfriend because of money. The girl had a relationship with Johnson's 'big man' and she got some money from him. Johnson told the girl that she must give him the money, but the girl refused. So Johnson grabbed his gun and killed the girl.

---

[23] I have discussed the term 'qwi' in relation to young girls elsewhere (Utas, 1999).

In their accounts Masa, Bintu and Hawa depict the structural trap of women during the civil war. To have a boyfriend or another protector in the right position in the war machine was of extreme importance; in Hawa's case it was her boyfriend's cousin that protected her. A civilian protector was of no use when the military strongman was out of town. Thus the ideal arrangement, despite the dangers, was to have several boyfriends simultaneously. As it was expected that fighters got killed, it was appropriate to have some kind of pre-arrangement with other fighters. The difficulty of rank among boyfriends has further to be stressed: to get a new boyfriend with lower rank than the previous one generally meant trouble. Likewise, to leave a high-ranking officer might turn into an incubus, because junior officers did not often dare to approach such a girl. Instead, she might fall prey to occasional sexual endeavours. The story of Johnson's girl-friend stands as a reminder of the maliciousness of the war system. Even when playing with great care, according to the 'rules', individuals within the system appeared to act quite unpredictably: the smallest of movements might threaten one's life.

Boyfriends – bonus

> You should make use of what you have (your sexual organ), because when you die the *bocabo* (termite) will eat it. (Young woman in Ganta)

> Q: Did the girls send their boyfriends or husbands to the front to go and bring goods for them?
> A: Yes, they would force them. You know, all these soldier boys when they went most of them would go on looting missions – they did not usually go and fight war. (Masa)

When the spaces of everyday life turned into battle zones and compatriot started to fight compatriot, social structures began to crumble. Many young girls were abandoned on their own for extensive periods of time in totally unfamiliar and novel settings, as in the cases of Hawa, Bintu and Masa. Even if these young people were involuntarily tossed into these situations, I would argue that, without the enthusiasm of these young men and women to get involved in war events, the war would never have been sparked off in the first place. The civil war was seen as a revolution in the eyes of many young people – a chance to become someone in a national system that had marginalized them, but also a chance to get rid of the load of work and expectations that the parental generation had laid on them (see Richards, 1995, 1996). Just as many young men took up arms, many young women participated in ways expected of them. Bintu was already flirting with the war before it brutally intruded into her life, for she was going out with a high official at the ministry of defence. This was a path towards independence from her parents who were too 'traditional' in her eyes.

> Milton Toe was the one that was supporting me. He took the whole initiative: I mean every-thing I wanted he was doing it for me. My parents never liked the idea. You know how Mandingo people are. I was just living that life because I wanted to live it. Do you understand? It was he and myself who were together until the war came.

A system of sponsoring young girls might be viewed as traditional in Liberia, where older men often sponsor young girls in the hope that they might become future wives. Important men have a wide assortment of young girls whom they provide for, in vary-ing degrees, in exchange for sexual favours, or social activities in the present or the future (see Utas, 1999; Fuest, 1996; Bledsoe, 1976, 1980a, b). Especially after the war, these boyfriends have become the most important source of paying school fees for young girls.[24]

Many young girls teamed up with fighters in the same way as they would have teamed up with older men – the difference now was that they teamed up with 'the homeboys' whom they earlier would have viewed as attractive but too poor to be considered of any help. Without a second thought most girls jumped into a swindling process that involved them in horrific occurrences. They teamed up with a novel but treacherous form of power. The new boyfriends were in general not used to having money. They felt so affluent that they could wash their cars in beer – a beverage most could not even afford to drink prior to the war – and that they could drive a car until it ran out of gasoline and then just dump it for another one. Likewise, the young girlfriends got hold of commodities that they had only dreamt of before. Here we enter the topic of loot. Some young girls deny that they ever looted anything or that they ever acquired any looted goods. Rather, they talk about what other young women did in order not to place themselves in an immoral appearance in the post-war setting. However, a lot of young women entered war relations with fighters for privilege, reaching out for 'the bonus of war'. As Bintu notes:

> Some of them really enjoyed being with commandos because they used to encourage the commandos to go and loot and because of that some of them have got money up till this day. Some of them looted to the extreme. They went to Bomi Hills and looted diamonds, gold and other things. But some of them suffered through the war like me. Some of them suffered a lot. But then again some of them were lucky to have a commando who understood. If not, they were beaten every day. As soon as you finished cooking them food – as soon as their bellies were full they would start beating you. They smoked *jamba* (marijuana) and then they would flog you – I mean most of us girls were living a mix-up-box-up life.

As is clear from Bintu's case, to be with a fighter certainly also had its disadvantages. Nevertheless, young girls teamed up with high ranking officers, even if these had more than five other girlfriends to cater for. In the case of Bintu, she behaved differently with different men. In the first case she seems to have been rather reluctant to join in the looting. She states that the reason for this was that she was feeling bad because her pre-war sponsor had been killed – and as a matter of fact her new boyfriend was amongst those who killed him. However, she explains how her 'mates' – his other girlfriends – used to pressurize the man to loot.

> I never forced him to loot but those other girls [Bintu's 'mates'] they used to force him to loot. Even when I was with him I used to hear them arguing when they were going on mission. They would tell him 'You must bring this, oh – you must bring that, oh'. These girls had not owned such things before and now they wanted to get rich over night – do you understand? So I used to hear them telling the man to bring such and such things for them and indeed he used to do so. He used to ask me why I didn't tell him to bring things for me, but then I said that his life was more important. I used to make him feel good by saying, 'If you just bring your life back it is alright'.
>   That man used to like me too much. For the looting business in Freeport [the commercial harbour in Monrovia] he always gave us arms. He would give us uniforms so that we could go and loot, but during that time I did not like the idea too much because my heart was spoiled

---

[24] In Monrovian schools, according to an expatriate aid-worker with experience in education, there are only slight differences between girls in the street and those residing with their families. Both categories depend totally on boyfriends for paying their school fees.

[because of the recent killing of her ex-boyfriend]. But the other girlfriends always joined him in fatigues. They used to return with looted videos, freezers, and all those other things. All good, good things you can think about. They looted the whole Freeport area. But for me I never used to like the looting too much during my time in Monrovia.

However, after her experiences in Gbarnga she changes her opinion and joins the looting missions. She states that it made her feel fine and also that it was necessary for her survival.

Q: But you used to like looting with Charles Taylor's men?
A: Yes, I used to like the looting with Charles Taylor's men, because during that time in the Gbarnga area if you didn't loot you didn't eat.

She is also framing her friends' activities similarly:

Q: But were your friends forcing their boyfriends to loot?
A: Some of them forced them to loot because they wanted to survive, do you understand? They would tell them, 'If you go bring this for me' or 'I want this because you see your friends' women have got it. They can wear this, I myself I want to be like them now.' If the fighter was fond of the woman and did not want to lose her to another fighter, then he would have to do what his girlfriend wanted him to do – if you want someone you need to satisfy her.

Hawa explains how she worked hard to stay out of the looting economy – how she was taking casual jobs for other people. Even so, it was with money from the war that she managed to start a business. She was making and selling cookies but she also had a small market stall where she sold miscellaneous things. She agrees that she sold looted commodities, looted by the same boy who gave her money to start her business.

In Ganta, now, I was struggling on my own. Working for people. The whole day I would work for them. When I worked for them I would get food. When they helped me with the food, then I ate. After I finished with the job I was doing in Ganta, I was working for different people going from place to place helping them with their water and such things. I did it for my own survival – that was how I was living in Ganta. After struggling this way for some time, I met up with another boy. The boy started helping me.
    The boy gave me one hundred dollars (JJ)[25] to start my own business. I started fixing cookies now. And I had a small business. I used to sell 'wallah' [having a small market stall]. I got my goods from the front. My husband and his friends used to go to the front. When they returned he could bring market goods for me. When he went to the front and they captured a place they busted people's stores. When they busted the stores they took the goods and put it in their car and brought it for me. But my business never improved because it was based on 'blood money'.

The fact that Hawa is connecting her failure in business with the fact that her goods had been looted – she was dealing in *blood money*, that was why her business never prospered – clearly points to her moral consciousness, even if it might be a post-war rationalization. She also states that she was trying to persuade the boyfriend to change his loot-

---

[25] During most of the war Liberia had two currencies. The JJ (so nicknamed because the late President J.J. Roberts' face appeared on the note) was the existing currency when the war started and was used throughout the war in 'greater Liberia'. The Liberty (with the national emblem of Liberia including the text 'The love of Liberty brought us here') was issued by the first interim government and used mainly in Monrovia. In early 2000 new notes replaced the old ones.

ing behaviour. Clearly she does not connect her business failure with the fact that most people lacked both money and items to barter.

> When he brought looted things home I used to tell him: 'Oh, that thing you are doing is no good'. Going around bursting other people's stores open, or going around putting people under gunpoint taking their money from them. But the boy never listened to me. After some time I decided to move my hands from his market business. When he sold his looted things he bought liquor for the money and got drunk. Then they bought beer and started washing their car with the beer. They said they were rich so they would only use beer for washing the car.

Even if Hawa condemned the looting, she was still active in selling the looted goods. Initially she was putting all the blame on her boyfriend and his friends and thereby pronouncing her innocence, but saying that she later took her hands away from the business clearly shows that she was aware of her own participation and thus recognized her own guilt. That young soldier boys were washing their cars in beer gives a glimpse of the looting euphoria of those days.

Looting and purloining of goods were key features of the Liberian Civil War. Young boys as well as girls were active agents in these doings as in most wars. Instead of teaming up with one fighter who supported his young women with looted goods, some preferred or were constrained to go around with several men. This would either be done in the form of direct prostitution, in a direct exchange of sexual favours, or in some more subtle form. Sexual favours might, for instance, be exchanged for food, house rent, goods or a market stall. When Bintu got out of prison she was forced to see other men to meet the needs, demands and requirements of the people she went to live with. Initially it was because the girl who had helped her out of prison lost her boyfriend because of her commitment to Bintu. Thus Bintu had a debt to pay back.

> Q: So you mean your boyfriend's cousin used to give you men to go out with?
> A: Yes. Because of my business she lost the contact with her boyfriend and he was the one that used to sustain her. Her man said she was too involved in my business. And if I was a 'reconnaissance' why then would she fight so hard to get me out of jail? Anyway, they then started accusing her too. That's how their relationship came to an end. The man told her that if she didn't take her mouth from my business it would be problem between them. She decided to take the problems in her relationship rather than leaving me. So she was facing problems because of me. And now I had the problem that men used to like me more than her. So that's why I started to do 'crocrogy' [Liberian English: immoral activities – prostitution, etc.]. I did it for us to survive.

Bintu's friend was now stuck with her reputation as the girlfriend of a 'big man' and thus had problems in finding another man whom she could rely on. Bintu became the solution. That Bintu went out with other soldiers was also something that her boyfriend had to bear, because he was just another powerless civilian when his cousin, Tom King, was not in town.

> I feel like my boyfriend used to know that I was going out with other men, but he just had to bear it because he never had any money and it was only Tom King who could help us. When Tom King was gone for two-three months, we did not even have money for toothpaste. These other 'small', 'small' boys and even other big men were afraid of going out with the girl [the one that had taken care of Bintu] because she had this relationship with a 'big man' earlier. So because of that I was the only person to 'mago-mago' (Krio: fighting for something by all means) at least to bring food home.

I never really used to enjoy going out with these fighters. I was doing these things because I wanted to survive – do you understand? It was no enjoyment at all. I just wanted to survive, because the crime they put on me was very bad. Reconnaissance – if they caught you for that they would kill you. So I was forced to make life 'sweet' for myself. Besides that, things were so difficult for the girl who had left her boyfriend because of me. So I just had to strain. You know, strain – to the full meaning of the word. For me it was not really any problem because I knew the life I had been living, but for her, she lost her whole home for my business. So I used to strain myself to satisfy her.

Bintu justifies her 'crocrogy' by saying that it was necessary for her own survival and because she owed the person who saved her life a lot, and this was a way of paying back some of the debt. Here we are at one end of a sliding spectrum between having several boyfriends and being a prostitute. During the war many young girls have been through various stages, especially in Monrovia. Being the capital, the commercial axis of the country, as well as the locus for international humanitarian assistance, more hard cash has been available in Monrovia, which has therefore become a magnet for girls 'selling' sexual favours. The lowest paid form of prostitution barely offers the daily bread for the young girls involved, however fortunate they might be at times. Whereas the best paid form would take the girls to a life of financial prosperity with the political and economical elite.[26]

★

Your ma is a hopo-jo (prostitute), don't cry baby. Your ma go look for food, don't cry baby. Your ma fucking for you, don't cry baby. Your pa is a useless man, don't cry baby. Your pa doesn't care for you, don't cry baby. (Liberian Lullaby)

★

Informal Polygyny

To give you an example: I would go and love to [have a relationship with] this commando. He would take me from my home and bring me to another town. When bringing me to this new town, he would take another girl from the street and bring her to our home. Then the girl and I would be sleeping in the same room and if I would complain he would kill me. Of course, I would agree with everything he is saying. And then the man would go and bring a third one – again you could not talk or they would shoot you. The only thing to do would be to take your hands from there. You would find your way. But if you would start to play jealousy they would kill you for nothing. (Masa)

The experience of sharing a man with several other women is not, of course, unique to the war years (Utas, 1999). The extent of such informal polygyny appears to be unprecedented, however. Young boys of 14-15 years of age might have five 'wives'/girlfriends or more. Older men who, prior to the war, did not have a single wife now secured ten. Girls from urban areas, where polygyny was viewed as a rural, backward habit (Little, 1973), were forced to get along with several 'co-spouses'. Female stories from the war years always relate to 'mates' and obstacles concerning this. One of my male informants in Ganta, who has two 'wives' himself, states that during the war years it was common

---

[26] I have discussed the 'loving business' of Liberian girls elsewhere (Utas, 1999).

among his friends to make two or three 'wives' pregnant simultaneously. To be 'entitled' to more than one 'wife' is a question of status and power. For young men and boys, the war created the possibility and deepened the urge to demonstrate newly found power through setting up polygamous households. Bintu first experienced this when she became the girlfriend of the INPFL fighter.

> Q: So the first commando you were having a relationship with was a Prince Johnson fighter. How many girlfriends did he have?
> A: We were seven. It wasn't easy to live with these girls because some of them had never been exposed to such a life, and lacked experience. They felt that they had met the best of men, because of all the looted things they got. They did not know that these boys were just doing these things because they had not been with nice girls before. They just used the gun to get relations with nice girls. Some of my mates just wanted to start confusion – to make palaver. I just used to play low [keep a low profile] because I was just doing it to save my life. Some of them would abuse me because – I mean – the boy used to like me best. That was because I used to play low and he also knew who I was going out with before I met him. Sometimes when they were cursing me I would call them and try to advise them. I would say: 'You stop cursing me' but I was not making a big issue out of it because these girls lacked experience and if I would talk too much they might have gone behind my back and told this man something. One wrong thing and he could have killed me. Rather, I used to talk to them in a kind of petting way. Sometimes when I cooked food for the man, some of them would take the pot and waste it on the ground because they were jealous of me.

Bintu learnt the importance of keeping a low profile. She was trying not to stand out too much. She says that her boyfriend valued her highly because of this, and one can assume that it made her unpopular in the eyes of the other girls. Later on during our interview she returns to the same topic but from a slightly different angle:

> You had your family and they did not have any food. If you did not have a relationship with a commando how would your family survive? You had your mother, father, brother, sister, uncle. If you didn't love to a commando, they would not get food. Any commando you would see with more than two, three women you would know that they were commandos with rank. If you had a relationship with one of these high rank commandos you knew that they had their own boys who would go loot for them and bring it back to you. When they went looting then you knew that you would at least be able to send something small back to your family. The soldiers without rank had, of course, also power but it was not like the others.

According to Bintu's experience, it was preferable to stay with a commando who already had several 'wives' because the bare fact that he had several 'wives' was proof that he could provide for them. Nevertheless 'mates' also meant trouble, as Hawa's case has illustrated. Because of these 'mates' she ended up in prison and was severely tortured. When Hawa came out of jail she still did not feel safe, and the danger actually came from within the premises of her 'home'. It was her five 'mates' that later, when the man was killed, got her jailed. Likewise, when she was living in Ganta, it was her 'mate' who, out of jealousy, informed other rebels of her ethnic status and thereby got her imprisoned again. At that time her 'mate' was having a relationship with a man from the Special Forces whom she persuaded to get her out of the way on his 'sweetheart's' account.[27] Jealousy was at the base of a lot of infighting. The mere fact that a girl risked losing her protection if she was dumped by her commando meant that the 'family' became a

---

[27] Up to the present Hawa and her husband are still sharing a bedroom with this girl.

hostile environment, where women fought and slandered each other behind their backs.

> Girls used to fight over men most of the time. They would fight like hell because sometimes the man did not even want to look their way. You know how men commandos were: they just picked the one they liked most for the time being, and the others they just ignored. So if one of the others had more strength than this favourite girl, then she would beat the hell out of her when the man was out. When the man went on mission and returned with all those things he would give most of it to his favourite girl. But if she were weak the other girls would beat her and take every goddamn thing from her. That's how it used to be. (Bintu)

As such, the pattern of 'mates' fighting for a good position inside the household was not unique to the war years (see Bledsoe, 1976, 1980a, b; Moran, 1988, 1990; Fuest, 1996). The one who arrives last, is the youngest or comes from the 'wrong' ethnic group, always had a hard time. Says Hawa:

> Being the youngest, I had to work hard for the others. Every morning I made sure to take the dirty clothes outside. I washed them. I cleaned up the place and then I had to cook. Sometimes I even went working on the farm. When the people were harvesting rice I had to go along. I used to do everything and after I arrived in the house the others did not do anything, but still they were against me. In all this my husband did not do anything to improve my situation.

In some cases women used pregnancies as a means to get permanent access to powerful men.[28] In other cases the mere fact that a young woman had a child meant that she had to find a fighter who could sustain her and her child. For men it was often proof of potency and power both to have many children and to have children with many 'wives'. But for a young woman a child is not always a successful route to the man, as in the case of Hawa:

> When I was pregnant for the man I too seized the man's money. When I seized his money then he fell in love with another girl. After he had fallen in love with the girl he started treating me really bad. The man did not even look at me. So I suffered a lot during my pregnancy. When I had given birth to the child I really started to regret that I had left the boy I was with before I went to this one.

Polygyny, in both its formal and informal fashion, was far from a new conformation in Liberia. The novelty was that increasingly young men tied up a whole assemblage of 'wives' or girlfriends. To a great extent this was a way of displaying their newly found powers. Girls originating from urban centres who regarded polygyny as a backward institution were equally forced to submit to war polygyny.[29] Capricious and often violent 'husbands' of limited maturity were clearly one obstacle, but young women seem to have had as many difficulties in relation to other women within the house. Jealousy games seem to have been a daily problem between 'mates', and little stopped them from committing horrible crimes against each other. To be a member of the 'wrong' ethnic group, the youngest or to arrive last had immediate consequences. Even so, young women preferred to team up with fighters who already had several women, as it was an indication that the man was successful and thus an adequate provider. As the war has receded and

---

[28] Pregnancies might be one of the main powers women have over men. Such had been the case long before the civil war (see Bledsoe, 1976, 1980a, b).

[29] It should be noted that polygyny is a controversial issue in Liberia. The habit is questioned not only in the urban areas but also among rural citizens.

many of the powerful, rich fighters have again become marginalized youth, young mothers now suffer severely.[30]

In Fatigues

> She was having a relationship with one of the commandos, that's how it started. Then she went with the man to the warfront and she saw how the man was fighting. Then the man gave her a gun. It was right there she became a fighter, but she never took any training on base. When the man gave her the gun he just said that 'you do like this and your gun will fire and like this and the gun will stop'. After that she always used to go to the front fighting along with her man. (Masa)

> Their [the female combatants'] aggression was mainly against women. They would strip you naked. They would shove the grenade somewhere up your private parts. They would put their hands where they're not supposed to go, saying they were looking for grenades. People were more afraid of them than the men, because the female combatants' temper was very quick. (Liberian girl interviewed by Olonishakin, 1995b)

> 'They are not just gun-toting women', Taylor said as we walked out of the small house into the sunlight, and the two women sentries stood briskly to attention, clasping their Kalashnikovs to their breasts. 'They are highly trained, and have become an important part of our fighting force.' (Huband, 1998:76).

A majority of the young women who fought in the civil war got involved through their boyfriends. Most of them never attended any formal training and many of them only went to the front with their boyfriends and thus were never part of the regular forces. However, both the INPFL and the NPFL had special female units. According to statistics taken during the disarmament (1996/97) less than 2 per cent of the fighters in the civil war were female (UNDHA-HACO).[31] During the civil war women soldiers were known to be at least as fierce as their male counterparts; men and women alike committed atrocities.[32] A young ex-fighter noted that 'it can be too fearful when you are fighting with a woman amongst you'.

Bintu's boyfriend was a civilian but she joined her boyfriend's cousin at the front line, and felt rather excited about being on the battlefield.

> Tom King was the rooster for us. Sometimes he would give me a gun and I would follow him to the front. I was just tired of all the talking and the raping in town, so when King gave me a gun and said 'let's go' I was relieved to get out of town. We went fighting – I used to join him in the bush. The first time we went all the way to Grand Gedeh. The second time we went there he got killed, but we went to so many other places before that. I remember when we fought in Kakata. During NPFL's first attack on Kakata I was there with him. This was when they attacked BWI [the Booker Washington Institute]. He gave me a gun and said, 'Today we will all go fight – do you understand.' So we all went into the battlefield that day. I will tell you

[30] UNICEF statistics reveal that Liberia has the highest rate of teenage pregnancies in the world. It should be noted that teenage pregnancy rates were alarmingly high even in the pre-war setting (see Bledsoe et al., 1993).
[31] The accuracy of these figures can be questioned. On the one hand, it could be argued that the figure is too high because the demobilization took place in urban areas, where women fighters were over-represented. On the other hand, it could be argued that women fighters would be less prone to attend demobilization because of the social stigma. Women fighters were often not part of the regular forces; as such they had no personal weapon to surrender at the demobilization centres. A former UNDHA-HACO staff member who worked on demobilization issues (1996–7) is of the opinion that the demobilization was 'just a number game', thus essentially invalidating the value of the statistics of the entire demobilization process (personal communication).
[32] The most ferocious atrocities during the war have often been ascribed to child and young soldiers.

one thing about fighting: to fight, to meet your enemy and to exchange bullets with them is not hard, but to retreat, that is the real problem. And I was not a military woman. It was God and nobody else that saved me that day. To retreat from BWI all the way to fourteenth street, that was problem. But God brought me out of that.

When in Monrovia with the INPFL boyfriend, she also wore fatigues. As noted earlier, Bintu was not too keen on the 'looting business' at that time. However, her boyfriend gave arms and uniforms to his other girlfriends, who took advantage of this. The girl who helped Bintu out of jail in Gbarnga also used to follow her man to the front, mainly for looting purposes:

> When she was with her boyfriend she went to the front with him. He used to give her arms too. She had war experience. She used to join her boyfriend because she liked him. It was just because of me that she lost the man. But she really used to like the man, so when he said 'Let's go to the front', she would join him. (Bintu)

Evelyn was 18 years old when the war started. She was in Monrovia when she first heard about the rebels. Like many others, she did not know what a rebel was; rumours had it that they had tails or that they had wings and could fly. A few months later Evelyn had her first encounter with the NPFL when they captured Bomi Hills, the area where her family were residing. A rapid course of events followed, turning her into a rebel. When she first met her boyfriend, a notorious commando nicknamed Bruce Lee, he accused her of hiding enemy soldiers. In front of her family he stabbed her with a knife and then started shooting at her. She survived the incident and later he demanded that she become a 'wife' of his. Evelyn accepted, being too afraid to say no. Then he wanted her to go to the front with him and again she was forced to agree. She not only went to the war front but also remained armed in town where she earned the reputation of a 'commando lady'. When Bruce Lee died, she continued in the same type of bargain with another fighter.

> He forced me to take up arms. He gave me a gun to hold; I used to be very scared. Sometimes he just sent his car up to my house to fetch me. Then we left for the war front. He always took me along on his missions and let me carry his arms. I had no other choice but to follow. In town they used to see me as a commando lady. They used to like me. They welcomed me, took care of me and served me. They used to like my business. Sometimes when some of the commandos did bad in town I would try to assist in solving the problem. For instance, when people were beating up other people who had been stealing things, I would go in between and tell the people to stop and to please forgive them. Sometimes when they wanted to kill somebody I would go there and convince them to forget about the issue. That was what I used to be doing, taking a responsibility behind the fighters. That was the reason why the civilians liked me.

Evelyn tries to legitimize her seemingly immoral behaviour by referring to the fact that she was helping to solve conflicts in town. Armed and backed by one of the important commandos in town, she possessed a certain power of jurisdiction. Whether people in town really respected her because of this care for the community is, of course, questionable. In most cases they had to comply with whatever the military 'desperados' decided. After the war Evelyn, like thousands of young women and men, has chosen not to return to her home, but to stay and live with a group of young people in a house in Ganta.

Even if actively taking part in the war machine, most women could not compete favourably with their men, in private or publicly. Masa recalls a woman fighter she used to know:

> She was a fighter and she found her boyfriend with a different woman and then she couldn't say anything. The man was above her – the man had a military degree. She didn't have a degree because she never went to base camp for training. Then the man went on training and then he [in his turn] trained her. She even used to call the man chief. But the chief thing is finished now [implying that now when the war is over he cannot continue to boss her around in the same fashion].

However, some young women who fought in the war turned it into a successful endeavour. These were most often fighting commandos, in some cases high-ranking officers.[33] With looted wealth they managed to build up business enterprises, and with contacts in the NPFL/NPP establishment they often had a plethora of 'big men' to back them. Naturally women who fought for other warring factions than the NPFL did not have the same political advantages. Probably the best known example is that of Julia Rambo who fought for the NPFL during the war and who today is the owner of a bar in central Monrovia, another on the beach and until recently yet another in Buchanan. Women who were successful in the NPFL have often been appointed to the civil service. For instance, a woman with a notorious reputation as Martina Johnson, General in the NPFL artillery and one of the brains behind the launching of the NPFL's Operation Octopus, was appointed head of security at Robertsfield International Airport (RIA). Julia Rambo, Martina Johnson, Agnes Taylor (Charles Taylor's ex-wife), Ruth 'Attila' Milton of the Liberia Peace Council (LPC) and other female fighters functioned as role models for many young females during the war. The power and integrity they upheld was in sharp contrast to the fragile positions in which most girls found themselves. The power that the barrel of a gun could achieve was certainly a tempting possibility.

Agency of Victims

Liberian national and regional politics has to quite a large extent been a male playground. If war is politics by other means (to paraphrase Clausewitz), then it falls quite naturally that the strategic agency of the war is mainly the property of men. But some women also participated in the war: they commanded soldiers, and upheld the war economy by trading with loot. Furthermore, they influenced their husbands and their sons to fight, and certainly young girls motivated boys of their own age to join the fighting forces. Men generally mediated female participation, but one has to remember that it was not men as a category, but rather a few men who mediated yet other men's participation as well. Just like women, most men were diverted into the war system by a few political actors – persons often referred to as 'big men', 'boss-men' or warlords (see Reno, 1998).

In this essay I have described how young women moved from a passive to a more active role. Entering into the civil war meant that young girls became involved with fighters for a number reasons. Most often it was a way of protecting oneself and one's family from intruders, i.e. the fighting forces, even if these were supposedly fighting for

---

[33] Paul Richards has noted that female participants in the NPFL seldom were as young as their male counterparts (1996:89). This observation contradicts UNDHA-HACO statistics.

the very same people. Families without close relatives involved in the fighting forces, were prey to the commandos. A young woman could be a successful broker for a family. In addition to protection, such a contact could prove necessary to secure food. For their own individual protection, many young women were also forced to team up with fighters. Likewise, some were left with no choice at all. As seen in the text, fighters abducted many young women from their home towns and later left them in unknown settings, forced to cope for themselves. A category of girls also teamed up with men because they felt that the advantages of being with an important man were something 'good' in themselves.

Whatever 'choiceless decisions'[34] introduced these young girls into the war system, they all had in common that they soon got used to the system and thus created different ways to master it. Boyfriends and looted goods came to have a central meaning in this complex. The struggles among the young women were over access to important fighters, mastering one's 'mates', the search for protection, etc. The wrong choice might end one's life. As such, women also triggered men to continue their actions. A boyfriend who did not loot, or wanted to pull out of the fighting system, was worthless indeed and would be promptly dropped for another more powerful fighter. Intelligent and smart young women were seen parading with the most powerful commanders. It was a matter of status among young girls to go out with high-ranking fighters. Thus the war created a category of 'war women' who skilfully mastered fighters and thus became economically prosperous. Many of these had the opportunity to move out of the war zone, but quite frankly felt that they could manage their lives much better in the vicinity of the battlefield, despite the dangers. When the fighting got too intense, they might follow their men to a safer location or take refuge in neighbouring countries.[35]

In this chapter I have tried to collapse the dichotomy of victim/perpetrator, not by trying to insert a third quantity in-between, but rather by demonstrating that even in war people are most likely both. I have argued that the Liberian Civil War limited most people's agency. People in general were limited to a 'tactical agency', using de Certeau's terminology. The minimal amount of a 'war agency' is what I have called *victimcy*, i.e. the agency of hiding one's actions in passive victimhood and reaping the benefit of other people's pity. Most young women in the Liberian Civil War have clearly had a much greater portion of 'tactical agency' than that, but even so they were victimized in the war. Tactical agency is the art of the weak (see Honwana in this volume), or the agency of the powerless (itself an oxymoron). I have described different modes of mastering the confines of war, the daily tactics of being a young woman or girl living in the war zone. Primarily this has been about obtaining security for oneself, and secondarily providing security for one's family and friends. The tactical agency of mastering the war zone from a young woman's perspective anticipated close contact with potentially dangerous rebel fighters or army men. If unwisely dealt with, it could lead to sexual encroachments, rape and in some instances loss of life. Basically, their agency was a manipulation of male combatants; about teaming up with the appropriate man, secretly seeing other men and having the right substitute prepared when the current boyfriend got killed on the battlefield.

---

[34] The expression is used by Aretxaga (1997:61), arguing that women in Northern Ireland exhibit both individual agency and simultaneously are victims of the social setting.
[35] During the April 6th war in 1996 I was living across the border in the Ivory Coast and experienced how many of these young 'war women' crossed the border. They arrived at the border towns in decent cars and posh clothing, only to continue down to Abidjan, or even further.

Fighters with high political and economic potential had numerous girlfriends or 'wives' and one tactical aspect of life was to deal with jealous 'mates' – mastering the game was also to master one's 'mates'. Playing it wrong in the house, disclosing secrets to the wrong person, etc. could have fatal outcomes. Tying up with fighters also implied achieving power. Many poor girls used the power of military fatigues and the barrel of a gun to lay hands on commodities of modern society that they would never have been able to obtain under normal circumstances. Their power put them in a position to rule communities and command individuals who had previously looked down on or ignored them. Many young women turned this into a life-style. Enjoying their newfound power meant that, even if they had the choice to leave and go into exile, they chose to stay – to 'enjoy' the war. Likewise, girls in exile moved back to the Liberian war zone, despite the obvious dangers entailed in such a move. In these instances their agency could be viewed as exceeding that of tactical agency. However, the most prominent feature of tactical agency is that it is 'for a limited time only'. De Certeau points out that a major difference between strategies and tactics is that, whilst strategies are long-term, tactics are only transient. Indeed, the end of the war became a brutal awakening for many of these young war-enterprising women, turning them at one blow into the pariahs of society.

Continuity or Change?

> During the war, I used to be out there doing business. My husband used to be at home taking care of the cooking. But now he is out there again. (Ganta/fieldnotes)
>
> The relationship between men and women is strictly financial in Liberia now. If you don't have money you have no true love. We just believe in the barter system that started during the war. You get the pleasure of my body, and I get the pleasure of your pocket. (Interview with high school graduate by Olonishakin, 1995a:22)

As social norms ruptured during the war, behaviours earlier regarded as immoral were now legitimized out of bare necessity. In two articles Funmi Olonishakin (1995a, b) argues that the war has caused young girls to care less about how the community conceives of them. In much the same fashion as urban youth cultures in the West, this is a response to a perceived stigma in the post-war society. A young 'war-generation' has constructed a loosely knit sub-culture with clear markers of opposition to broader society – created on construed markers of marginalization by a dominant culture. A more marked existence of such a sub-culture is seen in urban centres. In the quotation above a high school graduate argues that gender relationships in the Liberian war zone became entirely commercial. According to her, love was one of the war victims. Most women in pre-war Liberia would probably have reached the same conclusion but would have blamed economic hardship. But in war and post-war discourses it is the war itself that is given the blame.

Gender antagonism has been highlighted during the war. Men see women as prostitutes and women see men as careless beings who only crave insouciant sexual relations; this is only too often pointed out in popular discourse. The woman in the taxicab, with whose account I started this essay, stated that men were cowards during the war. Like her, women often claim that men were useless during the war. Quite often male family heads could not fulfil their commitments to their families. Instead, women stepped in as the main providers. To attach oneself to a fighter was one way of doing so; hence the statement that men see women as prostitutes. Many families were gashed open when women were forced to leave the domestic sphere to venture out into the public. In Monrovia the most prosperous relationship that a woman could engage in would be with ECOMOG personnel.[36] The crude wisdom related by these women to their husbands during the war years is said to have been 'You will chop (eat) when the ECOMOG leaves'. 'Eat' thus plays a double role by signifying both food and sex. Teaming up with an ECOMOG soldier, a rebel or a government soldier was also a technique to protect the very same man they were deceiving. For many men this issue was, and still continues to be, hard to deal with. During the war it also led to decisions to join the warring factions out of despair over loss of power and control over one's own wife, daughters and sisters. In some cases it also led to the expulsion of wives after they had been forced to have sex with soldiers or rebels.

Indeed, women were tragically excluded from their families and social networks because of being subjected to sexual encroachments and rape, but it is important to emphasize that more often than not husbands or parents chose to accept what occurred. Possibly they took their wife or their children to spiritual healers for ritual cleansing ceremonies (see also Honwana, 1999a, b; Nordstrom, 1997a). As rape was not an isolated occurrence during the war, but rather something that happened to all families and social networks, Liberians have generally chosen to accept it as a heritage of the war and thus something to be dealt with in the public process of reconciling and healing the nation. It is sometimes argued that the mere number of girls raped during the war is a reason why individual women will be mentally able to put a rape assault behind them. An inclusive mode in society will help to purge the wounds of rape victims. In opposition to the high school graduate, my experience holds that young girls talk about rape. Several of my informants have been very up-front with their experiences; however, the pathos of trauma is more intricate to talk about. The fact that many girls do not hide their personal experiences of rape suggests that rape is not as stigmatized in war and post-war Liberia as it was in the pre-war setting.

What has happened to those girls who had intimate connections with people in the fighting sphere or who themselves fought in the war? As stated above, many of them have chosen not to return to their pre-war setting, due to an experienced stigma. Cynthia Enloe talks about 'camp followers' in one of her books.

> The archetypal image of the camp follower is a woman outcast from society, poor but tenacious, eking out a livelihood by preying on unfortunate soldiers. She is a woman intruding in a 'man's world'. Skirts dragging in the battlefield mud, she tags along behind the troops, selling her wares or her body, probably at unfair prices. If by chance she falls in love with a soldier, she is destined to be abandoned or widowed (Enloe, 1983:1-2).

The images I have highlighted in this chapter are not entirely different from those offered by Enloe. Young Liberian women as well as 'camp followers' learned how to manage life under the difficult conditions of war. Some literally grew up in it and became dependent on the war fabric. Just like a 'camp follower' who stated after the end of the Thirty Years War 'I was born in the war; I have no home, no country, no friends; war is all my wealth and now whither will I go?' (Enloe, 1983:4), many young women knew little of life outside the reality of the war zone. War shaped the realities of life

[36] ECOMOG was a West African peacekeeping force. Although the salaries of these troops were quite modest, they often had access to other cash flows due to business with minerals, looted goods, etc.

for many of them. During the war they branched out into a public sphere because their fathers, husbands and boyfriends were in greater danger of getting killed out there. They too were in danger but, cruel as it might sound, they had something to trade with.

The civil war was an ugly process for most Liberian women. However, war often alternates periods of rapid change of both social and political conditions (Elshtain, 1987). War has often been seen as a period where processes of female emancipation take place (Massey, 1994; Stanton et al., 1985). As Meintjes et al. (2001:7)put it:

> It is a paradox that war offers opportunities for women to transform their lives in terms of their image of themselves, their behaviour towards men and towards their elders, and their ability to live independently.

Concerning Liberia, Ellis notes 'a radical shift in the position of women' and he states that '[s]ome women travelled widely to trade, and the effect has been a remarkable emancipation of women from their pre-war position' (1999:143). How durable are such changes? Just as in the various contributions to the volume *The Aftermath: Women in Post-conflict Transformation* (Meintjes et al., 2001), I observed a general inability of Liberian women to consolidate their wartime gains. If women came to occupy a part of the public space formerly unknown to them, I believe that the quotation at the beginning of this section has an important message to relay. During the war the woman took care of her family's public affairs, whilst her husband remained in the house taking care of food preparation and other domestic concerns. However, in the post-war setting this scenario is yet again reversed: her husband is out in the public and she is taking care of domestic life again. To a considerable extent, it signifies the post-war reality. Most women have moved back into the domestic sphere of the house and more young women live in polygamous relationships/marriages than before the war.[37]

Even if education is regarded as crucial, most young women do not stay in school for a longer period of time, if at all. According to statistics for 1999 available at UNDP, only 22 per cent of Liberian women are literate, compared with 54 per cent of men. Girls make up only 40 and 32 per cent of enrolments in primary and secondary schools respectively. Furthermore women occupy only 2 per cent of ministerial positions, 5 per cent of legislative seats and only 1 per cent of executive positions.[38] These are indications of a future much the same as the pre-war reality for women in Liberia. The war may have exposed young women to new realities, but to state that their roles in society have changed drastically seems somewhat far-fetched.

[37] Signe Arnfred makes a similar point concerning women who participated in the war in Mozambique (Arnfred, 1988).
[38] Cf. http://reliefweb.int/IRIN/wa/countrystories/Liberia/19990917a.htm

References

Aretxaga, B. 1997. *Shattering Silence: Women, Nationalism, and Political Subjectivity in Northern Ireland*. Princeton, NJ: Princeton University Press.

Arnfred, S. 1988. 'Women in Mozambique: Gender Struggle and Gender Politics', *Review of African Political Economy* 41: 5-16.

Atkinson, P. 1999. 'Deconstructing Media Mythologies of Ethnic War in Liberia', in *The Media of Conflict: War Reporting and Representations of Ethnic Violence*. ed. T. Allen & J. Seaton. London: Zed Books.

Bledsoe, C. 1976. 'Women's Marital Strategies among the Kpelle of Liberia', *Journal of Anthropological Research* 32 (4): 372-89.

— 1980a. *Women and Marriage in Kpelle Society*. Stanford, CA: Stanford University Press.

— 1980b. 'The Manipulation of Kpelle Social Fatherhood', *Ethnology* 19 (1): 29-45.

Bledsoe, C., P. Cohen, et al. 1993. *Social Dynamics of Adolescent Fertility in Sub-Saharan Africa*. Washington, DC: National Academy Press.

Butler, J. P. 1990. *Gender Trouble: Feminism and the Subversion of Identity*. New York: Routledge.

Card, C. 1996. 'Rape as a Weapon of War', *Hypatia* (Fall).

Certeau, M. de 1984. *The Practice of Everyday Life* (trans. Steven Rendall). Berkeley, CA: University of California Press.

Clausewitz, K. von. 1993. *On War*. New York: Knopf.

De Boeck, F. 1999. ' "Dogs Breaking Their Leash": Globalization and Shifting Gender Categories in the Diamond Traffic between Angola and DRCongo (1984-97), in *Changements au Féminin en Afrique noire. Anthropologie et littérature*. ed. D. de Lame & C. Zabus. Paris: L'Harmattan.

DiIorio, J. A. 1992. 'Feminism and War: Theoretical Issues and Debates', *Reference Services Review* 20 (2): 51-68.

Ellis, S. 1995. 'Liberia 1989-1994: A Study of Ethnic and Spiritual Violence', *African Affairs* 94 (375): 165-97.

— 1999. *The Mask of Anarchy: The Destruction of Liberia and the Religious Dimension of an African Civil War*. New York: New York University Press.

Elshtain, J. B. 1987. *Women and War*, Brighton: Harvester.

Enloe, C. H. 1983. *Does Khaki Become You?: The Militarisation of Women's Lives*. London: Pluto Press.

— 2000. *Maneuvers: The International Politics of Militarizing Women's Lives*. Berkeley, CA: University of California Press.

Fuest, V. 1996. '*A Job, a Shop, and Loving Business': Lebensweisen bebildeter Frauen in Liberia*. Münster: Lit.Verlag.

Goldman, A. 1998. *Snäckans sång: en bok om kvinnor och krig*, Stockholm: Natur och kultur.

Hay, M. J. 1988. 'Queens, Prostitutes and Peasants: Historical Perspectives on African Women, 1971-1986', *Canadian Journal of African Studies* 22 (3): 431-47.

Honwana, A. 1999a. 'Negotiating Post-war Identities: Child Soldiers in Mozambique and Angola', *CODESRIA Bulletin* (1 & 2): 4-13.

— 1999b. 'The Collective Body: Challenging Western Concepts of Trauma and Healing', *Track Two* (July): 30-5.

Huband, M. 1998. *The Liberian Civil War*. London and Portland, OR: F. Cass.

Jones, D. E. 1997. *Women Warriors: a History*. Washington, DC: Brassey's.

Keen, D. 1996. 'War: What Is It Good For?', *Contemporary Politics* 2 (1).

— 1999. 'Who's It Between?' 'Ethnic War' and Rational Violence', in *The Media of Conflict: War Reporting and Representations of Ethnic Violence*. ed. T. Allan & J. Seaton. New York: Zed Books.

Little, K. 1973. *African Women in Towns: An Aspect of Africa's Social Revolution*. Cambridge: Cambridge University Press.

Littlewood, R. 1997. 'Military Rape', *Anthropology Today* 13 (2).

Lucas, E. T. 1997. 'Sexual Abuses as Wartime Crime Against Women and Children: The Case of Liberia', *Liberian Studies Journal* 22 (2): 240-60.

Maček, I. 2000. *War Within: Everyday Life in Sarajevo under Siege*. Uppsala: Acta Universitatis Upsaliensis.

— 2001. 'Predicament of War: Sarajevo Experiences and the Ethics of War', in *Anthropology of Violence and Conflict*. ed. B.E. Schmidt & I.W. Schröder. London: Routledge.

Malkki, L. 1995. *Purity and Exile: Violence, Memory, and National Cosmology Among Hutu Refugees in Tanzania*. Chicago: University of Chicago Press.

— 1996. 'Speechless Emissaries: Refugees, Humanitarianism, and Dehistoricization', *Cultural Anthropology* 11 (3): 377-404.

Massey, M. E. 1994. *Women in the Civil War*. Lincoln, NE: University of Nebraska Press.

Meintjes, S., A. Pillay, & M. Turshen. 2001. *The Aftermath: Women in Post-conflict Transformation*. London: Zed Books.

Moore, H. 1994. 'The Problem of Explaining Violence in the Social Sciences', in *Sex and Violence: Issues in Representation and Experience*. ed. P. Harvey. & P. Gow. London: Routledge.

Moran, M. 1988. 'The Market Feeds Me: Women and the Economic Independence in Harper City, Liberia', *Liberia-Forum* 4 (7): 21-35.

— 1990. *Civilized Women: Gender and Prestige in Southeastern Liberia*. Ithaca, NY: Cornell University Press.

Moser, C. & F. Clark (eds) 2001. *Victims, Perpetrators or Actors: Gender, Armed Conflict and Political Violence*. London: Zed Books.

Newark, T. and A. McBride 1989. *Women Warlords: An Illustrated Military History of Female Warriors*. London: Blandford.

Nordstrom, C. 1997a. *A Different Kind of War Story*, Philadelphia, PA: University of Pennsylvania Press.

— 1997b. *Girls and Warzones: Troubling Questions*, Uppsala: Life & Peace Institute.

— 1997c.'Behind the Lines', *New Routes* (1): 3-7.

Olonishakin, F. 1995a.'Women and the Liberian civil war', *African Women* (March-September): 19-24.

— 1995b.'Liberia', in *Arms to Fight – Arms to Protect: Women Speak about Conflict*. ed. O. Bennett, J. Bexley & K.Warnock. London: Panos.

Omaar, R. A. & A. de Waal. 1995.'Rwanda: Rape and Abduction of Women and Girls', *African Woman* (March-September): 34-37.

Reno, W. 1996.'The Business of War in Liberia', *Current History* (May): 211-15.

— 1998. *Warlord Politics and African States*, Boulder, CO: Lynne Rienner.

Richards, P. 1995.'Rebellion in Liberia and Sierra Leone: A Crisis of Youth?', in *Conflict in Africa*. ed. O. Furley. London: Tauris Academic Press.

— 1996. *Fighting for the Rain Forest: War, Youth and Resources in Sierra Leone*. Oxford: James Currey.

Riley, S. 1996. *Liberia and Sierra Leone: Anarchy or Peace in West Africa*. London: The Research Institute for the Study of Conflict and Terrorism.

Rolston, B. 1989. 'Mothers, Whores and Villains: Images of Women in Novels of the Northern Ireland Conflict', *Race and Class* 31 (1): 41-57.

Ruiz, H. A. 1992. *Uprooted Liberians: Casualties of a Brutal War*. Washington, DC: American Council for Nationalities Service.

Schalk, P. 1992. 'Birds of Independence: On the Participation of Tamil Women in Armed Struggle', *Lanka* 7: 44-142.

Schalk, P. 1994. 'Women Fighters of the Liberation Tigers in Tamil Ilam: The Material Feminism of Atel Palacinkam', *South Asia Research* 14 (2): 163-83.

Sesay, M. A. 1996. 'Politics and Society in post-war Liberia', *The Journal of Modern African Studies* 34 (3): 395-420.

Sevenzo, R. & R. Omaar. 1999.'Why It's Much Better to Describe the Plight of Women in War Zones Without Seeking to Whitewash their Crimes', *London Review of Books* (18 February).

Stanton, E, S. Anthony, et al. 1985. *History of Woman Suffrage*. Salem, NH: Ayer Co.

Stiglmayer, A. 1994. *Mass Rape: the War Against Women in Bosnia-Herzegovina*. Lincoln, NE: University of Nebraska Press.

Turshen, M. 1998. 'Women's War Stories', in *What Women Do in Wartime: Gender and Conflict in Africa*. ed. M. Turshen & C. Twagiramariya. London and New York: Zed Books.

— 2001. 'The Political Economy of Rape: An Analysis of Systematic Rape and Sexual Abuse of Women During Armed Conflict in Africa', in *Victims, Perpetrators or Actors: Gender, Armed Conflict and Political Violence*. ed. C. Moser & F.C. Clark. London: Zed Books.

Turshen, M. and Twagiramariya, C. (eds) 1998. *What Women Do in Wartime: Gender and Conflict in Africa*. London and New York: Zed Books.

Utas, M. 1997. *Assiduous Exile: Strategies of Work and Integration Among Liberian Refugees in Danane, the Ivory Coast*. Uppsala: Department of Cultural Anthropology.

— 1999. 'Girls' "Loving Business" – Sex and the Struggle for Status and Independence in Liberia', *Antropologiska Studier* 64-65: 65-76.

— 2003. *Sweet Battlefields: Youth and the Liberian Civil War*. PhD Thesis, Uppsala, Uppsala University Dissertations in Cultural Anthropology (DiCA).

Virilio, P. 1989. *War and Cinema: the Logistics of Perception*. London and New York: Verso.

West, H.S. 2000. 'Girls with Guns: Narrating the Experience of War of FRELIMO's "Female Detachment"', *Anthropological Quarterly* 73 (4): 180-94.

4

PAMELA REYNOLDS
Forming Identities Conceptions of Pain
& Children's Expressions of it in Southern Africa

Introduction

This chapter is about the avenues through which the pain of some children in southern Africa is expressed. In working with children I have become mindful of their pain. I did not set out to examine their suffering, rather the opposite: I am fascinated by children's activity, creativity and development. Yet I have been made aware of their pain, particularly the pain caused by oppression, poverty and war. In working with children in southern Africa over the last fifteen years, I have observed that societies conceive of childhood variously; that they acknowledge children's pain variously; and that there is a contingency in the match between the kind of pain experienced and society's willingness to acknowledge and handle it. Societies pattern the ways in which children's pain is seen, responded to, ignored, given expression or attended to. Factors like age, gender, position in the family, the family's wealth, and individual attributes influence reaction. For example, societies sanction or forbid children the expression of certain fears, the articulation of certain nightmares, the speaking out of certain prophecies, and the demonstration of certain feelings of loss. The patterns accord with conceptions of childhood.

The description of children's suffering necessarily involves consideration of adults' roles in causing and alleviating their pain. Here I concentrate on the suffering experienced by children and youth in the contexts of political conflict, ranging from a community's stand against the forces of the state in the process of claiming the right to live in a squatter settlement in the Western Cape,[1] to the tensions experienced by a community in the aftermath of a war of liberation in Zimbabwe,[2] to the analysis by ex-pris-

---

[1] In 1979 and 1980 I worked with seven-year-old children living in a settlement of shacks known as Crossroads. The first shacks were erected in February 1975 on the sands of the Cape Flats. By 1979, when I began to work with children there, some 20,000 people were living in about 3,000 shacks. Almost every squatter was Xhosa. That they had to build shacks of zinc and scraps in the sand dunes among the wattle trees, and that they were classified as squatters and were vulnerable to imprisonment, expulsion from the area and loss of their homes arose out of their political powerlessness. A government that did not represent them controlled their movement through legislation to do with race classifications, migrant labour and Group Areas (see Reynolds, 1989 for more details). The struggle to secure the right of the people to stay in Crossroads was long and harsh. Despite constant threats of removal, many pass raids, shack demolitions and other forms of harassment, the people refused to leave. Crossroads still exists despite the change in government, in large part because there is an extreme shortage of housing in urban areas.

[2] For two years, 1982 and 1983, I conducted fieldwork with N'anga, Traditional Healers, in three areas of Mashonaland in Zimbabwe. My main interest was in healers' conceptions of childhood, and I focused on their treatment of children as patients and as acolytes, and on their understanding of morality, pain, healing trauma and the acquisition of knowledge. I worked with 60 N'anga.

oners of their fight against the apartheid regime of South Africa.[3]

In focusing on the recognition, interpretation and treatment of children's pain within communities, it is worth posing a number of questions in relation to children's hurts. Are there categories of pain that communities fail to acknowledge, with the consequence that the pain is denied, repressed, or channelled elsewhere? As conditions alter before the forces of rapid change, do some communities deny young people's suffering even once it suppurates openly? Does talk heal? Can children's talk cause too much pain to be given a hearing? If pain is not expressed, are hurts more likely to be cumulative and to affect whole communities? When communities' patterns of healing break down, do children suffer more? Are some hurts better healed by systems formulated outside the community? Are there hurts that cannot be healed by any system? Do communities, at certain times, invest in inflicting pain on children so that the infliction is over-determined? Systematic attention to questions like these may help us better understand children's experiences.

Anthropological research has documented the existence of culturally stipulated responses to pain, for example, the tendency of one population to vocalize cries and the tendency of another to suppress them (Scarry, 1987:5). Children learn what kinds of pain can be expressed under what conditions, in what manner, with what intensity, and in whose presence. That is, they learn what may not be articulated, in what situation pain must be suppressed, the forms of expression that cancel a hearing, and the categories of persons before whom certain pain should not be given voice. Implicit in the discourses about pain are assumptions about the relationship between personhood, gender identity and embodiment. Sets of culturally available discourses shape children's development, even as they resist or disagree with them (compare Moore, 1994:141).

I have listened to children expressing their suffering in dreams, in divination rituals, in physical and mental illness, in the display of wounds, in accusations of witchcraft, in the adoption of eccentric behaviour, in fear of the wild, of dogs, of armoured vehicles, of police, and in mourning the loss of kin, friends and homes. I have seen the consequences for children of destruction by the forces of the state – the negation of the possibility for establishing family structures valued and sanctioned by communities; of their basic trust – imprisoning them with their mothers for daring to visit their fathers without the permission, in writing, from state servants; of their security – bulldozers flattening their houses before their eyes; of their rights – to attend school or seek healing; of their dignity. Much of this destruction should have ceased as both Zimbabwe and South Africa have attained independence under democratically elected governments. Poverty remains, class distinctions will be exacerbated, faction conflict may continue and gender imbalances are unlikely to be levelled.

A basic assumption in Western discourses on pain is that talking helps relieve the dis-

---

[3] I conducted a study between April 1991 and December 1993 with students who had recently emerged from imprisonment as political activists or had returned from exile. It was a time just after the amnesty granted to political activists following President De Klerk's speech on 2 February 1990 announcing change in the South African state. The study involved 62 people, of whom 40 were students in tertiary educational institutions, and 22 were their kin, mentors or colleagues in political organizations. The focus was on the social means of support that the young drew on in surviving the consequences of political involvement in South Africa. We explored the nature of their experiences of childhood, the character of their families and their networks of support among peers and, later, comrades in political organizations. In doing so, we examined notions of childhood, the family and parenting. This was done through interviews and group sessions, all of which were unstructured, taped and transcribed, and some basic questionnaires.

tress. Richard Ellman says, 'Anguish described is anguish altered' (1989:235), while Elaine Scarry (1987:9), describing the work of Amnesty International, suggests that embedded in their work, as in medical work, 'is the assumption that the act of verbally expressing pain is a necessary prelude to the collective task of diminishing pain'. But talk is never unconstrained. As suggested above, communities direct the expression of suffering: few sanction girls' speech about sexual abuse, for example. The silencing of children is variously structured and monitored. As is the silencing of those who care for children.

The experience of suffering needs to be contextualized and its particular expression understood, so that locally healing can be effective. In order to examine generalizations about suffering, we need to match them against local interpretations of everyday experience and of crises.

Children in southern Africa often live on the edge of dreadful things – community violence, state oppression, warfare, family disintegration and extreme poverty. There are local ways of conceptualizing and managing children's suffering: ways that generate opportunities for children to participate in discourses about trauma because there are cues, metaphors, gestures, exchanges between people (especially mothers and children, children and children, and healers and children) that facilitate the telling. A child is already a participant in the social system so that induction into the means of healing need not begin from scratch. I have already suggested that societies can refuse to acknowledge certain kinds of suffering so that different systems may offer healing where local systems fail.

There are four sections in this essay. The first is about the recognition of pain even among the very young within the context of social violence. The second is on the experience of pain and its treatment. The third is on the young coping with extreme pain in isolation. The final section is about the cultural shaping of everyday pain.

Recognizing Children's Pain amidst Social Violence

Trauma and fears of seven-year-old children
In 1979 and 1980 I worked with fourteen Xhosa children who were living in Crossroads, an area of shacks in the Western Cape within the zone of Greater Cape Town (see note 1). I have drawn from that work the accounts of trauma and fear given to me by the children and their mothers. It was a time of extreme state oppression and it was the beginning of the final phase of the rebellion of youth that peaked around the middle of the 1980s with mass imprisonment and brutal repression.[4] The children with whom I worked were only seven years old and it is fascinating to learn how they interpreted the political situation as it impinged on their lives.

The women told me how they thought their children had been affected by their

---

[4] Gill Straker (1992:6) gives this description of the situation in the middle of the decade: 'During 1986 alone, the Detainees' Parent Support Committee estimated that approximately 10,000 children, some as young as ten and eleven years, were detained in jails. Allegations of torture and intimidation were commonplace. In addition, troops occupied many of the townships and intervened in the civil life of the young. Schools were frequently surrounded and access was strictly controlled. Troops supervised examinations and enforced discipline, often brutally. Between 1984 and 1986, figures show that 300 children were killed by the police and military, 1,000 wounded, 18,000 arrested on charges relating to political protest, and 173,000 held in police cells awaiting trial (Swartz & Levett, 1989). In addition, there was an increase in vigilante violence and in all forms of counter-violence. Children in the townships were thus living in a state of civil war (DPSC, 1986:114-41). Under these conditions it is difficult to retain one's concern for the individual as the statistics steadily mount. Yet each statistic has a name, a face, a history and a family.'

involvement in or witnessing of demolitions, riots, police raids or family distress caused by imprisonment. The children, too, told me how they had felt. The impression given by mother and child sometimes differed but far more often it dovetailed. I interviewed mother and child separately and on different occasions.

The children in the sample talked about various experiences during the troubles between 1975 and 1980. (Indirect accounts of the effects of these are given in descriptions of the children's play and dreams – see Reynolds,1989.) Three children were described by their mothers as being very fearful and the member in the family most disturbed by such events. Each had lived in Crossroads since its inception: each had been tied to the mother's back as she ran into the dunes chased by the inspectors who came to catch those without passes. Zuziwe was with her mother when she was arrested and taken away in a police van. Hintsa and Saliswa had been at home when their shacks had been demolished. Here is a verbatim report of Mrs Hleke's description of her daughter – she spoke in English:

> Zuziwe is very scared of riots and runs to hide. In December 1976, when the people fought, I carried her and she kept her eyes closed, being afraid of the things [curved knifes] that can cut off your head. The residents of Nyanga were fighting those in bachelor quarters when the children were closing the shebeens.[5] Houses were burnt. The people of Nyanga ran to Crossroads and they were kept out. It was bad: I think the people of Crossroads did wrong to keep others out as they were killing each other. Zuziwe is not naughty but very sensitive and screams if her rights are abused. She cried much as a baby. People said it was because I loved to listen to the radio while I washed when I was pregnant with her.
>
> If I die, I am concerned about her fastidiousness. She is a sensitive somebody. She hates quarrels. Runs from them. She goes to another house and hides her head on the bed. She has improved a little. She resents accusations and abuses and harps on her injuries.

Mrs Qasana described her child as follows:

> Saliswa has seen riots in Crossroads. They upset her: she was disturbed by the tear gas [she suffers from asthma]. I told her what was happening. When she was four years old, her father was imprisoned and the child was crying and asking for him. She understood that it was because of the pass.[6] Once I too went to prison : she was 1 year old and was with me. She was my bail as I was told to leave because of my baby. It was a bad experience.

The only fears that Hintsa admitted to having were these: 'Elephants make me afraid and dogs. Not you. I was afraid of you a long time ago.' His mother, Mrs Lusizine, described his response to trouble thus:

> Hintsa saw the riots at the school in 1978. He told me that a policemen had helped him and had told him to return home or he would be hurt. He went out of the school but was afraid

[5] During the 1976 student riots that originated in Soweto and spread to Cape Town and elsewhere, beerhalls were a main target of student anger. Some 67 were burned as early as the end of June (Geber and Newman, 1980:145). Students held the same attitude towards shebeens where liquor was illegally sold. Students' anger and frustration precipitated fights within black areas. Mrs Hleke is referring to one in this passage.

[6] A 'pass' was a reference or identification book that every citizen of the Republic of South Africa (including citizens of what were termed independent states, 'homelands', like the Transkei and Ciskei) were obliged by law to carry. For blacks, the pass showed whether or not the person identified had the 'right' to live and work in areas classified 'white' according to influx control legislation. Those charged under this legislation were detained in police cells and frequently sentenced to a fine of R60.00 or sixty days for being in the area illegally, and R10.00 or ten days for failure to produce a pass. A fine of about R70.00 represented approximately two to three weeks' wages for unskilled workers.

of the [police] dogs. He had bad dreams and was restless but the little girl [his sister] was worse. Still she does not want to go to school as she says she nearly died. I say nothing to them. I comfort them. Hintsa does not tell me his dreams. I think he dreams a lot. Our house was demolished at Brown's Camp when Hintsa was four years old. He was afraid. Later I was arrested on my way from work to Crossroads for having no pass. I went to jail for a night. Bail of R50.00 was paid by a Roman Catholic Sister. It happened in 1978. It was my only arrest. Hintsa cried and could not sleep that night. He was the most upset. My sister bought Complan to calm him. He is always the one to get the most upset. I don't know why.

These are the three who would not, could not talk directly about such experiences. They were the only ones who were described by their mothers as sensitive and particularly troubled by such matters, apart from Tozama whose own views and mother's opinion will be discussed shortly. Three mothers said that their children were untroubled by similar events. Lungiswa's mother said. 'She is not disturbed by riots. She is rather interested'; and Gwali's mother, 'He is not bothered by riots or other demonstrations'; and Yameka's mother's brother's wife, 'She is unaffected by riots or demolitions of other people's houses.' Yet the children did express fears. Lungiswa said, 'Mother has been to prison, She and others were going for training to Hanover Park and she was caught for the pass. I was very upset. I was well once she was out. I am now afraid of the police.' Gwali told me, 'I have seen houses knocked down and houses burnt down. I am afraid for my house. I do not dream about it. My mother's house was never burnt.' Finally, Yameka said, 'I have seen houses knocked down in Crossroads. I think nothing but I am afraid.'

Gedja and her mother both asserted that she had seen riots but they did not worry her. Mother and child were born, and their births were registered, in Cape Town and they have the right to live in the Peninsula. They left the Nyanga East township in 1978 to live in Crossroads and have not directly experienced pass raids or demolition threats. They have, however, been witness to many upheavals including the bus, school and meat boycotts of 1980. Nukwa expressed similar bravado saying, 'I am afraid of nothing'; but his mother said that he is afraid and that whenever there is trouble he asks to return to the Transkei.

The other six children openly expressed a variety of fears and they were confirmed in their mothers' understanding. Togu expressed fear of demolitions and of troubles in Crossroads. He added, 'I do not go into the forest as I am afraid of snakes. I am only afraid of snakes and policemen. I am also afraid of my teacher. I am not afraid of you.'

Cebo, for all his brash front, admitted fear of police and trouble in Crossroads. His mother was too anxious about his behaviour to worry about his reactions. She said, 'Cebo is naughty with his neighbours but not at home. I worry about his naughtiness and his nervousness. I am afraid that he will grow up bad.'

As on many topics, Tozama was articulate. In response to the query: 'Of what are you afraid, what worries you?' she said,

Sometimes father has no work. Nothing happens then. There is little to eat. People worry. I don't. I have seen both riots [1976 and 1978]. They worry me. I am afraid for myself.
   I am afraid of the teacher and of not doing well. I am afraid to play outside at night. If there is a thunderstorm, I just stand. I cannot run. I am afraid in the night of people going around and of the spirits. Even if I am with someone, I run leaving the person behind as they cannot help me against the spirits. No one told me about the spirits. I have not seen a spirit. Another child at school, Mandisa, said that a giant (ingqongqo) will eat you at night. I think it is true. I have not asked my parents. If someone is beaten at night, people will be afraid to come out and help. One day we were sent by mother to buy paraffin. As we rounded the corner, a

man in a black coat gestured to us with his finger to come. I ran. Nomvuyo was left. There were two men; one was hiding behind a pole. We did not buy the paraffin.

The children had been witnesses, victims and actors within contexts in which the infliction of pain had occurred. Below I give an example of a remarkable account by a seven-year-old girl who witnessed the killing of a man in Crossroads. At about 9.00a.m. on the morning of 11 August 1980, as I sat in the Hlekes' home, the loudspeaker that is used to convey messages from the Crossroads Committee to the community passed close by. The message was, 'If a member of your family left for work this morning via the Nyanga Bus Terminus, you should check if he/she is lying dead.' The people said that the police were forcing workers to violate the bus boycott by making them board buses against their will. Students reacted and a battle ensued. There was an atmosphere of unease in Crossroads that morning. Soon after 12.00 I was stopped by residents near the road to Nyanga East. They told me that as I was white I was in danger and that I should leave Crossroads, taking the Landsdowne Road not the Klipfontein Road, as trouble was about to break out. I left, and five minutes later the students came over the dunes singing. In the afternoon they gathered near the Klipfontein Road and stoned two cars. The driver of one, Mr Beeton, was stabbed and hit and he died at the scene of the incident. Another car driven by Mr Jansen was hit by the stones. His car stopped and the students overturned it and set fire to it. He managed to escape from the burning car and threw himself into a puddle of water. The police arrived and took him away – he died shortly afterwards. In the daily paper the next day, there was a picture of the man sitting in the puddle: a terrible picture. During the week, another man was killed by the students and a young boy was shot by the police. It was a week before Crossroads was quiet once again.

Tozama's account of the trouble follows. It is clear, vivid and moving. She told it all – the gore, the action, the response, the emotion, the humour – with a slight smile and intense concentration:

> The children of Black Power came from the Klipfontein Road across to near my house holding a red flag. There arrived a car with a white man. These children just ran to it and threw stones at the windows. The man was hiding himself with his hands. They turned the car upside down and lit it with fire while he was still in it. He tried to come out. He came out and was on fire and threw himself in the water. The soldiers arrived and the children ran to hide in Crossroads. The soldiers were trying to throw sand and water on the car and the ambulance arrived and took him. He was still alive. After a while we heard that he had died. My mother said that we must stay at the back of the house because she did not want us to see what was happening.
>
> I cried. I wanted my father. There were women who came to our house and they all cried. The blacks were not killed. Only whites. I don't know why. My parents did not tell me anything. My father was in the hospital during the trouble. He was getting tablets. I was afraid that my father would be hurt. It was right outside my house, near the tap at X4 [a church]. I was afraid at night after that. If we are sent outside at night, we are afraid to go past X4.
>
> I have not seen the children throw stones before. One child was shot by the policeman. The children removed the bullet from her knee. They removed it with a bottle top. I saw the child shot by the police. She ran away and the children gathered around her. This was near X4. The policemen saw them only after the bullet had been taken out. It was a girl from Crossroads, from house number –. She is not at school. She is an old child, over 15 years. She is fine now: no longer limping. A girl was the first to throw stones. I saw her throw stones. She is from Crossroads. The rest are from the townships.
>
> The newspaper said it was not the children from Crossroads but the township children who killed the man. I felt sorry for that man. My mother said, 'It seems as if that man is just like my child.' The other girls from the township, while the policemen were throwing tear gas, took off

their panties and peed on them then wiped their faces. The Crossroads children were here when the township children came along the Klipfontein Road. They joined them. They were mostly township children and some from Crossroads.

You would have been killed if you had come. The man was finally unconscious.

The child of number – was shot to death. The children went to that house. He was found at the hospital and brought back in a coffin. I did not see him being shot. The people from Crossroads and the teachers came to my house because they thought my brother was the one who had died.

[A little later during the same session, she told me how her uncle (*malume*) had tried to warn her family that trouble was coming]:

My uncle wanted to tell us what was going to happen that week. My mother took it easy and did not listen to him. He was afraid that you would be hurt. Now my mother wants to stay at his house in Guguletu because they hear things before they happen. Another lady from Crossroads saw a white lady coming towards the children after they had killed that man. She waved her hand to tell her to go. The children were angry and wanted to burn her house. She ran away.

The students were asking for petrol from a Crossroads man. They were not given it. My mother would have given it to them as she was afraid they would kill her.

My uncle came to my house and asked what is happening. He wanted to know the names of the children because he knows them. My brother would only give a name of a youth group. I do not know if he wanted to take them into prison. Only one boy from Nyanga, called –, mentioned all the names of those in his group. That was wrong because they were all taken to prison.

The township children came to school and made the older children join them. A teacher's sister was taken. She went. While they were going she said she wanted to pee. She was lying. They waited. She returned and then said she was thirsty. They said, 'We will wait.' She ran out the back [of the shack]. The children came and told her sister that she had gone and that they would punish her. They returned later and found her and forced her to join them again. They saw the police and the girl said, 'We must hide or we will be shot.' They hid and she escaped to another house. They did not get her again. My mother told us this story saying that we must not go to school. We stayed at home.

In the above account, Tozama expresses fear for her father's safety and pity for the white man; she observes with interest survival techniques (how to remove a bullet from the knee and how to avoid being overcome by tear gas); she analyzes the composition of the crowd; she expresses disapproval of informers and wonders about her uncle's knowledge and interest in the affair; and she recalls the details of an incident involving intimidation.

Her mother's account of the death of Mr Jansen represented the torn emotions of many adults in Crossroads. On the one hand, she was sympathetic towards the students and their cause, but on the other hand, she wept for those who suffered as a consequence. Mrs Ketshe was ill after the week of trouble and went on a visit to the Transkei to 'release' her body. She told of a woman who saw Mr Jansen being killed and had laughed and laughed and laughed. When she returned home and was cooking, her primus exploded and she was badly burnt on her face and hair and body. It was, said Mrs Ketshe, God's revenge.

Symptomatology of grief

From Crossroads, South Africa, we turn to Sultanpuri, India to examine another set of ideas on the recognition of the pain of children who have been caught up in violent social upheaval. Veena Das (1992) writes about children who were caught up in the riots that followed the assassination in 1984 of Indira Gandhi in Delhi. Das writes about the survivors in a refugee colony, called Sultanpuri, where she worked providing relief and rehabilitation. She details the great need on the part of the survivors to tell their story over and over again, and her paper is arranged so that the reader may 'listen' to the 'speech' of different women and children as they narrated the stories of the death of kin and neighbours. She suggests that a whole language about the 'symptomatology of grief' was available and shared by the community. It allowed them to offer some recognition of the grief and fear of the children even where parents' perceptions and interpretations about their children's behaviour following bereavement were not necessarily accurate. It was understood that the experience of tragedy can transform the body: the body can be broken and withered by grief and children's bodies are especially vulnerable to such effects. Extreme emotions, they believe, can be literally 'embodied'. Adults' protection, therefore, took the form of protecting the body rather than encouraging children to verbalize grief and fear.

Parents were sensitive to the manner in which children had been affected but did not feel that they had to provide any explanations to the children about what had happened, or even discuss with them anything of how they had experienced the loss of a parent. Children had to construct their own knowledge about the riots and what the future was likely to hold for them (*ibid.*: 378). Das argues that the cognitive needs of the children cannot be ignored. They tried to understand the events in order to make their world meaningful again. The time frame they used was invariably a mythic rather than a narrative one (ibid.: 379). Her account of the children's recall of their experiences is very moving. She describes their attempt to find symbols to express the brutalities to which they had been subjected and the effect that particular places or activities had in triggering children's articulation of their experiences. She encountered the children and their grief in two different contexts: one was in their community with adults and the other was in a bus on an hour-long drive between the children's homes and a summer camp that had been set up for them. In the first setting she encountered the children's grief primarily through the voices of adults and the children's narratives, in these contexts, seemed to have a very 'third person quality' (*ibid.*: 375).

> The children were brought to the summer camp in two vans. I would go in one of these to fetch them in the morning. I soon realized that the journey from home to camp, which took about an hour, was an occasion when many children began to talk about the riots. Often the memory was provoked by either the sudden recognition of a space where a parent had been killed, or by watching someone perform an activity in which a member of the family had once been engaged. The children who had seemed most unable to articulate their memories suddenly found language pouring out of their mouths. It is possible that groups of children had discussed these events amongst themselves but had been discouraged by adults from discussing them; or perhaps they found an assurance from my presence, so that these memories could indeed, be narrated.
>
> The children psychologically stood with each other in these remembrances. The more articulate ones often lent their voices to those who were numbed and could not speak. When remembering something, each would contribute to the story so that memory became a collective event. For example, a little girl, who was perhaps five years old, would not speak at all. But whenever we passed a particular spot the children would say, that is where Ballo's father was burnt. The crowd left him to burn and she ran to him holding his hand while he died. Ballo would nod shyly to affirm that the children were telling the truth, but could not be brought to put any of this into her own words(*ibid.*: 377).

The children sought categories with which to understand the grotesque forms of violence imposed from outside onto their communities.

The descriptions of children's experiences of trauma drawn from Crossroads in South Africa and Sultanpuri in India illustrate that there are differences among people as to the very notions of how to recognize what hurts children and the signs of hurt. Some are more practised than others in interpreting the signs: some feel under no obligation to notice them at all. Children (like mothers and healers) often notice distress in another child and draw attention to it. Often I have realized that a child's visit to me held within it, carefully folded into ordinary pleasantries and exchanges to do with common interests, a message about a friend's unhappiness. I wonder how often I failed to hear the invitation to attend to another's pain. My responses to children's suffering had to accord with local means for addressing them. The dangers to the child and to myself were real if local rules were flouted. Indeed, one has to earn trust before one can advocate on another's behalf. Where a child is at risk or where patterns of abuse (like school teachers' sexual abuse of school girls) exist and are not openly challenged, other measures may have to be taken with full cognizance of their possible consequences for the child involved.

The people of Sultanpuri hold that the experience of tragedy can transform the body, especially the body of a child. The Zezuru people of Musami, Zimbabwe, translate the effect of tragedy on the individual into a symbolic language that traces connections among kin, neighbours and spirits. Bodily pain and behavioural disturbances are interpreted as signs of disarray in the social and moral order. Zezuru attitudes are examined in the next section.

The Experience of Pain and its Handling by Others

Local means of paying attention
Among Zezuru people local means of paying attention to children's pain tend to ensure that a child is not rendered vulnerable (in the ways that victims often are) because metaphoric and ritual expression can skirt the need for confrontation and direct accusation. Implicit within Zezuru notions of children's welfare is a series of adult obligations. Adults are called to account for themselves when a child's distress is made public. Close kin are seen as the first ring of defence that secures a child within the stronghold of kin and community care. Misbehaviour, especially moral lapses by adults, is seen to be responsible for the child's exposure to outside forces, particularly those seeking redress or revenge. Zezuru people say that a child is frequently targeted by alien spirits and made ill or troubled so that family members will then quickly attend to the distressed child, search out the cause and seek to resolve the underlying stress in relations among the living or between the living and the dead.

In the following two examples a healer interprets children's ill-health as having been caused by spirits seeking to redress adults' wrongdoing. In September 1982 a healer called Chitate in Musami held a ritual for a girl aged ten. The girl had come from an area over 100 kilometres away with her brother-in-law and a woman. She said that she was ill and spoke no more until that evening when a ritual was held to consult the spirits about the cause of the girl's illness. During the ritual Chitate became possessed and so did the girl. The vengeful spirit (a *ngozi*) spoke through the girl claiming that a member of the girl's family had murdered him during the war. He had not been killed as part of the conduct of Zimbabwe's War of Liberation (that ended with Independence in 1980) but had been murdered. The spirit was making the child ill in order to draw the family's attention to his demand that five cows be paid to his kin in compensation for his death. The girl was treated and warned that she would fall ill again if the cattle were not handed over. This was the start of a process of negotiation between two families around the death of a kinsman. A child's ill-health was the trigger for a process of reconciliation between families that involved the living and the dead. In response to a query from me as to the fairness of using children as pawns in family negotiations, Chitate replied, 'There is no way to avoid it. It is part of the system.'

Another of Chitate's patients, a boy of twelve, was made ill by the spirit of a former servant of his father's father who had a grudge against his employer. It was divined that the spirit wanted to be 'chased with a cow', that is a cow must be slaughtered and the spirit propitiated. Family members had to drink the cow's blood mixed with medicine and eat certain portions of meat without salt. The boy, it was divined, would continue to fall ill if this was not done. The boy's illness, expressed in babbling and stomach pains, was seen by the healer to be part of his mother's sickness. His mother was diagnosed as ill because her mother had died bearing a grudge against her. When the sick woman was young and recently married her mother and father often quarrelled and her father would leave home and go to her (the daughter's) house. His wife was insulted and complained, 'Is your daughter your wife?' He would reply, 'Even if you die, I don't care as my daughter will look after me like a wife.' After one quarrel and departure by the man, a grandchild saw him returning home and informed his wife of his approach. She hanged herself with a rope. Now, years later, her spirit was causing her daughter to be ill and she was demanding that her daughter undergo the ritual of *kutiza botso*,[7] a ritual of humiliation carried out by those who wronged their parents. The ritual involves wearing tattered clothes, and being dirty as one wanders from household to household begging for grain with a small container. Children laugh at the beggar. Having undergone the ritual, the woman slaughtered a cow and brewed beer: she took a small pot of beer to her mother's family.

The boy was said to have been made ill by his father's father's failure to fulfil a promise to a servant and by his mother's wronging of her mother. He had been caught in a tangle of incestuous desires and conflicting duties that rendered the woman willing to humiliate herself in public and so retrieve health for herself and her son. (Did, one wonders, Cordelia in the love and service of her father overstep the boundaries that define the duties of a good daughter?)

During Zimbabwe's Liberation War, many children became messengers for the guerillas fighting against the Rhodesian army (see Reynolds, 1990 for a description of their roles). Children have a talent for escaping surveillance. They can move through the countryside undetected and thus serve admirably as messengers in times of war. Boys and girls aged between ten and sixteen who served the comrades were called *mujibha* and *chimbwido* respectively. They acquired positions of power in their communities because of their important and often dangerous roles. They were often viewed with wonder because of their bravery and with fear because of their arbitrary power. If a *mujibha* denounced someone as a sell-out, the comrades took action that sometimes resulted in that person's death. An estimated 50,000 young people acted as intermediaries between the comrades and the villagers during the war (Lan, 1985:125). The part they played was vital. The

[7] Hannan (1984:26) gives this definition of the ritual, using the plural 'vakatiza (or vakatanda) botso: they dressed in rags and went begging for millet with which to brew beer for the appeasement of the anger of a parent who died before they had asked forgiveness for an offence'.

Rhodesian Security Forces called them 'runners' or 'sympathisers' and treated them almost as harshly as if they were armed insurgents.

The experiences of these young people during the war, especially their acquisition of power and their subsequent loss of it, must have had a profound impact on their position in society. As communities began realigning power structures after the war, the position of these children was reconsidered. There was no simple return to the hierarchies of family, community or school, but the children did not retain their positions of power. Some children acknowledged the after-effects of trauma and sought various means of recovery. Others bore their pain silently. Many of them took advantage of local systems of healing to reveal their distress and seek ritual means to help them to come to terms with their experiences.

A healer called Simon treated many children after the war. He said that some of them were being driven mad by the spirits of those killed taking revenge on the children who had collected them to meet their death. Simon's treatment includes holding rituals that involve speaking to the spirit through the child in front of members of the family and community. If the persons who died were not guilty as charged (usually of informing against the guerrillas), the family of the child who led the person to his or her death is required to pay compensation. One spirit demanded seven cows, one goat, one chicken and a girl. If payment is not made, the spirit can cause havoc in the family, bringing about people's deaths. The girl demanded is usually a sister, aged between nine and twelve, of the one who caused the death. She is given to the family of the dead person and stays until she gives birth to a baby of the same sex as the one who was killed. Then, according to Simon, she is free to return home but must leave her baby behind, or she can remain as a wife of the man who impregnated her and, in some cases, bridewealth is paid for her. Only those given in compensation for war victims can return home. I asked how it can be justified that a girl should suffer for her brother's misdeeds and Simon replied, 'It is the way it works. It is the same as a girl who marries and the *lobola* (bridewealth) goes to obtain a wife for her brother.'

I once saw a girl, a cow and a dog walking in single file across the bush. There was something odd about the scene and, upon inquiry, I was told that she had been sent from her home to a family living not far away in compensation for the death of a member of their household killed during the war by the guerrillas on the instructions of the girl's brother. I doubt that she was given much opportunity to express her pain. Some years after the war there were so many cases of girls being given in compensation that the Zimbabwe Government enforced legislation against it. Custom is flexible and sometimes the girl is given symbolically and is replaced with cows. This depends on whether the exchange is acceptable to the receiving group. The child, I am told, will never be treated badly as she is feared having been sent at the spirits' command.

I expressed to a healer my concern about the well-being of a girl taken from her family and given in compensation for another's death, saying that many people would fear that the child might not develop well or might be unhappy away from her parents: he replied, 'In this case, the spirit will come for the child and transform the child's thoughts into believing that the new family is hers.' I asked how the pain of the mother is compensated for when she has to send her child away and he said: 'Nothing is done about it. She will believe that it is in the interests of the whole family.' Perhaps the examples I have selected show how harsh recompense and the soothing of relations among and between families and neighbours can be for the individuals whose lives are made part of the process of reparation. Perhaps I have failed to show how flexible ritual and custom can be and how malleable processes are in meeting new challenges in the soothing of damaged ties. For example, one healer negotiated an exchange of a cow for a girl in a case of compensation due to failure (two generations previously) to pay bridewealth. But who counts the cost? Against what standard? Whose time-scale – the child's, the adult's, the spirit's – is used as a benchmark? Reconciliation after war was, I believe, an extraordinary achievement: some people, like the young girls given in compensation, paid a high price. The pain of some was shifted on to others: one's hurt was healed by another's hurt.

Of children's pain we need to ask: to what social uses is it put? How is it given personal signification? How is it socially validated? Are there means for transforming it? The very concepts of pain can be differently weighted: emotional as against physical; individual references as against collective; idiosyncratic as against metaphoric discourse. Children participate in, and are inducted into, societies' constructions of truth, constructions based, in part, on the meaning given to suffering.

The Social Construction of Pain

Pain within an edifice of coercion

From 1991 to 1993, I worked with young political activists who, having been released from prison or returned from exile following the change in the political climate that began with President De Klerk's speech on 2 February 1990, were students in tertiary educational institutions in South Africa. Here, I shall touch on some of their accounts of suffering within the edifice of coercion of the South African state. Many of the young people who entered into political activity around 1976 had no weapons with which to fight and most had had but a sketchy introduction to politics. Some of those with whom I worked took up political activity while still at school, and some were convicted and imprisoned with hardly any exposure to political training. A few were trained in Tanzania, Angola, Mozambique and the Soviet Union. Most of them learned the tactics of political survival once they were charged and sent to prison.

Zolile, for example, had only just been recruited into the African National Congress when he was arrested, interrogated and charged; he was sentenced to ten years imprisonment. At the time of his arrest, he was still a school boy and had seen imprisonment once before for helping to organize a school boycott. He knew very little apart from the code name of the person who recruited him and the identities of the others in his cell. Here is a transcript of an interview with Zolile in which he describes his ignorance when he was arrested and his treatment by the police. The interview was conducted soon after his release from the prison on Robben Island. The hesitancies reflect his fragile state at the time.

> Ya, I didn't even know the correct name [of the person who recruited him] or, he was using a certain name, you know, like that. And I didn't even know how he got to know my name, or … So that was nothing, you know. So, although the police couldn't believe it, because they kept on beating me, torturing me, thinking that I am hiding others or big ANC people around the area, don't want to reveal them. But there was nothing I could say, you know. Except really admitting what I have done. So, of course, at that time, one was more, had a bit of experience being in the hands of the police, he could know what type of questions to handle, and what type of information to divulge, you know. So, although the beating was more serious, more than before, you know, because they took the ANC very seriously at that time, and … .

PR: What happened to you?

At that time, you know, they, they took me, I was kept in one of these farm police stations. You know, at one time I remember they took me to a cell, you know, and kept me with a pig in the cell. And ... .

It was very bad, you know, because the pig couldn't understand and it was very wild! To the extent that I had to shout, you know, to the police and one Coloured policeman came and actually opened up and took this pig out of the cell. And they used, of course, to take me in the middle of the night to interrogate me around the very dark places, around those farms, and sometimes in the beginning of the weeks the method that they used was to take me to one coast, you know beach, and put me into a sack, you know, where they will tie it with a rope into a Rover and pull it along the coast of the water in the sea, to get wet. And after that they will take me to this Landrover whilst I'm very much shivering cold, with cold, to this Rover, and open up an engine. They were using some machine which I couldn't understand at that time. Even now I don't remember, I don't understand what type of machine was that. But they will connect that machine to the battery of the car with wires and open ... In fact what they were doing first was to open it. It produced very much intensive heat, you know. The combination of that very much cold and heat I will be ... I'll feel very bad in my body and very painful, you know. Uhh, so that was one method they used to do, even shocks, you know? Choking me. So, that was types of torture I could remember at that time which they were using.

Zolile was eventually charged and sentenced and says that it took him three years on Robben Island to recover his equilibrium. I met men who had been broken by their maltreatment. The purpose of this kind of infliction of pain is not simply, or even necessarily, to extract information. Although the information sought in an interrogation is almost never credited with being a just motive for torture, it is repeatedly credited with being the motive for torture. But for every instance when someone with critical information is interrogated, there are hundreds interrogated who could know nothing of remote importance to the stability or self-image of the regime (Scarry, 1987: 28). People like Zolile had received little instruction from seasoned political campaigners or preparation for handling extreme levels of pain and humiliation.

A different account of suffering in prison was given by a young woman, Nomoya. She said that, apart from the physical pain inflicted on her, it was the conditions under which she was held that caused great distress. There the confined space, the lack of air and light, the refusal of the prison authorities to allow her a change of clothes for two months or to take her from the cell for exercise, the poor washing conditions, the sparse and inedible food (porridge at 5.00am, a slice of bread and a drink at 10.00am, and the same again at 3.00pm). She was in a cell near common-law prisoners and in one of these a woman who was mentally unsound was being held. This woman constantly made strange noises and shouted out her threats of suicide. Nomoya was deeply distressed. She says, 'I cried to be let out and interrogated rather than stay in that cell – just to have fresh air, to get out, even if they tortured me. The loneliness affected me so much and to think that it may be worse for those at home.' She never saw anyone else and had no news of home. Even if the warder took her to the nurse, she was kept out of sight of the other prisoners. This she experienced as a form of psychological torture. She found her situation of complete vulnerability difficult to handle. She felt that if she fell ill she might simply be left to die or that if the authorities wanted to they could do anything to her, even hang her in the middle of the night.

Eventually the police came and took Noyoma for interrogation. 'This time they didn't torture me physically. They would interrogate me psychologically for maybe more than six hours, and, really, it could not be worse. It was because they would come as big officers and put this one chair in the middle where I could sit and someone would ask the other one and the next thing was interpretation to such an extent that I didn't know what they were saying and afterwards I was taken back (to the cell). Of course I didn't just let them do as they were doing. I'd always put complaints to the prison warders.'

Despite her fear and bewilderment, Nomoya adopted the tactic of refusing to accept the conditions of her imprisonment without a fight. At every opportunity she put forward her grievances and made demands: some were met. Her first demand was for a Bible. She read it four times. Then she demanded books to read and eventually some were brought to her: mostly romantic novels of the Barbara Cartland kind. Next she pestered the authorities until they allowed her to select her own books from the prison library and, finally, she was given access to some academic books. She says, 'I won the struggle and I could study'. She won, too, the right to thirty minutes of exercise a day. One must not think that once one is imprisoned the struggle is over. Nomoya adds, 'You know, going into that place you must just start to wage another battle against the prison authorities. You don't have a chance of survival if you don't do that.' She expresses her sympathy for the illiterate prisoners who cannot benefit from privileges such as reading.

There are many other accounts of resistance. During sessions of torture, one young man would pull himself together when the white officers left the room for a break and lecture his black torturers on political consciousness and the need to take cognizance of their positions within the security forces. There are tales, too, of support among common-law prisoners who would violate prison rules deliberately in order to be incarcerated in punishment cells near political prisoners to whom they could send messages or pass letters or newspaper cuttings. Sometimes elaborate pulley systems of string were stretched out of cell windows to send small gifts – a sweet, a disprin, some soap – to boost morale.

The very discourse of resistance was one that was in the making. It had to be forged in a context of secrecy and isolation and of an excess of brutality that reached into every sphere of existence among the oppressed. There had to be a conscious effort to claim rights and there was a slow gathering in the momentum of consciousness among non-activists against the machinations of the state. Examples of resistance on behalf of activists follow.

Sipho was arrested in 1984 and thrown into a cell among hardened criminals who had been told to 'fix him'. The tactic backfired as the criminals merely demanded that Sipho give them lectures on politics. He was quite relieved to be removed from their cell.

Siyavuyo committed a political act of sabotage that secured him the death sentence. In the first month following his arrest he was severely tortured. During one session the soles of his feet were burnt and he was forced to stand for four days on wire mesh. While the officers were out of the room, a black policeman allowed him to get off the wire and lean against a wall. Such tiny gestures were placed, Siyavuyu said, alongside the pain of tiny betrayals by comrades that were intentionally revealed by interrogators in order to undermine any sense of trust or mutual support that the prisoner might be depending upon.

The students knew that just as the body is a political subject so is the mind. Siyavuyo said that it is harder to prepare the mind to resist, 'Because physical torture is terrible on the body but isolation is much more [terrible] I think on the mind'. He spent almost three years in solitary confinement, two of these on death row.

In South Africa there was an architecture of coercion that was terrifying in its diffu-

sion, abandonment, darkness. It encompassed farm prisons, border posts, high-rise build-
ings as sites of terror; it included pigs' ears to eat, wild pigs in cells, food like swill; it
involved state coercion to be a turncoat right up to the prisoner's entrance into court;
it ensured a denial of rights to health care, letters, visits, reading material that was arbitrary, long-term and petty. It was conscription into violence. It was a compulsion of violence.

As the architects of coercion, servants of the state used the bodies of young people
(sometimes of children) to humiliate, to punish, to control and to defeat them and so
quash political revolt. In turn, the young used their bodies to make political statements.

The pain that these young people suffered was experienced in isolation and in fear.
There was little chance of even receiving intimations of support until the actual infliction, or threat of infliction, of pain and its most immediate physical effects had passed,
because they were kept in solitary confinement and denied contact with the outside
world. Often kin were not even told that a member of the family had been arrested.
Even if it was known that they had been arrested, kin were not told where the person
was being held; the first signs of support from family, peers, political allies or community
members were often received only when prisoners were formally charged in court,
maybe months after their arrest. Sometimes signs came in the form of smuggled messages or were carried by voices calling from the inmates of other cells or even from outside prison walls, as kin, usually mothers, searched for their children. I have written
elsewhere (Reynolds, 1995) about the importance of support from others, especially
family members.

We know little about whether or not cultural constructions of pain influence individual resistance to its effects under such conditions. And little about 'the question of
how injuring creates an abiding outcome' (Scarry, 1987: 111). For some there were few
opportunities for envisaging their pain except alone even after release from prison, as
they felt its expression laid too great a burden of suffering on those close enough to share
it.

The large questions that need to be examined are to do with the infliction of pain
and its political use; the meaning behind its excess in its infliction; and the possibilities
for those harmed of reparation and the restitution of dignity. A full analysis of the findings of the Truth and Reconciliation Commission in South Africa and people's responses
to them may increase our understanding.

The Cultural Shaping of Everyday Pain

The oppressive states of Rhodesia and South Africa prior to Independence created political situations of great complexity for children. Choices had to be made not only in
opposition to the politics of the state but also to the politics of their elders. Commitment
to political action against the state involved, for many, the use of the body as the main
weapon against the force of state troops. It often called for alignment with groups that
were not necessarily the sanctioned representatives of their communities and that may
not even have drawn their members from the local area. In consequence, there were, for
many children, extreme tensions between belief and experience. For Raymond Williams,
important tragedy seems to occur in conditions when there is

... real tension between the old and new: between received beliefs, embodied in institutions and responses, and newly and vividly experienced contradictions and possibilities ... . But beliefs can be both active and deeply questioned, not so much by other beliefs as by insistent immediate experience. In such situations, the common process of dramatising and resolving disorder and suffering is intensified to the level which can be most readily recognized as tragedy. (1992:54)

The consequences of choices made have been profound for many of the children and, in accord with their actions and their pain, the common processes of dramatizing and resolving disorder and suffering have been intensified. Rituals and patterns of healing have been used in the recognition and treatment of young people's pain. There has been a remarkable flexibility in the response within communities in their attempts at healing and reconciliation.

An implicit pedagogy

Pierre Bourdieu (1977:95) writes about societies' tricks of pedagogic reason that ensure members' submission to the established order. He remarks on the way in which societies that seek to produce new sorts of members set great store by the seemingly insignificant details of dress, bearing, physical and verbal manners. They treat the body as a memory and so entrust to it in abbreviated and practical form the fundamental principles of the arbitrary content of the culture.

> The principles embodied in this way are placed beyond the grasp of consciousness, and hence cannot be touched by voluntary deliberate transformation, cannot even be made explicit; nothing seems more ineffable, more incommunicable, more inimitable, and, therefore more precious, than the values given the body, made body by the transubstantiation achieved by the hidden persuasion of an implicit pedagogy, capable of instilling a whole cosmology, an ethic, a metaphysic, a political philosophy, through injunctions as insignificant as 'stand up straight' or 'don't hold your knife in your left hand'.

Pedagogic reason exhorts the essential while seeming to demand the insignificant. 'The concessions of politeness always contain political concessions' (Bourdieu, 1977:96). Particularly in the socialization of girls. Bourdieu says that women and the young are disadvantaged by the symbolic order and that they ' ... cannot but recognize the legitimacy of the dominant classifications in the very fact that their only chance of neutralizing those of its effects most contrary to their own interests lies in submitting to them in order to make use of them ...' (ibid.:164-5). The mythico-ritual system, entirely dominated by male values, legitimates the division of labour and power between the sexes. Societies structure the passage of time defining the boundaries of age groups and imposing limits at different ages. The symbolic manipulation of age limits has a political function in defining a theory of knowledge. A major dimension of political power lies in the symbolic power to impose the principles of the construction of reality, in particular, social reality.

Bourdieu claims that, owing to a quasi-perfect fit between the objective structures and the externalized structures, the established cosmological and political order is perceived not as arbitrary, that is, as one possible order among others, but as the self-evident and natural order. An authority and necessity of the given order is attested to by the whole group. In consequence, 'Between the child and the world the whole group intervenes, not just with the warnings that inculcate a fear of supernatural dangers, but with a whole universe of ritual practices and also of discourses, sayings, proverbs, all structured in concordance with the principles of the corresponding habits' (1977:167).

This helps to make the world conform to the myth. Tradition is silent: what is essential goes without saying because it comes without saying. Bourdieu is, of course, describing orthodoxy – what he has termed doxa.

While his formulation fits the dominance of women and children across many societies and through much of history, it does seem too static, too mythical itself. Having watched healers conduct everyday matters among the Xhosa, Zezuru and Tonga, I query the extent to which groups, not directly controlled by powerful, centralizing authorities, accede to the unanimity of the orthodox. There is an attention to everyday matters at the local level that allows for a flexibility in the ordering of individual experience and in effecting change in the uses to which therapeutic practices and rituals are put. These suggest a greater malleability in relationships as negotiated across gender and age groups. But perhaps, as Bourdieu asserts, groups not directly controlled by powerful, centralizing authorities have already had their reputations laid open to questioning by dominant groups.

Nor does his formulation allow for the account of individual differences within groups. Moore points out that Bourdieu's concept of positionality is devoid of any notion of a multiple subjectivity constituted through multiple positions. He is unable to specify the consequences of the intersections of sets of different social distinctions for individuals in specific contexts. 'His strongly socialized and collective view of the body in its relationship to habitus means that he does not adequately theorize individual experiences and motivations' (Moore, 1994: 79). It is important to emphasize here because socialization theories frequently accept as unproblematic children's acquisition of identity. Young people in southern Africa questioned the legitimacy of dominant classifications. Many did not silently comply with tradition. Many young people in southern Africa rejected the established order imposed by undemocratic governments and, in doing so, they had to stand against much of the order represented by parents and other authorities at the local level. They drew on material and symbolic means in rejecting the definition of the real as imposed on them. They acted in the full knowledge that the likely consequences would be fear and pain, possibly death. Sometimes they acted in concert with others, especially peers, but often their decisions to stand against dominant forces were taken alone and their engagements in clandestine activities were necessarily secret. It is difficult to record the processes whereby a child involves himself or herself in acts that crosscut discourses that evoke obligations, loyalties, expectations and commitments at local and national levels.

Scarry (1987:109) affirms Bourdieu's emphasis on the presence of learned culture in the body as an imposition originating from without and adds:

> But it must at least in part be seen as originating in the body, attributed to the refusal of the body to disown its own early circumstances, its mute and often beautiful insistence on absorbing into its rhythms and postures the signs that it inhabits a particular space at a particular time. The human animal is in its early years 'civilized', learns to stand upright, to walk, to wave and signal, to listen, to speak, and the general 'civilizing' process takes place within particular 'civil' realms, a particular hemisphere, a particular nation, a particular state, a particular region … . The political identity of the body is usually learned unconsciously, effortlessly, and very early … . What is 'remembered' in the body is well remembered.

In her view, to the extent that the body is political, it tends to be unalterably political and if a new political philosophy is to be absorbed by a country's population, it is most easily learned by the country's children (1987:110). There is, for Scarry, a close interweave between body and state. And when there is a cleavage between body and state entrenched, as it was for blacks in southern Africa in their daily experiences, what implications does it have for the political identities of the bodies of the young?

Learning pain

The following piece drawn from the writings of Robert Levy (1973) offers an example of the cultural construction of pain. The pain here is not that brought about by social violence: it is more about social control and socialization, a culture's stance in the face of everyday pain. It is useful to consider as a counterpoint to individual responses to pain engendered in social crises or pain encountered in political actions. Levy (1973:435), working in Tahiti, observed how children's experiences are shaped, and how lessons are offered and learned repeatedly, lessons that may help explain the formation of some actions and some private meanings in adults. They influence adults towards a disposition that is brought to culturally structured situations, situations that are in themselves of considerable importance for maintaining private organization.

Levy gives examples of the effects of culturally influenced learning in psychological development and organization as it shapes expressions of pain by children. He observes that pain is a complex feeling state, involving more than elementary biological sensation. Differences in meaning seem to enter into perception itself and not only some later 'reaction' (1973: 309). As illustration, Levy describes an incident in which a child experienced pain:

> One day in Piri one of Uta's sons, eight years old, fell out of a tree at the other end of the village from his home. His upper arm was broken and clearly bent out of shape. Holding his forearm and elbow with his other arm, the boy walked to his family's house. His mother looked at him and, showing little emotion, told him to sit outside by the house. I asked her what she was going to do. She said that one of her brothers was good at setting bones and that when he came back from the fields he would take care of it. The boy sat for six hours before the uncle came home at his usual time. He sat quietly, obviously concerned, but looking neither anguished nor greatly frightened. When Uta himself saw the boy, he said to him, 'That will serve you right for climbing tall trees.'
>
> A few days later I asked Uta about his son. He said that they had not been able to make the arm straight when they set it and that it would be permanently curved. He laughed and said that would keep his son out of trees in the future (1973: 309).

Children in Piri, Levy adds, cry easily when they are punished or insulted, but those he saw in painful situations showed very little response to pain or were quiet and subdued (*ibid.*). He rejects explanations that hinge on 'comparatively gross behavioural inhibitions' like shame, and he looks for explanation of pain behaviour to more subtle aspects of the control and shaping of expression, to meanings given to injuries and illness, and to aspects of psychological organization (1973: 311). Adults' responses to children's pain form part ' … of a generalised socialization technique in which injuries and misfortunes are used for educational purposes and presented to the child as some deserved punishment by "nature", a punishment justly received for some wrong action of the child's' (*ibid.*). The socialization device makes use of only some pain-producing situations. Levy suggests that reactions to pain-inducing occurrences have something to do with the quality of the felt pain rather than only with the expression of pain. He cautiously wonders about aspects of symbolic meaning that might limit the troubling sides of felt pain (1973: 313). He suggests that, 'People suffered injuries, illnesses, and tooth loss not only with little expression of pain, but with little expression of anxiety or depression about any "threat to the body" ' (1973: 314). Levy suggests that questions of forms of conscience and fantasies of punishment, of body image, of attitudes about the body as an instrument for production and security, and of attitudes about the self in general, all come in here.

There are, he speculates, sets of convergent influences within particular societies that insure culturally-defined responses to selected situations. He imagines, further, that together with the sets of convergent influences go redundancies of control and that these are a necessary feature of most culturally determined behaviour (1973, 468). There are, of course, costs attached to all forms of control (or to lack of control).

A final example of the construction of pain, and the only one that is touched on here in relation to gender, is about the silence of girls in response to the infliction of pain on their bodies when they become sites of conflict. While working among young people in New Crossroads, an area of Greater Cape Town, Patti Henderson (1994:3) addressed the question of how the sexual expression of young girls is shaped by a particular style of parental discipline. The attempt by parents to circumscribe the sexuality of their daughters delineates the social spaces that young girls are expected to occupy. The space is inherently contradictory in the injunctions given to girls concerning their sexuality and in their variance with the social relations in which girls express themselves sexually. The physical person of the young girl becomes the site where contradictions meet and she becomes the object of blame and punishment. Henderson writes about the refusal of young girls to speak about the beatings or their sexual activities. The silence circumscribes the boundaries between generations and genders. She adds:

> Young girls, even though they often act defiantly in acting out their sexuality, are singularly silent about it. Their bodies become sites of punishment and their lack of verbal expression in asserting their sexuality and in response to punishment marks them as scapegoats for much larger social problems concerning reproduction in impoverished circumstances and the capacity of fragile and variable groups to care for the young …

In New Crossroads, male and female genders are naturalized through gender construction embodied in the way boys and girls are respectively taught to behave, their different spheres of work in the home, the different spaces which they occupy and the internalization of values attached to what is considered womanhood and manhood. The differences between the sexes are also marked through patterns of avoidance and respect even where these are contested in contemporary discourse.

Constructions of pain around the breaking of an arm are obviously quite different in quality from those around sexuality. However, in Levy's words, sets of convergent influences help to define responses in selected situations. Levy's questions of forms are pertinent in both Tahiti and New Crossroads. In the latter, the contradictions inherent in the girls' experiences are glaring and they revolve around issues to do with 'traditional' and contemporary sets of behaviour; fertility and virginity; obedience and self-assertion, none of which can be phrased in simple terms of either hierarchy or gender.

Conclusion

Drawing on three pieces of my own fieldwork and on other people's research, I have suggested that the hurts of children and youth are shaped and given expression (or hidden) by their context and cultural matrix. The hurts are often recognized and handled by particular persons like healers or mothers or other children who help those suffering to buttress themselves to withstand or explain these hurts often in practical, unsentimental ways. It is the close observation of instances and recognition of the subtleties of the commonplace that give these relationships their force. The relationships are given shape in everyday rituals, in the reaffirmation of bonds, and through links that form the active components of the support networks that are critical for children. The re-affirmation of bonds, expressed in small actions and in words, vary with context and age. And, as Moore (1994:77) suggests, actions themselves can be a type of critical reflection that does not necessarily have to involve conscious discursive strategizing.

Cultural contexts shape the experience and expression of pain. We have not examined carefully enough the effects of earlier handling of children's trauma on their ability to cope as young adults under stress. Is there a cultural imprint to the recognition and classification of suffering that modifies people's responses to a crisis like torture or solitary confinement? Or are other resources, not touched on by earlier experiences, called into play?

The theoretical questions that underlie these observations are to do with the cultural specificities of hurt and healing, and whether children experience and construct pain in ways that differ from adults. One question is the extent to which the rules, definitions and concepts originating in Western countries are applicable. I cannot answer such big questions. However, I suggest that actual experience, culturally shaped, has an input that significantly alters the outcome, that is, pain is not just 'pain'. Meanings, locally generated, alter that sense of pain. Besides, it is that local pain that is treated, not just 'pain' as universally defined. For children, the trivial, idiosyncratic inputs may be more significant, cumulatively, than the grand, obvious, exotic components of events: these inputs are only susceptible to micro-study. It is, perhaps, possible to see healers as contextualizing (and contextualized) therapists. I am suggesting the existence of theories of everyday experience at a level where local interpretations match up with wider generalizations.

I wish, quite simply, to draw attention to the need to recognize children's pain and the care that some communities take in handling it over a range of contexts and in keeping to a minimum ruptures of the lines of communication.

References

Agger, Inger. 1994. *The Blue Room. Trauma and Testimony among Refugee Women. A Psycho-social Exploration* (translated by Mary Bille). London: Zed Books.

Bourdieu, Pierre. 1977. *Outline of a Theory of Practice* (translated by Richard Nice and first published in French in 1972). Cambridge: Cambridge University Press.

Das, Veena. 1992. *Mirrors of Violence. Communities, Riots and Survivors in South Asia*. Delhi: Oxford University Press.

Dawes, Andrew & Donald, David. 1994. *Childhood and Adversity. Psychological Perspectives from South African Research*. Cape Town: David Philip.

Detainees' Parents Support Committee. 1986. *A Memorandum on Children under Repression*. Johannesburg: DPSC.

Dodge, C.P. & Raundalen, M. 1991. *Reading Children in War: Sudan, Uganda and Mozambique*. Bergen: Sigma Forlag.

Ellman, Richard. 1989. *Along the Riverrun. Selected Essays*. Harmondsworth, Middlesex: Penguin.

Epstein, Helen. 1979. *Children of the Holocaust. Conversation with Sons and Daughters of Survivors*. New York: G.P. Putnam.

Feldman, Allen. 1991. *Formation of Violence. The Narrative of the Body and Political Terror in Northern Ireland*. Chicago: University of Chicago Press.

Hannan, M. 1984. *Standard Shona Dictionary*. (Revised Edition with Addendum). Harare: College Press.

Harvey, Penelope & Gow, Peter. 1994. *Sex and Violence. Issues in Representation and Experience*. London: Routledge.

Heald, Suzette & Deluz, Ariane. 1994. *Anthropology and Psychoanalysis. An Encounter through Culture*. London: Routledge.

Henderson, Patti. 1994. 'Silence, Sex and Authority: the Contradictions of Young Girls' Sexuality in New Crossroads', *Vena* 6 (2).

Jones, A. 1994. 'Gender and Ethnic Conflict in ex-Yugoslavia'. *Ethnic and Racial Studies* 17 (2), January.

Lan, David. 1985. *Guns & Rain. Guerillas & Spirit Mediums in Zimbabwe*. London: James Currey.

Levy, Robert I. 1973. *Tahitians. Mind and Experience in the Society Islands*. Chicago: University of Chicago Press.

Lodge, T. B. Nasson et al. 1991. *All Here, and Now: Black Politics in South Africa in the 1980s*. Cape Town: David Philip.

Moore, Henrietta L. 1994. *A Passion for Difference. Essays in Anthropology and Gender*. Cambridge: Polity Press.

Reynolds, Pamela. 1989. *Childhood in Crossroads. Cognition and Society in South Africa*. Cape Town: David Philip

— 1990. 'Children of Tribulation: The Need to Heal and the Means to Heal War Trauma'. *Africa*, 60 (1) 1-38.

— 1995. 'Youth and the Politics of Culture in South Africa', in *Children and the Politics of Culture*. ed. Sharon Stephens. Princeton, NJ: Princeton University Press.

— 1996. *Traditional Healers and Childhood in Zimbabwe*. Athens, OH: Ohio University Press.

Riches, D. 1991. 'Aggression, War, Violence: Space/Time and Paradigm', *Man* (N.S.) 26: 281-98.

Scarry, Elaine. 1987. *The Body in Pain. The Making and Unmaking of the World*. New York: Oxford University Press.

Seremetakis, C.N. 1991. *The Last Word. Women, Death and Divination in Inner Mani*. Chicago: University of Chicago Press.

Straker, Gill. 1992. *Faces in the Revolution. The Psychological Effects of Violence on Township Youth in South Africa*. Cape Town: David Philip.

Swartz, L. & Levett, A. 1989. 'Political Repression and Children in South Africa. The Social Construction of Damaging Effects', *Social Science and Medicine* 28: 741-50.

Vittachi, Varinda Tarzie. 1993. *Between the Guns. Children as a Zone of Peace*. London: Hodder & Stoughton.

Westcott, S. 1988. *The Trial of the Thirteen*. Mowbray, Cape Town: The Black Sash.

Williams, Raymond. 1992. *Modern Tragedy* (first published in 1966). London: The Hogarth Press.

5

BRAD WEISS
The Barber in Pain
Consciousness, Affliction & Alterity in Urban East Africa

There can be little doubt that emerging understandings of the postcolony as a mode of 'illicit cohabitation' (Mbembe, 1992:4) have generated some of the most provocative and productive assessments of contemporary African culture and society. In their rejection of standard, oppositional dichotomies, scholars of Africa and elsewhere (Brown, 1996; De Boeck, 1996; Kaplan and Kelly, 1994) have turned their attention to the ways that dominant regimes and their dominated subjects collude in the production of spectacular, dramatic, and grotesque performances of power. Mbembe, in particular, emphasizes the postcolonial subject's ludic potential, the playful capacity for ridicule and ribaldry through which subjects both affirm the majesty of the *commandement*, and remake themselves, 'splintering' in Mbembe's terms, into myriad mutant personae (Mbembe, 1992). Most importantly, these 'subjects', the 'target populations' –the *cibles* – of officialdom, are not merely the mercurial witnesses and audiences for an absolutist authority. The 'conviviality' of domination demands that the preferences and values of the 'common man' are always already embedded in the banal performance of the *commandement*. We might ask, though, what form these 'common' and 'popular' values take. '[T]he official world,' writes Mbembe, 'mimics popular vulgarity, inserting it at the very core of the procedures by which it takes on grandeur' (1992: 10). To be sure, this critique directly confronts the fetishism of postcolonial hegemonies, and plainly demonstrates that even the most abstract authority fully realizes its efficacy in and through embodied representations and practices. Is the 'popular body,' though, of necessity banal and unbounded? Might popular consciousness be grasped in terms more compelling and complex than 'vulgarity' and 'down-to-earth realism'? Or are 'postcolonial subjects' bound to their regime to be likened to nineteenth-century French peasants, in Marx's celebrated phrase (Marx, [1852] 1978: 608), 'potatoes in a sackful of potatoes' glorified by Bonapartist splendour?

The elaboration of ever more disturbing, compelling, horrific, and uproarious exhibitions of command has clearly proliferated across the African continent (Ciekawy and Geschiere; 1998, Comaroff and Comaroff, 1999), and in our own backyard (Geschiere, 1998). It is the subjects' – and the subjective – participation in such spectacles of power that is the particular theoretical concern of this essay. Without wishing to disentangle the palpable entanglements of command, my aim is to shift the analytical focus from performances of statecraft which tend to take for granted the subjectivity of the state's subjects – more often a 'target population' subjected to authority than a people possessed of subjective intentions – and to investigate more closely the forms of consciousness that both motivate and are motivated by the spectacular. In particular, I am interested in processes of 'subjectification', the formulation, creation, and concretization of local and specific varieties of subjectivity (understood as lived experience, and capacities for action) that may be realized in the course of social life. As I hope to demonstrate, the generation of subjectivity is a crucial dimension of domination, for domination is itself a relationship between subjects endowed through their relations with different potentials for action.

The problematic possibilities of postcolonial subjects are only amplified when those subjects are postcolonial youth. The contradictory character of young people's lives, not only but perhaps especially in Africa, has been widely described. Simultaneously soldiers in the vanguard of social transformation and dangerous deviants, or 'social problems' par excellence, youth are often represented as – and even feel themselves to be – external to social totalities. This may be either because they are held in some ways to be 'unique' and thus transcend cultural and political forms (Malkki, 1997); or because they sense their own exclusion from sources of social value and power (Durham, n.d.). Central to this contradiction is the fact that, while cultural forms of popular practice often represent 'youth' as marginal and excluded – a theme that clearly resonates with many young men in Arusha today – 'youth culture' is absolutely *central* to the contemporary global production of culture. The implications of this contradiction are especially striking with respect to the forms of spectacle I shall be considering here, namely, the world of African-American hip hop and rap, and the compelling allure these have for young men in Arusha. In the musical and wider stylistic forms of hip hop and gangsta rap that are a central focus of Arusha's own 'youth culture,' the counter-hegemonic and oppositional possibilities of young people are *hegemonically* celebrated – indeed, sold – as icons of power and value of the highest order. Part of the argument of this chapter is that such ambiguities are central to the dynamic that characterizes the agency and experience of Arusha's youth. Their sense of themselves as 'submerged by power' (Coulter, 1998) is, I shall argue, also a *means* – perhaps one especially available to 'youth' among all the disenfranchised – to *engage* power.

It is certainly clear that the profusion of globally mediated images and expanding possibilities for mass consumption, which are central to the discussion that follows, have altered frameworks for social participation, fostering new alliances, modes of patronage, and generating novel – and contested – voices. All of these processes and institutions of interaction inform the new constructions of identity widely lionized in so much contemporary work. Again, without meaning to dismiss the vitality of these novel social constructions, I aim to show that not only identity – the forms of representation through which social beings come to know (i.e., to identify) themselves and others – but personhood – the relative ability to participate in, and so define oneself through processes of social construction (including identity formation) – can be usefully examined.[1] Exploring personhood further entails addressing both the shifting terms in which personhood can be recognized by means of new relations between persons and objects, and the engendering of new motivations and desires, as well as the dynamics of characterizing and enacting persons that resonate with more enduring patterns of sociality.

---

[1] My differentiation between identity and personhood as aspects of subjectivity is plainly an analytical construction. In practice, the ability to act on the world is ineluctably wedded to social agents' sense of who they are, and how others know and recognize (and authorize) the agents' acts – persons have identity, and this informs their personhood Nonetheless, I think it is useful to distinguish between the range of potential actions possible in a given context, and the enactment of particular actions that come to define, and so differentiate, particular kinds of actors.

Urban Scenes and Suffering

The ethnographic context for the consideration of these questions is at once broader than the postcolonial state and narrower than a complex, spectacular performance. In the summer of 1999 I began to hang out in barbershops – *kinyozi*, in Swahili (*vinyozi*, pl.) – in Arusha, in northern Tanzania. Arusha, a city celebrated in the almost completely obliterated history of African Socialism as the site of Nyerere's Arusha Declaration, the capital of the erstwhile East African Union, is now a thoroughly global cosmopolis. It is home to both the International War Crimes Tribunal on Rwanda and the current peace talks on Burundi, as well as the gateway to the Serengeti and Kilimanjaro. Thus, it abounds with UN representatives and tourists that range from the backpacking masses to the Abercrombie and Kent coterie. It is also a burgeoning, socially complex, inter-ethnic town. Commercial enterprise is still largely dominated by a prosperous Asian community (Peligal, pers. comm.); a rift between Pentacostal and Lutheran dioceses has torn Christian communities apart in recent years (Baroin, 1996); while WaArusha and WaMeru are the predominant peoples who reside on the farms ascending Mount Meru, Arusha itself is a town of relative newcomers from virtually every region in Tanzania, with especially large communities that retain ties to the Coast (from Dar es Salaam to Tanga), Tabora to the Southwest, and Kilimanjaro and the Pare mountains to the East.

Terms like 'the local' and 'the global' do exceedingly rough justice to the way in which the totality of these relationships can be articulated in Arusha. Nonetheless, these social threads *are* articulated, even in such mundane venues as the aforementioned barbershops. Indeed, barbershops are explicitly and self-consciously *about* creating and demonstrating these connections. The staff and clientele at most barbershops spend much of their time in the shop reading an assortment of daily and weekly papers, and listening to taped and broadcast music performed in French, Lingala, English, and occasionally Swahili. In a great many establishments one can watch satellite television broadcasts from the UK, South Africa, India, and the US. As others have noted (Ferguson, 1999), contemporary popular styles in much of Africa are never simply an appropriation of 'Western fashion'. For popular culture in Arusha includes: an interest in Congolese *bolingo* (née Rhumba; Remes, 1999) as well as (or, for some, in opposition to) gangsta rap music, Nigerian and West Indian footballers alongside American basketball stars (see Figure 5.1), soap operas from South Africa and the US, and religious education programmes infused with Saudi capital, or German and American evangelists. In barbershops the ubiquitous posters that display a range of hairstyles for clients are an apt icon of this polygenesis. Each poster is a pastiche of headshots, cut-outs from glossies like *Vibe* and *WordUp*, extracted from advertising copy for 'Dark & Lovely' hair-care products, or simply snipped from past years' barbering posters, then compiled, printed and reproduced (as was every such poster I saw in Arusha) in Nigeria.

There has been a true proliferation in this array of commodity forms during the last decade in Tanzania. Structural adjustment that liberalized a one-party socialist state led not only to a meagre influx of corporate capital; it also permitted wealthy Tanzanians to display accumulated fortunes without sequestering assets in offshore accounts – and with overseas kin. Predictably, the 'boom' of investment in the first years of this neo-liberal transition has given way to a massive 'bust', as inflationary pressures and unemployment today escalate to levels as perilous as any in the socialist era. Under these conditions a great many residents of Arusha are acutely aware of a radical rupture, not simply in their standard of living, but in their shattered expectations. Such senses of rupture are increasingly standardized in Africa's neo-liberal era (Comaroff and Comaroff, 1999; Ferguson, 1999; White, 1999). The growth of foreign and domestic media, and the introduction of new goods, and the veil that has been lifted from what was once hidden wealth, produce a clear recognition of the complex and compelling forms that value can take under globalization, as well as a pressing frustration that such values are only available to a fragment of the globalized world of which Tanzania finds itself a part. There is an ongoing commentary on the decline of resources – jobs, most particularly – throughout Tanzania, as well as a devastating understanding for many Tanzanians that the allure and promise held by the early 1990s may never be achieved again in their lifetimes. The presidency of Benjamin Mkapa is now described as *Ukapa* (lit. 'The era of defeat,' or 'downfall'), a tragically ironic pun that provides an all too accurate grasp of current (mis)fortunes.

Arusha's barbershops have also proliferated apace with the expansion of consumerism, and its increasing intangibility. It is no exaggeration to say that there are hundreds of barbers in town, most of which date to the last five years. Many blocks in town have a dozen or more such shops (the two square blocks around the central bus station are home to over thirty), and the tarmac road to Nairobi is lined with small commercial zones, each of which has at least one barbershop. Furthermore, the political and economic transformations just described are embedded in these shops. The barbershops' promotion of, and participation in, the spread of mass mediated imagery, objects, and motivations, as well as the economic conditions that permit such 'informal' enterprises to flourish (and rapidly wither) shape both the form and the content of the *kinyozi*. The barbershop, I shall argue, is a location – as well as a space of the imaginary – where clients and workers typically confront the hardships that their own social practice and position exemplifies.

Analytical attention to sites like barbershops in which consumption is grasped as a practice with a productive potential often focuses on the creative, dynamic, playful forms that consumption can take (Miller, 1994; Friedman, 1990a; Hansen, 1999). The fabrication and bricolage of consumerist practice have been seized upon by much of social science as perhaps the most central contemporary arena for mounting exhibitions of hybridity and creolization (Hannerz, 1996). In consuming, marginalized subjects are able to rework disparate signs, forms, and materials for the conveyance of powerful countermessages, subaltern identities, and disruptive mimicry, all of which demonstrate positive, assertive (and perhaps authentic?) voices. Young people, it is said, are some of the most important and the more complex subjects in this process. Again, the contradictions are to the fore: young people are both 'targeted' as 'audiences', and so made complicit cohorts in a global spectacle of 'popular' domination; yet they are also authorized by popular culture, presented with possibilities for creative assertion. Much of the activity in Arusha's barbershops could well be characterized in these terms, as young men – and more than a few young women – combine a diverse and (to a 'Western' observer, at least) unanticipated array of popular styles (country music AND hip hop clothing AND devotion to Islam, for example) in ways that incisively participate in what are often fractious, local political tournaments of identity. By now, studies of a vibrant popular cultural scene, insurgent in the face of global downsizing, important, compelling, and necessary though these studies may still be, have become something of a commonplace. In contrast, the socio-cultural (and not simply political economic) significance of subjugation is frequently approached simply as an absence of assertive capacity. Talk about subjugation often threatens to shatter the agency of those who endure it. If there are 'weapons of the weak', weakness *per se* is not often counted among them. Discussions of social misery all too easily reduce the experience and expression of oppression to mere evidence of dependency, if not deprivation; but the concrete forms in which such suffering is felt and lived are rarely explored in themselves as *meaningful* socio-cultural phenomena. Indeed, the forms of decline and anomie widespread in Arusha today are often taken as the very antithesis of meaningfulness. Ferguson (1999:19), for example, holds that this pervasive misery can

> confound one of the most basic anthropological expectations of fieldwork – the idea that by immersing oneself in the way of life of 'others,' one gradually comes to understand and make sense of their social world. What happens to anthropological understanding in a situation where 'the natives' as well as the ethnographer lack a good understanding of what is going on around them? What if 'the local people', like the anthropologist, feel out of place, alienated, and unconnected with much of what they see?

Aside from the fact that this challenge to a putative anthropology (one that asserts that 'the natives' constitute a uniform, stable community isomorphic with a set of clearly delineated, systematically organized cultural categories) amounts to the critique of a straw man (see Sahlins 1999), Ferguson's puzzlement seems curiously unfamiliar with the fact that anthropology, for as long as there have been anthropologists (and nowhere more than in Africa), has made attempts to comprehend the *experience* of rupture, discontinuity, and alienation of precisely the sort that Ferguson describes on the Copperbelt. We may certainly debate the merits of different approaches to the study of affliction, and ask whether theories of suffering and alienation, and the host of practices through which communities attempt to manage them, amount to anything more than functionalist explanations premised on social reproduction. Still, it is at least worth recognizing that not all anthropology proceeds from the same assumptions, and that questions like these may have been asked before.

There are further, and to my mind more fundamental, grounds for asserting that hardship and dis-ease deserve to be explored as cultural – which is to say, meaningful – forms of experience. Confusion and disarray are no less capable of being articulated, interpreted, and engaged with than are order and stability – indeed, they seem to *demand* concerted attention. Both the characterization of chaos and sustained efforts to remedy it can be communicated to others, and so form the grounds for active intervention. There are certainly ineffable and inchoate features to suffering, but cultural understanding need not require that all those who express their frustration have identical experiences. Moreover, distress is never simply an abstract or generalizable emotion or condition, but is always realized with respect to concrete circumstances. Surely Baudelaire's *ennui*, vague and indeterminate as it may have felt, is distinctly different from the fear and humiliation of losing a job, or the grief and disbelief of a lost pregnancy. The meaningful differences between these qualities of torment derive from the ways that affliction is inextricably grounded in a wider world. These grievances speak to the subjective perception that certain specific contours of a sensible world of well-being have been rendered senseless. Affliction is a phenomenon whose attributes are, themselves, significant, and so can be understood and acted upon in specific ways; and it further reveals, by negation, the lineaments of the taken-for-granted order called into question by affliction. An understanding of affliction and its management, perhaps especially in the Africa context, may help us to grasp the contemporary experience of rupture and distress in Arusha. To anticipate my concluding discussion more concretely, I shall argue that there are ways that the forms of subjectivity organized by 'spectacular' modes of domination, and the conviviality afforded by consuming these spectacles, resonate with the *constitution* and *transformation* of subjectivities often brought about in 'cults of affliction,' and possession cults, in particular. Participation in the practices of popular culture, like participation in cults of possession, provides a means of both defining and confronting powerful sources of oppression, and of defining one's self in relation to such masterful powers. This parallel builds on the indispensable observation that misfortune is always a potent index of an encompassing cultural reality – not a static 'system', rule-governed and uniform, but a world of meanings and values, broadly and unevenly *shared*, that makes sociality possible.

Kijiwe – A Place to Work, a Place to Think

If we are to explore this wider world within Arusha's barbershops, we might first ask: what kind of space is a barbershop?[2] To begin with, let me consider in turn two interrelated aspects of barbershops: they are both places of work and public spaces. As a site of business, the barbershop milieu bespeaks both the social crises of neo-liberal transition in Tanzania, already alluded to, as well as the *meanings* of these institutional shifts and the kinds of consciousness embedded in them, that is the pervasive sense of rupture, and especially of unrealized expectations. While anyone with scissors and a stool can establish themselves as a barber in the city's market (and not a few attempt to do so), maintaining a moderately successful barbershop requires some sources of investment, as well as cultural competence in the popular forms of barbering. Rents must be paid, infrastructural maintenance is required to assure an adequate supply of electricity, proper electric razors, aprons for clients, and hair care products all must be provided. And all of this independent of the costs of generating the sounds and scenes that make a barbershop attractive, the newspapers, radios and cassettes, even satellite TV that clients can partake of. What this means is that barbers and their clients tend to be young men with a significant degree of formal education (many spoke better English than some Tanzanian university graduates I know) and access to investors with small amounts of capital sufficient only to maintain an informal, and always quite tenuous, operation. There is, then, an intensely felt juxtaposition of a wider familiarity with not only the 'images' but also the material forms of success, as well as some – albeit limited – connection to persons who enjoy such success, in contrast with the declining real opportunities to enjoy these values and fully participate in the world they embody. Not surprisingly, this juxtaposition meant that all the young barbers I spoke to saw their jobs as a compromise. For some it was the best they could do until something better came along. For a great many, the tremendous promise of life in the city, especially for young men from more 'provincial' parts of Tanzania who had completed secondary school, was abruptly confronted with the reality of working in a barbershop. This juxtaposition of expansive potential and declining opportunities – perhaps the one unifying feature of 'African youth' (Cruise O'Brien, 1996) – is a central dimension, not only of these young men's biographies, but of the forms of social life they create.

At the same time, it must be noted that barbershops, as sites within a regional political economy, afford a degree of opportunity, and a sense of entitlement that is otherwise unavailable to an expanding disenfranchised population. As some barbers put it, a *kiny-*

[2] The account here is excessively brief, given limitations of space; see Weiss (2002) for fuller discussion.

ozi is a place where one can be independent, where you did not need to work for some 'boss'. While there are, as I have indicated, infrastructural expenses required to open a barbershop, these costs are significantly less than those associated with other businesses. Opening a retail shop or bar requires substantial capital to manage inventories and to pay for licence fees (which barbers are notorious for avoiding). Even the smallest hair salons (or 'saloons' in the orthographic preference of English-speaking Africans) require much more expensive machinery (for example, dryers, steamers, electric kettles for boiling water), and make much more extensive use of hair care products (virtually every customer at a salon will be treated with some commercial product, from relaxer to cholesterol, or other petroleum-based gels) than is needed for keeping a *kinyozi* afloat. Furthermore, I was struck by the fact that barbering is treated as a kind of 'profession' by young men with virtually no formal training in hair-cutting. For example, it is not uncommon for barbershops to close for lack of business, or the sudden withdrawal of a patron. Under such circumstances, young men who had initially taken up barbering simply because they could find no other work, will generally continue to look for work as barbers, rather than seeking some other kind of work. Many of these barbers indicated to me that they saw their work as a set of skills that they had 'learned' and they hoped to use this *elimu*, 'education', to get ahead in town. Moreover, these skills and the work of barbering were embraced as signs of a certain sophistication and, at a minimum, of a competence and mastery over the forms of urban living. Barbershops, as virtually all barbers told me, are never found in villages, where people have neither the electricity required for mechanized razors, nor the 'education' to appreciate a stylish cut. One barber told me, as he gracefully shaved a client's hair, 'My hands cannot even use a razor blade any longer'. Barbering, as this statement eloquently reveals, can be a testament to the skillful mastery of an urban lifestyle under conditions of material constraint.[3]

These political economic features of the barbershop as a place of work – a site of hardship and marginality, as well as urban distinction and entitlement – are directly relevant to the *kinyozi* as a public space. I use the term, 'public', knowing that it is ideologically fraught, immediately suggesting an opposition to a 'private' domain, but the public quality of the barbershop really transcends this opposition. Barbershops are 'private enterprises' but their existence depends upon their ability to participate in and to make a public. The display (and performance) of a barbershop is intended to publicize the shop in a dual sense; to promote it as an attractive, contemporary establishment, and also to demonstrate that the shop and its denizens are of the public, that they are hooked into a reality outside of the shop, beyond even the here and now of Arusha and Tanzania. It is surely no accident that the bus station and Nairobi Road, places of perpetual movement and connection, are the most visibly, densely concentrated sites of *vinyozi*.

An important part of the public character of barbershops is, therefore, their permeability, the ways in which they are ever oriented beyond themselves. This is made evident not only through the shops' representations – the images, sounds, and styles that explicitly reference Brooklyn, California, Liverpool, Kinshasa, Kosovo, etc. – it is equally true of the socio-spatial form that the shops take. A *kinyozi* is an exposed arena, its front door always open during business hours, and a social flow of staff, clients and visitors perpetually traversing a series of thresholds that encompass the shop. Clients getting haircuts joke with friends within earshot outside the door; next to the *kinyozi* door is a small

[3] For a compelling discussion of the ways that women's hair styling in contemporary Tanzania has been shaped by public discourse about both Tanzania's marginality, its efforts at economic self-reliance, and contemporary efforts to become 'modern' under conditions of liberalization, see Stambach (1999).

sitting area, lined with small benches, perhaps a chair or two; clients wait, idle barbers chat among themselves, with customers, with neighbouring shopkeepers, with passing friends in a continuous movement from barber's chairs to waiting area, outside the shop, and into the street and back again. Shoeshine stands are frequently adjacent to a shop, providing a service that contributes to the stylistic accomplishment of a good haircut, but also adding a venue for conversation, a place to wait, to watch, to talk (see pictures). *Vinyozi* actively insert themselves *mtaani* – 'into the street', with barbers and clients calling out to passersby, leaving their seats to accompany girlfriends and *fanya biashara* – 'do business' down the block before returning to the shop. Lest this 'public' character be construed in functional terms as simply 'good for business', it is important to point out that this public style is a specific feature of barbershops. The expansiveness unmistakably contrasts with women's hair 'saloons', which are closed off to the street, and always behind a curtain (typically), if not a closed door. Nor were there any salons at the bus stand in 1999 and 2000. The contrast is also clear in comparison with barbershops frequented and owned by Asians, on the high street of Arusha, with closed doors, and no visible publicizing of their establishment other than a simple barber's pole.

As an aspect of its public character, the barbershop also enfolds the street into itself. Passersby and clients do not enter into the social field of the shop indifferently, all must make their presence felt by shaking hands (always a performance that demonstrates semiotic virtuosity) and greeting everyone assembled at the *kinyozi* – gestures that must be repeated in reverse when anyone takes their leave. These gestures are crucial to the spatiality of the barbershop, for they establish that a shop, which is open and accessible in its attachments to the world, is also framed and circumscribed as a social field, never simply a motley array of people. In all of these modes of constructing space, the social practices of the barbershop confirm its character as a distinctive *place*.

In everyday parlance in Arusha, a barbershop, as a place, is a *kijiwe*, 'a little stone'. This diminutive harkens to rural social forms and places, a small stone, a recognized spot, around which (male) villagers gather to rest and relax, knowing that they are sure to find good company. The stylistic performances of a *kinyozi* are complex and changing, but every shop – like every *kijiwe* – is indispensably a place of conversation and companionship. They are places to be among others.[4] This kind of social interaction is explicitly described as important to one's sense of belonging, as well as well-being. The barbershop is a place to *punguza mawazo*, 'ease your worries'. *Mawazo* are a central concern of the barbershop – and of everyday life in Arusha – and are a semantically complex term. In the context just described, *mawazo* can be translated as 'worries', or 'troubles'. But in most contexts, *mawazo* are 'thoughts', and 'worries/troubles' are precisely one particular variety of thought.[5] As Fabian has perceptively noted for Swahili speakers in Shaba, equally consumed by *mawazo*, ([1978] 1997: 23), 'thought ... is not neutral ratiocination; it is active imagination'. While Swahili speakers in Arusha do not, to my knowledge, describe themselves as 'thinking', or use the verb *kuwaza* (in the Arusha vernacular, 'to think' is *kufikiri*) as they do in Shaba, men and women in Arusha do describe themselves as 'having thoughts' – *kuwa na mawazo*. This understanding of 'having thoughts' also

---

[4] The importance of barbershops as centres of sociality in the African diaspora has been widely noted; to my knowledge, little work has been done on barbershops in East Africa.

[5] In Luhaya, as well, 'worries/troubles' are characteristically described as 'thoughts,' *ebitekelezo*. Here, the term is not a cognate of the Swahili, so the term is not simply 'borrowed' by Haya speakers to describe their troubles. This suggests, if tentatively, that the link between 'thoughts' and 'worries' is a widespread semantic association in East Africa.

moves 'thoughts' beyond conceptualization, and points to a condition of activity – indeed, as I shall argue, a condition of bodily activity. What is further clear from commonplace discussion in Arusha about 'having thoughts [troubles/worries]' and 'easing thoughts [troubles/worries]' is that – paradoxically, perhaps, from the perspective of 'Western' forms of personhood – thinking is not only an active process, it is quintessentially a *felt* process.

As an active processes, 'thinking' or 'having thoughts' is never just 'thinking about' things, a detached contemplation of reality; rather, what is emphasized is a 'thinking *towards*' some anticipated (or dreaded) possibility. Tshibumba persistently describes his practice of painting as a form of 'thinking', Fabian tells us, and sees his paintings as realizations of *mawazo yangu*, 'my thoughts' (Fabian, 1996). Similarly, in Jamaa practice,[6] 'dreams', which are synonymous with 'thoughts', are sources of prophecy, revelations of things yet to come (Fabian [1978] 1997: 23). In all these ways, 'thoughts' are ways of *working through* life's circumstances, forms of creative practice that imaginatively select, organize, and communicate what is ultimately significant. In Arusha, and in barbershops especially, 'having thoughts' is not only about creatively working through present conditions so as to realize a meaningful future; it is about *confronting* the present as an obstacle to that realization. In 'having thoughts', one encounters an unknowable range of possibilities. For one who 'has thoughts', the future is an open prospect, and for that very reason thinking is demanded in order to *generate* the future as a knowable, viable certainty. For young men in Arusha today, in positions of such tenuous employment as barbershops, the depths of this uncertainty – the profound gap between one's severely limited, or intractable present, conditions, and the limitless prospects of the future – confront the 'thinking' subject as a formidable obstacle. So formidable, I would argue, that subjects (the young men gathered in the *kinyozi*) are less the agents of their own 'thinking,' than they are overwhelmed by 'thoughts' which *act on them*.

This formulation of subjectivity and personhood is central to much of the discussion that follows. I want to point out here that this characterization of 'having thoughts' means that 'thinking' is not only an imaginative and creative process; to think, in these ways, is to *suffer*, to be in pain. This pain is characteristically premised upon an absence, or a void. The chasm between now and later, the unknown prospect of the future, is one such absence, and it is one to which 'thoughts' incessantly return. One young man I met daily talked a good deal about his mother who had recently died. She had been a teacher, and before her death she had not only helped to educate five of her children, but also instilled in them a desire for education (and an expectation that education would provide for them in the future). This value was put into practice each day as my friend spoke to me in English, demonstrating how well he had learned, and how much he hoped still to learn. He also commented frequently on the fact that his mother had died leaving him, as her eldest child, to care for his siblings, all of whom were still at home in Central Tanzania. But the education his mother provided had not assured any of them the opportunities that she – and he – expected.

One day as I sat silently with him in the empty barbershop he revealed to me that he had dreamt that night of his dead mother. Without mentioning all of the responsibilities he shouldered, or plans he was pursuing – which were typical topics of discussion on other days – he simply told me '*kichwa kinajaa na mawazo*' 'my head is full of thoughts'. The dreams that Jamaa depends upon for prophecy (itself predicated on an unknown

---

[6] Jamaa is a charismatic movement in Congo (see Fabian, 1978).

future) are here dreams of loss, and distance, and separation, and unrealized possibilities – all manifest absences. This absence seems inevitably to flood with thoughts. Moreover, the felt qualities of thought, the painful process of being overcome by worries, are plainly embodied experiences – 'my head is full of thoughts'. Thinking is not just experienced as the active doing of thought, it is perceived as the accumulation of *mawazo mengi,* 'many thoughts', as thoughts that take on weight and mass. The volume of thoughts makes your 'head feel jumbled,' *kichwa kinachangayika.* Indeed, thoughts of this kind are *gumu* 'hard' and they are 'pain/bitterness' itself, *uchungu*; thus, productive social interaction works to *punguza* 'decrease' or 'lighten' one's thoughts. I once asked a painter I knew well to paint some portraits for me. Seifu, who was almost invariably smiling and joking with me, suddenly looked remarkably dour. 'Are you ill?' I asked him. 'No,' he said, 'when you get a job like this, your head starts to hurt' (*kichwa kinaumwa*). Even the creative process of working through the present and prospectively imagining the future is a source of bodily pain.

The Power of Pain

While suffering and bodily pain of the sort described often seem irreducibly personal, individuating, and isolating, it is important to recognize that they are also subjective conditions of encountering the world, and in this regard they are active *practices*. Pain, moreover, is a *social* mode of consciousness. It is about 'others' in a variety of ways. There is pain in sharing the injustices that characterize social life, in readying oneself with others for the hardships one has to endure. Pain also involves caring for others. The young men gathered in barbershops are familiar with one another's stories of the struggles they face everyday, not only because they face the same struggles themselves, but also because the *kinyozi*, as I have indicated, is a place where conversation works to 'ease your worries'. But suffering is social, not only because it is set in a collective context and shared, but also in the sense that it is itself a manner of *relating* to others and the world. As Asad notes in his discussion of pain in medieval Christianity, the monastic's body is made to testify to the truth of Christian virtues *by means of* social relationships (Asad, 1983: 313 ff.). The monastic's pain is truth as *revealed* to those who observe, authorize, and discipline him. Pain is the medium through which monastic brothers, and (in a radically different context) Arusha's youth, enact sociality. Never simply an internalized condition, a silent lament – nor a mere impediment to pleasure, or the 'repression' of the 'pain-free' self – suffering is a dimension of engaging with reality as it presents itself to the active subject. Pain, then, is being-in-the-world.

There are ways in which the phenomenology, or what we might call the generativity, of pain is realized and acted upon in young men's social world. Pain can be grasped as both a defining feature of personhood and the grounds for sustained sociality. In a conversation about local clubs in Arusha, I asked a young barbershop crowd about a place I knew to be especially popular. I was surprised to hear them dismiss the place as one they would never go to, and especially to show disdain for the typical clientele of the club. The men who frequent these places see themselves as 'special,' an English word in everyday use, especially to describe a manner of flashy and ostentatious dress – and a term which also betokens the *singularity* of one who sees himself as special, different and distinct from others. These club patrons were further characterized as *msenge*, current slang for 'fag,' who – somewhat paradoxically – are only interested in attracting women. The patrons at this club, I was told, 'would buy a beer for a girl before they would even buy one of their male friends a soda!' Wasn't this OK? I asked. Not at all! Even if a girl begged him, said one guy, he would only spend his money on his male friends.[7] A woman, he continued, did not deserve the respect of your 'boys', your 'niggas' (both words used in English) because '*tupo mitaani, sisi, tunaSURVIVE!*' – 'we're in the streets, we SURVIVE!' For this young man, and the group that laughed and approved of his account, the 'streets' and 'survival' are paramount features of a social world; indeed, they are icons of a world that is rife with *pain*, and so values survival. Most importantly, the capacity to 'survive' – to endure through struggle, to never give in to 'weakness' (especially a weakness for women) – is a central attribute of the person. 'Survival' is something one can only achieve through this social world 'on the streets', and it further *qualifies* one to participate in this world. Without a capacity to confront pain, one is less than fully human. Indeed, one guy described the indignity of slavery by saying, 'When the master says "I have an ache", the slave answers, "Boss, I'm in pain".' If I am subject to the pain of others in ways that strictly dictate my ability to face my own pains, my very existence as a person is denied.

I have been attempting to sketch an understanding of pain as a form of consciousness that can be grasped as a generative, productive, perhaps even positive attribute of persons and their social relations. If we approach the affliction of pain in this way it may be possible to see how the very *subjugation* of pain – the subject's sense of being acted upon by 'thoughts,' of struggling to 'survive' – may provide a means to its own resolution, if not absolute transcendence. As pain is an attribute of the person that bespeaks one's subjugation – without which one would not be in pain – pain can become a means of access to the source of that subjugation. In other words, the pain that a subject endures makes them *available* to some subjugating force, and may, therefore, provide a means of dealing with – if not overcoming – that force.

Let me offer a comparative example, worlds away from Arusha's urban barbershops, if not all that far from Tanzania's borders, that illustrates how this process of managing subjugation might work. Lienhardt describes the role of what he calls 'Powers' in Dinka experience, which are held to be 'the grounds of a particular human condition', which is to say responsible for human misery (Lienhardt, 1961: 148). In attempting to counter these deleterious effects, Dinka will not only try to identify the Power that has attacked them, they will further, and quite literally, identify *with* the threatening force. Hence, the (relatively) celebrated case of the man who, 'having been imprisoned in Khartoum named one of his children 'Khartoum' in memory of the place, but also *to turn aside any harmful influence* of that place upon him in later life' (*ibid.*, 1961: 149-50, emphasis added). Here, the one-time prisoner engages in what Lienhardt would call 'symbolic action', creating a model, or image, which captures an existential condition in order to act upon that model, and thereby transform the lived condition. In creating an image of Khartoum, this man produces an *identification* with the source of his enduring subjugation, and through that identification establishes a means to exert control over this oppressive force. Note, moreover, that the man does not attempt to *eradicate* the presence of Khartoum in his life, which will ideally endure long after him through his own children. Rather, he makes of Khartoum an image of self-identification (as a Dinka man's children are inexorably aspects of himself) so as to *partake* of the very power that Khartoum has

---

[7] The qualities of personhood and sociality iconically presented in 'pain' are unmistakably masculine qualities – as are the modes of display and consumption enacted in the popular cultural practices of the barbershop community. I address this in more detail in Weiss (2002).

to oppress him. In this way, the man becomes more like Khartoum, and his own recognition of the very subjugation to this threatening 'Power' provides a means of becoming more 'Power'-ful himself.

From a certain perspective the dynamics of 'pain' and 'survival', as I have described them, can be understood in similar terms. It is 'pain' itself that certifies one's standing as a person, an *mdumu* (literally, 'tough/hard person'), a *muhuni* (a 'wayward' person, today often eloquently translated as 'thug,') a 'street nigga'. Embracing this oppressive power as a means of self-identification thus provides a direct means of countering that oppression, as the recurrent discussion of 'pain', 'bitterness' and especially 'thoughts' enables the barbers in pain to engage more fully in a world that permits them to confront that pain, through 'survival' and, at moments, the 'easing of worries'. To experience, and self-consciously identify oneself, as one who suffers is, thus, simultaneously an act of diminution *and* an assertion of entitlement. Pain for the young male urbanites in Arusha is the bodily trace of injustice and oppression, but it also presents an affirmation of one's ongoing confrontation with obstacles, a process of grappling with life's troubles that defines existence itself. To suffer pain is to demonstrate oneself to be one who endures through adversity. By identifying themselves with pain, these young men thereby articulate and index the larger purposes – even the transcendent reality – for which they tolerate such hardship; for 'life in the street', the respect of one's 'thugs', as well as the care of one's kin. In this they are akin to the boxers Wacquant describes in Chicago, who 'have at their disposal a rich occupational vocabulary that enables them to confront pain . . . not with silent denial but with personal valorization and collective solemnization' (Wacquant, 1998:337). Pain, then, is not so much overcome as it is seized upon as a means of identification with the wider reality that is painful, and for which one faces pain.

Possessed by Pain

The predominant features of personhood, action, and sociality that are iconically expressed as pain go a long way, I would argue, towards elucidating the lived experience of everyday encounters for a great many urban youth in Arusha. Pain is an embodied quality, both produced by and generative of a kind of micropolitics of social life. This is a micropolitics found not only in barbershops but at the bus stand; in the breakneck competition of *dala dala* (minivan transport) crews; among the working staff of bars and *nyama choma* (lit, 'roast meat') joints; and the peddlers of *mitumbaa* (used clothing), all of whom scramble for a living, striving *kutafuta maisha*, 'to find a life', in town. Pain is the generative principle of the habitus of Arusha's informal sector. While this immediate, face-to-face lived reality is dynamic and even cohesive (if never systematically so), this micro-order of practice is only incompletely understood when considered exclusively at this level of social action. Pain is a very public discourse, and the barbershops have to be seen as one especially lively node in a *wider* public in which they participate.

This broader public projects the significance of pain in mediated signs and images that have a far-flung – indeed, global – circulation. For Arusha's young men perhaps the most compelling global signs and images of personhood – and especially of a public persona – are embedded in the world of rap and hip hop music and style. Barbershops throughout town are painted with icons of the most celebrated performers, and shops repaint (and re-paper their interiors) with new and different icons as fashions – and reputations – shift. Even those shops which do not blare gangsta rap music from their radios and tape decks, or cater to a clientele that prefers bolingo or R&B sounds, are still bedecked with images that derive from an African-American gangsta iconography. As I shall demonstrate below, the potency of these images, and the modes of personhood they exhibit, can and should be tied to the ongoing concerns with pain and suffering that characterize lived experience on Arusha's streets. I argue, therefore, that to fully grasp the import of pain, and to see how it motivates and formulates subjectivity and domination – to return to the 'spectacular' themes raised in my introduction – we need to situate the socio-cultural practices of thugs in barbershops in this context of a global imaginary, which is to say, within a wider cosmology.

Anyone with a passing familiarity with the sights and sounds, the lore and life of hip hop in the United States will recognize that pain is a widely proclaimed motif of this popular cultural scene. The violent deaths of Biggie Smalls (Notorious B.I.G.), Freaky Tah, MC Big L, and paradigmatically Tupac Shakur are not only evidence of the suffering characteristic of the rap and hip hop world. They are also comprehensible as inevitable – even predictable – outcomes of a life dominated by an intensely competitive struggle in a world of pain. Tupac is often described (in the American press) as having a 'messiah complex' with tracks like 'Only God Can Judge Me', 'How Long Will They Mourn Me', 'No More Pain', and 'Check Out Time'; his crucified appearance on the album cover of *Makaveli: The Don Killuminati*: the crucifix tattooed across his back; and his series of posthumous albums, including *Still I Rise* (or B.I.G.'s new release, *Born Again*). There are web pages dedicated to the Tupac 'Legend: Dead or Alive?' The suffering directly addressed in gangsta rap is never simply a way of decrying the social conditions of racial and economic struggle in the US (although this is not to be overlooked). Rather, pain is a focal point for constructing a social persona, for creating, enhancing, and demonstrating the viability of one's reputation. The reputation for pain – *Me Against the World*, 'So Many Tears' – that Tupac promoted, and that disciples like DMX profess in 'Ready to Meet Him' ('Lord, you left me stranded / And I don't know why / Told me to live my life, / Now I'm ready to die / Ready to fly / I cry, but I shed no tears ... I'm really tryin' to win, so where do we start? / (Thou shall not steal) /But, what if he stole from me? / (Thou shall not kill)/ But what if he's tryin' to kill me? / (Thou shall not, take my, name in vain, no matter how hard it rains, withstand the pain')) – challenges pain by working through it and identifying with it. Respect and reputation accrue not to those who project an implacable self-image, but to those who live with pain, and thereby show that they have the strength to endure – 'withstand the pain'. Again, such a world, and the kinds of persons that inhabit it, are dependent on the ongoing experience of pain.

It is clear that these models of subjectivity promoted and disseminated in the global imaginary of hip hop have profoundly shaped the consciousness of pain I have described in Arusha. Young men in town routinely describe and avow the hardships that they face by means of forms that derive directly from the world of hip hop. This avowal can be seen in slogans on *dala dala* such as '100% Pure Pain' and 'Suffer and Survive', and names of barbershops like 'Death Row Barberhouse', which not only evinces an image of oppression, but is a homage to the 'Death Row' record label founded by Tupac and his producer Suge Knight. Moreover, I often heard young men describe their *own* hardships as being 'just like' those endured by the rappers they admired, or discussing how Tanzanians were 'the same as "Black-Americans"' in their pain. The influence of these cultural forms is palpable, but how, exactly, can we *account* for this influence? Is gangsta rap, in spite of its revolutionary, outlaw promotion of struggle and strife, just one more version of cultural imperialism? Is the barbershop set in urban Arusha simply emulating American celebrity as emblematic of a self-evidently more powerful, and irresistibly more desirable, world? Certainly there are powerful interests that mine the commercial potential of hip hop and rap; but need this mean that the interests and motives of youth in Arusha are ultimately irrelevant?

There are a number of ways that studies of globalization have addressed precisely such issues. It is possible, for example, to argue that Tupac, Snoop, Dr Dre and others provide concrete material and meaningful forms through which the social experiences of those in places like Arusha can be imaginatively articulated. Suffering and pain enacted in the rhythms and rhymes of rappers could be said to provide a means of expression for the feelings of alienation and oppression that pervade this urban East African scene. The signifiers may be global, but the signified remains resolutely local according to this logic. The problem with this perspective is that it retains a fundamental (and insupportable) distinction between the cultural form and the social experience, as though the pain of urban life were ever present and simply waiting to be expressed in a powerful new language, This perspective fails to consider, as I have already outlined in some detail, that subjective forms of 'pain' and 'survival' do not merely represent social life, they actively *constitute* it. This means, at the same time, that the constitution of the world of persons, objects, and the relations between them as it is lived in the barbershops and street life of Arusha cannot simply be an emulation, or imitation of some other reality. The local is not merely *expressed* in global terms, nor are global images *defining* local experience in Arusha. What is needed in order to articulate these dimensions of total socio-cultural process is a recognition of the fact that as these particular Tanzanian young men consume popular global media (from gangsta rap to South African satellite TV) they are actively aiming to remake a world that they can fully inhabit.

In my earlier discussion of pain as a form of consciousness, I emphasized the fact that pain was not overcome, but seized upon as a means of identification through which Arusha's youth could qualify, or authorize themselves, to participate in their social world. In this regard, pain becomes a generative form of subjectification, that is, a constructive means of generating a subjectivity (inherently embedded in sociality) with which to confront a world of suffering. From this perspective, the identification with the themes, signs, and images of global hip-hop – especially in the form of figures like Tupac who publicly insist on their own suffering – becomes a way of asserting the positive value of pain as a means of access to a wider world, indeed, a world-wide community of affliction. In other words, pain becomes more than just the negative feeling of oppression, and more, even, than the foundation for a micropolitics of everyday encounters. The felt experience of pain, under these circumstances, becomes a way of situating the subject of pain in a powerful global order of meanings and relations. Popular cultural practices in a wide array of urban contexts serve to organize and realize what Foster describes as an 'imagined cosmopolitanism' (Foster, 1999), in which media consumers understand themselves to be participants in a world-wide scene. This imagined and imaginative reality is a potent, and spectacular, form of fantasy – and so it is a cosmopolitanism laden with subjective potential and imposing sources of domination. The possibilities of this situation, as in feeling one's self a subject in an overarching cosmos, are profound. For the barbershop crowd in Arusha, imaginative participation in this cosmos can be *daunting* enough to confirm their felt sense of suffering, but also powerful enough to *transform* that condition of suffering.

I would suggest, in fact, that popular cultural practices in Arusha oriented towards this cosmopolitanism are informed by *both* the dominating power of this global order – in Mbembe's terms, the fetishization of the spectacle – and its transformative possibilities; indeed, the former is a condition of the latter. For in imagining this world-wide reality, agents of popular culture in Arusha construct a complex relationship to this reality. In effect, these urban youth imagine that they may be *in* this world, but they are decidedly not *of* it. For example, as every Tanzanian devotee knows, gangsta rappers are split between East Coast and West Coast, a geography that can scarcely encompass East Africa. And so, barbershops characteristically take their names from this cosmic geography. There are 'Brooklyn Barbershops' and 'Liverpool Haircuts,' more than a dozen 'California' *Kinyozi* – even a 'Cosovo Cut' – but no Kilimanjaro, or Serengeti, no Dar, or even Nairobi, in spite of the fact that these East African places are routinely thought of as recognizable sites in a geography more cosmopolitan than Arusha. Virtually every person I met in Arusha was consumed with pursuing 'business', but none was consistently able to get access to the 'jack', 'benjamins', and 'cash money' that was part of the dollarized tourist and mineral economy. Instead, they hustled to get *mkwanja*, a euphemism taken from the piles of grass hacked up by landscaping road crews armed with hand-machetes, a plainly gruelling and debasing occupation. Such examples illustrate that the dynamism and force of the global world constructed by these urban actors is clearly felt to lie *elsewhere*, and crucial structuring principles and media of value that organize that world are inaccessible – or irrelevant – to life in Arusha.

Nonetheless, I would argue that this palpable distancing from these potent sources is essential to the productivity of the fantastical and spectacular processes of popular culture. In part, this distancing contributes in direct and substantial ways to the feelings of pain that shape subjectivity in Arusha. Many young men in town, for example, voiced their complaints about urban life to me in terms of the poor and uneven quality of the consumer goods that they desired, a complaint expressed by means of a contrast between the radios, cassette recorders (even hair clippers) they could get in Arusha, and the 'real' (*kwa kweli*,, 'true' or *haki*, 'honest') goods that were available in some imagined *kwenu* – 'your place' (i.e., America or Europe). This distrust of local goods articulates a sense of dissatisfaction that has both a local focus – with charges against the dishonesty of local retailers commonly heard – and a more global bewilderment at the plight of 'we Tanzanians' who, in a high-tech conspiracy of the first rank, receive only lesser quality goods, while the best of things are reserved for First World consumers. My point is not simply that Tanzanians have an acute (if largely imagined) sense of the contrast between 'we Tanzanians' and 'your place' as mediated by consumption, but also that this contrast is felt as part of the pain that comes increasingly to characterize social interaction in Arusha. I would add that this sense of the contrast between 'here' in Tanzania and 'there' in America/ Europe/elsewhere makes these highly valued and desirable consumer goods – as well as the multiply mediated images and practices of consumerism more generally – into powerful forces of *domination*. The intense desire for those things that are desirable *explicitly* because of their unattainability (for the desirable 'true/real/honest' goods are always projected to lie elsewhere) allows these highly valued products to *subjugate* the consumer in Arusha. That is, consumers can experience their desire as a source of constraint and limitation (Gell, 1988). In Mbembe's terms, the domination of command is achieved by means of its thoroughgoing fetishization.

Here, then, is a potent and creative paradox embedded in the fantasies of popular culture and the subjectivities of the youth who participate in it in Arusha: these young men perceive themselves to be marginal to, and so *subjugated* by, the global order of signs and values they intensely desire; and yet, this subjugation is experienced as 'pain' which – as a way of qualifying personhood and constituting sociality – can greatly contribute to the subjective sense of *connection* to that world-wide community. How might we resolve this paradox, and, more importantly, how might this paradox permit of a kind of resolution for those whose lives are defined by it? The dynamics of this dialectic in consciousness, I would argue, suggest that the lived feeling of subjugation, the pervasive and routinized awareness (which is to say, imagining) that vital sources of value, meaning, and power are always distant and seemingly inaccessible, make these cultural forms and forces seem *uniquely* real. If this is so (again imaginatively, or fantastically), then one's own existence must, by definition, be formed through its relation to this ontological order. From this perspective, pain becomes not only an expression of the subject's relationship to that unique reality, forming a conduit to this wider truth; it also becomes a way of seeing one's own subjugation as itself an *aspect* of this fundamental, ontological plan.

To use Lienhardt's language of 'symbolic action,' for the denizens of Arusha's shops and streets their own 'pain' is a model of their existential condition of marginality, a model through which they can act upon that subjugation so as to transform it. The trick, though, is recognizing that these practitioners of popular culture make *themselves* (that is, their consciousness of themselves as being 'in pain', 'having thoughts', etc.) models for their own action, turning themselves, in effect, into exemplars of an imagined transcendent, ontological realm. Identifying yourself as a person *acted upon* by overarching and unique forces, forces that are themselves characterized by pain and oppression (as the themes, images, sights, and sounds of the global gangsta make unambiguously clear) is to assert that you are commanded by an all-powerful reality – and that is a potent claim to agency and self-construction.

If we trace the implications of this language for the making of subjectivity to the specific field of *affliction* as a paramount socio-political concern – and a long-standing domain of 'symbolic action' – another way of describing these dynamics of consciousness (already alluded to in the earlier discussion) suggests itself: the barbershop crowd become 'hosts' for the Powers who, in their own obsessions with 'pain', come to 'possess' their alters. Arusha's youth routinely make themselves over in the form of some peerless 'others" (i.e., celebrity rappers) exquisite suffering. Their *own* suffering – the 'thoughts' that 'fill' and 'hurt,' and 'jumble' their 'heads' – is thus performed as simultaneously a core feature of *themselves* as suffering 'thugs', and of themselves *in the guise of* even more legitimate, 'real', and certainly powerful others (see Boddy, 1989 for an apposite perspective on the performative qualities of *zar* possession).

I am reminded, as an apt comparison, of the Sakalava tromba spirits described by Lambek (1998), returning to possess their hosts during festivals held at ancestral reliquaries. These spirits are royal persons, real historical figures, who inevitably appear in trance as they were at the moment of their own deaths. These most powerful of figures are available to their human alters in a condition of unsurpassed suffering, as death becomes 'the foundational moment' for these spirits' performances (Lambek, 1998:118). The (often traumatic) death of the tromba not only permeates their presence as spirits, qualifying them as powers, much as 'pain' qualifies persons in Arusha; the remembered death of the spirit also provides a substantial, corporeal connection between tromba and host. Hosts will prepare to receive their spirits 'by applying white clay to the parts of the body whose traumata lead to death' (*ibid.*:118). The embodiment of tromba is further elaborated in the ways that mediums make themselves the objects *acted upon* by these most powerful of spirits, as Sakalava hosts 'suffer when they speak the secrets of their spirits' (*ibid.*:123). Suffering, then, is both the embodied grounds of dominant social relations, iconic of the presence of the tromba in the bodies of their hosts, as well as a poetic trope of Sakalava history. Transposed into the practices of popular culture in Arusha, we might say that 'pain' is the presence of celebrated, fantastical global persons incarnated in urban youth, their heads filled with 'too many thoughts'.

If I suggest that participation in global popular culture in the specific context of urban Arusha can be likened to a modality of spirit possession, it might immediately be objected that none of the activities I have described ever entails trance or dissociation. While that is true, I think the more important point is that these practices do entail *embodied* forms of alterity, that is to say, a bodily consciousness of one's self as another. Though this consciousness may not be explicitly – that is, self-consciously – expressed as that 'other' (*wahuni* in barbershops may quote the rhymes of many a rapper, but they never, to my knowledge, claim to *be* those superstars), nonetheless, the subjectivity that they do present is closely attuned to the consciousness of these powerful figures. As so much of contemporary social and cultural theory has gone to great lengths to demonstrate that consciousness cannot be contained in overt self-awareness, or constructs of 'the mind', but is equally dispersed in embodied, implicit, and collective practices, it makes little sense to say that possession is a form of consciousness that depends upon the explicit self-awareness announced by possessing spirits.

Let me make it absolutely clear that I am certainly *not* suggesting that global hip hop in Arusha is the manifestation of some 'survival' cult of possession, the old wine of an 'authentic' African practice in new skins. There are any number of possession practices, both historical and contemporary, that have been associated with current residents of this region of Tanzania, from upepo spirits from the Swahili coast, to Waswezi spirits from Tabora and Mwanza, to modern-day Majini that afflict the town. The link I see, though, between popular culture and possession is less at the level of historical forms and more at the level of social action. Both possession and popular culture are ways of formulating subjectivity under conditions of domination in ways that use the subjects' position of subjugation as a vehicle to *articulate* and *identify with* the force of subjugating powers. A focus on the actional nexus of these relations of domination may therefore permit us to transcend the unproductive dichotomy between 'appropriation', and 'emulation', a view of popular cultural practices as 'quintessentially African' or 'slavishly' imitative of the West. Moreover, the terms of both possession and popular culture as modes of domination recall Mbembe's insights into the efficacy of 'conviviality'. Yet this view does not reduce such forms of subjectification to mere 'vulgarity', but instead sees them as productive forms of pragmatic action.

Possession as a potent way of expressing – and fantasizing – social relations that are at once intimately meaningful and overwhelmingly powerful is an equally cogent illustration of the way that globalization can be imagined and lived. Popular cultural practice performed by Arusha's youth – conceived of along the same lines – is not, therefore, the 'local' expression of a 'global' set of forces and institutions. Popular culture, like possession, is about the *connection* and co-presence of specific times, places, and persons, with encompassing powers, images, and relations. This co-presence is a *lived reality*, felt and worked through in the experience of 'pain', pain that is simultaneously your own and another's, embodied and objectified, specific and transcendent. It is pain as an organizing theme of consciousness and a mode of being – pain as a central criterion of persons that enables them to participate in the social world of Arusha's turbulent streets – that gives the practices of popular culture many of the definitive attributes of a cult of affliction. Urban youth, who simultaneously embody the social crisis of post-socialist Tanzania, the radical contrast of aspiration and opportunity, as well as the superlative power of global spectacle, are this cult's most proficient adepts. Amid the contemporary upheavals of this neo-liberal moment in Africa (and elsewhere), where once unimaginable wealth and well-being are now all too easily imagined (and instantaneously mediated), and therefore all the more painfully unattainable, we should not be surprised to find that cults of affliction (re)emerge as a persuasive means of 'illicit cohabitation' shared by those enraptured by these fantasies.

References

Asad, Talal. 1983. 'Notes on Body Pain and Truth in Medieval Christian Ritual'. *Economy and Society*, 12 (3): 287-327.

Baroin, Catherine. 1996. 'Religious Conflict in 1990-1993 Among the Rwa: Secession in a Lutheran Diocese in Northern Tanzania', *African Affairs* 95: 529-54.

Boddy, Janice. 1989. *Wombs and Alien Spirits: Women, Men, and the Zar Cult in Northern Sudan*. Madison, WI: University of Wisconsin Press.

Brown, M.F. 1996. 'On Resisting Resistance', *American Anthropologist* 98(4): 729–48.

Ciekawy, Diane & Peter Geschiere. 1998. 'Containing Witchcraft: Conflicting Scenarios in Postcolonial Africa'. Special Issue, *African Studies Review* vol. 41 (3).

Comaroff, Jean & John L. Comaroff. 1999. 'Occult Economies and the Violence of Abstraction: Notes from the South African postcolony', *American Ethnologist* 26 (3): 279–301.

Coulter, Chris. 1998. 'Youth After War. Emerging Influence or Submerged by Power', unpublished Research Proejct Proposal, University of Uppsala, Department of Anthropology.

Cruise O'Brien, Donal. 1996. 'A Lost Generation? Youth Identity and State Decay in West Africa', in *Postcolonial Identities in Africa*, ed. R. Werbner and T. Ranger. London: Zed Books.

De Boeck, Filip. 1996. 'Postcolonialism, Power and Identity: Local and Global Perspectives from Zaire', in *Postcolonial Identities in Africa*, ed. R. Werbner and T. Ranger. London: Zed Books.

Durham, Deborah. n.d. 'Youth and the Social Imagination in Africa'. Ms.

Fabian, Johannes. 1978. 'Popular Culture in Africa: Findings and Conjectures'. *Africa* 48 (4):315-34

— 1996. *Remembering the Present: Painting and Popular History in Zaire*. Berkeley: University of California Press.

Ferguson, James. 1999. *Expectations of Modernity: Myths and Meanings of Urban Life on the Zambian Copperbelt*. Berkeley, CA: University of California Press.

Foster, Robert. 1999. 'Marginal Modernities: Identity and Locality, Global Media and Commodity Consumption'. Paper presented at the German-American Frontiers of the Social and Behavioral Sciences Symposium, Dölln, Germany, March.

Friedman, Jonathan. 1990a. 'Being in the World: Globalization and Localization', *Theory Culture and Society* 7:311-28

— 1990b. 'The Political Economy of Elegance: An African Cult of Beauty', *Culture and History* VII: 101-25;

Gell, Alfred. 1988. Review article: 'Anthropology, Material Culture and Consumerism', *JASO* 19(1): 43-8.

Geschiere, Peter. 1998. *On Witch-doctors and Spin-doctors: The Role of 'Experts' in African and American Politics*. Working Paper No 4, University of Leiden.

Hannerz, Ulf. 1996. 'The Local and the Global: Continuity and Change', in *Transnational Connections: Culture, People, Places*. New York: Routledge.

Hansen, Karen Tranberg. 1999. 'Second-hand Clothing Encounters in Zambia: Global Discourses, Western Commodities, and Local Histories', *Africa* 69: 334-65.

Kaplan, Martha & John Kelly. 1994. 'Rethinking Resistance: Dialogics of "Disaffection" in Colonial Fiji', *American Ethnologist* 21(1): 123-51.

Lambek, Michael. 1998. 'The Sakalava Poiesis of History: Realizing the Past Through Spirit Possession in Madagascar', *American Ethnologist* 25 (2).

Lienhardt, Godfrey. 1961. *Divinity and Experience: The Religion of the Dinka*. London: Oxford University Press.

Malkki, Liisa. 1997. Children, Futures, and the Domestication of Hope. Paper presented at Humanities Research Institute, University of California, Irvine.

Marx, Karl. 1978 [1852]. 'The Eighteenth Brumaire of Louis Bonaparte', in *The Marx-Engels Reader* ed. Robert C. Tuckes. 2nd edn. New York: W.W. Norton.

Mbembe, Achille. 1992. 'Provisional Notes on the Postcolony', *Africa* 12(1): 3-37.

Miller, Daniel. 1994. *Modernity: An Ethnographic Approach*. Oxford: Berg Press.

Remes, Peter. 1999. 'Global Popular Music and Changing Awareness of Urban Tanzanian Youth', *Yearbook for Traditional Music* vol. 31. pp. 1-26.

Sahlins, Marshall. 1999. 'Two or Three Things That I Know About Culture'. *Journal of the Royal Anthropological Institute* 5(3): 399-422.

Stambach, Andy. 1999. 'Curl Up and Dye: Civil Society and the Fashion-Minded Citizen', in *Civil Society and the Political Imagination in Africa,* ed. J. L. Comaroff and J. Comaroff. Chicago: University of Chicago Press.

Wacquant, Lo¨c. 1998. 'The Prizefighter's Three Bodies', *Ethnos* 63(3): 325-52.

Weiss, Brad. 2002. 'Thug Realism: Inhabiting Fantasy in Urban Tanzania', *Cultural Anthropology* 17 (1): 93-128.

White, Hylton. 1999. 'Counting Stones: Youth and Ritual Politics in Post-Apartheid Zululand'. Paper presented at the annual meeting of the American Anthropological Association. Chicago, IL.

III Children, Youth & Marginality In & Out of Place

6 NICOLAS ARGENTI
Dancing in the Borderlands The Forbidden Masquerades of Oku Youth & Women, Cameroon

Nearly all culture is not original. (Ya Mary Nying, Baate member, Oku 12 July 1992)

Nearly all cultural forms are politicised and contested. (Abner Cohen, 1993: 126)

Introduction

The expression *nchiinen ebkwo* ('[the] law/culture [of] Oku') is often used in Eblam Ebkwo, the language of Oku, to discuss legal matters as well as masquerades (some of which are involved in judicial processes). The recent inception by the palace authorities of an annual week of festivities known by the English name of 'Cultural Week' – self-consciously displaying Oku masquerades and dances at the palace without reference to the funerary and memorial ceremonies they are meant to accompany – has done something to reify the concept of *nchiinen*, however, bringing it closer to contemporary popular Western notions of a body of timeless practices identifying a distinct people; a reification that is integral to the 'heritage politics' (Appadurai, 1990: 304; Herzfeld, 1982) I discuss below. Colonial administrators and anthropologists of the Grassfields, in collusion with the male lineage elders and palace elites who have provided the majority of their informants, have together constructed a discourse of place, identity and authority that is itself largely an invention – a discourse created by particular interest groups (both colonizing and colonized) to consolidate, rigidify and ultimately legitimize systems of power that were in fact volatile, in perpetual flux and subject to dissent (Rowlands, 1987; Warnier, 1985). In this chapter, I explore some of the means by which this discourse is questioned by those excluded from the benefits it has to offer – youth and women in particular.

I am very grateful to Jean-François Bayart and Jean-Pierre Warnier for inviting me to present the rudiments of this paper at their joint CERI-MàP colloquium, 'Culture Matérielle et Subjectivation Politique', at the Centre d'Etudes et de Recherches Internationales, Paris, in January 2000, and for their extremely useful comments. I am likewise indebted to Nadia Lovell and David Parkin for inviting me to present the paper at the EASA 2000 in Krakow, to Shirley Ardener, Elizabeth Ewart and Ian Fowler for inviting me to present it at the Oxford Institute of Social and Cultural Anthropology's Ethnicity and Identity Seminar the same year, and to Ulrike Davis-Sulikowski, Wolfgang Kraus and Anna Streissler for valuable feedback on the occasion of a presentation of the paper in Vienna in June 2003. Finally, my thanks go to Alex Argenti-Pillen, John Bah, Sally Chilver, Filip De Boeck, Deborah Durham, Peter Geschiere, Michaela Pelican, Toby Quantrill, Michael Rowlands and Brad Weiss for their invaluable comments. I retain the right to claim all shortcomings as my intellectual property.

121

I then go on to explore the processes by which certain performances are accepted as 'tradition' by the Oku palace authorities while others are proscribed, focusing on two cases of banned performances; those of Mondial, a new group of young male maskers, and Baate, a generic name covering a host of female masking groups of relatively recent introduction to Oku. This problem leads in turn to a further exploration of the means by which the youth and women excluded from positions of power and influence in the Grassfields now use subversive performances to embody subjectivities that operate to locate them anew within their political milieu. I finally suggest that these techniques of the body serve to question the models of place, identity and authority sedulously constructed by the palace elite in line with the latter's quest for modernist forms of authority.

Local Hierarchies, Exogenous Powers

Cameroon is notable for the density of its distinct social groups and languages – over 240 of them, according to some estimates. The Grassfields region alone, an area the size of Wales, boasts over 50 different polities or *fon*ships, each with its own *fon* or king, language, myth of origin, kinship system, cuisine, style of architecture and clothing, and performance traditions. Faced with this political complexity, the Germans of the 1889 expedition into the Grassfields, the first Europeans to arrive in the area, sought to make alliances, establishing which kingdoms would be their allies and which their enemies in their quest to gain influence in the region (Chilver, 1996). The effect of their intervention was to impose a new rigidity on what had until then been a fluid and dynamic situation of inter-chiefdom struggles for people and territory (see Chilver, 1963), characterized by Chilver (pers. comm.) as a Brownian Movement[1] rather than a clearly delineated hierarchy. The rigidifying effect that colonial rule had on inter-kingdom relations also had an impact on internal political relations within kingdoms. Struggles for power and dynamic reversals of fortune amongst ruling families were commonplace before the need for administrative rationalization discouraged open revolt and palace coups, and afforded unprecedented unilateral power to client *fons* seen to be amenable to the administration.[2]

As in many other Grassfields kingdoms, and indeed much of the continent (see De Boeck, 1994; Feierman, 1974; Herbert, 1993: 165; de Heusch, 1982; Drucker-Brown, 1992; Last, 1991; Turner, 1967: 93-111; Vansina, 1990), the dominant discourse of power put forth by the palatine elite of Oku represents the *fon* or king as a liminal figure – classically as a foreigner and a hunter. The *fon* of Oku thus represents a lineage said to have originated outside the kingdom in the distant Tikari plateau to the East of the Grassfields, and to have arrived and overpowered an autochthonous population of wild people (the Ntul) associated with the earth.[3] The early kings of Oku are closely associ-

---

[1] An irregular oscillatory movement first described by Robert Brown with respect to the movement of microscopic particles suspended in a limpid fluid.

[2] Geary (1988) and Tardits (1979) have recorded a struggle for supremacy by opposing factions within the palace of Fumban, on the eastern edge of the Grassfields, which followed the death of the *fon* prior to the arrival of the Germans in the late 19th century. The insecurity of the interim period they describe before Sultan Njoya finally attained power was not to happen again after his death, when the French colonial administration – who had previously exiled the Sultan – installed their own client ruler in his place.

[3] Marking the collusion between anthropologists and local elites, this historiography was until recently presented as *bona-fide* history by the chroniclers of the Grassfields. see *inter alia*, Jeffreys (1964a, 1964b) and Fowler & Zeitlyn (1996) for a critique.

ated with the elements, having had the power to become forces of nature such as water, or dangerous forest animals such as snakes, leopards, bush cows and elephants.[4] These diverse powers are glossed with the term *finte*, referring to the capability of metamorphosis and bi-location. Alternatively, *fons* are often represented as hunters.[5] Another early king, Mkong Mote, is closely associated with the sacred crater-lake Mawes in the montane forest that still clings to Oku's summits. The lake is appropriated as an alter to the body royal (both physical and political) by its circumambulation performed by all new kings, a walk that enacts the mythical descent of the legendary Mkong Mote into the lake (Argenti, 1996: 15-19; Bah, 2000). In keeping with the exogenous origin of the king's lineage and his close association with the forest surrounding the polity, the palace itself is not a single site, but the mirror image of another, secret palace hidden inside a part of the forest known as Lumotu. The palace of Lumotu is a miniaturized replica of the palace in the capital, and the king still makes a yearly retreat there with the palace *Kwifon* society. By means of myths of foreign or sylvan origin, feral forms of address, retreats to the forest, and the propagation of the belief that they are *finte*, the kings of Oku and their entourages are thus constructed as liminal figures, one foot in this world and the other in the chthonian, nocturnal world of the forest and its sacred lake.

Political organizations based upon myths of origin and local cosmologies tend, because of their emphasis on the supernatural and the imaginary, to be contrasted with rationalist Western colonial or postcolonial forms of governance in Africa. African kingdoms are thus often presumed to be discontinuous or incommensurate with the nation-states in which they exist.[6] In contrast to this presumption, I suggest that these apparently separate institutions have worked hand in hand to support one another in the Grassfields from the turn of the century onward. Specifically, I argue that the discourse of the exogenous origin of the kings described above has been adapted to the contemporary power relations in which the palace hierarchies now find themselves imbricated (see Bayart, 1999).[7] As Kantorowicz (1957) has described in depth with respect to early-modern European states, the rationale for liminal models of royal authority is that leaders are meant to negotiate between the *polis* and the world outside. The king's two bodies are taken to bring the polity into existence by the very fact that they are dual: for there to be an 'inside' or an 'essence', an 'outside' must be negotiated (and thereby defined) by a figure with a foot in each world. The king, in these models, plays the political role of skin on a body. The crucial difference in the case of precolonial African models of royal authority is that this body was not territorialized, but genealogical. Hence, if *fons* of the Grassfields were represented as 'containers' (Warnier, 1993a), it was because they contained people, not land. The 'boundaries' of the polity were thus negotiated in terms of

---

[4] One of the honorific titles with which *Kwifon* members answer the king is the exclamation *Mbeh!*, the call of the bush cow; another *Niam!*, 'The Beast'.

[5] Nyaya ('ever away from home') – a descendant of Chichi who first led a Tikari group out of their mythical homeland and one of the first kings of Oku – and his descendant Nei are both spoken of in many versions of the Oku myth of origin as hunting in the forest for an extended period of time before settling down to rule the kingdom (Argenti, 1996:17).

[6] For a recent discussion of this tendency across the continent see Perrot and Fauvelle-Aymar (2003), and with particular reference to the Cameroon Grassfields, see Warnier (2003).

[7] The latest *fon* was chosen not only because he was eligible in the line of descent (many others also were) but because he was the national secretary of the Baptist Church of Cameroon. Although he lost this office upon becoming *fon* (largely as a result of inheriting over sixty wives from his predecessor), his Baptist connections were presumed by the palace elite to have provided him with valuable connections with the new business and bureaucratic elite and the postcolonial state. Literacy is highly valued as an attribute of Grassfields *fons* for the same reason.

alliances between groups of nominal kin rather than inscribed on the landscape. If the myths relating to divine kingship depicted the king as a liminal figure transcending the boundaries of the polity, it was because his anomalous duality served to forge alliances with potential enemies and to incorporate foreigners.

The arrival of the colonial powers in the region had the effect of reifying this genealogical discourse into a territorial model that emulated Western, modernist models of political authority (see Bopda, 2003: 42-4). As Grassfields *fons* became conversant with the new colonial discourse of territorial authority, they actively collaborated with colonial administrators to make their hegemony take concrete form on the landscape. In a clear instance of this strategy, they regularly called upon the anthropologist and colonial officer Jeffreys to try cases of land disputes in court. Jeffreys would force the losing kingdom to provide labourers to mark the established boundaries on the land with stone cairns, thus objectifying inter-kingdom boundaries that had previously been affirmed in people. The discourse of royal monopoly on the exogenous and its attendant model of wealth in people thus came to be essentialized and reified by Western colonial administrators and their postcolonial successors, who turned a complex heterogeneous aggregate of local subjectivities into a modernist extension of the fledgling nation and its homogenizing ambitions for national unity.[8]

This process has continued to the present day, with the role of the colonial administration being taken over by the postcolonial state. Concerned as it is with the task of establishing a strong state in the midst of linguistic and cultural diversity, the Cameroonian government now looks to Grassfields rulers as an extension of its influence at the local level, using them as administrators and party supporters whenever possible (Argenti, 1998; Fisiy, 1995; see Geschiere, 1993 for the francophone case). The *fon*ship is thus gradually made to resemble an anodyne sub-category of the nation, with *fons* now officially ranked by the government into 'First Class' and 'Second Class', with 'First Class' *fons* earning state salaries.[9]

The collusion between palace hierarchies and colonial and postcolonial authorities has never been uncontested, however. Young men's and women's identities, in particular, are

[8] When I discuss modernist political models in this chapter, I am referring to a discourse that promotes bounded notions of space, place and identity that are historically specific characteristics of the Western European nation-state and the colonial and postcolonial expansion of the state outside the West in the course of the 19th and 20th centuries. I do not therefore use the term to refer to technological advances (as Fisiy and Geschiere [1993] point out, 'modernization' is anyway associated with witchcraft in Cameroon), or to the increasingly rapid and complex exchange of cultural practices that characterizes many aspects of contemporary experience the world over. Rather, I argue here that the plurality of cultural forms that global networks facilitate are in fact incompatible with modernist concepts of place, culture and identity, which are by contrast fixed, monolithic and universalistic. Ramanujan (1989) and Argenti-Pillen (2003) have developed these ideas in relation to South Asia in terms of context-sensitive vs. context-free (modernist) cultures. In the terms of this model, Oku identity seen from the elite perspective – like German, French or US identity – is context-free: immutable and absolute. From the perspective of those excluded from the palace elite, however, identity is context-sensitive, and portraying oneself as an Oku person is contingent upon many factors that are liable to change from day to day.

[9] Clearly illustrating the government's hegemonic project to extend its 'tentacular grip over civil society' (Fisiy, 1990:60, my trans.), Grassfields polities are gradually being incorporated into normalized national territories. Oku was thus 'granted' sub-divisional status in 1992. Since then, the government has taken to mimicking the rites of investiture of *fons* with a parallel ceremony of its own. These ceremonies are attended by the Senior Divisional Officer, the local mayor, the heads of the gendarmerie and of the frontier police – all in dress uniform (Pelican, pers. comm., May 2003). In one of the most striking examples of the appropriation of Grassfields cultural practices by the central government, President Paul Biya had himself enthroned as '*Fon-of-Fons*' of the Grassfields soon after his state investiture. During the ceremony, officiated by a number of the most prominent Grassfields *fons* with ties to the CPDM ruling party, the President wore a full *fon*'s outfit, complete with embroidered gown, cap and assorted regalia.

seldom as unidimensional or localized as myths of origin and administrative – or indeed ethnographic – accounts would have it. Many Grassfields people live in disputed border territories between kingdoms or regularly travel between kingdoms. They speak several languages, marry into different kingdoms from those of their birth, and bear children who speak different languages from them and settle in different kingdoms again. In addition, many family heads foster children from friends, relations and business partners in other kingdoms as a means of bridging language barriers and building external alliances.[10] Within this regional system, it is women and youths who are particularly likely to transgress local identities in the creation of filial and business partnerships (see Nkwi, 1986:55). At the performative level, the panoply of masquerades of any one kingdom turns out upon scrutiny not to be discrete, but rather, following the Brownian model, a local re-working of a finite and recurring set of masks and dances belonging to a pan-Grassfields genre. This is the sense in which the discourse of locality, ethnicity and unity is belied by the experience of the majority – an experience that the youth and women excluded from influence are willing to embody, if not to voice.

Illustrating the close relationship not only between the national government and local elites in the Grassfields, but further between these two groups and modernist Western forms of territoriality, the cairns that Jeffreys had erected along the Oku-Kom border were restored in 1992 by a British forestry project working in collaboration with the Oku palace and the District Officer.[11] However, as it was to the palace hierarchy and local administration alike, the assertion of such modernist authority is more of an exception than a rule. The great majority of the cairns set up during the colonial period have been dismantled over the years by protagonists in border disputes. Even in the places where such boundary markers are left standing, they suffer from the same deficiency as the palatine discourse of power: they bespeak an elite ideal (as does the myth of royal hegemony) but fly in the face of political reality. The majority of Oku's borders are in fact made up of no-man's lands of fallow fields, abandoned villages and secondary forests: mobile buffer zones that separate adversaries one from another, and clearly belong to neither party in a dispute.[12] The people of Mbok-Keve, home to the masquerade Mondial I discuss below, are nominally within the boundaries of Oku, but speak of 'going to Oku' when setting out on the journey across the montane forest to the capital, Elak. They do not, however, mention they are 'going to Babungo' when attending the neighbouring kingdom's market just a few minutes' walk from their village. Grassfields kingdoms are thus not generally experienced as clearly bounded sites by such groups, but rather as permeable zones of relative influence that weaken and fade as they gradually merge with neighbouring zones of influence (see Drucker-Brown, 1989; Mbembe, 1999: 14-15; Rosaldo, 1988: 87). Just as the people of the Western Grassfields close to the border with Nigeria – only visited by Cameroonian politicians and District

---

[10] Warnier (1975:374-7) has provided evidence that in the late precolonial period too, an average of 30% of the married women in a Grassfields chiefdom had come from another chiefdom. Added to the intense migration of groups throughout the area due to slave raiding and internecine disputes, he concludes that 'the population of each chiefdom was a blend of all other populations around it' (1975:386).

[11] The Kilum Mountain Forest Project was run by British staff and employed local staff. It is now run exclusively by Cameroonian staff provided by the Ministry of Environment and Forests (MINEF). The project was part-funded at various times by Birdlife International, the ODA (now DfID), WWF and USAID (Quantrill, pers. comm. 19 June and 9 July 2003). One of the reasons why the late *fon* of Oku granted permission to the project to establish itself was so that it might save the narrow corridor of forest remaining around the sacred site of Lumotu, then threatened by encroaching farmers (c.f. Argenti, 2002b).

[12] Mbembe (2000:263), following Kopytoff (1987), notes that this was also the case in many precolonial African polities.

Officers by helicopter because of the lack of roads connecting them to the provincial capital and the rest of the nation – attend Nigerian markets and schools and use Nigerian currency, so too those living on the peripheries of Grassfields kingdoms share their allegiance with more than one fonship.

Furthermore, from the arrival of the Germans and the installation of plantations on the coast, and increasingly in the modern nation-state, the adult life of many Oku men and women has been spent outside their kingdom, gaining an education to earn a living in the new monetarized economy of the emerging nation (Warnier, 1993b, 1995), or indeed in Western Europe (Bouly de Lesdain, 1999). Given this reality of flux, sprawling no-man's lands, pluri-lingualism and pluri-locality, the discourse of the bounded, homogeneous kingdom espoused by palace elites is perpetually confronted by commoners' daily experience of a shifting, conditional affiliation to one or several unbounded, amorphous and permeable polities. As Friedman (1994: 89) notes in a general argument on culture and identity, 'There is clearly a tendency for economic success to seriously weaken ethnic identity as individuals find new and rewarding identities in the expanding career possibilities of the growing national society'. In the Grassfields as in much of Africa, 'career possibilities' may have dried up some time ago, but urban centres have lost none of their allure.

In the Grassfields case, however, palace elites counter centrifugal patterns of outmigration with centripetal responses. As the elite, and the *fons* in particular, become increasingly dependent upon the national government for their power, they bolster mythical allusions to the wild with bureaucratic discourses of modernist power, effecting a slippage between these two realms of exogenous power.[13] The palatine hierarchies of the Grassfields thus clearly evince highly ambiguous relations to the nation they are now dependent upon. On the one hand, they promote cultural identities that are inherently at odds with the nationalist project. On the other hand, the methods they use in the promotion of these identities are borrowed from the nationalist discourse of the state, thus leading to the promulgation of modernist state ideology and social organization, or simulacra of them, at the local level. Belonging to a kingdom is thus increasingly made to involve the adoption of a micro-nationalist identity, with kingdom or state on the one hand, and nation on the other appearing as cannibalized versions of one another (see Mbembe, 1999; Lemarchand, 1997).[14]

Delineating the problematic relation of contemporary states to nations, Appadurai

[13] In an insightful study that encapsulates many of the features of exogenous models of power, Atkinson (1984) outlines the use of *kiyori* by the Wana of Central Sulawesi, a poetic form which emphasizes relations to external political orders (see also Strathern, 1980: 193ff. on the Hageners' model of exogenous power). Because it has become a place of refuge from the armed forces, the forest has become a symbol of resistance to the central government in more recent *kiyori*, which now 'conjure a sense of a Wana polity in opposition to the external and foreign state' (1984: 61). Thus, 'What we see in the case of the Wana is the partial merger of the powers of the wild and powers of the state' (*ibid.*: 66, see McKinley, 1979). This slippage between the wild and the state allows a shared sense of ethnic identity to emerge in what is in practice a scattered set of hill communities. The Wana thus imbricate contrasts between their farming communities and the surrounding forests, on the one hand, with those between the upland Wanna region and the power centres on the coast, on the other. The first contrast poses an opposition between humans and spirits, the second between Wana and Indonesian society (see Bloch & Bloch, 1980). In both cases, authority is built by referring to external powers, while identifying these as sources of danger.

[14] Informants close to the palace often tried to explain the palace hierarchy to me by translating the various palace titles directly into government titles. The *fon* was thus 'the president', the highest-ranking *Kwifon* members his 'ministers', and so on. This model would always collapse relatively quickly, however, as the complexities of the palace hierarchy proved difficult to accommodate. Most importantly, however, the presidential model artificially petrifies relations of power that are in fact a constant source of struggle and flux within the palace.

(1990:303) points out that states not only constitute, but also threaten the nations in which they exist.[15] The relation between Grassfields polities and the Cameroonian nation is accordingly characterized as much by agonism as by mutual dependence. The kingdom is not engaged in this struggle with the nation on behalf of its people, however, but in an elitist bid for political influence that increasingly excludes those who are already disempowered by the local hierarchy. Youth and women accordingly reject the struggle for power between the nation and its constituent states by engaging not in the sort of open revolt or verbal dissent easily identified as a political movement, but rather in embodied practices modelled upon the masking traditions that the palace seeks to appropriate to its own discourse of 'culture'. The innovative forms of masking I now turn to offer young men and women the opportunity to construct alternative ways of being in the Grassfields that reject the palace's modernist discourse of a timeless 'Oku culture' in favour of performances that embody and objectify the deterritorialized experience of the majority.

Mondial

The group-masquerade Mondial was founded by Mathieu Nshiom of Mbok-Keve in 1992, during the protracted death celebrations for the late king (*fon*) of Oku (Argenti, 1999). Although based in a peripheral border-village, this masquerade's performance at the palace in the capital Elak not only enabled it to fulfil the obligation all new masquerade groups have of performing at the palace to be approved by the king, but it also marked the first public appearance of a group which was to achieve a reputation as a highly accomplished dance group within a few months of its inception. Having seen their first appearance at the palace, I set out for Mbok-Keve to interview the group leaders and photograph one of their rehearsals in November 1993.

  In contrast to the older lineage masquerades, in which the office-holders are nearly always married men with children and compound or lineage heads, the Mondial dancers are all young men between the ages of about twenty and thirty-five – their leader Nshiom included – and the group is notably devoid of the vast majority of offices and titles that characterize lineage masquerades.[16] Mondial dancers are also all members of another organization: the Mbok-Keve Youth Group. This is a voluntary organization of a type found in many Grassfields villages, with a mixed-sex membership that organizes community work and credit schemes (*njangi*) for its members. Although youth group members are often middle-aged, they are defined as 'youths' or 'children' insofar as they tend to be unmarried and have yet to found their own compounds. In the anthropological and political science literature, they have been defined as 'social cadets' (*cadets sociaux*).[17] Youth groups thus organize those normally excluded from the longer-established

[15] As Appadurai puts it, this ambiguous relation between states (*fon*ships or kingdoms in this case) and the nations that encompass them is not one of identity or homogeneity so much as of struggle: 'The relationship between states and nations is everywhere an embattled one. (...) While nations (...) seek to capture or co-opt states and state power, states simultaneously seek to capture and monopolise ideas about nationhood' [1990: 303].

[16] While the majority of the dancers in established masquerades are usually young men as well, they are strictly controlled in their performance and their place in the hierarchy of the masquerade by elders who preside over the society's initiation rites, the payment of membership fees and fines, and the punishment of those who commit offences.

[17] For an analysis of this in Cameroon, see the discussion concerning 'social cadets' in Argenti (2002a), Bayart (1985, 1989), and Warnier (1993b). Young men of the Grassfields have been characterized as social cadets because they are unable to marry until they have negotiated the tortuous route through the traditional

palace-affiliated societies based on hierarchies run by elders into more inclusive and egalitarian associations designed to by-pass dependence on gerontocratic authority. In my interview with him, Nshiom emphasized the youth of the Mondial dancers rather than downplaying it, explaining that 'this masquerade is cool (zeele) (...) [it] dances with children (ghonde)[18] because their blood is still strong (taan), still new (mfëë)'. 'Coolness' is one of the most highly prized qualities of good dancers throughout the Grassfields, and medicated libations are often poured over the feet of the dancers just before a performance to ensutre that this property is achieved. In some respects, Mondial operates like the youth group that provides it with its dancers. It uses half the gifts it receives during a performance (faale, gifts of food, drink or cash) to help those in charge of the death celebration at which they perform. This act of generosity even surpasses that of the youth groups, which typically make loans rather than gifts to people having to host large celebrations.

Though recently founded and self-consciously egalitarian and avant-garde, this masquerade shares some characteristics with longer-established 'traditional' masked dance groups. In the first place, it dances with costumes and wooden helmet-masks in the style of established Oku lineage masquerades. Secondly, the history and structure of its leadership and patronage resemble those of the established groups. Like older masquerades, Mondial is headed by a bamkum, a masquerade leader or 'father' (bâ), and its dancers are assigned places in the procession of masks according to the usual Oku formation, including a lead dancer (kam), one to bring up the rear (kam ebam) and one (the keshiengene), whose role it is to ensure the others stick to the current dance step. Furthermore, the group is based in an established lineage-head's compound (kebey kerarene), just as 'traditional' lineage masquerades are. Mondial is not a traditional Oku lineage masquerade, however, but rather one amongst a new group of masquerades found throughout the Grassfields and known generically as styles groups in Pidgin, and in Eblam Ebkwo as emkum mekale (sing. kekum mekale): 'foreign' or 'European' masquerades (see Argenti, 1998).

The word mekale is generally used in Oku to refer to that which originates outside the polity, in particular to machinery, pharmaceutical medicines, or any object of industrial manufacture. Apart from material objects, the term is also used to refer to forms of knowledge or behaviour perceived to be of foreign, and especially of Western, origin. The English language, for instance, is often referred to as Eblam Mekale – the mekale language, and Europeans and Americans alike are often called ghel mekale (sing. wel mekale) – mekale people. Unlike the Eblam Ebkwo term balak, which applies to roughly the same semantic field but has pejorative overtones (by association with its original use to denote raiding Fulanis in the nineteenth century), the term mekale has generally positive connotations, emphasizing productive, fertile power as evinced in wealth, progress, growth (kekwiye) and development. Despite the fact that the word is widespread across Cameroon and dates back to the early nineteenth century, when the Bakweri used it to

hierarchy which enables them to acquire the influence to build a compound – a pre-requisite to being seen as a marriageable man (Warnier, 1993b; Shanklin, 1985). However, despite the fact that the state in Africa refuses to recognize the fact that 'youth' is not monolithic, there are many categories of cadets (Mbembe, 1985). Women can equally be depicted as cadets because they can own crops but not land (Goheen, 1996), and run businesses but not possess wealth (Malaquais, 2000). Durham (forthcoming) shows how youth operates as an indexical term in Botswana; rather than marking biological age, it is used alternatively by different groups to protest against social exclusion, to make claims to status and responsibility, or – by the state – to justify alarmist stereotypes regarding the disenfranchised.

[18] The term ghonde (children) in this case should be understood not as a literal description, but as a hyperbolic statement used to emphasize both the virile youthfulness of the dancers and their exclusion from authority.

refer to Europeans (see Ardener, 2002), Oku folk etymologies suggest it was coined locally, formed from the Eblam-Ebkwo term *kāle-kāle*, 'to go round', supposedly referring to the curious circular, repetitive trajectories of the German and then British colonial officers on tour in the Grassfields. I was also occasionally told, however, of what seems to me to be a later derivative of this core meaning: that *mekale* refers to the way in which Europeans have encircled the earth with their colonial expansion and their technological prowess. This statement was made enthusiastically and with approbation, and is in keeping with the long-standing view of 'youths' or social cadets in Cameroon that the European conquest represented not a threat, but an opportunity to by-pass the local hierarchies that excluded them. This folk etymology thus pointedly evokes similarly positive globalizing connotations to those elicited by the term that Mathieu Nshiom chose for his *mekale* masquerade: Mondial.

Asked why he decided to found the group, Nshiom talks of progress, advancement, and development: 'The village had not opened [before I founded Mondial]. [Now] it will not be lost in the bush any longer, it will be strong.' 'Opening' (*edisen*) is a thick term alluding to change perceived as a generally positive force whereby access is gained to some source of external power, knowledge or influence beyond the territory of the polity. For example, one who acquires a television set or a car, or founds a school or other public institution, or introduces a new cash crop is said to be 'opening' the kingdom or the village. The term can also be used ironically, however; for instance, by those in traditional positions of power who stand to lose from the introduction of new forms of access to power and wealth that by-pass them. Fay Keming of Eghok Ntul, one of the most highly placed palace *Kwifon* regulatory society members, once explained to me that the gods had left their traditional dwelling places in the forest because the kingdom had 'opened', and *balak* (negatively valued *mekale*) had been permitted to enter. In keeping with the modernist, territorializing discourse espoused by the palace elite, 'opening' here takes on negative connotations, signifying not a form of progress, but of damage or contamination to a perfect, healthy body politic. Unlike Fay Keming, however, the youthful Nshiom and others of his generation see *edisen* or 'opening' as an unambiguously positive phenomenon enabling them to have a stake in a political economy which otherwise tends to exclude them from power and influence until late in life. While Fay Keming sees the forest as the proper site of power to be tapped by the palace hierarchy for the benefit of the kingdom, Nshiom re-interprets the forest as a barren, untenanted wasteland that he has the power to connect to an external world of technological power and wealth. This may be a modernizing view, but it is not a modernist discourse.

Masquerade groups are almost all associated with what might be termed foundation charters or oral histories that record the founder's life story. The founder of a masquerade group is frequently a man who has spent a protracted period of time outside the kingdom, and is returning from abroad. Such men have typically gone abroad to make money or learn a trade, sometimes also to obtain a wife, and they do in fact often mark their return to Oku by founding a masquerade group. Such men are said to have 'brought the masquerade with them', an expression which can have several senses. By becoming initiated into a foreign group, they may have negotiated with the compound head of a neighbouring kingdom to give them the right to replicate the group that they have joined when they return to Oku. Alternatively, a man may have invested some of his new wealth earned while working abroad in organizing the production of masks and costumes needed for a masquerade group that he then literally carries back with him on his return. In this scenario, the masquerade has typically been performing for some time at the residence of its patron while based away from Oku. A third possibility involves a more metaphorical use of the expression to denote the fact that the patron or prospective patron of a new masquerade has amassed sufficient wealth while abroad to organize the production of the material culture of the masquerade, but that he in fact only commissioned the objects from local craftsmen once he was back in Oku. It is in this latter sense that Nshiom 'brought the masquerade back' with him from Bamenda, the provincial capital, after having been working there for thirteen years. In fact, Nshiom did not even claim, as most Oku masquerade patrons do, that his wealth brought the masquerade to the kingdom, but emphasized that all the members contributed to help pay for the production of the necessary gowns and masks. All the masks were then commissioned together from one carver: Joseph Nsa of the village of Ngashie.

However local the material culture of the masquerade might be, however, its name obviously emphasizes a cosmopolitan – not to say global – outlook. In addition to its connotations of worldliness, Mondial is the name of one of the biggest hotels in Bamenda, the provincial capital. It was built and is run by a successful private businessman of commoner origin. It therefore stands not only as a monument to his legendary success, but also as a sort of ideal for the thousands of young men who go to Bamenda from the rural kingdoms seeking the wealth with which to subvert their inferiority in the traditional hierarchies of their places of birth. Nshiom is aware of the hotel, and when I asked him, he confirmed that it influenced his choice for a name, but he also emphasized that he chose it because his group 'would please the whole world with its dancing'.

When Nshiom 'brought the masquerade back' to Oku, he did not set it up in his father's compound, but rather in that of Ba Tedji, a village elder to whom Nshiom is not related. This compound already had another (traditional) masquerade in it, and thus a masquerade house (ndamkum) in which to house the paraphernalia of Mondial.[19] Justifying this decision, Nshiom explained that he is a young man, without his own compound yet, and that Ba Tedji's compound is an old, established one in which one could expect to find a masquerade. Placing Mondial in an established masquerade house, he went on, was a good way to present the group as a serious one, as opposed to a 'children's game'. Oku children (between the ages of around three and thirteen) in fact perform their own masquerades known as kesum-body (Argenti, 2001). Kesum-body dancers wear costumes made from reclaimed discarded items of industrial manufacture found around the compound, such as sheets of beaten aluminium, soap-bar wrappings and nylon coffee bags. They play percussion instruments made from old tin cans, sing songs in gibberish, and dance in imitation of popular bar-room dancing. As such they are the subject of much hilarity among adults. Adolescents (between the ages of about twelve and seventeen) in Mbok-Keve and a few other villages of Oku had also during my stay (from 1991 to 1994) started to perform a new type of masquerade imported from the neighbouring kingdom of Nso'. These were known as nton, and were patronized by young men and boys from minor compounds without the means or the influence to start a group lineage masquerade. Nton were single masks as opposed to groups, with simple, perfunctory costumes devoid of wooden headdresses, and were therefore cheap to produce and organizationally simple to run, necessitating few powers of delegation. Adults were on the whole sceptical about them, however, tending to see them as a nuisance or a failure.

[19] Speaking in Eblam Ebkwo, one would not, of course, refer to the paraphernalia per se, but to costumed figures as integral wholes, as if speaking of real creatures rather than masked dancers.

While, as mentioned above, Nshiom had referred to his dancers metaphorically as 'children' in order to emphasize their virility and their exclusion from power, he was nevertheless understandably concerned that his group should not become identified with these children's performances. In his own words, he placed Mondial in Ba Tedji's compound 'because it is still a new thing, and [new things] should be placed in the hands of elders'. This statement obviously begs the question as to why a group supposedly resisting elite power should submit to gerontocratic authority structures. The point is that Mondial's means of resistance is not to oppose eldership in general, but rather, by boring from within, subtly to redefine it as a system amenable to change and difference, distinct from the palace discourse of culture and ethnicity. In other words, Mondial does not attack tradition so much as the palatine elite's centralization of power by means of its appropriation of tradition to nationalist ends.

This point is illustrated with respect to Mondial's performance, which is characterized by two distinct styles of dance. On the one hand, the dancers know how to perform in a traditional lineage masquerade style similar to the long-established masquerades of large compounds. Since their masks and costumes are themselves 'traditional', when dancing in this style they are indistinguishable from many of the older groups in Oku. However, Mondial has another performance style altogether which it did not indulge in on the occasion of its first palace performance in front of the king, and which is much closer to a *kekum mekale* type of dance. Before returning to Mondial, let me therefore say a word about these recent innovations in Grassfields masked dance. Despite their name, *mekale* groups dance most often to long-established Grassfields xylophone tunes, albeit to many different tunes in a single performance, and to 'foreign' tunes borrowed from other Grassfields kingdoms. While the established lineage masquerades are almost always identifiable by the tune of their xylophone, *mekale* xylophone music, composed as it is of an amalgamation or a collage of tunes borrowed from up to twenty-five different groups in a single performance (the majority of which will be unknown to Oku people), results in a musical pastiche rather than an identifiable and homogeneous tune. Certain fragments of these pastiches, like medleys or jazz melodies, are, however, recognizable to the audience. One of the fragments played by Mondial, for instance, is taken from the musical introduction to the prologue to the daily news programme on Radio Buea – itself taken from a xylophone tune played in South West Province.

In addition to their musical pastiche, *mekale* or 'styles' groups differ from lineage masquerade groups with respect to their choreography. While the latter perform a limited set of steps to two or three xylophone rhythms, the new *mekale* groups break the dancing line into several couples or trios of dancers, or perform with four to eight dancers in total, executing a series of complex dance steps to rapidly changing xylophone rhythms (see Argenti, 1998). This style of dance is said to have been developed in the 1970s by Oku groups run by wealthy new-elite patrons, based outside the kingdom in the urban centres of the country. The local exegesis emphasizes pragmatic considerations as the prime cause of the innovation. The style is said to have developed in response to the emerging national competitions in which these groups began to participate. Because performance time was strictly limited and groups were now dancing for points, as it were, technique was of the essence. As a result, as many tunes and dance steps as possible were crammed into a single performance, and a new virtuoso aesthetic was born. Unlike the majority of the xylophone tunes, many of the new dance steps were borrowed from African popular music videos played on national television rather than from the available Grassfields masquerade dance-steps. This popular choreography first won national repute for Subi, the Oku people of Bamenda's *mekale* group (which has gone on to perform in Korea and Spain), and then spread to other groups, rapidly superseding those with choreographies identified as 'traditional' or 'local' – referred to with the adjectival use of the Pidgin term 'country'; an expression often connoting a lack of sophistication, or a poor local substitute for a foreign luxury.

It is thus the rapid switching between many different tunes – many of them from different kingdoms – the popular music *styles* choreography of the steps, and the association of this type of performance with national competitions and the national government that organizes them, that led Mondial to be associated by its founder with the 'opening' of the kingdom to sources of knowledge and power perceived to be foreign or external to the kingdom. As far as its *mekale* dance is concerned, however, Mondial goes further still than any of the other Oku *mekale* groups in acknowledging the politicized nature of its external referent. As I have suggested, all *mekale* groups make use of musical pastiche and the appropriation of African popular styles of dance to refer in their performances to a pan-Grassfields (and thus minority Anglophone) and even a pan-African or globalized identity. At least for a short while before being banned by the palace, however, Mondial was unprecedented in Oku for overtly introducing the theme of party politics to its performance.

During its *mekale* performance, for the brief period before it was forbidden, the lead dancer (*kam*) would reach into a bag on the ground and pull out aluminium stencils of upper-case lettering. The first read 'OKU', and the next two represented the acronyms of the ruling and main opposition parties: 'CPDM' (Cameroon Peoples Democratic Party) and 'SDF' (Social Democratic Front), respectively. He would then hand these out, both as single letters and as whole sets, to the members of the audience, who would in turn dance with them on the periphery of the masked dancers to the music of the xylophone and drums. For comic effect, the *kam* would give the most stalwart party supporters present the acronym of the opposing party to the one they identified with, and then cajole them into dancing with the stencil. At Mondial's initial performance at the palace in honour of the deceased king in 1992, and later at the practice session I also witnessed in November 1993, the audience members seemed to enjoy the joke, with CPDM 'Big Men' merrily dancing with the 'SDF' stencil and SDF 'party militants' holding up the 'CPDM' stencil they were handed. During the practice session, a certain comic effect was also achieved by handing the stencils to those who are traditionally divorced from the passion and divisiveness of party politics: the elders.

Unlike the great majority of the other masquerades one might choose to describe in Oku, however, this performance was to be short-lived. Mondial returned to perform at the palace a second time on 11 December 1993, once again obeying the call to all masquerades to perform at the palace along with all the other masquerades of Oku, this time for the late king's memorial or 'old die' (*ekwo ewuie*). In the mêlée of the crowd and the many simultaneously performing masquerade groups, Mondial managed to secure a performance space not in the large outer courtyard where the majority of the groups were dancing, but in the smaller inner courtyard directly facing the palace veranda where the king's throne stood. Since the king was seated on his throne at the time, this ensured a royal audience for the Mondial dancers.

This time, unlike its first palace performance the previous year, it engaged in a version of its *mekale* performance. The music and the dancing began, and Mondial had amassed a good-sized crowd when its leading masker (*kam*) pulled two of the aluminium stencils out of the bag on the ground: first 'OKU', then 'CPDM' (Figure 6.1).

6.1 *The lead masker of Mondial brandishes the 'Oku' stencil in front of the fon. (©Nicolas Argenti)*
6.2 *'Nearly all cultural forms are politicised and contested': Mabu, the kwifon society's lictor mask, scatters the dancers and their audience as the fon slips away to fetch him a cock. The 'CPDM' stencil is still on the veranda step, and Mondial's lion-shaped collection box is just visible on the ground, far left. (©Nicolas Argenti)*

The *kam* tried uncertainly to hand them to the king, but the latter showed no interest in taking them from him, so the *kam* placed them at the king's feet on the palace veranda step instead. He was just bending down to take out the third 'SDF' stencil when Mabu – the palace *Kwifon* lictor mask known in the past as the executioner of this policing society and still used on punitive expeditions today – stormed out of the palace *Kwifon* compound, rushed up behind the *kam* and scattered with its spears all the stencils and the offending bag in a great fury, not even sparing Mondial's lion-shaped wooden collection box on the ground close by the bag or the *kam*'s ceremonial spear planted next to it (Figure 6.2). In the ensuing havoc, the king quietly slipped back inside the palace to fetch Mabu the live cock that he traditionally offers the mask when it performs. Meanwhile, the musicians and the masked dancers alike all fled in search of shelter.

Baate

Baate, possessing the only women's masks in Oku, is still more transgressive than Mondial and yet less unprecedented. It is more transgressive in the sense that it breaks rules that are quite explicit in Oku: that women should not engage in masking, and that they should not hold meetings *in camera* or handle medicines. Mondial, by comparison, breaks no explicit rule since nothing has ever been said before about the relationship between masking and party politics. On the other hand, Baate is less unprecedented than Mondial in that it is based upon similar groups that have existed for some time in the neighbouring kingdom of Nso' and that go by the same name but are entirely legitimate there (Goheen, pers. comm. November 1996). On the basis of the legitimacy of these groups in a neighbouring kingdom, groups of Oku women have periodically attempted to inaugurate their own Baate groups, only to have them banned by *Kwifon* soon after their inception. As with Mondial, fledgling Baate groups tend to make their first public appearance at a large palace death celebration (in honour of princes, king's wives or mothers, or of the king himself). This simultaneously satisfies the palace requirement for new groups to present themselves for approval to the king and *Kwifon*, and offers the groups the opportunity to try to avoid incurring censure under the aegis of the celebratory mood and the confusion of the moment.

Baate groups are not exclusively composed of young people, as is the case with Mondial, but potentially of women of all ages. Even the men of compounds that own a Baate group sometimes join in their performances as accompanying musicians. In practice, though, the core of their membership and their masked dancers tend to be middle- to late middle-aged women. Baate societies possess masked figures that are categorized as such in the nearest Eblam Ebkwo word (*kekum*), and these figures wear masks made by men specifically for them. Baate masks look nothing like men's masks, however. They are not carved of wood, but made of raffia fibres. They are not monochrome, but particoloured. They are not representational, but abstract. The 'masks' of Baate are in fact hoods, though highly decorative ones that effectively obliterate the identity of the wearer. The hoods consist of cylindrical sleeves of woven raffia fibres, closed at the top, from which long strands of stiff raffia are made to protrude outward in the manner of a porcupine's quills. These quills are dyed in bright colours and clipped into the form of a globe at a length of approximately 45cm, giving the dancer's head an appearance of enormity (see Plate 3). The height of the headdress also makes the figure stand out head and shoulders above its company. The Baate maskers wear gowns – also made by men: tailors used to making men's masquerade gowns – which tend to be printed replicas of the blue-and-white wax resist-dyed cloth known in the Grassfields as *kelanglang* or *fentshii*, and normally reserved for members of the royal family. The masked figures dance in pairs, accompanied by a few musicians and a relatively large retainerdom of acolytes, numbering two to three dozen, the great majority of them women.

The music of Baate is played largely on different instruments from those of male masquerades. The only instruments they have in common are the long drum (*ntshum*) and the clapperless double bell (*ngem*). All the other instruments of Baate are borrowed from non-masking groups, some male and some female. The large standing-drum (*kentom*) some Baate groups use is primarily associated with *manjong*, the male military society. The various rattles they use are also played by women's dance groups which have no masks (*njang*). The long blow-pipe they use is borrowed from *fembien*, the established and legitimate female secret society closely associated with the palace. While the *fembien* version of the instrument is cryptically referred to as '*fembien*'s drum' (*ntshum fembien*), however, the same instrument when used by Baate orchestras is referred to literally as a *kefung*.

While it is generally agreed that Baate groups have had a presence in Oku for up to 30 years, at which point they were introduced from Nso' under various names, they have had a history of bannings (*bunle*) by the palace *Kwifon* society followed by temporary re-appearances. There seem to be several reasons why Baate groups have managed – however precariously – to establish themselves in Oku despite the ban on women engaging in masking activity. The first reason has to do with actions vs. norms or representations (Holy and Stuchlik, 1983), or practice vs. rationalization (Giddens, 1984). That is to say that, in spite of the overt ban on women masking that Oku men and women all agree upon in principle, the fact is that *fembien* – a strongly established, legitimate and powerful female palace organization with ramifications at the village level throughout the kingdom – has a masquerade and secret objects of its own.

Interestingly, the rule against masks is side-stepped by *fembien* in that their 'mask' is never actually seen.[20] Even during a public appearance for the death of a *fembien* or *Kwifon* society member (the two are seen as sibling organizations), the *fembien* 'masquerade' processes from the bush beyond the compound into the compound courtyard completely hidden by green branches that the members of the society have collected in the bush and hold up around it in a tight formation. As the group approach the women's quarters in the compound, they dance outside the door briefly as the 'masquerade' slips inside the house, and the branches all suddenly fall to the ground to reveal the emptiness in their midst. Invisible as it is, this is nevertheless a masquerade (*kekum*) in the structural sense. It is referred to as such, has secret instruments associated with it in the manner of the secret objects revealed to initiands of male masquerade societies, and joining the society involves an initiation ceremony similar to joining a male masquerade society. Like night masquerades that need no costume but the darkness to hide them

---

[20] Cameron (1998:58), following Adams (1986, 1993), has pointed out the incapacity of Western terminology applied to masking to account for the social and cosmological equivalence in many African societies of masking with phenomena that fall outside this linguistic category. The effect of the resulting concentration on masking-with-masks at the expense of any performance alluding to alternative identities and forms of power is to exclude the wealth of women's performances that tend not to make use of carved masks, while nevertheless achieving similar ends.

(Peek, 1994: 484-6), *fembien* masquerades are defined by their invisibility. Moreover, the resonating stone they play hidden from view of all men but *kwifon* society members – referred to elliptically in terms of the drum (*tshum*) used by male masquerades – has many of the characteristics of acoustic masks that are heard but not seen. Baate members therefore sometimes refer to *fembien's* masquerade when arguing for the legitimacy of their own.

Discovering the other reasons for the relative degree of success Baate societies have had in spite of the explicit ban on women masking calls for a brief history of the groups. Few informants agree on the details of the early history of Baate groups, but they all paint roughly the same picture. The groups were first introduced from Nso' in the 1950s (during the late *fon* Sentie's reign 1956-91). At this stage they generally went by the name of *jofke chëklë* ('good hospitality/entertainment'). Like Mondial, Baate first ensconced itself in compounds along the borderlands of Oku, but from there a group was quickly established in Chung Bëy in Keyon, one of the most highly placed royal family (Mbele) compounds in the kingdom, the head of which is a senior *Kwifon* member and one of the few 'king-makers'. From the beginning, Baate groups were thus associated with the royal family, and they managed to gain the approval of the last *fon* on this basis. At a palace appearance, the Baate of Chung Bëy was officially recognized by the late *fon*.[21] From then on, the women of many other compounds throughout the kingdom began to acquire their own Baate groups.

In line with being associated with the royal Mbele lineage, however, the masquerades also eventually became associated (in people's conception of the groups, if not in fact) with the princes' society, Ngiri or Ngele. And just as the princes were closely associated with the Christian church in Oku at this time, so too Baate groups became associated with the church. This is widely seen as another reason for their having become accepted. People felt that any group belonging to the church would not be likely to harbour medicines or engage in witchcraft. This association was also, however, what led to the anxieties the groups elicited. As in many other kingdoms of the Grassfields, the princes' society was seen as subversive and dangerous to the king and the general well-being of the kingdom. It is for this reason that the princes are thought to have joined the early church in Oku, because it offered them an alternative hierarchy in which they could acquire knowledge and power while bypassing the hierarchy under the control of the *Kwifon* society. Furthermore, the Ngiri society members regularly flaunted their subversive attitude to the palace authorities by appropriating copies of *Kwifon* society masks, or creating types of mask that went against the canons of Oku style. For instance, the princes appropriated their own version of *Mabu* (*Mabu Ngele*), the executioner masquerade mentioned above, created a Janus-faced mask (*Mbui-n'ebame*; 'Front-and-Back') and began using paints to colour their masks, even though all of these things are proscribed in Oku.

By the early 1980s, people were openly comparing Baate groups to Ngele/Ngiri's transgressive masquerades, calling Baate 'the female branch of Ngiri'. This coincided with increasing accusations against Baate groups of harbouring medicines. As the groups began to spread, they were no longer confined to the churches. Rival groups began to compete against one another, singing antagonistic songs about certain compounds and organizing themselves more hierarchically. Finally, as they began to adopt the rites

---

[21] Official approval of Baate took the same form as that afforded to male masquerades: the *fon* would watch the performance, and then re-name the group, usually giving it a proverb or riddle as a name, such as the group Mbekenkveui which had its Lam Nso' name replaced with *Jabse Ndë*? 'Who is discriminating?'

of male secret societies such as Samba, anxieties grew regarding their supposed occult powers.

Having originally had a motherly, nurturing image (*baate* means 'to gather' or 'to unite', of crop harvests, etc. as well as of family members), they began to demand more respect from non-members. At first they entered their meeting-house without ceremony, but as they gained influence and established themselves, people were expected to step off the veranda for them, as when a lineage elder (*fai*) or king (*fon*) enters a house. Then they began passing through doorways backwards. Everyone I spoke to about Baate (members included) was of the opinion that they did so because they were holding medicinal concoctions in their bags. 'Only bad masquerades do that', I was told by one informant, 'it is a sign they are already carrying something dangerous. They had dangerous medicine.' The act of entering a house backwards relates to the euphemistic expression used by men's secret societies to refer to their medicines in Oku. These medicines are called *nda ebam* ('house behind'), referring to the back of the house, to a hidden (masquerade or secret society) house, and by extension to something buried under the floor of the house, or to the inversion of the normal domestic order of a house. Out of anxieties provoked by this sort of inversion, it used to be illegal to have a back door to one's house in Oku. Entering a house backwards is not only a sign that one is in possession of *nda ebam*, it is a means of actively inverting the house and one's normal physical relationship to it; and again by extension, it is a way of transforming the domestic space of the house into a site of occult power.

Around 1986, soon after *fon* Sentie and the *Kwifon* society had banned certain Ngiri society masquerades, one of the Baate groups was also banned for the first time. Informants disagree as to which one; some say it was the one from Chung Bëy, others that it was one from the village of Ngashie. Be that as it may, the result was that all Baate groups came to be seen as illegitimate; 'they have banned [the masquerades of the Princes' society] Ngiri', one informant told me, 'and those people are bringing another one'. Once one group was banned, the members of all the others began re-organizing their societies as straightforward *njang* groups without masquerades for a time. Then in 1991-92 came the 'loss' of the *fon*, and the protracted celebrations marking the installation of a new one (Argenti, 1999). This presented an opportunity to Baate members to re-present themselves at the palace in the hope of gaining an amnesty and official approval from the new *fon*. Throughout the month of June 1992, dance groups from all over the Grassfields performed at the palace in honour of the new *fon* and to offer their respect to the late one. Amongst these, Baate groups performed almost daily, on occasion several times a day. These, of course, could not be banned by the Oku *Kwifon* society, who had no jurisdiction over them, and so the Oku Baate groups were encouraged to re-emerge.

On 29 June, the first two Oku Baate groups performed without incident. Then, on the morning of 3 July, a Baate group from the village of Ngashie attempted to perform. They danced with elaborately decorated spears and poles topped with cowrie shells and a multi-coloured fringe of strings which flew outward as they spun the poles in their hands (Figure 6.3). While they were still dancing, three members of *Kwifon* came out of the palace wearing loincloths, their ceremonial attire, and shouted a public announcement in front of the group and the hushed public (Figure 6.4). The message was phrased in 'high' language, rhetorical questions and esoteric proverbs. It announced that the group had not existed in the past, that it was foreign to Oku, and that women do not have the right to own masquerades in Oku, or to be involved with medicines and witch-craft. In addition, the claim was made that the women were dancing with the spears of the male secret society Samba. Because these women were breaking these rules, the announcement went on, the ban enforced by the late *fon* was re-established today. This formalized message was in itself a ritual act of interdiction known as *bunle*. Once it had been performed, the *Kwifon* members confiscated the spears from the dancers and took them into the palace.

The Predicament of Cultures

It is not only anthropologists and historians who are privy to the deconstruc-tionist insight that tradition is invented – many ethnographers' informants know this full well themselves. Thus Ya Mary Nying, speaking to me about the origins of Baate, felt it necessary to qualify my naïve reading of the local term *nchiinen* as 'culture'. 'Almost all culture is not original', she retorted to my suggestion that the palace authorities may have banned her women's masking group because it was not part of 'Oku culture'. To support her argument, she brought up the example of the many 'tra-ditional' male military and secret societies of Oku that sing songs and recite prayers in the languages of distant kingdoms. While Oku people generally take the opacity of these societies' secret languages as proof of their age, pedigree and other-worldly powers (*kediar'*), thus setting them firmly within the realm of 'Oku culture', Ya Mary turns such claims on their heads by calling attention to the foreign origins – and hence the recent introduction – of these societies.[22] In so doing, she introduces a discourse of het-erogeneity with which to counter the palatine discourse of boundedness and homo-geneity.

By means of movements such as Baate and Mondial, social cadets who are excluded from the palatine hierarchies of the Grassfields and their micro-nationalist discourses of cultural-territorial integrity increasingly assert their own claims to access to exogenous sources of power. These excluded cadets are forced during the course of their lives to bypass the palace and develop multiple allegiances to places, social groups, economic practices and political orders in order to make a living, marry, and bring up children. These allegiances in turn foster the acquisition of multiple languages, bodily practices, 'homes', 'ethnicities', 'identities' and other complex forms of belonging. The resulting plural experience of place, belonging, and indeed of self, is inherently inimical to the imposition of essentialized and monolithic state-like discourses by the palace hierarchies.

In this section, I argue that performative events such as those staged by Baate and Mondial performers provide evidence that liminal models of divine kingship – especially in their newly reified versions in the Grassfields – are best understood not as 'cosmologies'

---

[22] Likewise, 'country fashion', the nearest Pidgin equivalent of *nchiinen*, has ambivalent connotations (with 'country' often pronounced *kontele* with tongue-in-cheek rusticity). Although referring to a rite as one's 'coun-try fashion' can be invoked as the reason to adopt a reverent and submissive attitude towards it, more often than not the expression is used in a derisory or belittling manner, emphasizing the inferiority of the practice (due to its local origin) in relation to a practice of colonial or postcolonial origin presumed to be more pow-erful or efficacious. Likewise, 'country chop' is seen in certain contexts to be inferior to imported food, 'coun-try soap' to industrially produced soap, 'country medicine' to pharmaceutical medicine. The Francophone Cameroonian joke that Warnier reports gains its humour from this opposition: A woman is told at the doctor's that she will be given a local anaesthetic for a small wound. 'Oh! No, Doctor', she pleads, 'not a local anaes-thetic. Please give me an imported one!' (Warnier, 1993:164, my trans.).

6.3 'Nearly all culture is not original': The Baate masks approach the palace veranda with their entourage. (©Nicolas Argenti)
6.4 Bunle: Three kwifon members make a public announcement banning the Baate group from performing again. The women of the group are huddled behind their few male members on the right. The two maskers' headdresses and the offending spears are visible just behind the drummers. (©Nicolas Argenti)

equally and unreservedly shared by all members of a homogeneous and bounded 'culture', but rather as discourses of power produced by a local minority elite engaged in a perpetual struggle to maintain supremacy. In the case of Oku, the discourse of the liminal king that fosters the model of the bounded polity is not shared equally by the entire population, but rather contested by those whom it excludes from power. Liminality, in other words, is not (nor in all probability was it ever) the exclusive preserve of the nobility of Oku, where even the pyramidal model of the palace hierarchy is itself the relatively recent result of an imbrication between the local elite and the nation-state. Those who do not share the palace hierarchy's experience of a bounded polity – youth and women, in particular – contest the palace's hegemonic quest for liminal authority as a form of boundary mediation protecting an enclosed centre. As in the past, and despite their annexation of modernist models of power espoused by the nation-state, Grassfields *fons* are therefore forced to negotiate power within an embattled or contested field in which they and their acolytes are not unambiguously positioned as 'leaders' in the Western sense.[23]

Outside the palace, the totalizing discourse of royal liminality is rapidly confronted by various levels of dissent, many of them enacted at the level of the very practices which otherwise constitute a sense of locality and discrete 'culture', and hence of royal power. Masked performance – the realm of transformation and the mediation of the exogenous – constitutes one such practice. African masking is often presented in the literature primarily as a conservative phenomenon supportive of the status quo (see Argenti, 1997 for a critique), and the majority of Oku masquerades – memorialized in local historiographies as if they were timeless and grounded in the space of the kingdom – could be interpreted as upholding the palatine discourse by lending Oku an apparently discrete genre of masking that would seem to differentiate it from neighbouring polities. In the Grassfields as elsewhere, however, new forms of masking periodically emerge that represent political platforms for groups of dissenters to the hegemonic discourse. Such masking traditions tend to be innovative, flexible, avant-garde and potentially critical of authority (Argenti, 1997, 1998; Cameron, 1998; Cohen, 1993; Kapferer, 1991, 1997; Kasfir, 1988a, 1988b; Nunley, 1987; Picton, 1990). The cases of Baate and Mondial underscore this point. If these two groups were banned in Oku (and yet continue periodically to re-surface), it is because their embodiment of exogenous forms of knowledge expresses Oku cadets' experience of a plural existence between kingdoms, between political economies and between 'cultures'. This embodiment of plurality is perceived by the palace elites as a subversion of the palace's negotiation of all things exogenous – whether from the realm of the wild or of modernist hierarchies – and its monopoly on the domestication of the exogenous into the local, and thus on the reproduction of the kingdom as a homogenous and bounded polity. While the *fon* plays the role of skin on a body, these new practices question the need for skin in a disembodied political context.

In the opening section to this chapter I argued that Grassfields kingdoms, despite their representation by members of the palatine hierarchies, colonial officers and ethnographers alike as static and territorially bounded 'cultures', in fact owe their existence to discourses of power that imbricate them – precisely by way of these representations – within the Cameroonian nation rather than in any primordial forms of local 'culture' or 'tradition'. These hierarchies therefore represent a subtle graft of precolonial models of divine kingship onto the modernist reifications of culture

---

[23] The *fon* is in fact a member of *Kwifon*, and therefore a servant of that society within the palace. In many ways, both formally recognized and relatively covert, the *fon* is one who is beholden to others around him to wield any sort of power (Dillon, 1990).

adopted by contemporary nation-states anxious about the security implications of their predicament of cultures. In the case studies of Mondial and Baate, however, I have provided evidence of performative practices that contest this micro-nationalist discourse of territorial integrity by breaking local elite proscriptions against the introduction of exogenous forms of knowledge and power without reference to the palace. The palace uses *Kwifon* society masquerades, on the one hand, and the British-funded forestry project and local administrative officers, on the other, to police the forest as its own monopolized zone of access to the exogenous. The national government, similarly, anxiously polices its highways with paramilitary road blocks every few kilometres, breaking the national space into zones of scrutiny, control and domination between which physical movement, trade, and communication are greatly restricted for ordinary citizens.

Performances such as those of Baate and Mondial might just be so contested because they successfully transcend the fragmentation and expropriation of space practised by the Grassfields states and the national military apparatus alike by establishing what we might term inter-states: multi-dimensional zones of contact between the local and the exogenous, the traditional and the modern within which the subject is free to forge new aggregates. The people of the Grassfields negotiate power in its relation to space in terms of zones of relative influence between which they forge multiple allegiances during the course of their lives. In the resultant multi-dimensional space of syncretized and partial identities, Mondial and Baate match the inter-territoriality of life in the Grassfields with a pastiche of composite musical and choreographic compositions that offer the subject free access to the wealth of social and political experience denied by modernist discourses of bounded culture. Inter-states traduce the road-blocks and other policing mechanisms of state and nation alike by introducing new trans-cultural spaces that transcend modernist practices of territorialization.

The notion of deterritorialized 'borderlands' that has recently emerged in the social sciences (Appadurai, 1990; Bhabha, 1994; Deleuze and Guattari, 1992; Gupta and Ferguson, 1992), clarifies my suggestion that Mondial and Baate performances are forbidden because they successfully contest palatine hegemony by introducing what I call inter-states as new ways of being in the Grassfields, ways of being that question bounded, micro-nationalist models by embodying plural identities and multi-dimensional allegiances, not only reflecting but constructing alteric subjectivities in their performers. If we understand palatine discourses of culture in the Grassfields not as essentialized and timeless objects, but as part of a process or movement toward nationalist integration designed to secure ever greater power for the state and local hierarchies alike (see Friedman, 1994: 90), then practices that offer the means to alternative forms of self-construction can be seen to interrupt or to moderate this hegemonic project, and therefore to operate as counter-hegemonic processes.[24]

---

[24] Rather than get caught up in the thorny question of whether such practices amount to resistance if they do not lead to the demise of palatine hierarchies in the Grassfields, one ought instead to ask another question: what would these hierarchies look like if they were not contested? In terms of an argument I have previously made with reference to new masking groups (Argenti, 1997), the two contradictory forces of the hegemonic discourse of locality and cultural identity, on the one hand, and counter-hegemonic practices such as those of Baate and Mondial, on the other, can be conceived of as tectonic plates opposing each other isometrically along a fault line that only occasionally becomes visible as fracture, but the hidden forces of which are always at work. Lack of radical socio-political change, in other words, does not entail lack of effective opposition; and just as tectonic plates shift not only in dramatic earthquakes but also imperceptibly over long periods of time, so too in the Grassfields the effect of such groups as Baate and Mondial lies not in the immediate moment of a single performative event, but rather in the longue-durée within which they enable the construction of new subjectivities.

The alteric subjectivities that Mondial and Baate performances facilitate can thus be seen as means of introducing a force with which to counter the centralizing pull of the palace hierarchy. I grant that this counter-hegemonic project cannot be successfully encapsulated within a centre-periphery model of resistance by the marginalized, which could not account for the multi-locality, the trans-locality, or the local complexity of the situation in the Grassfields (see Appadurai, 1990; Bayart, 1999; De Boeck, 1996 and Mbembe, 1992 for critiques).[25] As Deleuze and Guattari put it, 'Even the authors who stress the role of the peripheral and the acquired at the level of releasing stimuli do not truly overturn the linear arborescent schema, even if they reverse the direction of the arrows' (1992: 328). Nevertheless, one can read counter-hegemonic practices by the light of the rich heterogeneity of inter-states, or imagined 'ethnoscapes' (Appadurai, 1990), with which the cadets of the Grassfields counter palace and national models of place. Even Appadurai's notion is still too essentialistic in its emphasis on ethnic identity (imagined or not) to do justice to the exogenous subjectivities of extroversion (Bayart, 1999) that these groups foster. In the Grassfields, it is the palace hierarchies that emphasize ethnic identity as the basis for a grounded, localized form of belonging (and exclusion),[26] while those excluded from this hierarchy question any notion of ethnic purity and its attendant territorialization in line with their experiences of cultural and filial miscegenation, movement and transformation.

The experience of translocality that characterizes the lives of those excluded from Grassfields palatine hierarchies cannot be lived in terms of palatine discourses of locality and belonging. The need therefore arises for new practices that confront this ideology and locate young people and women in the very *lack* of place in which they live their lives. Bhabha (1994: 9–18, 1989) describes this confrontation effectively by calling attention to the Heidegerrian *presencing* effect of bridging the boundaries constructed by modernist power structures and homogenized historiographies. Far from fostering national or ethnic identity, texts and practices that *presence* emphatically deny the hegemonic historicity of the homogeneous myth of origin, replacing it with the estranging, heterogeneous and 'unhomely' actuality of life in an inter-cultural, pluri-local, hybridized space. Presencing in the Grassfields thus takes the form of an embodiment of unhomeliness that ironically relocates young people and women in the world from which they are alienated by micro-nationalist and nationalist discourses. The world one is returned to by means of these practices is an unhomely place, but not a place of homelessness. It may be a place of disquiet or even of terror (Argenti, 1998) – disorientating and disembodied – but this is only because it is a place in which the disjunctions of one's political existence are made plain.[27]

[25] Warnier's (1993b) explanation of the defection of cadets from the Bamileke kingdoms of the Southern Grassfields highlights the conditions that give rise to the adoption of the 'exit option'. From a local perspective, both groups seem marginalized by a palace hierarchy that excludes them from opportunities, while, from a larger perspective, both groups can be depicted as marginal to a world capitalist system that alienates them. The model of marginalized women and youths begs the question, however, of what 'centre(s)' they are marginal to, and whether such discrete centres really exist as anything other than discourses in the Grassfields or the Cameroonian nation as a whole (on the 'challenge' of integration that Cameroon faces, see Bopda, 2003).

[26] The *fon* of Oku, when speaking publicly in English or Pidjin, is fond of referring to the Oku 'clan' (a borrowing from the ethnographic literature), by which he promulgates a micro-nationalist naturalism that presents 'associations of people and place as solid, commonsensical, and agreed upon, when they are in fact contested, uncertain, and in flux' (Gupta and Ferguson, 1992: 12).

[27] Gupta and Ferguson (1992) likewise explode the myth of the homogeneous place and the bounded culture, criticizing 'the isomorphism of space, place, and culture' (1992: 7) promulgated in the social sciences, and again introduce instead an emphasis on the 'borderlands' as a place *between* places for the inhabitants of which 'the fiction of cultures as discrete, object-like phenomena becomes implausible' (*ibid.*).

In the Cameroon Grassfields, young men and women did not wait for Jameson's (1984) 'post-modern hyperspace' to forge links heterogeneously with neighbouring and distant communities, nor to move from place to place, nor to question their local hierarchies and thereby change their relations to them. The experience of space described by Gupta and Ferguson or encountered in the performances of Baate and Mondial is at odds with the modernist forms of territorialization introduced by the state and emulated by the palace hierarchies of the Grassfields. Gupta and Ferguson accordingly call attention to the deterritorialization characteristic of the post-Fordist era that pulverizes the space of high modernity and – like Ya Mary – radically questions what anyone might mean by 'cultural identity' (1992: 9, 20). Following Deleuze and Guattari (1992), however, Gupta and Ferguson also call attention to the *re*territorialization of space that any deterritorialization entails (1992: 20). Specifically, they call for the replacement of the old geographical grid on which culture used to be mapped with multiple grids capable of accounting for trans-local allegiances 'differentially available to those in different locations in the field of power' (*ibid.*) and resulting in variant representations of territory. Subversive masquerades in the Grassfields presence their participants in the inter-state between polities, cultures, political economies and nations, offering those excluded from power access to one such multiple grid. I would not argue that Baate and Mondial demonstrate that space, place and identity no longer matter. Rather, in their multi-perspectival, context-sensitive approach to these issues, Baate and Mondial reveal the limits of modernist, universalizing, context-free discourses both as political processes and as analytical devices.

States of Mind, Contested Nations

Notwithstanding royal edicts against them, Mondial and Baate still perform today in Oku. These ongoing performances expose the naturalist model of exogenous power exclusively monopolized by the ruling elite and funnelled through the sole channel of the palace as a discourse that is more often contested than not, and therefore as a form of negotiation or struggle for power in which the palace hierarchy is forced to engage as one amongst several groups of protagonists. The model of the bounded kingdom is therefore not a historical fact, nor is it a totalizing hegemonic system. Rather, it is a rhetorical device used by the palace authorities and the national government alike in their attempts to foster modernist forms of nationalism and micro-nationalism. As mentioned at the outset, the naturalist reification of 'culture' as the practice of containment that micro-nationalism involves is exposed by Baate and Mondial's performances of extroversion by means of which young people and women self-consciously embody exterior influences in the fashioning of new, hybrid modes of being that celebrate rather than hide their exogenous exemplars.

In the 1980s, a large concrete billboard stood at the gateway to Leh, the capital of Ladakh, that read 'Remember you are Indians first, Ladakhis second'. Highlighting the agonism of micro-nationalism, the *fon* of Oku often seems at first glance to invert this slogan when addressing his subjects, admonishing them that 'political parties come and political parties go, but Oku is here to stay'. Just as nations fear state identities, the rulers of Grassfields states are suspicious of strong national identities (especially those fostered by opposition parties) and the damaging internal conflicts and divisions these may lead to. Grassfields elites' anxieties regarding the state should not, however, be mistaken for total rejection; while the *fon* of Oku admonishes others to stay clear of political involvement, the palace hierarchy is nonetheless modelled upon national political structures and the *fon* himself plays a role in national politics at the local level. The process of democratization of the 1990s has thus not shaken the fundamental principle according to which access to government resources is but the latest currency in the prestige economy monopolized by the palace. Just as leopards, guns and slaves were in the past, political influence – the latest exogenous luxury good – is now largely controlled by the palace.

One might wonder whether the exogenous appropriations practised by Baate and Mondial are not themselves modernist replications of the palace's discourse of power. Mondial's leader might be said to see himself and his group in modernist terms: not only does he speak of the 'opening' of the village that he aims to achieve, he has introduced contemporary dance steps to the group's repertoire and given it a distinctively avant-garde name. Similarly, the appropriation of exogenous forms of power attempted by Baate dancers might be conceived of as according with the logic of the palatine discourse of power and its preoccupation with the accumulation of exogenous prestige goods as a source of legitimation. In both cases, however, these dance groups evince a marked contrast with the political project of the palace. What makes the political practice of the palace modernist is not only the fact that the elites engage with state forms of national identity, but that they replicate the territorializing effects of these at the local level, giving birth to micro-nationalist discourses of ethnicity. In contrast to this, the appropriations that Mondial and Baate effectuate do not reproduce so much as traduce the logic of their exemplars. To follow on from the brief discussion of modernity in note 8 above, Mondial and Baate promote a discourse of modernization, but reject the universalizing, context-free principles of modernity.

Mondial engages in mimetic appropriations of national political structures, but it is not straightforwardly party-political, nor does it aim uncritically to reproduce the forms of power that inspire its dancers. Unlike the palace, Mondial transcends the sectarianism characteristic of current Cameroonian politics by commenting humorously on the party system. Moreover, by making itself laughably inauthentic and irreconcilable to 'Oku culture', Mondial goes a step further to reveal the role of 'culture' in nationalist and micro-nationalist formations. By engaging its performers ludically in syncretic appropriations of the paraphernalia of state power, Mondial offers them new techniques of the body (Foucault's '*travail de soi sur soi*') with which to side-step royal admonitions to leave national politics to the palatine elite. The refusal to reproduce an exemplary reification of 'Oku culture' (heritage politics) and the direct physical engagement with undomesticated exogenous powers offer a wry commentary on the imbrication of Grassfields palatine hierarchies with modernist state structures, but they do more. They also mark young men's experience of their own trans-local existence in several fields of power simultaneously.

The discourse of palatine hegemony presents the *fon* as the only meaningful filter through which external forces trickle down to the people, who are thereby constituted as homogeneous subjects, but the young men who dance Mondial embody their experience of the world as it appears to them: raw, messy, undomesticated, heterogeneous and incommensurate with discourses of state and national integrity and centralized, arborescent models of power. Mondial's appropriations of foreign musical and dance forms serve to expose and to negotiate what it means to be *ghel Ebkwo*, 'Oku people', while also being young and disenfranchised in a plural, heterogeneous space. Not only is the dance a commentary upon the participants' experience, it is itself a bodily engagement with the world, a means of presencing oneself firmly within the unhomeliness of the

Grassfields and the nation without waiting for the inclusion that the elite periodically grant to the few. In the words of Mondial's leader Nshiom, Mondial offers the youth of this border village a means to open (*edisen*) their polity to exogenous forces (*mekale*). While this may look like what the palace also does, its consequences could not be more different: While the palace produces discourses of culture that replicate state forms of power of which it purports to be the source, Mondial playfully refracts images of authority and identity from diverse sources, claiming none but exposing all to scrutiny, thereby exchanging bounded discourses for the multiple grid of the inter-state.

Just as Mondial breaches the boundaries that the palatine discourse erects, Baate members' practices of walking backwards through doors, making men step off the veranda, wearing masks, and dancing with Samba spears to the sound of men's military society drums represent simultaneous breaches of both gender and cultural-territorial boundaries. Baate dances are obviously acts of transgendering, and appropriations of power as such,[28] but they also represent appropriations of exogenous cultural practices (often under the aegis of the Christian church) into the kingdom, and it is this latter fact that leads to their regular censure. As Adams (1986; 1993), Adler (1982), Cameron (1998), Phillips (1995), Röschenthaler (1993; 1998), and Weil (1998) have all recently shown, many African women do 'mask' legitimately, whether with or without masks. While the illegitimacy of Baate groups is justified by their critics in Oku on the grounds that they use masks, this is more an *ex post-facto* rationalization than a full explanation. Rather, Baate groups' insistence upon their own lack of 'tradition' or 'culture' and their celebration of the transgendered and translocal syncretism of their performance would seem to be the real threat in a setting in which the female *fembien* society's transformational performances – openly referred to as masquerades (*kekum*) – are not only legitimate, but widely respected.

As with Mondial and the adolescent masquerade Nton, Baate groups first gained a foothold in the border villages of the kingdom, those zones of ambiguous suzerainty farthest away from the control of the palace. Rather than become included within the palace as an accepted part of 'Oku culture', Baate groups then forged a strong association with the Christian church, on the one hand, and with the dissenting princes' society (Ngele), on the other. As Baate moved to the centre of the kingdom, in other words, it retained its alteric identity rather than become domesticated, and increasingly came to offer a field of power not amenable to palace control. This position was accurately sensed by those who accused the group of acquiring medicines and of dancing with the paraphernalia of a male secret society. Since medicines and secret societies are the preserve of men, their

---

[28] Taking the appropriation of male military regalia a step further, the maskers of one of the Baate groups that performed at the palace during the enthronement celebrations wore headdresses adorned with a few long red touraco feathers – prestige objects reserved as insignia of office by titled leaders of the Manjong and Mfu military societies, who are entitled to wear a touraco feather in their caps. In addition to the transgender elements of the female maskers' costumes, the men who often perform as the musicians for Baate groups could also be seen to be blurring gender boundaries in the very fact of belonging to a women's society. Johnson (1997) clearly delineates the means by which acts of transgendering in the Philippines are inherently acts of political dissent and counter-nationalist forms of alteric identification with imagined foreign countries. In Oku, the only overtly transgendered figure is the *fon*, who is represented by a female statue during royal installations (Argenti, 1999). In an event remembered locally and recorded in the German colonial archives, the *fon* who ruled when the first German patrol entered the borderlands of Oku went out to meet them dressed as a woman, an ambiguous gesture which the Germans took to be a sign of submission. The transgendering of Baate groups may therefore be seen by the palace authorities not simply as an attempt by female Baate members to appropriate male social roles, but as an abuse by male and female Baate members alike of the royal monopoly on the capacity to encompass both genders.

usurpation by women marked an appropriation of male power, or rather an attack on the integrity of that boundary. As Kasfir (1998:24) notes, the legitimacy afforded to women's masks stops where their failure to be mediated by men begins. The fact that the Baate members I spoke to never offered me a myth of origin for the group in the manner of legitimate Oku male and female masquerades also underscores the groups' deconstructionist orientation. Rather than seeking acceptance as part of an elite hegemonic construct, Baate members question the dominant historiography by emphasizing their debt to the exogenous 'cultures' and global social networks in which they work and live.

While Baate appropriate the material culture and the bodily practice of masculinity, and Mondial appropriate the material culture of national party politics, both primarily embody exogenous forms of power, knowledge and alterity, thus usurping from the *fon* the exclusive claim to do so himself. However, rather than create a cultural identity by domesticating these exogenous forces as the palace does, Mondial and Baate reveal the plurality of worlds in which Oku people exist. Whereas palatine and national discourses of power mobilize myths of authentic origin (of 'Oku culture' and the Cameroonian nation-state, respectively), Baate and Mondial refer to the plurality of spheres in which Oku communities now exist. The palace is therefore best understood not *a priori* as a localized place bounded by a container-king (the self-presentation of the palatine hierarchy that Warnier (1993a) has accurately described), but rather as a flux of negotiations and struggles for power engaged with alternative, globalizing relations of power which by turns threaten and reinforce it. The subversive potential of performances such as those of Baate and Mondial is not that they resist a self-reproducing centre of power, but that they fundamentally question the 'arborescent', functionalist ideology of power that would privilege certain locales and lineages in favour of a 'rhizomatic' schema emphasizing a co-ordination between multitudinous, plastic and ephemeral zones of influence.

Those to whom the 'imagined communities' (Anderson, 1983) of the Grassfields mapped onto physical locations still matter are those with something to gain from identification with the state in Cameroon: the elite. Those without a toe-hold in the modern discourse of power – the young, women, and commoners of the Grassfields – express their incommensurate experiences of space and place by means of counter-hegemonic practices that presence them in the multi-dimensional network of cultural flux and meagre opportunity that is their *true* milieu, their genuine political experience. If their performances evince an 'unhomely' or interstitial cultural syncretism, it is because they expose the illusion of a natural and essential connection between space, place and culture, thereby deterritorialising their identities in relation to the palatine hierarchy and the nation alike, and reterritorializing themselves in a counter-hegemonic space that is the one in which they exist in fact. Stuck uneasily between the mutually cannibalizing state and nation and their largely commensurate discourses, those without opportunities in either the local or the national hierarchy forge new practices of extroversion in order to bypass the gate-keeping mechanisms of divine kingship and national unity alike, both of which emphasize exogenous dangers as the justification for internal fragmentation, domination and violence. By dancing in the borderlands and travelling along interstates, Mondial and Baate performers embody a social reality that belies the paranoid symptomatology of state and nation building alike.

References

Adams, Monni. 1986. 'Women and Masks among the Western Wè of Ivory Coast', *African Arts* 19 (2): 46-55.

— 1993. 'Women's Art as Gender Strategy Among the Wè of Canton Boo', *African Arts* 26 (4): 32-43.

Adler, Alfred. 1982. *La mort est le masque du roi: la royauté sacrée des Moundang du Tchad*. Paris: Payot.

Anderson, Benedict. 1983. *Imagined Communities: Reflections on the Origin and Spread of Nationalism*. London: Verso.

Appadurai, Arjun. 1990. 'Disjuncture and Difference in the Global Cultural Economy', *Theory, Culture and Society* 7. Reprinted in Appadurai, Arjun. 1996. *Modernity at Large: Cultural Dimensions of Globalization*. Minneapolis: University of Minnesota Press.

Ardener, Shirley. 2002. *Swedish Ventures in Cameroon 1883-1923: Trade and Travel, People and Politics*. New York & Oxford: Berghahn Books.

Argenti, Nicolas. 1996. 'The National Culture of Power in Oku, North West Province, Cameroon', PhD dissertation, University of London.

— 1997. 'Masks and Masquerades', *Journal of Material Culture* 2 (3): 361-81.

— 1998. 'Air Youth: Performance, Violence and the State in Cameroon', *Journal of the Royal Anthropological Institute* 4 (4): 753-82.

— 1999. 'Ephemeral Monuments, Memory and Royal Sempiternity in a Grassfields Kingdom', in *The Art of Forgetting*, ed. Adrian Forty and Susanne Küchler. London: Berg.

— 2001. '*Kesum-body* and the Places of the Gods: The Politics of Children's Masking and Second-world Realities in Oku (Cameroon)', *Journal of the Royal Anthropological Institute* 7 (1): 67-94.

— 2002a. 'Youth in Africa: a Major Resource for Change', in *Young Africa: Realising the Rights of Children and Youth*, ed. Nicolas Argenti & Alex de Waal. Trenton, NJ & Asmara: Africa World Press.

— 2002b. 'People of the Chisel: Apprenticeship, Youth and Elites in Oku (Cameroon)', *American Ethnologist* 29 (3): 497-33.

Argenti-Pillen, Alex. 2003. *Masking Terror: How Women Contain Violence in Southern Sri Lanka*. Philadelphia, PA: University of Pennsylvania Press.

Atkinson, Jane Monnig. 1984. '"Wrapped Words": Poetry and Politics among the Wana of Central Sulawesi, Indonesia', in *Dangerous Words: Language and Politics in the Pacific*, ed. Donald Lawrence Brenneis & Fred R. Myers. New York & London: New York University Press.

Bah, John. 2000. 'Some Oku Rituals: Western Grassfields, Cameroon'. Privately circulated document.

Bayart, Jean-François. 1985. [1979]. *L'Etat au Cameroun*. Paris: Presses de la Fondation Nationale des Sciences Politiques.

— 1989. *L'etat en Afrique: La politique du ventre*. Paris: Fayard.

— 1999. 'L'Afrique dans le monde: une histoire d'extraversion', *Critique Internationale* 5: 97-120. (Published in English in *African Affairs* 99 (395): 217-67.

Bhabha, Homi. 1989. 'Location, Intervention, Incommensurability: a Conversation with Homi Bhabha', *Emergencies* 1 (1): 63-88.

— 1994. 'Introduction: Locations of Culture', in *The Location of Culture*, ed. Homi Bhabha. London: Routledge.

Bloch, Maurice & Jean Bloch. 1980. 'Women and the Dialectic of Nature in Eighteenth-Century French Thought', in *Nature Culture and Gender*, ed. C. MacCormack & M. Strathern. Cambridge: Cambridge University Press.

Bopda, Athanase. 2003. *Yaoundé et le défi Camerounais de l'intégration: à quoi sert une capitale d'Afrique tropicale?* Paris: CNRS.

Bouly de Lesdain, Sophie. 1999. *Femmes Camerounaises en Région Parisienne: Trajectoires Migratoires et Réseaux d'Approvisionnement*. Paris: L'Harmattan.

Cameron, Elizabeth. 1998. 'Women = Masks: Initiation Arts in North-Western Province, Zambia', *African Arts* 32 (1): 50-61.

Chilver, Elizabeth. 1963. 'Native Administration in the West-Central Cameroons, 1902-1954', in *Essays in Imperial Government*, ed. K. Robinson & F. Madden. Oxford: Basil Blackwell.

— 1996. (1966). *Zintgraff's Explorations in Bamenda, Adamawa and the Benue Lands 1889-1892*. ed. E.W. Ardener. Oxford: Friends of the Buea Archives.

Cohen, Abner. 1993. *Masquerade Politics: Explorations in the Structure of Urban Cultural Movements*. Oxford: Berg.

Comaroff, Jean. 1985. *Body of Power, Spirit of Resistance: The Culture and History of a South African People*. Chicago and London: University of Chicago Press.

De Boeck, Filip. 1994. 'Of Trees and Kings: Politics and Metaphor among the Aluund of Southwestern Zaire', *American Ethnologist* 21 (3): 451-73.

— 1996. 'Postcolonialism, Power and Identity: Local and Global Perspectives from Zaire', in *Postcolonial Identities in Africa*, ed. R. Werbner and T. Ranger. London: Zed Books.

Deleuze, Gilles & Félix Guattari. 1992 (1980). *A Thousand Plateaus: Capitalism and Schizophrenia*. Brian Massumi, trans. London: Athlone.

Dillon, Richard. 1990. *Ranking and Resistance*. Stanford, CA: Stanford University Press.

Drucker-Brown, Susan. 1989. 'Mamprusi Installation Ritual and Centralisation: a Convection Model', *Man* (N.S.) 24: 485-501.

— 1992. 'Horse, Dog and Donkey: the Making of a Mamprusi King', *Man* (N.S.) 27: 71-90.

Durham, Deborah. Forthcoming. 'Disappearing Youth: Youth as a Social Deictic in Botswana.'

Feierman, Steven. 1974. *The Shambaa Kingdom: A History*. Madison and London: University of Wisconsin Press.

Fisiy, C.F. 1990. 'Le monopole juridictionnel de l'état et le règlement des affaires de sorcellerie au Cameroun,' (trans. Jean Copans) *Politique Africaine* 40: 60-71.

— 1995. 'Chieftaincy in the Modern State: An Institution at the Crossroads of Democratic Change', *Paideuma: Mitteilungen zur Kulturkunde* 41: 49-62.

Fisiy, C.F. & P. Geschiere. 1993. 'Sorcellerie et accumulation, variations régionales', in *Itinéraires d'Accumulation au Cameroun*, ed. P. Geschiere & P. Konings. Paris: ASC-Karthala.

Fowler, Ian & David Zeitlyn (eds). 1996. *African Crossroads: Intersections Between History and Anthropology in Cameroon*. Oxford: Berghan Books.

Friedman, Jonathan. 1994. *Cultural Identity and Global Process*. London: Sage.

Geary, Christraud. 1988. *Images from Bamum: German Colonial Photography at the Court of King Njoya*. Washington, DC: Smithsonian Institution.

Geschiere, P. 1993. 'Chiefs and Colonial Rule in Cameroon: Inventing Chieftaincy French and British Style', *Africa* 63 (2): 151-75.

Giddens, A. 1984. *The Constitution of Society: Outline of the Theory of Structuration*. Cambridge: Polity.

Goheen, Miriam. 1996. *Men Own the Fields, Women Own the Crops: Gender and Power in the Cameroon Grassfields*. Madison, WI: University of Wisconsin Press.

Gupta, Akhil & James Ferguson. 1992. 'Beyond "Culture": Space, Identity and the Politics of Difference,' *Cultural Anthropology* 7: 6-23.

Herbert, Eugenia. 1993. *Iron, Gender and Power: Rituals of Transformation in African Societies*. Bloomington & Indianapolis: Indiana University Press.

Herzfeld, Michael. 1982. *Ours Once More: Folklore, Ideology and the Making of Modern Greece*. Austin, TX: University of Texas Press.

de Heusch, Luc. 1982. *The Drunken King, or the Origin of the State*. Bloomington, IN: Indiana University Press.

Holy, Ladislav and Milan Stuchlik. 1983. *Actions, Norms and Representations*. Cambridge: Cambridge University Press.

Jameson, Frederic. 1984. 'Postmodernism, or the Cultural Logic of Late Capitalism,' *New Left Review* 146: 53-92.

Jeffreys, K.D.W. 1964a. 'Who Are the Tikar?', *African Studies* 23 (3–4).

— 1964b. 'Le berceau d'une grande civilisation Camerounaise. Le pays Tikar', *Semaine Camerounaise* 58.

Johnson, Mark. 1997. *Beauty and Power: Transgendering and Cultural Transformation in the Southern Philippines*. London: Berg.

Kaberry, Phyllis. 1952. *Women of the Grassfields*. London: HMSO.

Kantorowicz, Ernst. 1957. *The King's Two Bodies: A Study in Medieval Political Theology*. Princeton, NJ: Princeton University Press.

Kapferer, Bruce. 1991 (1983). *A Celebration of Demons: Exorcism and the Aesthetics of Healing in Sri Lanka*. London: Berg.

— 1997. *The Feast of the Sorcerer: Practices of Consciousness and Power*. Chicago: University of Chicago Press.

Kasfir, S. 1988a. 'Masquerading as a Cultural System,' in *West African Masks and Cultural Systems*. ed. S. Kasfir. *Sciences Humaines* 126. Tervuren: Musée Royal de l'Afrique Centrale.

— 1988b. 'Celebrating Male Aggression: The Idoma *Oglinye* masquerade', in *West African Masks and Cultural Systems*, ed. S. Kasfir. *Sciences Humaines* 126. Tervuren: Musée Royal de l'Afrique Centrale.

— 1998. 'Elephant Women, Furious and Majestic: Women's Masquerades in Africa and the Diaspora,' *African Arts* 32 (1): 18-27.

Kopytoff, Igor, (ed.) 1987. *The African Frontier: The Reproduction of Traditional African Societies*. Bloomington, IN: Indiana University Press.

Last, Murray. 1991. 'Adolescents in a Muslim City: the Cultural Context of Danger and Risk,' *Kano Studies* (Special Issue on Youth and Health in Kano).

Lemarchand, René. 1997. 'Patterns of State Collapse and Reconstruction in Central Africa: Reflections on the Crisis in the Great Lakes Region', *Africa Spectrum* 32 (2).

Malaquais, Dominique. 2000. 'An Architecture of Desire: Sex, Seduction and Constructions of Identity in the Bamileke Highlands,' unpublished manuscript presented at the joint CERI-MàP colloquium 'Culture Matérielle et Subjectivation Politique', Paris, 10–11 January.

Mbembe, Achille. 1985. *Les Jeunes et L'Ordre Politique en Afrique Noire*. Paris: L'Harmattan.

— 1992. 'Provisional Notes on the Post-colony,' *Africa* 62: 3-37.

— 1999. 'Migration of Peoples, Disintegration of States: Africa's Frontiers in Flux,' (Trans. Derry Cook-Radmore), *Le Monde Diplomatique*, November: 14-15.

— 2000. 'At the Edge of the World: Boundaries, Territoriality and Sovereignty in Africa', *Public Culture* 12 (1): 259-84.

McKinley, J. Robert. 1979. 'Zaman Dan Masa, Eras and Periods: Religious Evolution and the Permanence of Epistemological Ages in Malay Culture', in *The Imagination of Reality*, ed. A. Becker & A. Yengoyan. Norwood, NJ: Ablex.

Myers, Fred. 1979. 'Emotions and the Self: A Theory of Personhood and Political Order among Pintupi Aborigines', *Ethnos* 7: 343-70.

Nkwi, Paul Nchoji. 1986. *Traditional Diplomacy: A Study of Inter-Chiefdom Relations in the Western Grassfields, North West Province of Cameroon.* Yaoundé: University of Yaoundé.

Nunley, J. 1987. *Moving with the Face of the Devil: Art and Politics in Urban West Africa.* Urbana, IL and Chicago: University of Illinois Press.

Peek, Philip. 1994. 'The Sounds of Silence: Cross World Communication and the Auditory Arts in African Societies', *American Ethnologist* 21 (3).

Perrot, Claude-Hélène & François-Xavier Fauvelle-Aymar. 2003. *Le retour des rois: les autorités traditionelles et l'état en Afrique contemporaine.* Paris: Karthala.

Phillips, Ruth. 1995. *Representing Woman: Sande Masquerades of the Mende of Sierra Leone.* Los Angeles: UCLA Fowler Museum of Cultural History.

Picton, John. 1990. 'Transformation of the Artifact: John Wayne, Plastic Bags, and the Eye-That-Surpasses-All-Other-Eyes', in *Lotte: The Transformation of the Object.* ed. C. Deliss. Graz: Grazer Kunstverein.

Ramanujan, A.K. 1989. 'Is there an Indian Way of Thinking? An Informal Essay', *Contributions to Indian Sociology* (n.s.) 23 (1): 41-58.

Rosaldo, R. 1988. 'Ideology, Place and People without Culture', *Cultural Anthropology* 3: 77-87.

Röschenthaler, Ute. 1993. *Die Kunst der Frauen: zur Komplementarität von Nacktheit und Maskierung bei den Ejagham im Südwesten Kameruns.* Berlin: VWB Verlag für Wissenschaft und Bildung.

— 1998. 'Honoring Ejagam Women', *African Arts* 32 (1): 38-49.

Rowlands, M. 1987. 'Power and Moral Order in Precolonial West-Central Africa', in *Specialization, Exchange and Complex Societies*, ed. E. Brumfiel & T. Earle. Cambridge: Cambridge University Press.

Shanklin, Eugenia. 1985. 'The Path to Laikom: Kom Royal Court Architechture,' *Paideuma* 31: 111-50.

Strathern, Marylin. 1980. 'No Nature, No Culture: The Hagen Case', in *Nature, Culture and Gender*, ed. Carol MacCormack & Marylin Strathern. Cambridge: Cambridge University Press.

Tardits, Claude. 1979. *Le Royaume Bamoum.* Paris: Armand Colin.

Turner, Victor. 1967. *The Forest of Symbols: Aspects of Ndembu Ritual.* Ithaca, NY: Cornell University Press.

Vansina, Jan. 1990. *Paths in the Rainforests: Toward a History of Political Tradition in Equatorial Africa.* London: James Currey.

Warnier, Jean-Pierre. 1975. 'Pre-Colonial Mankon: The Development of a Cameroon Chiefdom in its Regional Setting'. Unpublished PhD thesis, University of Pennsylvania.

— 1985. *Echange, Développements et Hiérarchie dans le Bamenda Pré-colonial (Cameroun).* Studien Zur Kulturkunde 76. Wiesbaden: Franz Steiner Verlag.

— 1993a. 'The King as a Container in the Cameroon Grassfields', *Paideuma* 39: 303-19.

— 1993b. *L'Esprit de l'Entreprise au Cameroun.* Paris: Karthala.

— 1995. 'Around a Plantation: the Ethnography of Business in Cameroon', in *Worlds Apart: Modernity Through the Prism of the Local*, ed. Daniel Miller. London: Routledge.

— 2003. 'Chefs de l'Ouest et formation de l'état au Cameroun', in *Le retour des rois: les autorités traditionelles et l'état en Afrique contemporaine*, ed. Claude-Hélène Perrot & François-Xavier Fauvelle-Aymar. Paris: Karthala.

Weil, Peter. 1998. 'Women's Masks and the Power of Gender in Mande History,' *African Arts* 32 (1): 28-37; 88-90.

7

DEBORAH DURHAM
'They're Only Playing'
Song, Choirs & Youth in Botswana

Mama wandji, indji yandjera
Oku nyanda Tjiherero (repeat)
Tu na tjo, tu na tjo, tu na tjo, Tjiherero.

My mother, let me
Play Herero
We have it, we have it, we have it, [being/doing] Herero.[1]

On Christmas Day 1988, I walked with my husband into the centre of Herero Ward in Mahalapye, a complex urban village in Botswana, to have my first unscheduled ethnographic encounter with Herero people. In the ward centre, we found a large number of people, ranging in age from their late teens to their forties: members of the Herero Youth Association preparing for a Christmas evening party and meeting, and other young people watching the preparations hopefully. While some busied themselves in the December heat with preparations for the party, most sat in the shade of the spreading acacia trees on rickety benches, old buckets, and other impromptu seats, and sang selections from the Lutheran Herero-language hymnal, to the accompaniment of a pounding walking stick. I walked up and introduced myself as interested in Herero song.

It was a fortuitous introduction to the right group. Although the leaders of the Herero Youth Association (HYA) often described their goals of reviving Herero culture, educating Herero about state resources, and providing moral leadership for the young, much of the Youth's activity revolved around singing and the HYA choirs. (Herero often referred to the group as 'Oyouthi' or as 'Omitanda,' which means youth in Otjiherero, or more fully as 'Otjira tjOmitanda', youth association.) The group had started, by most accounts, as a choir in 1981, and throughout the 1990s the association's leaders struggled to distinguish the choral activities from the other aspects of the association. A June 2000 meeting of the Gaborone branch, which I attended while visiting the country, focused primarily on how to separate choir practices, choir meetings, and choral performances from the 'general' association business, and to allow non-singing youth to feel part of the association. But the choral activities seemed somehow still to predominate, and to infil-

---

[1] A little song sung by members of the Herero Youth Association and others in the late 1980s. It was modelled directly on a song sung by an older Herero commemorative group, Otjiserandu, about playing at Otjiserandu activities and having the flag of Otjiserandu. Youth stopped singing the song and by the early 1991 some professed never to have sung it.

trate other activites. Even non-choir business meetings spent hours debating the uniforms to be worn by the choir (six-gore or four-gore skirts? sky, or navy, blue?), along with other business. When members of the HYA undertook an 'educational tour' of Namibia over the Christmas holidays in 1994, the tour was largely occupied with choral performances to Herero households, on Namibian radio and TV (singing many Setswana songs, to the Herero and larger Namibian audience), and to the Botswana embassy to Namibia (singing many Otjiherero songs to the Tswana staff). In Mahalapye HYA choir also moved Herero performances outside of the ward and Herero community to the large, multi-ethnic town's community hall, entering choral competitions and even singing not only in the national language of Setswana, but in Otjiherero as well.

In spite of the latter successes, the predominance of singing and of choral performances in HYA activities, the number of parties they held for just their own members, like the one we intruded upon that first Christmas, and an ambivalence about the Youth's failure to organize other projects, prompted many Herero from the Mahalapye community to dismiss them and their other goals as 'just playing'. 'They're just playing', said an urban Herero woman in a senior civil service position, an age-mate of some of the Youth leaders, 'what have they actually done (accomplished)?' 'They're only playing', said an elderly and impoverished village woman who belonged to another Herero association, the pan-Southern Africa Otjiserandu, known for its August 'games' (*omanyandero*) commemorating the Herero past. 'They're only playing', said a committed churchwoman and community participant, whose daughter wanted to marry one of the HYA leaders, with sharp disapproval. *Mave nyanda uriri.* I heard it again and again.

What does it mean, this insistent refrain, they're only playing, made about a group whose goals were a rather approved ethnic revival and the promotion of projects to benefit the entire community, a group whose leaders held well-respected jobs in the civil service or in the private sphere, and whose activities and meetings were at the least more organized than those of other Herero associations? And why do choral activities seem to be at the centre of the accusations? Clearly, the claim that the young people were just playing is a form of containment, a strategy that reminds them of the limits of their local powers and agentive potential, and holds in abeyance claims made through song as well as in their business meetings, unrealized educational programmes, and other activities. But what claims could the songs – generally unremarkable verses about God's love, about being children of Herero, about travelling and greeting others, set to, or based on, familiar tunes from the local repertory of southern African gospel and folk-traditional music, sung in Otjiherero, Setswana, Sesotho, and English – be making to prompt such containment?

The innocuous songs, the well organized meetings, the carefully planned parties, and the Youth themselves entered social space as alternately entertaining and supportive of the community, and as potential saboteurs of political topographies within the Herero community, and of the political space of Botswana within which that community recreates itself on a daily basis. Such activities, posed as they are between the two overlapping spaces, are recomposed along lines of work and play, accomplishments and inconsequentialities, Mahalapye-based homes and nationally dispersed lives. Diouf has described how in Senegal youth groups have 'redefin[ed] the spaces and logics of sociability and public places' (1996:235). Associations there based on religion and ethnicity, as well as other social and athletic associations, reclaimed neighbourhood sites abandoned by the government, or sites and services entrenched in a prebendial political logic, and started services – often educational – of their own. Such projects subverted the centralizing logics of power of the state, and initiated new strategies of self-definition that circumvented attempts to monopolize identity through state-centred clientelism. Like the youth associations of Senegal, the activities of the Herero Youth Association struck at the space of intersection of state and community, and hit both. But, as Abu-Lughod (1990) has pointed out for the defiant clothing choices of young Bedouin girls in Egypt, such acts can only be understood within the intersecting discourses of power through which they are made, and the multiple identities contested and at stake. An examination of the intersections reveals complex enmeshed agencies and shifting dependencies, rather than clear-cut acts of challenge, resistance, and empowerment.

As elsewhere in the the world, shifting topographies of social power have focused in Botswana considerably on youth – who they are, what the grounds of their actions might be, and how and where multiple contexts of agency and subjectification will intersect (see Durham, 2004). As with any topography, that of youth in the social imaginary is composed of innumerable equations and axes (Durham, 2000). Two of these intersecting axes are of particular relevance to understanding the constant refrain that the Youth were 'just playing'. One is the state-centred reconstruction of youth as liberal citizens, and the other encompasses the modes through which ethnicity is acknowledged in Botswana's overtly civic nationalist discourses. Both come together in the songs – and the well organized meetings, educational plans, and parties – that characterized Youth activities, tracing shifting lines across work and play, social maturity and youth, community and state, songs and sabotage.

In the last two decades, the ages of those who may be considered youth has been shifting noticeably downwards. In 1996, a National Youth Policy, along with new regulations established by various political youth wings, anchored an officialized discourse on youth as a younger group of people, now in their later teens and twenties, than had previously been the case, or than continues in other spaces such as the Herero community. Of course, these policies have been responding to shifts in employment and unemployment, demographic changes, various international media, and a wide range of other factors; the policies make concrete statements about what are much more uneven and contested processes.

At the same time, discourses on youth development programmes and educational initiatives in the later 1990s/early 2000s were offering new conceptualizations of youth agency. While 'agency' is often a factor in anthropological investigations of youth these days (see, for example, Amit-Talai and Wulff, 1995), we must remember that social agency is not a uniform, homogeneous, or generalizable phenomenon. In Botswana, youth agency, formerly distinctive and differentiated from other social agentive positions, is rapidly being reconfigured in the terms of a radically liberal citizenship that characterized Botswana's national development discourse as a whole. Youth programmes now focused on 'empowering' the young, much as state and non-governmental development discourse has turned to talk primarily of economic 'empowerment' of the citizenry (see Durham, in press). Many young people, especially in the schools, universities, and urban contexts, now claimed the social agency and power of the universal, undifferentiated citizen, demanding spaces of recognition as full and equal members of society. People formerly considered too young and unconfident to do so were standing up in *kgotlas* (chiefs' courts) to contribute opinions or even to question ministers and other political seniors; students rioted for independence and recognition (Good, 1996; Durham, 2004); and members of the political youth wings protested against their exclusion from party positions or complained about the 'deadwood' of various party seniors. For those who attempted to seize the promise of empowerment, the activities that typify youth in Botswana seem problematic. Students interviewed by one university student researcher complained about the Botswana National Youth Council's political empowerment programmes that the BNYC held 'talk shows and music festivals and [is] not interested in political education' (Kemodimo, 2000:30). And within the government Department of Youth and Culture, with youth and culture each having its own administrative apparatus and budget, so many requests submitted to the Youth programme officers are for choral or song-drama (*reetsaneng*) performances, that there is ongoing argument within the department over budgetary responsibilities, with youth administrators wanting culture to fund the more playful aspects of youth programming.

The second axis that undoubtedly prompted Mahalapye Herero to contain Youth activities as 'just play' concerned the place of ethnic mobilization and ethnic performance in Botswana. The leaders of the HYA often told me that the association was 'non-political' (they meant uninvolved in party-related politics). Yet, not only in addressing the role of youth in society, but also by being a specifically Herero association, the Youth could not but be political. Indeed, the claim that they were non-political was about as political a statement as could be made. The nature and place of ethnic identity have been a feature of life for groups such as Herero in the Tswana-dominated national society, and have surfaced since the late 1980s as a troubling question for the state sphere in Botswana, officially predicated on a civic nationalism that refuses to acknowledge ethnicity as an aspect of citizenship (see Durham, 1993, 2002a; Solway, 1994, 1995; Werbner, 2002; on 'civic nationalism' see Greenfield, 1992). The civic questions about ethnicity and citizenship have been most sharply posed to the state by a series of ethnic associations, including notably SPIL (Society for the Preservation of Ikalanga Language) and Kamanakao (a Yei group). In such a national discourse, the Herero Youth Association cannot fail to be political, although they may not recognize the political claims they make in their very denial of politicking. And while the leaders, telling me that the association was 'non-political,' referred to the domain of national parties and electoral politics, the political nature of the group within the local community of Herero from Mahalapye cannot be understated. In the midst of this non-political politics, the shifting line between 'just playing' and serious work is drawn across the business and organizational meetings the association was known for, its parties for members and the rare 'educational' trip, and the singing and choirs that seemed to dominate many members' interest.

Indeed, the choirs themselves carve out a very special ambiguous space between work and play, local community and a national public sphere, and youth and society, that is key to understanding the hot debates over the condition of youth in Botswana today, and the place of ethnicity in the civic sphere. The oft-heard refrain that Herero Youth were 'only playing' suggested that, in spite of their claims to the contrary, they were entering serious political space with their choral and organizational forms. At the same time, however, young people complain and complain vociferously, to those who interview them, that they feel marginalized and alienated from the political process. At least one student activist in Gaborone (the capital) complained that youth who attempted to participate in political parties were relegated 'to sing in choirs', thus marginalized from more serious business (Kemodimo, 2000:28). To understand the force of the critique of Herero Youth, and the debates of ethnic and age identity that shape their particular space of just playing and choral performance, I shall discus in the following sections the Herero Youth Association, discourses of youth in Botswana, including the significance of play and work and youth agency, and the place of song and choirs as an ambiguous space for evaluating youth.

The 'Local' Context

At the outset, I must make clear that 'local context' refers to a community within which ties are dense and deep, but whose 'location' is dispersed across Botswana, southern Africa, and occasionally as far as the United States, Britain, and Germany. The Mahalapye Herero community was founded by refugees from the Herero-German War of 1904 in what is now Namibia. In the wake of the war, Herero refugees settled in communities across the Bechuanaland Protectorate, although primarily in the west and north. Settling in Mahalapye, a central-eastern village, in the 1920s, Herero followers of Samuel Maharero established a ward of their own in the outer ring of the village, and cattleposts to the east and, later, west. By the 1980s, Herero Ward had become a multi-ethnic ward, with a Herero headman who heard disputes among Herero and also the Tswana, Kalanga, and other residents of the ward. (A Herero chief also sat in the village's main *kgotla*.) Herero have moved out of the ward, living in several of the adjacent wards and indeed some of the far-flung seventeen wards that make up the village (called an urban village for its urban downtown and the increasing dependence of residents on non-farming subsistence activities). Herero have also moved to the major cities of Botswana (Francistown and Gaborone, and their outskirts), to the diamond mining towns such as Jwaneng, and to rural areas in other parts of the country where they establish cattleposts near non-Mahalapye Herero relatives. Herero from Mahalapye move around the country for education, jobs, marriage, or long-term visiting. Many become fairly inactive members of the Mahalapye community. Even these remain members, in the sense that their names are continuously circulated in gossip and inquiries about the health of relatives and acquaintances of more active members. Others remain deeply involved, returning for funerals and weddings and for family reasons, to build homes in the village or to visit relatives (often children left with older female relatives), and to attend meetings and choral events such as those held by the Herero Youth Association.

Mahalapye Herero, although they remain convinced of the ultimate truth of a Herero identity, in the 1980s and '90s by and large accepted with enthusiasm the premise of equal, non-ethnic, citizenship in Botswana. While on rare occasions they voiced suspicion of ethnic bias in government affairs (Durham, 2002a), and consistently decried Tswana arrogance in daily life, most of their activities and orientations, from wearing Herero dress (see Durham, 1999a) to pursuing university education, are shaped by their uncertainty about Herero relationship to any national culture. Herero-ness is something that is negotiated primarily in domestic spaces and in local activities whose audience is primarily other Herero and scattered non-Herero neighbours and friends. Of prime importance, then, are the transitional public spaces of funerals (Durham and Klaits, 2002), and the village *kgotlas* and community halls, where Herero-ness as embedded in language, dress, and difference is confronted most directly. Many of these confrontations take place in sites that are by nature oppositional and at the same time designed to build consensus and co-operation: the funerals, in their embedded discourses of love and hate (see Durham, 2002b); the *kgotla* in which cases are pressed between parties of various sorts; and the community hall, where choirs compete before local or imported judges.

While Mahalapye Herero of all ages find themselves living across the country, young people are particularly pressed to move out, either for education, for employment, or to live with supportive (and sometimes exploitative) relatives. Many of these live in or near the larger urban centres of Gaborone and Francistown, and since the early 1990s the Herero Youth Association members have introduced local branch activities in these centres.

The Herero Youth Association at Work and Play

During a short visit to Botswana in June 2000, I found the Gaborone branch of the Herero Youth Association (now much expanded from the group I met in 1988) discussing their forthcoming annual conference. A major issue of discussion was the relationship of the meetings of the HYA choir and the general meeting of the HYA as a whole. This involved issues of uniforms to be worn (the choir sports two it wears for performances, in addition to the HYA uniform), but also the difficulties many members (and, also quite importantly, community observers) had in separating choral practices and performances from the goals and activities the Executive Committee had for the HYA as a whole. There were many people who joined the HYA and did not join the choirs; for them youth activities were dominated by series of meetings – business meetings, conferences, organizational and planning meetings – throughout the year, decreasing in regularity and participation in the mid-1990s but of renewed frequency and organization by the end of the century. The organization and these meetings are unremittingly bureaucratic, filled with offices and committees, motions and minutes. Even the parties they held had a bureaucratic air: a catering committee was in charge of procuring and preparing food; a group was specifically assigned to dishwashing (ongoing so that the dishes could be used by those still waiting to eat); another group was assigned to locate and borrow iron pots, utensils, and tables. At one event, members were openly chastised for straying from their assigned tasks to work at others. In their careful choreography, and the importance put on co-ordinated performance, these meetings and activities have something in common with the more public performances by the HYA choir since the 1990s.

Beyond the highly structured meetings and assignments of roles, occasionally the Youth – both choir and general membership – 'did something' (in the words of one of their critics mentioned above) – organizing a visit to Botswana's Chobe Game Reserve, or a trip to Namibia, or cooking and serving food, and cleaning at a public event. These accomplishments, always accompanied by all sorts of choral activities, sometimes raised community opinion of the HYA for a period of time, especially insofar as they recalled the older patterns of youth service to the community. The last age regiments (*mephato)* formed in the Ngwato chiefship, in which Mahalapye lies, were formed in the 1950s. Many older Herero were members of the age regiments, and when the village hosted a large party to celebrate the opening of the national Railway Workshops (repair facilities), the Malekantwa regiment, the last to be formed, worked as fundraisers, and prepared and served food. The Ngwato age regiments formed groups of people who performed community services or, what was seen as ideally the same thing, services for the chief. They might be sent after stray cattle, work on roads, or punish wrong-doers. In the past, too, Ngwato and other chiefs sent age regiments to work in South Africa to raise money for schools for the polity, or for other 'tribal' projects (Wylie, 1990; Schapera, 1940). So when the Youth prepared food in the Herero ward centre on New Year's Day, or at a wedding, or sang as a choir at a village celebration, they were indeed doing the kinds of work associated with youth in the past. The contributions they made to weddings and funerals were referred to by Herero at large as 'work' (*oviungura*). But important as these acts were both for the community and for members of the HYA, the actual 'work' of the association designed by its leaders and approved by its members was much more ambitious, and much more insidiously situated between non-complementary structures of power and authority.

As members of the Executive Committee (the President, Chairman, Secretary, Treasurer, and other officers) talked to me about the goals of the association during 1989 and 1990, a frequently recurring term was 'consciousness-raising' (used in English). While these Committee men (all men) did not explicitly make the comparison, their statements and goals complemented vividly the statement I heard frequently among Herero of all sorts in Mahalapye during those two years, *matu kara uriri*, we (Herero) just live, or, in effect, are doing nothing (to improve ourselves). The consciousness-raising that the HYA officials described (rarely articulated by other members of the association who deferred to the leaders' authority) included both developing awareness of Herero identity, culture, and history, and improving community awareness of the development problems, and the programmes and opportunities offered by the state.

Most of these goals were understood as educational: the Youth said they would like to provide Herero language education at weekends, to teach youth and younger people especially about Herero dress, distinguishing cultural practices, and such 'cultural markers' as place praise names or *oruzo* (patrilineage) histories. They also talked about providing crèche (nursery school) services for women who worked. While these ambitions were frequently spoken of in presentations to outsiders (such as me), in debates over the constitution that would be the cornerstone of registering the Herero Youth Association as a society under the government Societies Act, and occasionally in other conferences and meetings, they were taken up only very sporadically, and with mixed success. During the New Year's party/meeting for 1989, a Herero elder who was the acknowledged local expert on Herero history, was invited to address the Youth on Herero tradition. As he admonished the young women to wear the distinctive Herero dress (see Durham, 1999a), the women and some men exchanged glances and tittered during his brief address (certainly under five minutes), and hurried on to financial, membership, and organizational business, and into their elaborate party meal. The next actual effort to learn more about Herero 'culture' that I know about occurred in December 1994/January 1995, when a small number of the Youth went to Namibia and during the trip collected Herero place praise names, the histories of *otuzo* (pl., patrilines) to which they belonged, and attempted to visit the graves of the Maharero line of chiefs. Far more important to most of the participants on this trip, however, were the choral performances they gave throughout, which I will describe below.

The other educational, and 'consciousness-raising', goals the Youth Executive described were to educate the Herero community about government assistance programmes, and the problems that these were designed to address. For example, Youth members talked about possibly getting someone from the Ministry of Health to address the young people of the community about the dangers of teenage pregnancy and sexually transmitted diseases, or the community at large about other health problems. They wanted to sponsor presentations on the FAP (Financial Assistance Policy), which provided loans for small business start-ups; on livestock inoculations and health, and range management; on the agricultural programmes of ALDEP and ARAP. None of these presentations was ever organized or made, to my knowledge, but the idea remained a mainstay of the association throughout the 1980s and '90s. The goals of community improvement were consistent again with other forms of youth 'work,' and yet at the same time seized and transformed community political space in ways deeply disturbing to many in the community in the early 1990s. It was undoubtedly this threat that prompted some to dismiss Youth activities as a whole, and not only the choir practices and elaborate banquets for themselves, as just play.

The leaders of the HYA were mostly employed, and most of them (though by no means all) were employed by the government in various ways. A number worked for the veterinary department; some were teachers in primary or secondary schools; others worked for private industry or ran small businesses on their own. All of these, and some of the unemployed as well, considered their experience in government and in the working world to be formative to their leadership and management skills. 'We are the leaders,' I was told by one, 'because we know how to conduct meetings, and to plan projects, and to get things done.' In 2000, these leaders and doers were trying to train new members in these skills; at the meeting I attended in Gaborone, old leaders were clearly coaching their successors. Although very little of their plans seemed to come to fruition, their commitment to bureaucratic models of governance, to the development goals of the national government, and to the educational strategies through which knowledge could be transmitted in forms that they had learned through the state, was striking. For example, their plans for a crèche were based upon models of a nuclear family, with a working mother unable to afford domestic help in the home, where she kept her own children, a practice which was quite uncommon in the village where children were most often cared for by grandmothers and other female relatives of their mothers (working, or not).[2] The crèche plan also, implicitly and never in a manner voiced by any of the Youth, implied that better upbringing and care might be afforded by a community institution (modeled on crèches run as businesses, or by churches) than by the older women of the village. In the crèche, children would be taught learning skills and some basic numeracy and English to prepare them for the educational ladder. Similarly, the plans to teach younger Herero the Herero language (possibly in the crèche) were, in fact, plans (as one HYA member put it to me) to teach it to them 'properly' – that is, along models of language regularity and grammaticality such as they had learned for Setswana and English in school, and not the haphazard speech that they thought they learned at home.

Claims to leadership in the community based on education, on skills, and on highly specialized knowledge in officialized forms established outside the community itself, were both recognized by all – including older – members of the Herero community, and also fairly subversive of older forms of political power and social authority in the ward. Processes of bureaucratization and specialization had been ongoing in the Ngwato policy since early in the century (Wylie, 1990), and had accelerated considerably since Independence in 1966. The technocracy of Botswana's government was supported by a widely accepted doctrine of liberal individualism in which individual accomplishments, skills, and initiative were seen to anchor action – although these ideas were in tension with other concepts of personhood and agency rooted in relationships and community orientations (see Durham, 2002a, 1999b). But within the Herero community, authority based on (social) age, inherited status, cattle patronage, and on a knowledge of Herero

---

[2] This is not to say that people did not struggle with child care. They did. One older woman cared for up to nine children each day, who came from other compounds.

ways based on experience (and the capability to improvise that comes with participation in a variety of circumstances) was being challenged by the HYA through the more bureaucratic and liberalist forms they used. This can be seen in their treatment of the Herero chief and headman, and in the ways in which they conceived of and planned to promulgate 'culture'.

The Herero chief was chief by (maternal) birth – and the open respect older people offered him based on that birth contrasted with the lack thereof of younger Herero. While such doubts as older people voiced were based on his age (he was, in 1989, only 33, not much more than a child) and patterns of behaviour associated with youth (performing manual labour himself, wearing 'herdboy' clothes, chasing girls, resisting marriage, not listening to his uncles), the younger Herero noted his lack of education. In the early 1990s, many suspected that he could neither read nor write (he could), and described him as 'brought up at cattlepost'. After one of their annual elections in which the Executive Committee was re-elected (although shuffled in its positions), one of the HYA members told me that, in the 1980s, soon after the chief's installation in fact, they had elected the chief to the position of Chairman, 'out of respect'. She said that was the last time they elected him to anything – although they regularly nominated him. 'He was stupid', she said. He had been, she said, unfamiliar with the responsibilities of the chair in following agendas, guaranteeing orderly debate, and moderating, and had dominated the meetings with his own pronouncements and decisions. Members of the Youth were less openly scornful of the Herero headman, who heard cases in the ward court and who led most ward meetings,[3] but they paid little attention to him and expected no leadership from him (except perhaps in resolving family disputes before they got to court). He was illiterate and unfamiliar with the government forms that came his way.

The Chairman, Secretary and President of the HYA were often called upon to act as the 'Masters of Ceremony' at funerals, but more remarkable was their outspokenness at ward (*kgotla*) meetings held over Herero affairs in the late 1980s, when these men were still relatively young to be speaking so, and saying the things they did. At one 1989 meeting called by the chief, the problem of poor attendance led the discussions (a common issue at the time). The HYA Chairman challenged the chief by saying that the poor manner in which the meetings were organized and held led to poor attendance, and directed him to be more business-like with them, explained how meetings should be conducted, clearly drawing upon the model of how meetings were conducted in his government affairs. Within their own households, moreover, while the Youth leaders (who came to typify the association to the community) continued to defer to their fathers and uncles in matters of religion and ancestral practices (many of the leaders were openly sceptical of witchcraft, where elders would also maintain authority, see Burke, 2000), they often dominated economic decisions and decisions about the schooling, training, or residences of younger members of the household.

Much like the young Pentecostalists described by van Dijk (1998), who challenged the grounds of morality and authority of gerontocracy, the Herero Youth Association and its leaders challenge very strongly the ability of the more traditional authorities of the community to direct community affairs, both through their own discounting of the older sources of authority and through their introduction of new models. Herero had throughout the nineteenth century adapted and adopted a variety of models of organization, drawing upon the chiefships of Nama to their south, and on the military

---

[3] The chief sat as one of three chiefs – the most junior one – in the main Mahalapye *kgotla*, which served as a court of appeal for the whole village.

metaphors of Germans (see Durham, 2003; Werner, 1990; Gewald, 1999). Herero Youth were therefore challenging not so much an age-old set of traditions as the particular grounds upon which older people in their community had claimed authority, managed subordinates and younger people, and mobilized projects in their own lifetimes. One of the ways in which older people attempted to contain the subversive claims of the Herero Youth to better direct projects and to improve the community, was to discount their activities as play. They were better able to do so, because most of the HYA energies were devoted to the organizational forms themselves, and very few of their plans were actually implemented or projects successfully undertaken. In dismissing them as playing, moreover, other Herero were not only pointing to their lack of actually accomplishing 'anything', they also suggested that the things they did accomplish were not things 'for the community'. This idea I shall discuss in the next section.

These new bureaucratic models, however, were possibly most subversive where they were least obvious: in the ways in which the HYA were reconfiguring what 'being Herero' was and what and how 'culture' would become an emblem of being Herero. One of the distinctive features of Herero cultural practices – the idea being used fairly uncritically for the moment – was their embeddedness in doing things for various social purposes. Because Herero communities in Botswana are dispersed, and because Herero in nineteenth-century Namibia were not united politically (except, fairly uneasily, under German rule), Herero practices were never controlled by any one authority, and were continuously adapting as Herero individuals moved from group to group (and into and out of non-Herero groups). In the terms of Deleuze and Guattari (1987), Herero culture was and has been markedly 'rhizomatic' – or decentralized and yet connected by ongoing webs of interaction that guaranteed innovation and migration of ideas and practices (see Durham, 2003). But the models of culture in which the Youth wanted to educate other (younger) Herero were based on ideas of correct, final and authoritative knowledge, a knowledge that would be inscribed in books, perhaps, and which displayed the kind of 'centralizing' and homogenizing tendencies of the bureaucratic models they espoused in their organization.

The models of culture, what would be included, its codification in authoritative and correct forms, and how and where it would be enacted, were to a large extent borrowed from the way in which 'Setswana culture' was taught in schools (where, like choral pieces, it could be judged as right or wrong). Perhaps the most dramatic enactment of this, for me, was during a stroll downtown, when a young Herero woman described – in terms straight out of Isaac Schapera's mid-twentieth-century ethnographies – the 'normal' Tswana funeral to a young Tswana former schoolmate, to his great enjoyment and approbation. She had learned the funeral, he said, better than he. For the HYA, the elements of 'culture' were selected, and while some were integral to older Hereros' everyday lives – such as the long Herero dress – many were items from a resurrected past, collected and recorded, such as the *otuzo* histories and praise names for places in Namibia that HYA members collected while they were there.

But even more 'bureaucratic', and more playful too, was the way in which the Herero Youth Association seemed to produce special places and times in which to be Herero, while spending other parts of their days being just citizens of Botswana. As noted, almost all of the leaders of the association had jobs. Most occupied these jobs not as Herero, but as the unmarked liberal citizens of which Botswana is ideally – although never really – composed. When I visited one Youth member in her office in the district capital, her office colleagues expressed surprise to discover that she spoke Herero and came from the

Herero community (an ingenuous surprise, no doubt, as they also knew of her engagement to a Herero man, but the expression itself was significant). Another Herero told me
of going on a trip for his job up to Ngamiland, where many Herero live. Herero women
whom he was assisting began to speak to each other in Herero, discussing how to get
the government workers to do some of their work. As he told this story, it was clear that
he thought it reasonable that he would be seen as non-ethnic, or at least non-Herero, in
his government job.

The lecture by the old man to the Herero Youth, exhorting the young women to wear
the Herero dress, was itself significant in this respect. Most of the women he addressed,
with the exception of two somewhat older ones, dressed in the Western-based styles that
Herero call 'setswana' dress (see Durham, 1999a) at work and in their daily lives. Many
of them, however, did put on a Herero dress for specific occasions – for weddings, for
funerals, and increasingly throughout the 1990s for Herero Youth public performances.
Especially in the earlier part of the decade and the late 1980s, putting on the dress did
seem something of a game for them. They would borrow dresses from older female relatives (who would tie the complex headscarf known as the *otjikayiva*), and then dress
together for the event in question. There would be much laughing and assisting one
another with the layers of underskirts, the fastening of the difficult buttons along the side
of the bodice, the tight cinching of the belt, and adjustments to the *otjikayiva*, as well as
with (also uncommon in daily dress) make-up. While in the dresses, they would osten-
tatiously draw skirts over ankles that were normally exposed – the ideals of the long dress
were that ankles and legs remain hidden, although many women looped their skirts up
with their belts while working in their compounds or at the cattlepost.

All this playfulness with the dress is less significant, though, than the way in which the
wearing of the dress, and the activities of the Herero Youth Association, seemed to partition being Herero. The dominant members of the HYA had come to live in Gaborone,
Francistown, Palapye, Serowe, and other parts of Botswana, and were very invested in the
national public sphere of work. Their returns to Mahalapye and to participation in
specifically Herero activities, including domestic and inter-domestic interactions, as well
as projects of community reproduction, were largely confined to spaces carved out
around their other activities. Indeed, these visits home often coincided with HYA meetings or activities, mostly scheduled during the four-day holidays that punctuate the work
year, or other weekends.[4] In some ways, being Herero, for these youth, with their broad
involvements with the larger national society, becomes something confined and specialized, something identified with certain expertises that must be transmitted in highly regularized ways, and yet which takes place outside of their jobs.[5]

This bureaucratization not only of culture, but also of identity, the setting off of distinct offices and places for its performance, the increasing definition of narrow and regularized attributes, or responsibilities of culture, are picked up in the treatment of the
dress not so much as playful, but in its development as a uniform. The sartorial landscape
of Botswana is a patchwork of uniforms: most of these are put on and off for specific
performances, although some mark more permanent and consistent identities. For
example, most churches have uniforms that many men and women wear when they go

---

[4] In June 2000, I found the Gaborone branch of the HYA scheduling regular meetings on Wednesdays, after
work. This also adheres to the pattern of scheduling activities in 'non-work' hours.

[5] Unlike the period and place described by the Comaroffs (1987), people in Botswana today do not distinguish linguistically between 'work' and 'labour,' *go dira* and *go bereka*. But one dimension of the distinction
remains, as I describe above for Herero (who speak Setswana, and Otjiherero). Herero do not feel, however,
that jobs/labour are less valued than community-oriented work.

to services; uniforms mark out jobs and the expectations of people in them; and choirs, including the choirs of churches, social choir groups, and the HYA choir, have one or more uniforms that they will don for performances, competitions, and fund-raising activities. Some uniforms may be worn in such a way as to suggest a permanent identity for the wearer that is continuous across all his/her fields of activity. Members of the ZCC, for example, wear a little ribbon and pin all the time, reminding them of their essential grounding in church doctrines and policies (they also have a variety of more complete uniforms for church performances). Widows and mourners wear clothes and ribbons as the outward expression of their mourning. These clothes invite recognition from passers-by of the fundamental identity of their wearers at all times. ZCC members are always likely to be greeted with the recognitions of their church – 'kgotsong' (a greeting meaning 'to peace', used only by the ZCC and not by Botswana society at large). The Herero dress is also worn by many women as a continuous affirmation of their identity – and, less remarkable but nonetheless parallel, older men with their walking sticks and hats (sometimes ordered from catalogues from German makers).

But the youth – young people in general, as well as members of the HYA – do not wear their Herero identity so continuously. They are not recognizably Herero in many of their activities, but only in delimited ones. The Herero dress becomes for them like a uniform, worn to distinguish particular activities. Herero-ness is less a continuous state of being than one that is integrated into national society and their much broader lives and range of activities in distinguished and limited ways. While, to some extent, their 'being Herero' grew more continuous and their life projects became more embedded in the Herero community as they aged (by the year 2000), they did in fact introduce a new model of being Herero in their bureaucracy, uniforms, and creation of performative moments. These models accorded with other movements being made by ethnic minorities for representation in the public sphere, promoted by other groups at the end of the twentieth century, and to which I shall return in the conclusion. And they were indeed profoundly subversive of ideas of being Herero, sabotage not only of the ways and places in which authority would be claimed and sustained, but also of the ways in which everyone's identities in Botswana's public sphere would be recognized. And yet, with all these intimations that Youth activities could be called play, when, in 1991 and later in 1994, I asked members about the song quoted at the beginning of this essay, which was sung in 1989/90, they were all quite put off by the idea that what they were doing was 'play'.

Playing Herero

From the start, I found the idea that the Herero Youth were 'playing' Herero captivating because of its resonance with ideas of Johann Huizinga (1950), whose study of play suggested that it was a crucible of experiment and creativity out of which culture itself was forged.[6] Huizinga defined play as voluntary activity, taking place 'outside ordinary life' and distinct from the driven necessities of satisfying immediate material needs, marked off from the ordinary in both time and space by framing devices that set up a space with

---

[6] Huizinga, defining play as opposed to the mundane activities directed at mere 'appetitive' necessity, comes to identify culture substantially with play: the 'play function' is the 'culture function' (1950:9). It should be noted, given Huizinga's definitions, that he identifies ritual as a form of play. It is important that the 'fun' aspect, and the suspension of material drive, is extremely important to Huizinga, and he bemoaned the loss of that element in many activities that should be 'playful' in Western modernity.

its own set of rules that are imaginative and creative, and within which are novel kinds of order, order with an affinity to the aesthetic, an order that is itself a counterpoint to the messiness of the everyday, and which clarifies the ethical nature of behaviour. Play, too, Huizinga notes, although circumscribed by time and place in its performance, tends to become repetitive and so to extend itself temporally; it also creates 'play communities' that perdure as 'us groups', against which there are others. Unnecessary for survival, but an embellishment of creative whimsies and imaginative experiment, creating order, play is, for Huizinga, the very source of culture (or, for his purposes, civilization). The introduction of each new cultural form, each institutional development, must have been unnecessary in terms of the ordinary routes to survival and material satisfaction, and hence a playful activity that might later become regularized into mundane duty and needful activity.

The appeal of Huizinga's approach for an understanding of the HYA activities is apparent. Song is used for their activities, as in most public events, to frame certain spaces in which a particular order is presented. The bureaucratic games that the Youth 'play' seem, to others in the community, to 'accomplish nothing'. And yet their activities are imaginative and actively engaged in forming new kinds of order, and new kinds of 'us' and 'others'. But we need to take seriously, too, the Youth claims that what they are doing is both work and very serious work indeed. Huizinga is able to sustain such a rich definition of play, and to explore its constitutive character so fully, by ignoring, perhaps, the subtleties of work, by relegating play's structural opposite to an idea of very basic appetitive human needs.

The 'work' of the Herero Youth Association incorporates for its members two ways of understanding work. The idea of 'work' in Botswana and in Setswana has a complex history, as explored by the Comaroffs (1987) and Hoyt Alverson (1978). It was no longer the case in the 1980s and '90s that Setswana, the national language in Botswana, distinguished terminologically between *mmereko* (to labour in a job for another) and *tiro* (work that builds oneself as a social being with complex interdependencies); these distinctions were sharply drawn in the recent past and in other parts of Botswana to articulate the interface between the extractive and alienating migrant labour economy of South Africa and the self-making processes of cattle-herding, agriculture, dispute settlement and political debate, and the work of funerals, weddings, and other community rites that build enduring and negotiable relations between people. The idea that working in a salaried or contract job does not do the latter is not strong in the Herero community, or in Mahalapye more widely as I encountered it, since most salaried or contract workers use their incomes in ways that enhance or develop social personhood in one recognized way (narrowly, focusing on self and/or nuclear family) or another (more broadly, to effect various kinds of interpersonal dependencies). Notions of work, and of play, are complex and dispersed across the semiotic activity landscape. And yet, the idea of working to enhance broad community relations as a distinctive moral kind of work does remain important, and is the basis for the ambiguity and ambivalence about whether the activities of the HYA are play or work.

The Herero language distinguishes between to work, *oku ungura*, and to play, *oku nyanda*. As described above, the Youth see their activities as performed for community enrichment – the educational programmes, the consciousness-raising, all work. And to some extent, the Youth take the forms of their activities themselves to be proof of their seriousness and status as work. The bureaucratic systems, the rules of order, the careful following of agendas and committees and assignments – all these are highly significant.

They are the forms associated with the jobs that many Youth hold, and so bear the imprint of 'seriousness' and determination that *kgotla* meetings, and meetings of other groups, often rambling and without clear result, seem to lack. The seriousness that these forms impart to activities is met in the idea that these forms enable productive accomplishments – that the forms of activity are necessary to 'doing something', whether it be revitalizing being Herero, or putting together a banquet for themselves.

And much of what the Youth did *was* work in a more generally recognized sense. At funerals and weddings, the Youth arrived – sometimes simply as members of the Herero community, but often in uniforms and as a collective unit – to do the work, the *oviungura*, of the event. The taskness of this work – its mundane and burdensome nature, its fulfilling of need and lack of pleasure – was self-evident to Herero, and the washing of dishes, preparing of tea and cooking of fatcakes, the serving of food without eating oneself were usually the subject of much tension and complaint about shirkers, among the women who usually executed these tasks.

When the Youth took up these chores, they did so occasionally for the kin-based obligations of one or several of their members, but sometimes for 'the community' at large, much as their goals of consciousness-raising/education were intended for the benefit of the community at large (although such educational projects as they did achieve were in fact for themselves narrowly). In this way, as I suggested above, they were taking up the classic 'work' of youth under the older Tswana polities in which they lived for most of the twentieth century. Newly formed age regiments among the Ngwato were called *majafela* (they only eat; setswana), 'because they have not yet done any work for the tribe' (Schapera, 1938:108). The activities of the Herero Youth Association today not only continue some of this ethos of age-regiment activity, they also parallel similar such 'work' by other youth associations. In 1995, for example, the chairman of the Botswana Democratic Party Youth Wing of the ruling party discussed the various activities of the wing with me. These included prominently, in his representations, community projects with educational and upliftment goals – building village garden plots to demonstrate home income-earning potential and good horticultural techniques, establishing craft-making projects (these projects all failed either initially or soon after starting), and fundraising for flood victims or hospitals. Both this Youth Wing, and the Youth League of another major party engaged extensively in mobilizing voters for their party (in a way, a project much like 'consciousness-raising'). Youth Leaguers complained extensively about this, seeing in it only service to the party and to the big men of the party without any self-advancement or benefit for themselves – in effect, while what they were doing was 'work' of the sort associated with youth specifically, it was only playing, when seen through the ambitions of self-development of the liberalist individual.

Playing is an activity associated prototypically with children (a younger age group than youth), and one hears the term most often, indeed very often, used to refer to them. Playing is, to Herero, self-indulgent and not directed toward accomplishments or goals. 'Oh, this one just plays', say grandmothers and mothers (indulgently) about the small children running around their homes. The children were being accused of not doing their many household chores diligently – of carrying wood or water dilatorily, of running around in the lanes with other children when they should be cooking or cleaning, of playing little games around the compound when it has not been swept, of failing to listen when called. Playing, in this sense, refers prototypically to the shirking of domestic responsibilities, and to the pursuit of pleasures that do not contribute to a domestic economy or sociality. When older women complained that the Herero chief was chasing girls and not looking for a marriage, they accused him, too, of 'just playing'.

The activities of the HYA do indeed seem to many Herero to be 'play' in the sense that they take place on the margins of domestic spheres and indeed draw the members away from some domestic or other obligations that are seen as driven by duty and responsibilities to others. Members often have to make a choice between an HYA meeting, trip, choral competition, or other activity and a matter of concern to their parents' households, a funeral in the community or a wedding. When, in 1994, the HYA scheduled a 'conference' (annual meeting) at the same time as the annual Otjiserandu August ceremonies, in which members of the commemorative society visit the graves of ancestors and the founders of the community and recall broader Herero history, they were fiercely criticized. When several members of the HYA opted to go on a tour of Namibia at the time the wedding of one of their leaders was scheduled,[7] there was broad scepticism in the community about the actual value of the so-called 'educational' tour. After the tour, in spite of overt approval of their ability to 'accomplish something', there was considerable covert suggestion inside and outside the Association that they had been just singing and 'not serious' on the trip. The sense that 'play' is activity that distracts from domestic engagements and responsibility is very important, I think, to the repeated claims that what the Youth were doing was 'only playing'.

Another sense that may surreptitiously creep into the notion of 'play', and recognizes the potential sabotage of such practices, is brought out in the causative form of *oku nyandisa*, to play with, to make fun of, or to tease – a carnivalesque upending of expected relations. When Herero or Tswana children teased me as I passed by, calling out the phrase *mo i pi?* (where are you going?), a phrase that many Tswana knew and called out to passing Herero (to Herero annoyance), adults would tell me that *mave ku nyandisa*, they are teasing you. When an older 'uncle' talked to a younger woman, he might also joke and tease her, threatening to come and visit her at night (meaning a sexual visit), or to choose a husband for her. This sense of playing, of teasing and causing playfulness, directly addresses issues of identity. When the children called out to me, they were playing with my ambiguous identity as a white woman who was also, to them, Herero, speaking the Herero language and participating in a range of Herero events in Herero dress and as a worker. When the 'uncles' tease their young nieces, they too play with the potential in their relationships, compromised by age or by parallel lineal connections, or with the nearing maturity of the young woman.

And this is indeed what the Herero Youth Association does (as does Otjiserandu, the other group that claims sometimes to 'play'): it plays with the identity of being Herero. Demarcating Herero-ness to specific performances and clearly delimited times, establishing dress, language, certain songs, wedding and funerary practices, they create – with the enjoyment, the fun, also critical to all definitions of play – novel ways of being Herero, ways that incorporate a bureaucratic imagination. And, like the children reprimanded for shirking domestic responsibilities, what they do takes place outside of the household and domestic space. But it is not, in fact, only 'outside' that space: indeed, where the Herero Youth see their activities taking place, and where they do in fact have their effect, is very important for understanding not only why they are 'work,' but the special work of youth – and why, indeed, they are so potentially subversive. For while the recognized 'work' of Youth, the assistance at weddings or funerals, the provisioning

---

[7] Members complained that the mother-in-law had set the date for the wedding after they planned their trip; the mother-in-law was one of the association's most vocal critics, and one of those I quoted at the beginning of this essay.

of a feast at New Year, does take place within domestic spaces and the community itself, much of it is also very markedly situated in broader public space. Indeed, the activities of the Herero Youth Association are directly interpolated into the space *between* the kin-based networks of the community and the broader national sphere defined by liberalism and citizenship. And it is here that their subversive potential takes place, disrupting the boundaries and rewriting both, sabotaging politics with the morality of community, and re-inventing identities and representations. And, at the same time, containing their effects through the marginalizing discourse of youth-work and play.

Choirs and the Containment of Youth

In 1995, I interviewed the chairman of the ruling party's Youth Wing; it was an interesting time for youth as the new National Youth Policy was being issued (after many years drafting), and the Youth Wing, moving in tandem with their government, were introducing age limits on their membership, and then debating whether the upper limit should be 35 or 39 (or 29, as the National Youth Policy defined 'youth'). There had been a rising chorus of complaints in the 1990s about a Youth Wing dominated by men in their forties and even fifties, as changes in the economic, educational, social, and globalized discursive landscape of Botswana transformed ideas of who (people of what age) could claim the political space of youth (see Durham, 2004). As he described the various community-assistance projects that local youth wings had initiated (demonstration plots for vegetable gardening, crafts marketing initiatives), he admitted easily that only choirs and choral fundraising had had any long-term success and perdurance. But for these choirs, and the concerts through which they raise funds, he reserved a special comment. While the main Youth Wing activities, including offices and projects, would be restricted to designated 'youth', he thought that the choral activities should be open to 'all youthful members'. Choirs and choral performances somehow, then, encapsulated an important aspect of youth – or youthfulness – in ways that exceeded any attempts at official regulation.

Singing and choirs are integrated into a wide variety of activities and sites for Herero of all ages and for others in Botswana. Singing passes the time between eating and formal ritual at weddings and feasts, moving the heart joyously and bringing people into a form of happy communion. At Herero celebrations (*omikande*, parties), a wide variety of song may be heard. At a wedding, for example, the young people – small children to predominantly girls in their teens and early twenties – will gather into tight but disorganized groups performing the traditional Setswana (and some Otjiherero) wedding songs that tease a bride and groom about their sexual, marital and parental future. Older women join in, laughing, now and again, and retreat to watch the children. If the wedding involves one of their members, the Herero Youth may also form a more organized young people's choir that, along with the child singers, escorts the bride from site to site throughout the weekend of the wedding. During the evenings and nights of the wedding (and some days), men and women from their later twenties to their seventies, sit around tables or in chairs together, sometimes drinking beer, singing appropriate selections from the Herero Lutheran hymnal and other well-known Herero hymn-like songs, while someone beats time with a stick and calls out the lines rapidly before they are sung. And if one is looking, one might see in the darker corners of the party, sitting on the ground and occasionally rising for a little dance, older people in their sixties to nineties, well inebriated, singing the 'traditional' Herero songs about horses and cattle and history (see Alnaes, 1989), that they and everyone else in the Mahalapye community claim to have forgotten entirely.

At funerals, the singing is more sombre, but equally pervasive, ranging at Herero funerals from the distinctive Herero laments sung by older women in the mourning house, which merge autobiography with collective mourning, to hymns that punctuate prayers, carry the mourning community through the night of the wake and help move the body ultimately to the grave, to hymns organized into choral performances by uniformed voluntary associations (see Durham and Klaits, 2002). While the wedding songs are clearly integral to the purpose of the events, but are considered a pleasurable facet of the process, at funerals the singing is more unambiguously considered 'work' and not play.

Choirs punctuate social space and action well beyond spheres of domestic reproduction. Evening singing sessions of groups of young people – which is what most choir practices look like, although some choirs are more disciplined in their rehearsals (such as the renowned KTM choir in Gaborone) – have long been part of village life in Botswana and a prototypical activity for young people (see Schapera, 1940). These evening gatherings formed consociational spaces that bridged different households. Local branches of the political parties form choirs that perform at political rallies, church choirs sing at church services, school and police and hospital choirs join the others to sing at a variety of community events. All these – along with groups formed exclusively to be choirs – compete in community halls, join in fundraising concerts in neighbourhoods, and perform at the national stadium on national holidays. The competition in some of these events mingles with the sense of harmony and synchrony to produce a sense of fun and engagement. Such performances often framed political gatherings such as the visits of government ministers and secretaries: people listened attentively to the oratory, but with critical ears and sensible of the undercurrent of dispute and disagreement. When the choirs sang, however, more people joined the audience to watch; they crowded tightly around; their enthusiasm merged with the songs, critical ears still attuned to the performance (and approval often shown in the same ululations that grace the political oratory), but not for its divisive undercurrents as much as its potential to represent the sensibilities of all there.

What the Youth Wing chairman loved, and where he found his youthfulness realized was in the 'concerts' – a form of fundraising that probably has its roots in early church practices, and built up momentum in the competitive social arenas of towns (Coplan 1985; Erlmann, 1991). Concerts start after dark, a time of mixed sociality in Botswana when men, women and children congregate together, a time when social complaint and arrangements are made (an older brother goes to his sister's lover's place to discuss her pregnancy, an irritated woman complains to the chief about her husband or son), when amorous adventures are initiated or carried through. In the villages, where electricity was scarce in the 1990s, night was not a time for labour-work, but for the work of social negotiations, and for such play as choir practices and concerts. Concerts generally feature several choirs, who will split the proceeds (the organizing choir often taking more).

After an initial presentation of songs that introduce the choirs and show something their repertory (which includes 'traditional' Tswana wedding and work songs, song copied from gospel tapes in South Africa or popular at choral competitions in th region, and pieces composed by the choirs along these models), a master of ceremonies starts fielding requests from members of the audience (and choirs). By paying 5 thebe (about one US cent), or a pula or more (about 20 cents or more), one can request that a certain song be sung, or more likely that it be sung in a certain manner, with the men absent or standing in front, with another member of the audience conducting, or that it be sung 'better'. These bids and requests interrupt songs, so that, after the initial introductory singing, no song is ever sung right through and the choirs and individuals within them are constantly sitting down and getting up. The chairman recalled cheerfully being asked – for a large bid of 50 pula or more – to go outside and run around the parking lot; the play of concerts is not limited to the stage and choirs, and is often directed at the audience as well.

One cannot refuse a request – though one can outbid the original, and ask to be allowed to sing again, or that someone else run around the parking lot. The joking, and the small flirtations that occur in the dark corners of the candle-lit space in the village, provide talk and smiling memories during the subsequent days, as well as money for a project (a planned trip) or community service (donation to a charity or event). When at midnight (usually) the MC stops the singing and counts the money and announces the sum collected, everyone claps vigorously and leaves for home chatting happily – all perhaps youthful for the evening. In these events, the sense of playfulness, the lack of seriousness, the suggestions of activities taking place on the borders of domestic space but not yet political, the ideas of 'work for the community', the clearly demarcated space of the performance, are all merged, and choirs do indeed become the epitome of youthfulness for all youthful people.

While singers vary widely in age, and at any event may include a broad range, choral song is particularly associated with youth, and also with women. Through youth (and women, who also often come to bear the burdens of representing ethnicity), it is also associated with ethnic 'culture' – both subject positions whose status is uneasily being confronted in Botswana today. (Indeed, with age, ethnicity, and of course gender, all hotly contested throughout society, and class beginning to be so, Botswana seems a laboratory for contemporary sociological analysis.) An annual 'eisteddfod' is held for school choirs each July, and the schools compete vigorously throughout the year to secure a place in the final national competition. There is a 'Western' choral competition, but the highlight is the performance of 'traditional' dance/song by the various school choirs (arranged in grade categories). The young women and men don traditional clothing – either made locally specifically for these groups, or ordered from South African manufacturers – and perform a variety of recognized dance styles. Since the 1980s, Sarwa (Bushman) styles have been very popular, performed by schools from the west and north (see Lee, 1993); I also noted a distinctive style performed by a few choirs from the northeast (where many Kalanga live). The judges are brought in from South Africa; they judge the authenticity of the performance, measuring it against broad regional standards of 'traditional' dance/song. Innovation is not appreciated by the judges, though the audience I watched was captivated by the imaginative and polished performance of one lower-ranking school (their lead dancer, I was told by an audience member, was certainly a herdboy who spent most of his time out dancing and drinking at cattleposts).

For the Herero Youth Association, as well, the choir is an opportunity to introduce Herero song (and dress) into the national public sphere. But they do so with a sense of risk, risk to the various ideas of citizenship, of liberalist opportunities and judgments, and

of identity. In 1990, the Youth entered a village-wide choral competition, held in t
Mahalapye Community Hall. The competition was well attended by young and old, a
much of the affair was conducted like a concert (with bidding for song variations, p
marily). The Youth choir had been directed by a member of the KTM choir fr
Gaborone: the KTM choir was widely acknowledged to be the country's premier ch
had won regional competitions, and had toured in the US (going to Atlanta a
Montana), and Scandinavia. Their performance was (to my mind) the most polished a
musically sophisticated. But they sang a few songs that (they later felt) disqualified th
from winning. One was a stunning, precisely performed piece with complex harmon
and rhythm changes, sung in Sotho (a language close to Tswana, but with some voca
ulary differences; several choir members did not know what several of the song's wo
meant), that brought the house down with excited applause. Others were in Here
including an entrance song in which they introduced themselves as '*owete ovan*
Ovaherero' (it is us, the Herero children). After being placed third (much lower than th
had hoped), members of the choir were insistent that it was not the Herero *per se* (wh
I rather suspected) that lost them the competition, but their selection of songs that w
outside the judges' (and much of the audience's) repertory, making the songs difficult
judge according to uniformly recognized standards.

Song (choral song) was a good medium in which to play with identity and the pu
lic spaces in which songs were entered. Herero Youth who went on the trip to Namil
in December 1994/January 1995 made the most of this potential – singing Tswana-la
guage songs to Herero hosts and as their highlight composition performed on t
Herero-language radio and TV stations, and then singing Herero songs to workers at t
Botswana embassy to Namibia, which the Youth felt they should visit as Botswana ci
zens. Choirs and choral performance always retain the sense of play, and of containm
from the more serious 'work' of forging social relations (no matter how much th
effects resemble that work). The choirs that frame and punctuate political events do
contained in a playful, enjoyable space that demarcates their work for the commun
from the work of developing powerful socially connected (and divisive) personas a
political programmes. Choirs invite into political space those most marginalized fr
political work – youth (most typically), women, and increasingly minority ethnic grou
But they do so in ways that marginalize these groups and what they represent from t
open arena of political debate – bureaucratizing, in effect, youth, gender, and 'cultu
difference' to specific times, places, and possibilities. But the community work – t
which typifies youth – is real, and the effect can be profound. By 1996, following t
popularity of the Youth choir within Mahalapye at concerts and the like, and the incre
ing popularity of minority performance styles in the national eisteddfods, non-Tswa
song was welcomed into Mahalapye public performances, and the Herero chief v
asked to persuade the Youth, or a junior choir (the Happy Choir), to perform at villag
wide celebrations.

The movement of non-Tswana ethnic performance into public and political p
formance space paralleled the demands made in formal political space for more rep
sentation of the non-Tswana 'tribes' in Botswana. These demands were made
opposition parties throughout the later 1980s (and from which, one might note, t
HYA specifically distinguished themselves as non-political), and in the later 1990s b
lawsuit by one of the 'tribes' for permanent representation in the House of Chiefs,
advisory but significant part of government. The movements of minority performar
into spaces defined as 'play' were more easily accomplished; the debates, often quite b

ter, about minority representation in an overtly political sphere continue today. And yet, if the efforts to introduce new 'tribal' chiefs into the House of Chiefs *are* successful, the effects are likely to be not very different from that of introducing non-Setswana songs into choral competitions. The chiefs, who have a tremendous rhetorical impact on national debate and opinion, stand, within the political space of the postcolonial nation, ideally opposed to the politics of elected and competing parties (see Durham, 2002a). One reason that their positions are currently under attack is that they, perhaps like the youth choirs, ostensibly represent communities, or their polities, as a whole; their mandate is for consensus, commonality, and communality. But their presence in the national government is only advisory, and while people listen closely to what they say, their power to enact, and to act within the sphere defined by the allocation of state resources, jostling for power, and implementing policies that enable people to develop themselves, is limited, or contained, in a bureaucratization of chiefship and its sphere of action.

Perhaps even more telling about the parallels between youth containment and the containment of minority ethnicities are projects currently under way to document and record minority cultures in Botswana, and past ways of recognizing and displaying them. The documentations and displays will set up certain categories of practices – practices that may seem to differentiate (such as matrilineality, or different kinds of marriage payments), but in fact through organization in a series of parallel charts will make each 'culture' a mirror of the others, with differences categorized and subject to government recognition and intervention. And all of this is to the end of making all members of all minority groups *equally* citizens, equally able to participate in the liberally defined political space of political actors and means of advancement in a non-ethnic state. 'Culture' and cultural identities will be recognized, but allocated their own spaces for performance, spaces which allow the undifferentiated citizen to be the grounds of political action. These spaces are now epitomized by song, and although other practices and activities will be recognized and introduced, they too will share the ambiguous nature of youthful play, posed against serious adult work.

Conclusion

Youth have entered political spaces across the globe in dramatic and often violent ways. Student protests and actions, as well as recriminations against them, were instrumental to the recent overthrow of the Suharto regime in Indonesia; student protests have been registered with varying intensity on the political ground in China; it is significant, surely, that challenges to politics-as-usual is associated with so-called 'Young Turks'. Youth, that is, people *claiming* the specific political-rhetorical space of youth, have been equally prominent across Africa as well, have violently entered the public sphere and issued direct and unmistakable challenges to political order and social *status quos*. It is not difficult to recognize the potential for youth appropriations of political space, the challenges they levy or the subversions accomplished, in the student riots that swept Senegal in the 1980s and '90s (see Diouf, 1996; Cruise O'Brien, 1996; also issues of *Jeune Afrique Economie* from that period). Witchhunting, moral crusades, and the lynching or policing of thieves or other perceived public enemies, are often taken on by groups of young people in direct challenge to the abilities of elders and the state to guarantee public safety and moral society (see Auslander, 1993; Niehaus, 1998; Diouf, 1996; van Dijk, 1998).

While student riots, violent and threatening enough to bring out the army and its hel-

icopters, did rock the civil politics of Botswana in the mid-1990s (see Durham, 199
Good, 1996), people marked out as youth have been by and large, on the surface, pol
ically quiet. The Botswana National Youth Council emphasize in their projects the go
of youth 'empowerment', suggesting that the primary predicament of youth in Botswa
is their lack of power. (Youth regularly note the irony that they are further subordinat
to the leadership and financial support of government and older people in these pr
grammes.) The programmes target primarily social (through public displays of yout
such as marches and *reetsanang* drama), economic (through skills and training) and pol
ical (through political education) empowerment. The sense that youth are not acti
politically was confirmed to those who define political involvement as direct entry in
the recognized political spaces occupied by government and chiefs during the 19
national elections. This was the first election since the voting age was lowered from
to 18. Nonetheless, very few people in the 18-21 age group voted; by some estima
the turnout for this group was as low as 4 per cent. In the past, youth, like other su
social minors as women and, in some areas, ethnic minorities, and Basarwa (Bushmer
were not allowed to speak for themselves in the village chief's courts; current politi
participation is sometimes seen as continuous with past practice, and young people re
ularly complain that they are not listened to either at home or nationally. Except, pe
haps, as choirs.

And yet the constant insistence by members of the Herero community that t
Herero Youth Association were *just* playing suggests that choirs, and the activities of t
youth group, were something potentially disturbing, something that needed to be co
tained through the liminal designation 'play'. At the same time, such criticisms al
imply, double-edged, that the Youth Association should be doing *work*, real work, and tl
they were failing to do so. In order to understand the disruptive potential of singing a
the youth choirs, and to understand how seemingly inconsequential songs borrow
from weddings, from school repertoires and a body of familiar songs sung in natio
choral competitions, from the pop radio, and especially modelled on South Afric
gospel tapes, can threaten to remodel political space, it is important to understand t
potency of play in the hands of youth – and why the category of youth, of who c
claim the political role of youth, has been so contentious in Botswana in the 1990s.

References

Abu-Lughod, Lila. 1990. 'The Romance of Resistance: Tracing Transformations of Power through Bedo
    Women', *American Ethnologist* 17 (1):41-55.
Alnaes, Kirsten. 1989. 'Living with the Past: The Songs of the Herero in Botswana', *Africa* 59:267-99.
Alverson, Hoyt. 1978. *Mind in the Heart of Darkness: Value and Self-Identity among the Tswana of Southern Afr*
    New Haven, CT: Yale University Press.
Amit-Talai, Vered, and Helena Wulff (eds). 1995. *Youth Cultures: A Cross-cultural Perspective*. London: Routled
Auslander, Mark. 1993. '"Open the Wombs!" The Symbolic Politics of Modern Ngoni Witchfinding',
    Modernity and its Malcontents: Ritual and Power in Postcolonial Africa. ed. Jean and John Comaroff. Chicago,
    University of Chicago Press.
Burke, Charlanne. 2000. 'They Cut Segametsi into Parts: Ritual Murder, Youth, and the Politics of Knowle
    in Botswana', *Anthropological Quarterly* 73(4): 204–14.
Comaroff, Jean & John Comaroff. 1987. 'The Madman and the Migrant: Work and Labor in the Histori
    Consciousness of a South African People', *American Ethnologist* 14:191-209.
Coplan, David. 1985. *In Township Tonight! Music of South Africa's Black City Music and Theatre*. Johannesbu
    Ravan Press.
Cruise O'Brien, Donal. 1996. 'A Lost Generation? Youth Identity and State Decay in West Africa', in *Postcolo
    Identities in Africa*. ed. Richard Werbner & Terence Ranger. London: Zed Books.

Deleuze, Gilles, and Felix Guattari. 1987. *A Thousand Plateaus: Capitalism and Schizophrenia*. Minneapolis, MN: University of Minnesota Press.

Diouf, Mamadou. 1996. 'Urban Youth and Senegalese Politics: Dakar 1988-1994'. *Public Culture* 2 (2):225-50.

Durham, Deborah. 1993. 'Images of Culture: Being Herero in a Liberal Democracy (Botswana)'. Ph.D. dissertation. University of Chicago.

— 1998. 'Mmankgodi Burns: Missing Youth in Botswana', Paper presented at African Studies Workshop, University of Chicago, 3 March.

— 1999a. 'The Predicament of Dress: Polyvalency and the Ironies of a Cultural Identity'. *American Ethnologist* 26 (2):389-411.

— 1999b. 'Civil Lives: Leadership and Accomplishment in Botswana', in *Civil Society and the Political Imagination in Africa*. ed. J. L. Comaroff and J. Comaroff. Chicago: University of Chicago Press.

— 2000. 'Youth and the Social Imagination in Africa: Introduction' [to a theme issue]. *Anthropological Quarterly* 73(3): 113-20.

— 2002a. 'Uncertain Citizens: The New Intercalary Subject in Postcolonial Botswana', in *Postcolonial Subjectivities in Africa*. ed. R. P. Werbner. London and New York: Zed Books.

— 2002b. 'Love and Jealousy in the Space of Death', *Ethnos* 67 (2): 155-80.

— 2003. 'Passports and Persons: The Insurrection of Subjugated Knowledges in Southern Africa', in *The Culture of Power in Southern Africa: Essays on State Formation and the Political Imagination*. ed. C. Crais. Portsmouth, NH: Heinemann.

— 2004. 'Disappearing Youth: Youth as a Social Shifter in Botswana'. *American Ethnologist* 31(4): 587-603.

— in press. 'Making Youth Citizens: Empowerment Programs and Youth Agency in Botswana', in *Generation and Globalization: Family, Youth, and Age in the New World Economy*. eds J. Cole and D. Durham. Bloomington, IN: Indiana University Press.

Durham, Deborah, and Fred Klaits. (2002). 'Funerals and the Public Space of Mutuality in Botswana', *Journal of Southern African Studies* 28 (4): 777-95.

Erlmann, Veit. 1991. *African Stars: Studies in Black South African Performance*. Chicago: University of Chicago Press.

Gewald, Jan-Bart. 1999. *Herero Heroes: A Socio-Political History of the Herero of Namibia, 1890-1923*. Oxford: James Currey.

Good, Kenneth. 1996. 'Towards Popular Participation in Botswana', *Journal of Modern African Studies* 34 (1):53-77.

Greenfield, Liah. 1992. *Nationalism: Five Roads to Modernity*. Cambridge, MA: Harvard University Press.

Huizinga, Johann. 1950. *Homo Ludens: A Study of the Play-Element in Culture*. London: Routledge and Kegan Paul.

Kemodimo, Monica Goabaone. 2000. 'Youth and Political Participation in Elections in Botswana. Case Study: University of Botswana'. Senior Research Paper. University of Botswana.

Lee, Richard B. 1993. *The Dobe Ju/'hoansi*. 2nd edition. Fort Worth, TX: Harcourt Brace.

Muller, Carol Ann. 1999. *Rituals of Fertility and the Sacrifice of Desire: Nazarite Women's Performance in South Africa*. Chicago: University of Chicago Press.

Niehaus, Isak. 1998. 'The ANC's Dilemma: The Symbolic Politics of Three Witch-Hunts in the South African Lowveld, 1990-1995', *African Studies Review* 41 (3): 93-118.

Schapera, Isaac. 1938. *A Handbook of Tswana Law and Custom*. London: Frank Cass.

— 1940. *Married Life in an African Tribe*. London: Faber and Faber.

Solway, Jacqueline. 1994. 'From Shame to Pride: Politicized Ethnicity in the Kalahari, Botswana', *Canadian Journal of African Studies* 28 (2): 254-74.

— 1995. 'Political Participation, Ethnicity, and Multiparty Democracy in Botswana', in *The Politics of Change in Southern Africa*. ed. D. O'Meara. Montreal: Canadian Research Consortium on Southern Africa.

van Dijk, Rijk. 1998. 'Pentecostalism, Cultural Memory and the State: Contested Representations of Time in Postcolonial Malawi', in *Memory and the Postcolony: African Anthropology and the Critique of Power*. ed. R. P. Werbner. London: Zed Books.

Werbner, Richard P. 2002. 'Introduction: Challenging Minorities, Difference, and Tribal Citizenship in Botswana', *Journal of Southern African Studies* 28 (4): 671-84.

Werner, Wolfgang. 1990. '"Playing Soldiers": The Truppenspieler Movement Among the Herero of Namibia, 1915 to ca. 1945', *Journal of Southern African Studies* 16 (3): 476-502.

Wylie, Diana. 1990. *A Little God: The Twilight of Patriarchy in a Southern African Chiefdom*. Hanover, NH: University Press of New England.

IV Past the Postcolony

8

IBRAHIM ABDULLAH
'I am a Rebel'[1]
Youth Culture & Violence in Sierra Leone

Introduction

On 18 January 1967 a high school student by the name of Louis Farmer was stabbed
death by his peers. The accused, all high school students in Freetown, were arraigned
a celebrated murder trial that ended in acquittal/imprisonment (*Daily Mail*, 10 Octo
1967). On 8 June 1973, six years after the murder of Farmer, a group of working-c
youths in the West End were convicted and hanged for the murder of the proprietor
Travelers' Lodge, a low-priced motel in the city centre (*Daily Mail*, 9 June 1973). O
March 1974, less than twenty-four hours after the execution of those involved in
murder of the proprietor of Travelers' Lodge, another murder took place at Mam
Yoko Street in the rough and densely populated East End. The victim of the fatal st
bing was a bartender named Unisa Sesay (*Daily Mail*, 1 March 1974; *We Yone*, 1 Ma
1974). All six accused were found guilty of murder, lost their appeal, and were hang
their corpses displayed outside the maximum security prison.

These events could be read as instances of violence among youths, but they are a
about what different categories of youth did or could do under certain circumstanc
Murder or violence was something youths engaged in, irrespective of class or cultu
differences. The three murders implicating youths from middle- or working-class fal
lies are a window through which we can begin to understand the complex connectic
between youth culture, criminality and violence. The first murder involved high sch
students, the second, working-class youths in their twenties, the third, youths in their
teens and early twenties, some of whom were high school graduates or dropouts (*D
Mail*, 10 October 1967; 9 June 1973; 1 March 1974).

The murder of Louis Farmer took place after an athletic event – a high school tra
and field competition – an important component of mainstream youth culture
Freetown. The murder of the proprietor of Traveler's Lodge was a botched operation;
accused were not hardened criminals but marginal/working-class youths with regu
low-paying jobs. The principal accused, Johnny Grant, was a road transport worker. T
third murder took place shortly after midnight when some youths in the East End ca
ally strolled from their popular rendezvous to the pub on Mammy Yoko Street. Th
intention was to get a few drinks and, if possible, some cash. Their adventure ended
the death of the bartender.

[1] This title is taken from one of Bob Marley's songs popular among youths in the 1970s.

172

These three events represent different layers of an evolving youth culture. They bring together the motley experiences of youth – from the mainstream high school student to the dropout in the neighbourhood – and their collective relationship to 'the other', the external world of adulthood and of authority. As the murders reveal, these were different categories of youth – high school students, dropouts and working-class youths – occupying seemingly different social and cultural spaces. These socially constructed borders marking the different sites, I argue, began to shift, to collapse, in the late 1960s and early 1970s under the heavy strain of political repression, the emergence of an 'imagined community' constructed around the *odelay*,[2] the *pote*,[3] pubbing, reggae music, and the neighbourhood. The result was a kind of fusion, a hybrid of sorts, which brought different categories of youth together, and inaugurated a political conversation anchored on the use of violence. If the late 1960s and early 1970s witnessed the emergence of this imagined community of youth, the 1980s revealed a matured community with a distinctive imaginary that was contestatory and subversive of the *status quo*. My central argument revolves around the role of subaltern culture in the making of an alternative political route to power in postcolonial Africa. The first part of this essay discusses the origins of *rarray boy*[4] culture; the second is a sympathetic reading of aspects of their cultural practices as strategies of negotiation from without; the third outlines the path leading to the 'revolutions' of the 1990s – the wasted decade.

Youth Culture and Violence: A Conceptual Statement

The extant literature on youth culture and violence suffers from a chronic lack of understanding about how divergent youth experiences converged to produce an imagined community with seemingly common symbolic signposts that were subsequently transformed into deadly 'weapons of the weak' in pursuit of a fuzzy political agenda (Richards, 1995; 1996; 2002; Reno, 2002). This transformation – from divergent experiences with specific cultural sites to the emergence of an imagined community with seemingly common symbolic signposts – not only witnessed the repackaging of violence as an individual/collective act directed against other youths in the emergent community, but more importantly its elevation, via pan-africanism, as the most important medium of political change. As the murders referred to above demonstrate, different categories of youth were engaged or involved in violence for a variety of reasons.

Rarray boys/lumpen youths, mostly pickpockets and petty criminals, engaged in violence in their everyday life: they attacked their victims and were prone to violence in their regular turf wars over control of territory. The latter were conducted within the burgeoning community of youths centred around *odelays* located in different areas of Freetown. This type of violence was strictly non-political, and it involved lumpen youths in densely populated enclaves in the city but particularly the seaside areas in the East and

---

[2] *Odelays* are masquerades organized by youths in specific neighbourhoods. Introduced by liberated Africans from Yorubaland in the nineteenth century, they were later appropriated by marginal youths in the mid-1940s. They are arguably the most popular form of urban leisure for Freetown's marginal youths. See Nunley (1988).
[3] The word *Pote* comes from the Temne – one of the two major ethnic groups in Sierra Leone – word *an-pot*. It was originally a place to relax after a hard day's work. The American word, Ghetto, is now used to refer to these popular rendezvous created by rebellious youths to use drugs, listen to music, and just talk!
[4] The origin of this term is obscure. It is normally used in reference to dropouts, rebellious youths, drug addicts and criminals. When used with reference to women – as in *rarray gial* – it simply means sex worker/prostitute. It serves as a catch phrase for non-conventional as opposed to mainstream youth.

West End. 'Hanging out' in these areas was risky for those perceived as outsiders/non-initiates. This rough lifestyle was an aspect of masculinity that only 'street-wise' youths could negotiate. It was the litmus test for 'manhood', and the most notorious of these youths were those who engaged in violence – mostly stabbing their victims – – and got away with it. It was petty criminality on a small scale, and, arguably, a dress rehearsal of some of the monstrosities that would be visited on innocent civilians/communities. These thugs, as they were collectively referred to, would become useful tools for the political class in the late 1960s and '70s when electoral politics became an exercise in political thuggery.

What was missing in these everyday forms of violence within the emergent youth community was a clearly articulated discourse on which such violent acts might be anchored. The authors of this violence were predominantly unlettered and therefore lacked the intellectual capital within which such a discourse could have been constituted. The transition from random individual/collective violence to collective social violence as a political project took place in the late 1970s amidst political repression dwindling mining revenue and the collapse of the multiple cultural barriers separating mainstream and marginal youth culture. This collapse led to a fusion between the mainstream and the marginal; it was marked by the evolution of a common language, a shared cultural space and the emergence of a political discourse which privileged violence as the medium of social change. The authors of this discourse were not marginal youths. They were college students who had by then positioned themselves as the inform opposition to the decadent one-party dictatorship. They freely mixed with their less fortunate brothers – there were no sisters – in the numerous *potes* in Freetown and elsewhere to smoke and to 'conscientize'. These ideological sessions were the assembly line wherein rebels were made.

The valorization of violence by student radicals was a short cut to legitimizing its use as the political weapon. It gave a new meaning to the hitherto random individual violence in so far as it was directed against the perceived enemy. In this warped appropriation, violence simply meant revolution; and revolution was understood as violence writ large. It was this reading of violence as the only route to revolutionary change that produced the Revolutionary United Front(RUF), the National Provisional Ruling Council(NPRC), and the Armed Forces Revolutionary Council(AFRC).

The Origins of *Rarray Boy* Culture

Like elsewhere in Africa, colonial officials in Sierra Leone did not design a formal policy for youth. What evolved in the Department of Social Welfare after 1945, when the colonial powers rediscovered Africa, was a project of social engineering targeting two groups: youth in formal educational institutions and those considered socially deviant (Cooper, 1996). Rediscovering Africa simply meant providing welfare institutions geared towards improving the standard of living of the people. Attempts were therefore made promote formal leisure and recreational facilities vigorously in schools, and reform institutions were established to tackle the problem of juvenile delinquency. While the former was designed to promote a sense of civic awareness and adherence to mainstream culture and society, the latter was devised for purposes of rehabilitation. Both approaches shared a common assumption. They denied agency to youth in transforming their own lives and foreclosed the need for a dialogue or conversation between youth and adult hood (Austin and Willard, 1998). More importantly, they failed to problematize a key youth category: *rarray boys* and their vibrant culture in the city of Freetown. These assumptions about youthhood survived the colonial era and were reproduced ad infinitum in the national discourse about youth in postcolonial Sierra Leone.

The postcolonial discourse on youth was therefore anchored in a colonial duality: the mainstream versus the unacceptable. The mainstream was typified by official acceptance, the unacceptable by its opposite, official disapproval. The mainstream was the abode of respectability as constructed by officialdom and middle-class society. It was the world of the law-abiding student/youth – those who would rather play by the rules. The unacceptable, seen predominantly as the dregs of society, was the world of the school dropout, the unemployed, the dope pusher, the shoeshine boy, and the illicit miner. How these seemingly opposite and conflicting official imaginaries about youth are deployed in the everyday site of the marketplace, the street/neighbourhood, the pub, and the school/university, constitutes the most important element in understanding the fusion which eventually emerged as a result of the conversations between these seeming opposites (Skelton and Valentine, 1998; Amit-Talal and Wulff, 1995).

The origins of *rarray boys* as a social group date back to 1890-1900. There are numerous references to criminals and vagabonds in middle-class/colonial/official discourses in the late nineteenth and early twentieth centuries. Mostly unemployed young males on the edge of society, working on the side, or living by their wits, *rarray boys* became an item on the official register throughout the early twentieth century. And like the lumpen proletariat in nineteenth-century Europe, they simply refused to go away. Initially the *rarray boys* were predominantly young men from Freetown, but their ranks were soon swelled by migrants from the Sierra Leone hinterland, who survived in Freetown by moving in and out of casual jobs as labourers, domestic servants, and night-watchmen. As early as 1917, the Freetown reading public was informed about the existence of organized gangs of youths. One of these was identified as *Foot-A-Backers*, a branch of another group called *A-Burn-Am*, whose leader was a certain Generalissimo Yonkon. These gangs were located on the seaside along with another called *Arms Akimbo* (*Sierra Leone Weekly News*, 17 May 1917).[5] As is usual with subalterns, they only entered the official mind in the form of criminal statistics. Officialdom was content to view them through Victorian lenses: it was simply what to do with the residuum or dangerous classes (*Census Report*, 1921).

A creation of colonial modernity, *rarray boys* emerged in colonial cities at about the same time as the working-class was being made (Van Onselen, 1982; La Hausse, 1990; Abdullah, 1998b.) The backwardness of the colonial economy before 1915 and the worldwide depression of the 1920s witnessed an increase in the number of migrants and vagabonds in the city of Freetown. In spite of this, suggestions of a Poor Law similar to that in England was turned down by government officials. Even with the abolition of slavery in 1926 and the opening of the mines in the early 1930s, poverty and acute overcrowding remained a major social problem in Freetown.

The segregated residential pattern in the city – based on race and ethnicity – did not affect *rarray boys*. Partly because they were officially labelled as migrants who could be repatriated to the hinterland and partly because they were involved in casual work, they could move in and out of the migrant residential area. Thus they bunched together in the city's East End and waterfront areas where they engaged in petty theft and as labour-

---

[5] It is not clear what these names/terms represent/mean. But during the 1940s and even beyond, *A-burn-Am* became synonymous with petty crooks and thieves.

ers in the rickety warehouses they also used as dwellings. The official cost of living sv
vey and the slum clearance report, commissioned during this period, underlined v
general poverty and appalling living conditions of the working-class and the urban po
From the margins of colonial modernity, *rarray boys* eventually snaked their way to v
centre through cultural forms seemingly rooted in resistance.

The exclusionary cultural landscape in the city of Freetown might provide a clue
the origins of what later became a central pillar in the architecture of *rarray boy* cultv
the *odelay* societies. From about 1915 to the end of the Second World War, a cultural re
aissance gripped the city. Its hallmarks were the introduction in 1915 of what was cal
the electric cinema, the proliferation of dance halls, and the formation of voluntary c
tural groups called *Ambas Geda* among the Temne, an ethnic group. The dance hall c
ture was popular among the Krio ethnic group, while the voluntary cultural gro
occurred predominantly among the Temnes. The *Ambas Geda* (We Have United) wa
popular and well-respected form of urban leisure among the working-class, wh
quickly gained official acceptance. The *Ambas Gedas* sponsored open-air dances a
singing competitions among working-class Temnes. These two leisure sites – the dan
halls of the Krios and the *Ambas Geda* of the Temnes – were ethnic-specific and exc
sionary. The *Ambas Geda*, although originally a working-class creation, came to symb
ize Temne interests in general, as opposed to working-class interests in particular. T
popular dance halls of the Krios were too middle-class and snobbish to accommod
rarray boys. *Rarray boys* who were of different ethnicities could not gain access to th
sites, primarily because of their social position. Nor were they accepted as members
another popular leisure form, namely, the *ojeh* and *odelay* societies imported fr
Yorubaland.[6]

Excluded from participation in these leisure/cultural spaces, the *rarray boys* evolve
kind of urban leisure patterned on the *odelay* societies. These societies consisted of you
men who periodically celebrated national public holidays in carnival fashion, at the ce
tre of which was a masquerade decked in animal hides and/or imported fabrics. Th
celebrations were intensely competitive and resulted in violence on several occasio
From the time of their inception in the early 1950s, the two *rarray boy odelays* – East
Paddle and *Lawd Da Masi* – were greeted with hostility by the middle-class and city c
cials.[4] The fact that members of these societies were from the working-class, the une
ployed and the urban poor, made it impossible for them to gain any respectability
official acceptance. By the 1960s *rarray boy odelays* had become arguably the domin
form of leisure among the urban poor, the working-class and some sections of the lov
middle-class.

Rarray boys were visible as pimps, pickpockets and petty criminals in interv
Freetown. The Second World War provided brisk business for them. Brothels sprang
on the waterfront, at Custom Bay, Sawpit, Magazine and other areas which later beca
the abode of Freetown's proletariat. The darker side of their existence is brought to l
in Graham Greene's narrative of life in wartime Freetown, *Heart of the Matter* (Gree
1959). In spite of official hostility, an 'imagined community' evolved around the cultu
space carved out by the *rarray boys*. This community was gender-specific, a kind
macho-male bonding constructed around the *odelay*. It was rooted in territoriality,
specific neighbourhoods, at the centre of which was the *pote*. The *pote* is a meeting poi
a place to hang out, a rendezvous, where youths congregated to smoke, gamble, and j

[6] The *Ojeh* and hunting societies were imported from Yorubaland in the nineteenth century by recaptives f
present-day Nigeria.

talk. *Potes* originally sprang up as *rarray boy* abodes in peri-urban areas far away from the eyes of the law. As *rarray boy* culture matured, *potes* were established as legitimate businesses with liquor licences. This was the cover used by the proprietors of the numerous working-class/marginal youth pubs, which sprang up in the 1960s and 1970s. *New Time Garden* in the West End, *Masiyanday* in the central area, and *Happy Corner* in the East End were among the most popular.[7]

Independence saw the proliferation of *odelay* societies, *potes*, and an increase in the number of *rarray boys*. The establishment of more *odelay* societies in the city suggests that this form of leisure had become the most popular form of cultural relaxation, not only amongst *rarray boys*, but also amongst some sections of the working-class and increasingly the urban poor. There were noticeable changes in the leadership structure in the late 1950s and 1960s. More working-class elements joined the leadership cadre. Prominent among this group were sea-faring men, dockworkers and road transport workers. These groups played a key role in the making of modern *rarray boy* culture. It is perhaps not unexpected that the two modes of living to which *rarray boys* commonly aspired were sea-faring and driving. *Rarray boys* did not produce any constructive critique of society. Like the *rude bwoys* in Jamaica, who are seemingly only interested in the good life while maintaining a violent and anti-social culture, this group remained on the margin of Sierra Leonean society, appearing bereft of any constructive ideas about social change.

The anti-social aspect of *rarray boy* culture alienated them from mainstream society. Their violence, mostly within the group, was occasionally directed at members of the public. Violence, gambling and rough living are integral aspects of *pote* culture. Violence was common within or between *odelays* during their periodic carnivals on public holidays. This violence largely consisted of turf wars centred on territoriality and control over space and, not infrequently, women. These youth communities were constructed around specific territories, and *odelays* functioned like criminal gangs with rituals and initiations (Schneider, 1999). Bars, public spaces, and neighbourhoods in the rough East End, and the densely populated areas in the West End, usually belonged to a specific *odelay*. 'Tresspassing' in a rival *odelay* 'territory' was a risky venture undertaken at one's peril. Through these and other ways *rarray boys* affirmed and defined their masculinity. By the early 1960s a *rarray boy* image had been invented: unemployed, uneducated, violent, uncouth, crude and anti-social.

The violent aspect of *rarray boy* culture made them an electioneering asset for politicians. *Rarray boys*, now christened 'youth', became more visible politically when the All Peoples Congress (APC) was voted to power in 1967. The *rarry boys'* involvement in large numbers as thugs for the ruling party further alienated them from the sober citizenry. Even so, their culture and institutions were appropriated by the new kids on the block in furtherance of a fuzzy political objective: the radical transformation of society.

Culture: A Subversive Life-style?

The exclusion of subalterns – women, slaves, lumpens, and other marginals – from grand narratives about history and culture is arguably as old as the art of history writing itself. Not only have they been excluded from history but also their contributions have remained largely undocumented. The contribution *rarray boys* have made to the devel-

---

[7] These were strictly speaking *pote*-pubs where liquor and marijuana could be purchased. Music and dancing featured prominently in their daily activities.

opment of Krio language and culture belongs to this genre. The oral texts they have p
duced and continue to reproduce in conversations with rebellious youths in the
form an essential critique of the postcolonial moment from their marginal standpo
Their multiple discourses, both covert and overt, reveal cultural resilience and creati
as they come to grips with the existential reality of everyday life in the city. As peddl
struggling artisans, hawkers, or plain unemployed in the so-called informal sector, t
engage in cultural production: various art forms, from which we can recover their me
ories/dreams about the political. These cultural sites are the urban texts from whence
can understand their grammar of protest. In the context of Freetown, these te
embrace the spheres of music, language, art, and, of course, the periodic carnivals of
odelay societies.

The *rarray boy* contribution to Krio language raises a fundamental question in the
of socio-linguistics. Under what circumstances does a subaltern and disempowe
group become the dominant voice in the development of a *lingua franca*? What are
likely political implications of a situation where *rarray boy* images and symbols becc
national icons/signposts? These questions revolve around subversion and counter-c
ture; they conjure up an image of a disempowered group forcing its way to the cen
The *rarray boy* contribution to Krio language forces visitors and residents alike to le
new words and expressions, unlearn old sayings, and pick up the fashionable new wo
which inevitably envelop a cultural landscape in transition. Terms like *chap* (make a
buck), *e dae bush* (she/he is bankrupt), *ah don embalm* (beyond the pale) and *put for*
(grease my palm), emanate from *rarray boy* culture and have been gradually absorbed i
mainstream Krio. What distinguishes middle-class or mainstream Krio from *rarray boy*
working-class Krio is that the former uses a lot of English expressions, perhaps as a p
tentious mark of worldliness. Thus a middle-class Krio speaker would say, '*Me wife p
nant*', instead of '*Me wef get belleh*' or '*Ah go see yu tomorrow*', instead of '*Ago go see
tumarra*'.

The contributions from below reflect the structural position of this *rarray boy* gro
and their everyday existence in a situation of extreme privation has made them the m
compelling voice of the economic hardship in Sierra Leone. The notion of *chap* or
for me, a metaphor for corruption, comes from the game of craps; the expression *ah
emblam*, another metaphor for stoicism, underlines the grim reality of everyday surv
and their resolve to soldier on against all odds. The war has added a new set of voca
lary, particularly military terms, to the language. For example, expressions like launch
(as in to launch a missile) and deploy (as in deployment of troops), are now part of
new Krio. Even such grisly acts as the rampant amputation of civilians' limbs practi
by the Revolutionary United Front (RUF) are referred to as 'long sleeves' or 'sh
sleeves'.[8] The social networks spawned by participants in this culture, both in Freeto
and elsewhere in Sierra Leone, ensure that the *rarray boy* contribution to the *lingua fr*
remains the most dynamic force shaping the creation and recreation of the Krio l
guage. It is hardly surprising that the standard Krio currently spoken in Freetown is
rarray boy Krio of yesterday. Can this cultural subversion be read as the civil takeover
so-called civil society *sans* violence? What does the conversation between college s
dents and *rarray boys* tell us about this cultural subversion?

Fourah Bay College (FBC) students were the major link between *rarray boys*
mainstream society. Their social networks in the *potes*, the neighbourhood/junction,

---

[8] 'Long sleeves' refer to amputation of the hand from the shoulder joint, and 'short sleeves' to amputation
the elbow/wrist.

the drug culture in the college residence had, by the late 1970s, created a Krio language on the college campus that was similar to that of *rarray boys*. Students gave respectability and legitimacy to the vocabulary emerging from below. But the process of making/re-making the language occurred in dialogue with the original group: the *rarray boys*. Terms like *patta* (copulation), *pwell am/bwell am* (have fun), and *ib am* (to tease) are contributions from students as they interacted with their less fortunate allies in the world of rebellious youth culture in Freetown. The college students give a stamp of respectability to the Krio of the *rarray boys*; they are the cultural bridge between this evolving community and mainstream society.

In the area of popular culture *rarray boys* have contributed to the development of an indigenous musical form popularly referred to as *milo*. Like the *odelay* societies, *milo* music was considered a *rarray boy* pastime when it emerged in the late 1940s. The snobbish Krio middle-class did not patronise these musicians. Instead, they engaged the services of the respectable Ebenezer Calendah, Pa Wilson and Peter Nah Lepet. 'Meringue music' was therefore referable to *rarray boy* music. The fact that most of these musicians were attached to some *odelay* did not give them any respectability in society. The persistence of *odelay* societies as a form of urban popular culture and their grudging acceptance by mainstream society went hand in hand with the development of *milo* as a musical form. The acceptance and patronage of *milo* musicians by the working-class and the non-Krio population contributed towards its acceptability in the eyes of the middle-class. But *milo* music did not carry any social message about their conditions in society. The lyrics dealt with the vulgar and the profane. *Milo* musicians initially appropriated most of their songs from female circumcision festivals. The change from the vulgar to the popular praise singing took place at a time when politicians became interested in the *odelay* as a pool from which they could get a regular supply of thugs.

There is nothing on the West coast of Africa that compares with the *odelay* societies in Freetown. The two original *odelays* – Eastern Paddle and Lawd Da Masi – emerged in the 1950s (Nunley, 1988). They were established by working-class Krios – Remi and Scott-Olu – but with a predominantly non-Krio membership. The exclusionary cultural landscape in pre-war Freetown and the refusal by the more respectable middle-class *odelays* to recruit/accept *rarray boys* as members, were key to the emergence of these societies. In a sense they represent a form of protest against their collective exclusion and can therefore be read as a refusal, by *rarray boys*, to accept the kinds of leisure in which they could engage. From this marginal position they gradually made their way to the centre through politics. Prior to the APC electoral victory in 1967, *odelay* societies were tolerated by city officials and the police in so far as they were able to control their members during their periodic carnivals. There were as yet no formal links between *odelays* and aspirant politicians. Their debut in politics probably started with the 1962 City Council elections when members of an *odelay*, Rainbow in central Freetown, voted *en masse* for the APC candidate, S.I. Koroma.

A major change took place after the APC came to power in 1968. The following year two leading youth politicians, both members of the APC youth wing – Leslie Patrick Allen and Alfred Akibo-Betts – were given the honour of leading two *odelays* – Firestone and Eastern Paddle. This new development symbolized the close links between politicians and *odelays*. The high point of this acceptance and respectability came sixteen years later when President Joseph Saidu Momoh (1985-92), was given the honour of leading the Eastern Paddle after his inauguration in 1985. Seven years later, in 2002, President Ahmad Tejan Kabba, went out to 'greet' Eastern Paddle on the day of their carnival.

The revelling in *odelay* carnivals constitutes an important barometer with which measure popular opinion. These are normally moments of mass protest, of popular op sition, in the form of songs, against injustices in society, particularly after the declarat of the single-party state in 1978 and the consequent stifling of organized political op sition. The carnival crowd was now representative of the general society, so that the ly of the numerous songs composed for such events became essential in understanding only rebellious youth culture but also popular consciousness. The lyrics of the so range from a critique of the Lebanese *comprador* minority to the price of rice, the natic staple; from the corrupt practices of successive heads of state and their ministers to un and unpopular actions by the government. The protest lyrics of some groups in *Eastern Paddle* carnival in 1986 (this carnival remains the most politically explosive t Freetown has ever experienced) led to the proscription of *odelay* carnivals the follow year by the police chief. The personal attack on the president was primarily because the increased price of rice – the national staple. This, according to the refrain of songs, was not what he had promised during his inauguration a year earlier.

If these popular negotiating strategies could be read as cultural subversion of the *tus quo*, *sans* violence, how do they relate to the wasted decade, 1991-2001, which lec three violent upheavals in six years and left more than 30,000 people dead?

Violence and 'Revo(loot)shon'

The transition from random individual violence to collective social violence in the na of an idea has never been a *rarray boy* project. Although the composition of *rarray l* kept changing in the 1960s and 1970s as more youths dropped out of school and joi the *odelays* societies hanging out in *potes*, *rarray boys* could not inaugurate a national c course on violence and revolution, nor could they make the transition from an alter tive culture to an oppositional one. An alternative culture could co-exist side by s with a dominant culture, but an oppositional culture might confront the dominant c ture through strategies designed to undermine its hegemony. The major wherewithal such a transition – intellectual capital – came from college students who had carve social and political space for themselves in the ongoing conversations between the c ferent categories of youth in the 1970s. College students appropriated aspects of *rai boy* culture – particularly the *pote* and the new Krio language – and transformed th sites into a solid oppositional culture. The result was a rebellious youth culture and c course founded on pan-Africanism, national liberation, and violence. It was from t common cultural pool, this same youth constituency, that the three 'revo(loot)shc were to fashion their respective projects and language of protest in the wasted decade the 1990s (Abdullah and Muana, 1998a; Rashid, 1997). Ironically, the college stude who initiated this process of transformation from an alternative into an oppositional c ture were not involved, nor did they participate in any of these 'revo(loot)shons'.

The driving force in the world of rebellious youth culture, not *rarray boy* culture, always been the perennial lack of job opportunities and the means to acquire necess skills. Without a well developed vocational education to incorporate high school gra ates and dropouts or a system whereby small loans could be made available to aspir petty traders, young men had little choice but to join the increasing army of the une ployed. But they were not all lumpens. By lumpens, I refer to the largely unemploy and unemployable youths, mostly male, who live by their wits or who have one foo what is generally referred to as the informal or underground economy. They are prone to criminal behaviour, petty theft, drugs, drunkenness and anti-social tendencies.

From the 1970s and 1980s onwards, the new crop of young men who were swelling the ranks of the unemployed were predominantly literate. Some had special skills, but no jobs. They drifted in and out of the numerous *potes* in the urban centres. The increase in the number of lumpens and the unemployed took place at a time when the number of *potes* in the city was also increasing. Dope peddling became a full-time job for some of these youths. This new group came with all sorts of contradictory tendencies. While some were politically conscious and also very critical of the *status quo*, a particular group in the East End were only interested in the proverbial good life. This group was the lumpenproletariat *par excellence*. They lived by their wits and were implicated in the murder at Mammy Yoko Street. Their emergence spawned a particular style or mode of getting by which made pickpocketing, purse snatching, street violence and petty theft, a city-wide problem. Their victims were always traders and European tourists. Their brief appearance in the early 1970s was marked by the formation of a new *odelay, Liner*, at Magazine, a high-density neighbourhood in the East End.

Unlike the original *rarray boys* who were not particularly concerned about their looks, this new sub-group acquired a petty bourgeois taste, together with a particular dress code. Instead of the typical haggard-looking *rarray boy*, this cohort was into the latest fashion. They shopped at the most expensive stores in town: *Boutique Colisée, Madam Sheriffa's*, and *Elegant Store*. Their two most distinctive artefacts were ultra-violet sunglasses and a pair of white shorts. A polo top completed the outfit. Their money came from petty theft – at home and on the street – and gambling. Some of them came from wealthy and influential families in the East End. Their flamboyant reign was cut short by two tragic events: the murder at the Traveler's Lodge and the one on Mammy Yoko Street. The execution of those found guilty opened a new chapter in the history and sociology of youth culture in Freetown. This chapter coincided with the proliferation of reggae music and the inauguration of an intense but fuzzy political conversation among youths in general.

From the late 1960s to the early '70s, developments in music, pubbing and the drug culture created a situation that brought middle-class, working-class and lumpen elements together. This movement was not specifically Sierra Leonean. Rather, it was a global trend which spawned such groups as the hippies, the beatniks and the rock-and-roll generation. And they all came with a drug culture and the slogan of free love (Hobsbawm, 1994). By 1970 all high schools in the city had their respective *potes* where truants could hang out to smoke marijuana and gamble. The formation of *Purple Haze*, a rock 'n' roll musical group, *Afric Jessips, Superb Seven* from Liberia, *Super Combo* from Bo, all in the late 1960s and early '70s, contributed to the proliferation of the drug culture particularly amongst the middle-class school-going youth. Many middle-class youths became participants in this culture; it was fashionable to be a *savis man,* to be hip, especially if one frequented the usual hangouts, and took part in the ritual of smoking, dubbed 'sessions'. The *savis man* was street-wise, attended school and also hung out with the crowd; it was the 'hip' thing to do. Those who did not were called all sorts of names: square, dead, ball head, amongst others. The musical group, *Purple Haze*, was predominantly composed of middle-class youths. Those implicated in the murder of Louis Farmer were to be found among this group.

Partly because these new groups had some formal education and were exposed to what was unfolding elsewhere in the world, they were more politically conscious than the original *rarray boys*. They appropriated the rock 'n' roll culture from the West, w Mick Jagger, Curtis Mayfield, Jimi Hendrix and Sly Stone, established the Gardene Club at Fourah Bay College, a forum for radical nonconformist students in the 19 and '80s, and were arguably the first to establish *potes* in the College residence. Th arrival transformed the *pote* culture by making it more political, in the image, I wo add, of the working-class pubs in nineteenth-century England. The *pote* is to *rar boy*/rebellious youth culture what the pub in England is to working-class culture. T new group appropriated *rarray boy* culture and inaugurated a rebellious discourse w vague hints at political transformation.

What marked *pote* culture during this period was the intense but fuzzy political cc versation centred on the state of the nation. The influence of Bob Marley, Peter To Bunny Wailer and Fela Anikulapo Kuti was evident in *pote* discourse. The conversatic about the state of the nation became centred on the corrupt practices of the politi class, the stifling political atmosphere under the single-party dictatorship, and the ov whelming dominance of the Lebanese minority. A sub-group within this new gro predominantly of working-class origin, who were not college students, became the f to try their hands at organizing *rarray boys*/rebellious youths. By this time the drug c ture was silently gaining grudging acceptance from officialdom and parents alike. L Rastafarians in Jamaica and elsewhere, the new tendency extolled the imagined virt of the weed and considered it acceptable *Inna Babylon*.

The first attempt at organization took place in 1975 with the establishment of the Youths Organization (AYO). Its headquarters were in central Freetown at Matadi, a in the city centre, with branches in Babylon, another *pote* in the East End. The A recorded more than 200 members but later fizzled out after its founder and princi organizer, Khalil Sesay, left Sierra Leone for further studies. The remaining leader Mohamed Sanu and Eddie Gomez – continued with the organization while others to start new groups elsewhere in the city and the hinterland. AYO was explicitly pol cal; it was an attempt to articulate the frustrations of its largely unemployed membe 'The AYO project was about empowering unemployed youths to enable them to p ticipate as citizens in the nation-state', Khalil Sesay recalled in a recent interview.[9]

The changed environment in the *pote* made the drug culture a *sine qua non* for ra calism and nonconformity. Those who did not participate in the ritual of drug use w not considered radicals or conscious brothers (there were no sisters); they were sim impostors dubbed as *bellahs*.[10] The *pote* continued to attract high school graduates, th awaiting their Ordinary and Advanced Level examination results, and those retaki their exams. The *pote* was friendship, camaraderie, a revolutionary cell, all rolled into o There was good music, reasonable beer, and at times women, but always company, son one to talk to, brothers to 'conscientize'. Here, youths came into contact with new id from 'advanced revolutionaries' who had read some Marx, some Fanon, some Rodr and knew a little about Nkrumah, pan-Africanism, and of course, Marcus Garvey, Fi Castro and Che Guevara. They could connect the writings of these political think with the lyrics of the *reggae* musicians, and some were able to draw examples fr African history in the era of slavery and colonialism to demonstrate the exploitation Africa's resources, and its continuation in the postcolonial era.

This period was marked by the development of a new kind of politics at Fourah I College. The new radical students strengthened the tradition established by the rock

[9] Interview with Khalil Kamara, London, 3 July 2000.
[10] An outsider, someone who does not belong.

roll group. It was an exemplary fusion between town and gown: FBC students and *man dem* in the city, especially in the *pote* and some working-class pubs. This unity between town and gown, markedly absent elsewhere in Africa, was the critical factor, which gave meaning and a 'sense of direction' to the cultural upheaval from below. It brought in some undigested ideas from some 'advanced revolutionaries', with which this movement was able to establish a degree of legitimacy in its quest for a radical political transformation. The intellectual origins of rebellious youth culture could be dated to this period, for *rarray boy* culture, even with its vibrant contribution in the cultural sphere could not inaugurate any form of discursive regime that would qualify as rebellious culture. It was certainly contestatory, and an alternative to the mainstream, but it was never rebellious, precisely because it could not muster the relevant social capital and resources to be so. So it was left to radical students and other 'organic intellectuals' to develop this rebellious youth culture, particularly its grammar of protest. Yet none of the students or activists involved in this 'conscientization' took part in the formation of the Revolutionary United Front (RUF) or in the violence that characterized the three 'revo(loot)shons' in the wasted decade of the 1990s.

From *rarray boy* to *savis man* – note the growth and maturity from adolescence to adulthood – a new era dawned in the 1980s: the era of *man dem* and *me man*.[11] This was the era of the *Green Book* and the *Juche* Idea of Kim Il Sung, the Socialist Club, and the Pan-African Union (PANAFU). These organizations were well established in FBC in the early to mid-1980s; they were the dominant political craze in the College and elsewhere in the major urban centres. Ghaddaffi's *Green Book* was discussed in *potes* and the student residence. The PANAFU brought students, the unemployed and lumpens together. It was different from other student organizations, because its leadership, especially after 1985, condemned the drug culture and refused to accept that a revolution was imminent. PANAFU was more concerned with educating its members about neo-colonialism in Sierra Leone/Africa and apartheid and Zionism in South Africa and Israel, than with the capture of state power. If AYO had organized the unemployed in the 1970s for explicitly political ends, PANAFU went further: it organized youths in general within a pan-Africanist framework by establishing regular study groups. PANAFU had a political and an intellectual agenda; AYO was more into activism and control from above.

The new groups were neither involved in petty theft – this had ceased being an aspect of lumpen youth culture – nor were they interested in legitimizing the postcolonial order by offering their services as thugs. They were also far removed from the *odelay* societies. The change in language is significant. Whereas the earlier change from *rarray boy* to *savis man* was to gain respectability, the move from *man dem* to *me man* signified group solidarity as opposed to individuality within this predominantly masculine culture. The notion of *man dem* captures the binding collective spirit of the emerging imagined community, while *me man* underlines the spirit of brotherhood – there was no sisterhood in this exclusively masculine adventure – inherent in the new-found community. It was a script that laid great emphasis on oneness; a spirit of give and take; and a unity founded on an imagined common interest freely translated into an opposition to the *status quo*. Put differently, the script was the collective speaking with one voice: the voice of an imagined community with identical interests and destiny. The new quest for equality reflected in the new language amongst youth directly challenged the entrenched patron-

---

[11] This was the beginning of the community of common interest and the emergence of the imagined community. *Me man/man dem* captures the camaraderie in this new-found community; it was selfless service in the name of an ill-defined ideal loosely referred to as Revolution!

client relationship in the society. What this group craved for in their quest for equal and change was total transformation; in a word, a revolution and nothing less. The maj ity of them had no clear idea how this revolution would come about and they did theorize or even explore an alternative to violent change in Sierra Leone, because t was impossible under the one-party state. By then violence, more specifically politi violence, a central feature of the revolution-to-be, had become the common property all who called themselves 'revolutionaries' – and there were many – who claimed tl were against *de sistem*.[12]

But the language of protest, of revolution, was palpably ambiguous, reflecting, perha the different categories of youth and their numerous experiences with talk about rev lution and violent change. Revolution meant different things to different groups. Eve happening or action by students against the college administration or the governm was smuggled under this catch-all 'abracadabra'. 'Revolution' was the buzzword for an thing anti-establishment or anti-system. Under these circumstances, a student demo stration against the undemocratic APC regime in 1977 was dubbed 'revolutio Similarly, a radical student leadership takeover of the student union in 1985 was ce brated as a revolution. This infantile reading of what constitutes a revolutionary proj was appropriated by rebellious youths in the city and elsewhere. It was to be reprodu in grotesque forms in the 1990s under changed conditions, leading to the loss of m innocent lives in the name of an imagined revolution. The genealogy of the language protest, of revolution, which is found in the Revolutionary United Front (RUF), National Provisional Ruling Council (NPRC), the government of the military sub terns who overthrew the APC regime in 1992, and the Armed Forces Revolution Council (AFRC) which came to power after a bloody uprising in May 1997, has to sought in the conversations about violent change in the late 1970s and early 1980s. T reading allows us to understand why widespread looting was dubbed liberation, why abduction of innocent children was considered a rescue operation, and why collect gang rape was seen as remuneration for combatants! Grotesque appropriation of w constitutes a revolutionary project produces grotesque results.

Lacking any clear-cut ideas about the political goals of an armed uprising, and m merized by the individuals who set themselves up as guardians of the revolution-to-some of these youths were convinced that they had arrived at a level of political ma rity that would usher in the much talked about revolution. Those who were involved these conversations about revolution/violent change were impatient with the protrac process of political education and ideological transformation, which normally con with a revolutionary project. They were convinced that all that was needed was gu guns, not even military training or political education. Their impatience, others say ang led some of them out of Sierra Leone to acquire military training to make a revoluti Others joined the army in pursuit of the same goal: the capture of state power in name of a revolution. The conversations about revolution and violent change amo rebellious youths, produced youths obsessed with the necessity of violence in chang *de sistem*, not conscious revolutionaries.

This obsession with violence as the midwife of change spawned the so-called revo tion of the Revolutionary United Front (RUF/SL) in 1991 and the *coup* of the Natio Provisional Ruling Council (NPRC) subaltern officers in 1992. Five years later, the t groups – the RUF and the Sierra Leone Army – were united in the Armed For Revolutionary Council (AFRC), which was in reality a dictatorship of the lumpen p

---

[12] *De sistem* was a catch-all term for the *status quo*.

letariat. The leader of the first revolution was a functionally literate corporal in the Sierra Leonean Army, cashiered for his alleged involvement in a *coup d'état* in 1971; the leader of the second revolution was a high school graduate turned disco dancer who later joined the army; the leader of the third revolution was a major sprung from prison where he had been incarcerated for acts of treason. The leadership of all the three revolutions were young men in their twenties and early thirties who were participants in the rebellious youth culture. Neither the radical students nor the 'advanced' revolutionaries in Freetown took part in this mimicking gimmick dubbed revolution. Starved of ideas that might have helped them market their monstrous creations as revolutions, the leadership of the three revolutions had to rely on violent rhetoric and acts of incomparable brutality to compensate for the lack of popular support. Their lack of ideas forced them to fall back on their natural constituency: lumpen youths in the cities, the mining centres, and the rural areas.

The wanton and indiscriminate violence that marked the arrival of the RUF when it launched its revolution in 1991 from bases deep inside neighbouring Liberia would remain the most distinguishing feature of this nihilistic movement throughout its existence. Slaughtering women, children, community elders and government workers in the border district of Kailahun and Pujehun, the movement quickly established itself in this enclave with the help of Liberian combatants from Charles Taylor's National Patriotic Front of Liberia (NPFL). The widespread violence initially attributed to the Liberians deprived the movement of support from the local population, so that by the end of 1993, the Sierra Leone Army, with the help of Guinean troops across the border, was able to force the RUF to retreat to whence it came. The RUF's rhetoric of power to the people was lost in the violence and brutality that marked the first phase of the war. When the movement returned in early 1994, however, it re-emerged with a renewed determination to capture power by all means. By systematically targeting strategic areas like the mines and Bo, the second largest city, coupled with the establishment of bases all over the country, the RUF was able to stretch the Sierra Leone Army to its limit. A war without frontline ensued, so that by 1996 a new civilian government was forced to negotiate with the rebels. The following year, a group of junior non-commissioned officers in the Sierra Leone Army seized power and invited the RUF to join them. The new regime, the AFRC, lasted only nine months before it was kicked out of power by the regional intervention force.

The RUF and its allies, the renegade Sierra Leone Army, retreated to the countryside where they unleashed a reign of terror on innocent civilians. The two campaigns of terror – Operation No Living Thing and Operation Pay Yourself – forced thousands of civilians to flee to neighbouring Guinea. And then in January 1999 the Sierra Leone Army and the RUF invaded the city of Freetown, killing thousands of its inhabitants and abducting several hundred women and young girls.

The three 'revolutions' are products of the same historical and sociological processes. Their so-called revolutionary scripts are markedly similar, but they chose different routes to achieve the same objective: the capture of state power. It is not coincidental that their support base remained largely amongst lumpen/rebellious youths on the margins. The RUF, the most notorious of the three, initially recruited the bulk of its fighters among urban/rural lumpens in Freetown, Monrovia and the border districts with Liberia. Once the war got under way they devised another recruiting strategy: conscripting under-age boys and girls who are forced to commit horrendous crimes in their communities and are then continuously fed with drugs. The bulk of the RUF combatants are press-ganged

youths and children who have no clue about what they are fighting for. The social ba
of these so-called revolutions needs to be emphasized. To read them otherwise is to su
vert the evidence (Richards, 1996).

Conclusion

The wasted decade of the 1990s started with an insurgency movement in 1991, a cc
d'etat by young military officers in 1992, followed by a bloody uprising in 1997 in whi
the elected government was overthrown. These events unfolded against a background
war, general insecurity and the total collapse of institutions of governance in both ru
and urban areas. Central to understanding this drama is the role of youth culture, pa
ticularly rebellious youth culture, the evolution of an imagined community centred
the *pote* and the *odelay*, the fusion of different categories of youth in the 1970s, and t
inauguration of a political discourse anchored in violence. Neither the *rarray boy* cultu
which provided the foundation from which the movement was to evolve, nor the reb
lious culture from which it later sprang, was equipped to fully understand what cons
tutes a revolutionary project. The language of revolution was not only ambiguous, it v
also misunderstood by those who claim to speak that language on behalf of the peo
who ironically became their prime target. The 1991 insurgency movement that herald
the beginning of the war in the name of revolutionary change, the 1992 *coup d'état*
subaltern officers in their twenties that proclaimed a revolution in pursuit of a purita
ical ideal, and the bloody *putsch* in the name of peace in 1997 reproduced the same und
gested and ambiguous 'revolutionary texts'. The end result was a grotesque caricature
revolution, one that left thousands of Sierra Leoneans dead, thousands of others maim
for life, and a country ravaged and stripped in the name of an elusive but least und
stood ideal.

References

Abdullah, I. 1998a. 'Rethinking African Labour and Working Class History: The Artisan Origins of the Sie
    Leonean Working Class'. *Social History* 23 (1): 80–96.
— 1998b. 'Bush Path to Destruction: The Origin and Character of the Revolutionary Uni
    Front(RUF/SL)', *Journal of Modern African Studies* 36 (2): 203-235.
— 1999. 'The Role of Youth in Conflicts'. in *The Role of youth in Conflict Prevention in Southern Africa*. ed
    Palme, Kauhava, Finland.
— 2004. *Between Democracy and Terror: The Sierra Leone Civil War*. UNISA Press/CODESRIA.
Abdullah, I. & Bangura Y. (eds). 'Lumpen Youth Culture and Political Violence: The Sierra Leone Civil W
    Special Issue. *African Development*, 23 (3&4).
Abdullah, I. & P. Muana. 1998. 'The Revolutionary United Front: A Revolt of the Lumpen Proletariat'.
    African Guerrilla. ed. C. Clapham. Oxford: James Currey.
Amit-Talal, V. & Helen Wulff. (eds). 1995. *Youth Cultures: A Cross Cultural Perspective*. London: Routledge.
Austin, J. & M. Willard. (eds). 1998. *Generations of Youth: Youth Cultures and Histories in Twentieth Century Ame*
    New York: New York University Press.
Cohen, P. 1999. *Rethinking the Youth Question*. Durham, NC: Duke University Press.
Cooper, F. 1996. *Labour and Decolonisation in Africa*. Cambridge: Cambridge University Press.
Greene, G. 1959. *Heart of the Matter*. London: Penguin.
Hall, S. & T. Jefferson (eds). 1976. *Resistance Through Rituals*. London: Routledge.
Hobsbawm, E. 1994. *The Age of Extremes*. New York: Pantheon Books.
La Hausse, P. 1990. 'The Cows of Nongoloza: Youth, Crime and Amalaita Gangs in Durban, 1900-1930', *Jour*
    of Southern African Studies, 16.
Nunley, J. 1998. *Moving with the Face of the Devil*. Urbana-Champaign, IL: University of Illinois Press.

Rashid, I. 1997. 'Students and Rebellion'. Paper presented at CDD Strategic Planning Workshop on the Peace Process in Sierra Leone, Lomé, Togo.
— 1999. 'Subaltern Reactions: Lumpens, Students and the Left'. *African Development* 23 (3&4): 19-43.
Reno, W. 2002. *Insurgencies in the Shadow of State Collapse.* Roskilde: Roskilde University Press.
Richards, P. 1995. 'Rebellion in Liberia and Sierra Leone: A Crisis of Youth?' in *Conflict in Africa.* ed. Oliver Furley. London: Tauris Academic Press.
— 1996. *Fighting For The Rain Forest.* Oxford: James Currey.
— 2004. *No Peace, No War: An Anthropology of Contemporary Wars.* Oxford: James Currey.
Schneider, E. 1999. *Vampires, Dragons and Egyptian Kings: Youth Gangs in Post-war New York.* Princeton, NJ: Princeton University Press.
Sierra Leone Census Report. 1921. Freetown.
Sierra Leone Weekly News, 1919, May 17; 1919, October 11; 1939, December 25; 1940, October 26; 1942, March 14; 1945, May 5.
Skelton, T. & G. Valentine. (eds). 1977. *Cool Places: Geographies of Youth Cultures.* London: Routledge.
Van Onselen, C. 1982. *New Babylon.* Johannesburg: Ravan Press.
Wyn, J. & R. White. 1997. *Rethinking Youth.* London: Sage Publications.

9

FILIP DE BOECK
The Divine Seed Children, Gift & Witchcraft in the Democratic Republic of Congo

Introduction: 'Siting' the Imaginary

In Congo, as elsewhere in Africa, there has always lurked, in a rather unproblematic w
another reality underneath the surface of visible reality. Movement and stagnation, soc
or physical reproduction and death, the diurnal and the nocturnal, have always exist
in and through each other. 'More precisely,' states Mbembe,

> the invisible was not only the other side of the visible, its mask or substitute. The invisible v
> in the visible, and vice versa, not as matter of artifice, but as one and the same and as exter,
> reality simultaneously – as the image of the thing and the imagined thing, at the same time.
> other words, the reverse of the world (the invisible) was supposed to be part and parcel of
> obverse (the visible), and vice versa. And in this capacity to provide a basis for, and state
> inseparability of, the being and nonbeing of persons and things – that is, the radicality of th
> life and the violence of their death and their annihilation – lay the inexhaustible strength of
> image. (Mbembe, 2001: 145)

Witchcraft is one of the mechanisms in which this inseparability and simultaneous mu
tiplicity most clearly come to the fore. 'The efficacy of defensive fetishes and aggressi
sorcery', notes Devisch, 'relies on the principle of the subversive capacity of "catastroph
retroflexion" (see *pli-catastrophe* ...), otherwise described as the homeopathic rever
mobilized in the "floating signifier" ... proper to residue, detritus, or excretio
(Devisch, 2001: 116). In Congo today, however, something seems to have changed in t
slippage between reverse and obverse, visible and invisible, reality and its double,
shadow, spectre, reflection or image. In contemporary (urban) Congo the societal cri
seems to have embedded itself in the changing function and qualities of junction a
disjunction (such as the disjunction between life and death), and hence of the role of t
imaginary, which operates that disjunction or *dédoublement*. Put in a different way, t
societal crisis in postcolonial Congo essentially revolves around the increasingly pro
lematic positing or 'siting' of the double (for example, death as the double of the livir
or the double as the living and familiar figure of death).

Setting out from an ethnographic focus on a recent but widespread phenomenon, t
of witch-children in the Congolese capital of Kinshasa, this chapter intends to discu
the changing nature of the urban imaginary. This change seems to express itself prim

I wish to thank Jaak Le Roy and Adelin N'Situ for their comments during the many conversations we had
the subject dealt with in this chapter. Thanks are also due to Jean Comaroff for her helpful comments.

rily through a *liquidation* of the double. As a consequence, it produces a new epistemological breach, which is basically appearing in what is a growing indiscernibleness between the first and the second world, or between reality and its double (De Boeck, 2002). This other, second world (*deuxième monde*), second city (*deuxième cité*), pandemonium world (*monde pandemonium*), or fourth dimension (*quatrième dimension*, i.e. one of the multiple invisible worlds of what is referred to as *kindokinisme*)[1] increasingly seems to push aside and take over the first world of daily reality. A term which is currently used in Lingala to describe this change, this quality of mounting *Unheimligkeit* and elusiveness of the world, is *mystique*. In the postcolonial *Afrique fantôme* that Congo seems to have become, it is increasingly frequent to designate people and situations as *mystique*, difficult to place, interpret and attribute meaning to. The changed status of children in Congolese society is symptomatic of this more general change (De Boeck, 1998, 2001).

In his insightful chapter on the 'thing' and its double in Cameroonian cartoons, quoted above, Mbembe remarks upon 'the new experience of speech and things' which I have indicated above. Despite the scale of the transformations and the discontinuities, he nevertheless assumes that an imaginary world has remained. One of the leading questions throughout this chapter, however, points in a different direction: what happens if the very nature of the imaginary as a flexible but organized field of social practices has become disorganized and has lost, at least to some extent, its localizing force and its capacity for creating continuity, for producing sociality? The imaginary is the dimension of the invisible, but what if the invisible becomes, or takes over, or pushes aside the visible? What if the imaginary is no longer the socially productive phantasmagoric but constantly crosses the boundaries and invades the real in an unmediated, non-symbolic way? What if the imaginary is no longer the 'irréel' but the *indiscernibleness* between 'réel' and 'irréel' (see Deleuze, 1990, quoted by Bayart, 1996: 138)? What, in other words, when the dual and therefore non-alienated relationship with the double, which until recently certainly existed in local Congolese experience, most notably in relation to the witch, is becoming problematic and leads to alienation instead? If death, as the double of the living, belongs to the realm of the imaginary, and if the imaginary thus operates the disjunction between life and death, what then does it mean for a societal constellation when that distinction ceases to exist? Can we say that Congolese reality seems to be losing its capacity to undouble itself into multiple others to (re)institutionalize itself through this act?

In dealing with the phenomenon of witch-children, I propose to tackle these complex questions by looking at the relationships between the growing presence of death, the notion of the double in the articulation between the imaginary and the symbolic level, and the forms in which continuity, exchange and gift are spelled out in Congolese towns and cities, and particularly in Kinshasa, today.[2] In these urban worlds the frenetic

---

[1] *Kindokinisme* is derived from the Lingala term *kindoki*, 'witchcraft'. The use of the neologism is significant in that it illustrates how the unpredictable transformations of reality constantly seem to require new conceptual frameworks.

[2] The material presented here is based on several periods of field research in Kikwit (between 1994 and 1998) and Kinshasa (1999-2000). For five weeks in August and September of 1999 and again in May and September 2000 and April 2001, I did research on the phenomenon of child witchcraft in Kinshasa, and more particularly in the context of prayer movements and healing churches, most of which had links with Pentecostalist churches and other 'fundamentalist' branches such as Watchtower and Jehovah's Witnesses, as well as Seventh Day Adventists. I frequented churches mainly in the neighbourhoods of Masina, Bandalungwa, Lemba, Selembao, Ndjili and Kintambo, and conducted interviews with children, church leaders, parents and other relatives of the children involved. In Kikwit, where the phenomenon of child witches is a much more marginal reality than in the capital, at least with regard to the numbers of children involved, I worked with a group of girl-diviners and child healers. Most of this material, however, will have to be dealt with in a future publication.

construction of local modernities goes hand in hand with the expectations and promises of a millennial capitalism that finds its – sometimes fanatical – expression in the
thousands of independent churches operating and proliferating in the urban context of
Congo and elsewhere in sub-Saharan Africa today (see Corten and Marshall-Frantani,
2001; Laurent, 2003; Tonda, 2002; van Dijk, 2000). It is in these locations that the social
and cultural imaginary, as interaction in time and space (between heritage and innovation, between past, present and future, between rural and urban realities, or between
Congolese and the global world) is most strongly active.

More and more, children and youngsters emerge as, and form the crucial sites of, identity in which all of these interactions take place. Children and youngsters appear as the
ultimate focal points of the contemporary Central African imaginary. Children, as *opus
operatum* and as *modus operandi* of crisis and renewal, form the identity locations in which
the ruptures and fault lines of an African world in transition become manifest. As part of
a wider transformation of the socio-cultural, political and economical architecture of the
urban landscape, children and youngsters thus are at the heart, or better still, the *frontier*
of the reconfiguration of geographies of inclusion and exclusion, or private and public.

Children of the street have always existed in Kinshasa, but in recent years their numbers have swollen dramatically. One phenomenon that has greatly contributed to the
growing presence of the street child, variously referred to as *phaseur, moine* (monk),
moineau (sparrow) or *shege/chegue*, is the changing pattern of witchcraft accusations
which may be currently observed in the capital. The incessant re-invention of the
Central African urban lived environment is not at all marked by a Weberian
Entzauberung. It is, on the contrary, enacted and produced most strongly, not only in the
'enchanting' spaces of Christian fundamentalism, but also in the frenzied and often
obsessional production of discourses and practices surrounding witchcraft. Both are, of
course, intimately related. Overall, observers have remarked upon the general increase of
witchcraft accusations in Congo over the last decades (see, for example, Douglas, 1999).
Although this remains to be proven, it is clear that the dynamics of witchcraft themselves
have undergone some dramatic changes over the past years. One of the most disconcerting phenomena that highlights this evolution is the central role that children are
nowadays given in these developing witchcraft discourses and practices. In contemporary Kinshasa, thousands of children are implicated in witchcraft accusations.[3]

After a brief description of this spreading phenomenon in the streets, homes and
churches of Kinshasa, I shall begin my analysis by arguing, first, that children and young
adolescents have never before occupied a more central position in the public spaces of
urban life, whether in the popular urban music culture, the media, the churches, the

---

[3] In 2000 the NGO 'Save the Children' gave an estimate of 2000 children who are the subject of such accusations in Kinshasa, but it recently reviewed its estimate upwards to 20,000 (BBC report, 17 January 2003). In
my view this recent estimate is more accurate because it seems to take into account the high turnover of children in those churches and the constant production of new child witches. For the rest, the joining of children
and witches is of all times and all places. While in Europe, before 1600, witches were mostly elderly people,
children were increasingly accused of witchcraft after that date. Not only were children victims of bewitchment, as in the case of seventeenth-century Salem, Massachusetts, but they were also accused of bewitching
others. In seventeenth-century Europe, children were regularly burnt as witches, as attested by Midelfort's
analysis of the Würzenberg witch trials of 1627-9, in which ten children between the ages of six and twenty
were killed on account of witchcraft (see Midelfort, 1972: 179ff). The phenomenon of child witches is not
new to Africa either. For comparative material in recent years see, for example, Geschiere's analysis of *mbati*, a
reportedly 'new' type of child witchcraft which started to appear among the Maka of South-east Cameroon
in the beginning of the1970s (Geschiere, 1980). What therefore seems to be exceptional in the Congolese case
that I am dealing with here is above all its expansive scale.

army, the street, or the bed. Occupying such a prominent social position, children are not only victims but have also become active impact factors in and on Congolese society. The newly generated, central but ambivalent, societal status of children seems to have crystallized most clearly around the figure of the witch, which is the materialization of a cultural imaginary of crisis on the crossroads between, for example, money, power, kinship and sexuality.

Secondly, 'new situations demand new magic'. Due to the increasing impact of the global media and of globalization *tout court,* the newly arising tensions between traditions and modernities are being defined most powerfully, and sometimes resolved, in the field of witchcraft. First of all, the heritage of colonialist modernity as embodied by the postcolonial state is sometimes perceived to be itself a source of witchcraft and evil. As one preacher of a healing church explained:

> The late Mobutu brought witchcraft from the village to the city. Now everything is destroyed in Congo, not because of the incapability of the Congolese, but because of witchcraft. Our country has been sold somewhere; it has been sold to a mysterious world (*monde mystérieux*), to museums abroad, and even in France, Egypt, Morocco and the United States. These are strategic places of evil. And this witchcraft even brought us the war. All of this happened because our leaders and our government touched fetishes in India and elsewhere. (Interview, September 1999, Church of Beth Shalom, community of Masina, Kinshasa)

In this interpretation the post-independence state, the heir and propagator of a certain colonialist model of modernity, but also the forces of globalization (from the United States to France and India, a Congolese version of the 'axis of evil') are at the origins of witchcraft. On the other hand, there is not only the witchcraft of modernity (see De Boeck, 1998). As has been noted by Geschiere and a growing number of others since (Comaroff and Comaroff, 1999; Geschiere, 1997; Moore and Sanders, 2001), witchcraft practices in Africa have also been gradually reformulated to come to represent one of the major gateways to 'modernity', in a rapidly developing space of 'expectations' and desire in which an 'economy of the occult' (Comaroff and Comaroff, 1999) has become the means to win the 'war of dreams' (Augé, 1999). This nocturnal economy of desire, which forms the hyphen between a fast growing local economy of violence and the violence of a penetrating global economy (see Lutz and Nonini, 1999), is also increasingly being accessed and shaped by the young. Children have started to occupy a more central position in the public realm. Here they appear not only as passive consumers, as in the West, but also as major societal players with access to these new global economic fields, and often in direct opposition to the generations that precede them.

Thirdly, the austere living conditions of Congolese urbanity have caused a profound transformation of existing idioms of witchcraft. The ever increasing poverty of the population of Kinshasa and other cities and towns throughout this vast country, is being accentuated by the war in the east of the country, and adds to the pressure that existing structures of kin-based solidarity are currently undergoing in the urban context. I shall argue that the linkage between children and witches is related to a profound de- and re-structuration of the notions of motherhood, gerontocracy, authority and, more generally, the field of kinship itself. These transformations are themselves grounded in an even more profound crisis that punctuates urban life: that of the logic of reciprocity and gift as the most constitutive part of the basal structure that underpins the field of kinship at large.

Finally, the crisis of the gift, in its Maussian sense as 'total social fact', also embodies the crisis of the symbolic, the increasing impossibility to 'site' the imaginary in unproblematic way. The crisis of the (structuring of the) symbolic, the capacity to syr bolize, I argue, reveals itself in the unravelling and tearing apart of two interdepende levels: the level of the symbolic, the first world, the reality of reciprocity, contract a representation, and the level of the imaginary, to which the second world also belon; and which informs the social logic and the symbolic as internalized social structur Because these two levels no longer operate as two sides of the same coin (hence the m tiqueness of the Congolese world, the awareness of 'displacement', the experience of t world as a 'dislocatory presence' which evolves from the more general rupture betwe signifier and signified, or from a change in the ways in which the floating signifiers op ate), the imaginary no longer underpins and legitimizes reality. Typical for the Congol postcolonial reality that is increasingly acquiring and being marked by an oneiric dime sion, ever larger chunks of the fields of kinship, reciprocity, money, market, sexuali power and violence are thus pulled out of the symbolic realm back into the imaginar

Witch-children in the Streets of Congo-Kinshasa

My name is Mamuya. I am 14 years old. I became a witch because of a boyfriend of mi Komazulu. One day he gave me a mango. During the following night he came to visit me my parents' house and threatened that he would kill me if I didn't offer him human meat return for the mango he had given me earlier. From that moment I became his nocturnal co panion and entered his group of witches. I didn't tell my mother. In our group we are three. night we fly with our 'airplane', which we make from the bark of a mango tree, to the hou of our victims. When we fly out at night I transform myself into a cockroach. Komazulu is t pilot of our airplane. He is the one who kills. He gives me some meat and some blood and th I eat and drink. Sometimes he gives me an arm, at other times a leg. Personally I prefer to (buttocks. I keep a part of the meat to give to my grandmother who is a witch too. Komazu is a colonel in the 'second world', and he has offered me the grade of captain if I sacrifice a pe son. That's why I killed my baby brother. I gave him diarrhoea and he died. With our group ` have already killed eight persons. Our victims haven't done any harm to us. Sometimes, thoug we judge them. If they don't defend themselves well, we kill them. Sometimes when a man buried in the cemetery, we go there and say a prayer. That prayer makes the dead person wa up and then we eat him. Now I have come out of the world of shadows, thanks to the pray of the preacher who treats me in church. But the others who are still in the 'second world' ke pulling at me. They want to kill me now for fear that I betray them. (Interview in the Chur of the Holy Spirit, Selembao, Kinshasa, September 1999)

In 1994 I accidentally came into possession of a video-tape which triggered my intere in witch-children. The video-tape featured three Congolese children between the ag of eight and twelve. They were being cross-examined by a number of Congolese adu and two Belgian men, members of a Pentecostal prayer movement in the Congole diaspora setting of Brussels, Belgium. The three children had recently left Kinshasa come to Belgium. The tape shows how the three are accused by the adults of the dea of a number of their relatives in Kinshasa, one of whom is the mother of one of t accused boys. During the (at moments rather violent) cross examination, of which t tape is a one-hour-long summary, the three children acknowledge that they indeed 'a a number of people in Kinshasa. In a story that much resembles Mamuya's, they expla

---

[4] For an insightful treatment of these themes in relation to the gift see Baudrillard (1976) and, more recen Godelier (1996).

in detail how they exited their body to 'fly' to Congo in a 'helicopter', which they had made out of a match-stick. In Kinshasa they had been helped by older witches and nocturnal friends, and most prominently among them the grandmother of one of the three boys. Finally, the three give a morbid account of how they killed their victims, chopped them up, and distributed the body parts amongst witch friends to 'eat' during a nocturnal feast in which the grandmother participated, dancing naked around the victims' houses. The taped testimony was later sent to the boys' relatives in Kinshasa to corroborate the existing suspicions.

Such stories have become part and parcel of the daily life in a city like Kinshasa. In fact, there are now so many children involved in similar rumours and accusations that even the international press agencies have started to report on them.[5] One immediate effect has been that the city streets have started to abound with ever growing groups of street children (see also De Boeck, 2004 for a more detailed ethnography of street children in Kinshasa). Until recently this phenomenon of street children restricted itself to the more important traffic arteries of areas such as Gombe which are part of 'La Ville,' the 'white' colonial heart of the city where embassy personnel and other expatriates still mostly live today. In recent years, though, street children have become a familiar aspect of street life in all parts of this vast city. Many of these children were forced to take to the street after being singled out by family members in a witchcraft accusation. Such accusations against children within one's own family have become a common occurrence that transcends all rank, class and ethnic divisions and differences that characterize Kinshasa's urban context. Increasingly, children, from babies to teenagers, are being accused of causing misfortunes and mishaps, as well as the illness or death of other children and adults in their family and neighbourhood environment. The following is an account given by a thirty-year-old AIDS patient, a mother of three children. At the time of my interview with her she was being treated in a healing church together with her four-year-old daughter, Nuclette, accused of witchcraft:

> I have suffered a lot in my life. I sold vegetables at the market. The father of Nuclette was deeply in love with me but now he has left me. I was responsible for this separation: all of a sudden I could not return his love any more.
>
> One day, I noticed that my market money had disappeared. People told me that Nuclette had stolen it, but I wouldn't believe them. But then, Nuclette began to be suspected as a witch by our neighbours. Apparently, Nuclette had tried to bewitch a woman who lives in our neighbourhood. Nuclette had changed herself and appeared as an adult woman when she went to harm this neighbour. One day, when I was out, this neighbour came over to our house and started complaining to my mother: 'How can you accept to live together in one house with the same witch-child that has tried to bewitch and kill us in our home? We are no family of yours; we didn't know that this child is a witch. Why does she try to harm us?'
>
> My mother and I decided to take the child to a prayer session at Pasteur Norbert's. That evening I washed my two other kids, and we all went together to the 'prayer control'. The preacher started to prophesy and it was affirmed that Nuclette was a witch but that the two

5 See Barthélémy Bosongo, 'Les "enfants sorciers", boucs émissaires de la misère à Kinshasa' (Agence France Presse, 13 October 1999). During the same period BBC 2 Newsnight devoted a whole programme to the phenomenon of witch-children in Kinshasa. More recently APA (Agence Presse Associée) reported (28 March 2000): '108 enfants abandonnés par leurs familles pour cause de sorcellerie ont été présentés dimanche à la presse au Centre d'exorcisme et de récupération des enfants, à Masina Pascal au cours d'un culte organisé par l'Eglise évangélique de Jésus-Christ au Congo. Ces enfants dont l'âge varie de 5 à 15 ans (filles et garçons) sont exorcisés et encadrés par le révérend Kikutu Kamboma en vue de leur insertion utile dans la société.' See also the Dutch NRC *Handelsblad*, 'Mothers in Congo give birth to "witches"', 24 March 2000; and Mark Dummett's report for the BBC, 'D.R.Congo's Unhappy Child-witches', 17 January 2003.

other children were not touched by this evil. Then the Pasteur asked me where my husbar
was. I told him that he had left our neighbourhood and was now living in a different area
the city. I didn't tell him my husband's name, but he cited it and said: 'It was Nuclette wh
caused your marriage to break up. She made your husband leave. And when you were sleepi
in your bed at night she came with other witch-children and injected you by means of a di
bolical needle with contaminated blood.' This is how I started developing AIDS. I became ver
very thin. People started saying that I had AIDS. Thanks to the preacher of this church, we no
know that the AIDS is diabolical. I have been here in the church for over a month, and tl
preacher has purified me. I was dying when I arrived here but now I am cured of AIDS.

In other cases little girls are suspected of transforming themselves into stunning
beautiful women to lure their own fathers and uncles into their bed, to snatch away the
testicles or penis, and to cause their impotence or even death. This illustrates the fact th
Congo's current societal crisis is, to an important degree, also an etiological crisi
Children are also believed to be at the origin of madness, cancer, or heart attacl
amongst their relatives and parents. Other kids appear to be three- or four-year-olds :
the 'first world', but in the nocturnal, second world they have themselves already give
birth to many children. These in turn become witch-children roaming through tl
streets of Kinshasa. Others still transform themselves into 'mystic' serpents, crocodiles «
mami wata sirens (see below).

Most of the time all these hidden suspicions and open accusations erupt into a vi«
lent conflict within the accused child's family. Often the child in question is severe
beaten, in some extreme cases even killed by family members or neighbours:

A man frequently dreamed about the thirteen-year-old son of his landlord. The landlord ar
his family lived in a separate house in the same compound. In his dreams the boy harassed a
threatened to strangle him. Soon everybody in the neighbourhood was informed about the
strange dreams. One morning some young men, all neighbours, gathered in the compound ar
started throwing stones on the corrugated iron roof of the owner's house. The boy was insid
When they started throwing the stones, the boy appeared. People started to stone him. A stor
hit him on the head. The child fell down, bleeding profusely. Some men put a tyre around h
neck and set fire to it. When the boy's parents arrived, their child was already burning to deat
The parents did not interfere for fear that they would undergo the same fate. (Field notes base
on eye-witness accounts, Mombele, May 1997)

Although such forms of extreme violence are by no means the rule, most of these chi
dren are, however, disowned and repudiated. Displaced, disenfranchised, but feared l
most, the alleged witch-children (called sheta, tsor or tshor, from the French sorcier, witcl
end up in the street, where they often team up after a while with other abandoned chi
dren to form their 'stable' (écurie), usually a group of up to seven or more persons. The
gangs have a varying lifespan (from a few weeks to some months, rarely longer than
year). Often, several of these 'stables' associate to form a larger, more loosely knit grou
Witch-children are believed to adopt the same form of organization in the world of tl
night. 'Stables' of witch-children also fashion themselves after a military army model. I
their nocturnal army, witch-children accord grades to themselves, from sergeant to ge
eral, and one climbs in rank with every victim that one has killed and 'eaten'.

Often the children who end up in the street as the result of a witchcraft accusatio
already occupied a structurally marginal position in their own family environmen
Owing to the AIDS epidemic and other causes related to the poor living conditions i
Congo, many of them were orphaned at a very early age. Others were abandoned l

their mothers, often teenagers themselves, and grew up amongst, sometimes distant, relatives: (classificatory) grandparents, uncles, aunts, cousins, or one of their father's co-wives. When one or both parents are still alive (and average life expectancy for the Democratic Republic of Congo is less than 50 years – as low as 47 for men), they are often absent, an absence which is increasingly due to patterns of displacement, migration and diaspora under the pressure of economic factors, political instability and war.

Witchcraft and the Churches

The spiral of violence that erupts in the kinship group because of the pattern of witchcraft accusations directed at children is partly countered by the church and prayer movements that are flourishing everywhere. As has been argued for different African contexts, fundamentalist churches, and foremost amongst these the Pentecostal churches and apocalyptic movements that may be found throughout sub-Saharan Africa nowadays, devote a lot of attention to the figure of the Satan, to demons, and to the struggle between Good and Evil (see, for example, Meyer, 1999 on Pentecostalism in Ghana). Beyond any doubt the churches' contribution plays a crucial role in the ceaseless production and increasing centrality of the figure of the witch in the collective imaginary of Congolese society, which is itself being restructured in terms of an Armageddon, a second world in which demons have gathered in an all-out war against God (see the Book of Revelation 16:16).

Paradoxically, then, the *Verteufelung* of the figure of the witch in the discourse of these churches makes the witch itself more omnipresent in the social field. Therefore, the position of the churches in relation to evil, straightforward as it may seem at first sight, nevertheless produces contradictory tensions in the social field. The churches' role with regard to the child-witch phenomenon is an equally ambivalent one, which makes them both part of the witchcraft problem itself as well as of this problem's local solution. On the one hand, the space of the churches is one of the most prominent sites in which the coincidence of the figure of the witch and the child is produced. During the masses and collective prayers, children are urged to make a public confession in order to reveal their true nature as witches and to confess the number of victims they have attacked (see further below). Rather than being a perversion, the naming of the witch offers an opening to solving the crisis, as it has always done in more traditional settings. Before this public moment they have usually been sniffed out or recognized as witches by the church leaders and *pasteurs* during more private consultations. In these meetings more 'traditional' divinatory models are often blended in with the church discourse to create a ritualized moment of witch-finding.

As a consequence of these denunciations, however, international aid agencies and NGOs such as Save the Children, in their struggle against the marginalization of children, accuse the church leaders and *pasteurs* of child abuse. These organizations usually treat the problem of witch-children in Kinshasa as a humanitarian problem of street children, while choosing to disregard totally the cultural implications of the witchcraft aspect. And yet, one could argue that the churches, in providing and authorizing this type of diagnostics, offer an alternative for the violence and conflict that occurs in the family as the result of a witchcraft accusation. The church leaders do not themselves produce these accusations, but merely confirm and thereby legitimate them. In doing so, the space of the 'healing' church enables the relocation and reformulation of the – sometim extreme – physical and psychological violence that the accused children have to underg within their kin-group.

The child is removed from the threatening family context in which its place h become highly problematic, and is left in the care of a *pasteur*. Here, the often equal tough treatment starts with an initial period of seclusion and quarantine, either indivie ually or collectively with other child witches. As I observed myself, some churches tal in up to a hundred children a week. The period of seclusion, during which these chi dren usually live in rather poor conditions in terms of food and hygiene, may last fro a couple of days to some weeks or even months, depending on the seriousness of tl case in question. During their seclusion the children are subjected to a period of fastin and ritual purification. The lavish administration of laxatives and emetics aims at clean ing the witch-children's bodies from the meat of the victims that they have eate Undigested pieces of meat or bone, but also objects of all kinds which are found in tl children's vomit and faeces, will be used as corroborants during their public confessie before the assembled members of the church. During the period of seclusion, the chi dren are regularly subjected to interrogations, sometimes alone, at other times in tl presence of one or both of the child's parents or other related adults if the latter are wil ing to co-operate. Many adults, though, are too afraid of their children to maintain clo contact with them.

During these more private sessions that evolve between the child and the preacher one of his or her assistants, there slowly emerges a narrative of disruption and descei into evil which will also help to structure the 'outing ritual' of confession in the publ space of the church later on. Not often mentioned or written about, this period is nev ertheless a crucial point in a whole process of 'emplotment', which helps to shape t the imaginative task of modelling an experience of crisis and drawing a – quite standar – narrative configuration out of a simple succession of illnesses and deaths. As part of therapeutic narrative process, which eventually leads to the children's rather stereotyp cal story of confession, the emplotment that takes shape here gives the experience of cr sis a direction, it mediates disruption and promotes self-healing (see Becker, 1997), eve though the children themselves are not, or only in certain ways, free in their choices how to plot their narratives.

Some days after the crucial moment of public confession the *pasteur* proceeds by orgar izing a number of exorcizing moments, referred to as *délivrance* (deliverance) or *cure d'âr* (soul-healing). This ritualized exorcism is often carried out collectively in prayer grou; under the guidance of female church members known as *intercesseuses*. The child is place in the middle of a circle of praying, often trancing, women who regularly lapse ini speaking in tongues, a sign of the Holy Spirit's presence. The focus of this powerful pray ing ritual, the child is then repeatedly subjected to exorcizing prayer and the laying on hands. Usually one woman takes the lead in prayer, while the others sustain her by regu larly punctuating her preaching with religious songs and hymns. Depending on the tyj of church, these praying sessions unfold in collaboration with the child's mother or son relatives in the hope of facilitating a reintegration of the cleansed witch-child within i family. In many cases, however, parents are not very collaborative and such reintegratic remains problematic: the child's parents and other members of the kin-group ofte remain too afraid to accept such a child back into their midst. It is usually in these all tc frequent cases that the children are subsequently forced to take to the street.

Esther's 'Soul-healing'

The following text is a translated summary of a deliverance session, originally in Lingala, for a six-year-old girl, Esther, formerly known as Falone, who looks as if she is only three (see photograph). This fact was interpreted as a clear indication of her *mystiqueness*. When I met Esther, she lived with her maternal grandparents. As her grandmother explained to me, Esther's mother had travelled to Angola to try her luck in the diamond traffic there (see De Boeck, 1999a/b). Her father had been a soldier in Mobutu's army. When Kabila came to power in 1997, the father was arrested and sent to Kitona, a re-education camp in the Lower Congo. He never returned to Kinshasa. One day the grandmother found Esther in the street where she had been beaten up by the neighbours on account of her being a witch. The grandmother, however, continued to care for Esther and even took her to several hospital centres after Esther became ill. No clear diagnosis of her ailment was ever given by any doctor, but Esther herself had started to look 'like a 70-year-old woman' and had completely stopped speaking. In one hospital, and with the financial support of some European nuns, Esther and her grandmother stayed for nine months of sustained treatment, but to no avail: Esther did not get better. Finally, the grandmother turned to prayer.

During one intensive prayer session at home, Jesus revealed to her 'the thing' in Esther's body. During the same period the grandmother had started to dream that Esther and her witch friends were trying to kill her. At this point, the grandmother decided to entrust Esther to a *pasteur* for more professional prayer help. With his assistance, the whole terrible truth about Esther slowly started coming out. Also, many of the misfortunes that had recently befallen the family suddenly began making sense. It turned out that, in the second world that Esther was inhabiting at night, she was an adult woman, with a husband, a certain Papa Bukafu, with whom she had had eleven children, six 'to the right' (boys) and five 'to the left' (girls). Esther and her witch family lived in a river under water. At night she transformed herself into a *mami wata* siren. Esther became a witch after having received a piece of dried salted fish from a neighbourhood woman, Mama Losiya, in the marketplace. Afterwards this woman started paying nocturnal visits to Esther. They started 'hunting' together, both in Kinshasa and abroad in Europe. During these travels Esther walked around with a stick that she used to kill people.

It also appeared that Esther had apparently 'blocked the way' (-*kangisa nzela*) of her mother and her two maternal uncles who were hunting for diamonds in Angola but had met with no luck so far. When news arrived in Kinshasa that one uncle had been killed by a UNITA soldier, his death was quickly attributed to Esther as well. Similarly, she was believed to have blocked another maternal uncle who had a university degree in economics but still had not found a job after two years. In the meantime her grandfather, who had worked all his life at the national airport as a warehouse-man, was also fired. When Esther's mother finally returned empty-handed from Angola and found that her daughter was the source of her misfortune, she almost killed her. In the meantime, Esther herself had started to look like an old woman and had totally stopped speaking.

In September 1999 when I met Esther and her grandmother they were still deeply involved in deliverance sessions. Thanks to the 'soul-healing' during which she had also received her new name, Esther had regained some of her former looks, although she had not grown at all. She was still closely monitored by the church community who feared that she might collapse back into the world of shadows. Each week her grandmoth took Esther to the church to participate in a session of deliverance, led by an old woman who acted as the *pasteur*'s personal emissary (see Photo 9.1):

In a vision I see a big river, like an ocean. Some trees are long, others short. This water hold lot of power, in this place there is a whirlpool. A big river, I say, with black water. And I see snake who sits where Mother Mary is, a snake which is fixedly looking her in the eyes. And also see a little girl with untidy hair. In one of her eyes there is a white spot, while the oth eye is totally white, as if she were blind. This child's name is Falone. We have given her the nar of Esther. She has the power of the water in her. She moves powerfully and calls herself *ma wata*. Summon all the compassion that you find in yourself and pray for this child. Open yo eyes, for she has a strong power residing inside her. [Speaking in tongues]. This other woma they showed her a snake. The snake is her witchcraft. There is a woman who sells on the ma ket. She is the one who gave fish meat to Esther. The powers of the water come from a m who is their neighbour. On his land there is running water coming out of a stone. There is spring. In this river a white man used to wash himself. Let us pray for God's grace for He is t only One who is King and who can save this child from the powers of witchcraft and mag Speaking in tongues. Stand up! Destroy! Cursed be the day this child received the meat out this woman's hands. That the bewitched meat she ate remains without effect! In the name Jesus Christ! Her grandmother tells us this child travels to Europe. In her hands she holds stick, a stick to kill people. God's grace! You, you are mothers, you know how to give birth, y know the pain of childbirth, help this child, block the path of the devil, and tie all the perso who wish this child harm and who visit her at night. Block the path of Mama Losiya, destr her in Jesus' name. Let us pray now for the weapon she uses to kill people with. Disarm her Jesus' name.

The spirit tells me that Esther is communicating with other witches through her little fing at this very moment. Cut all communication lines, all the radars, all of her signalling with h arms. Close down the place where Losiya is. Block all evil in heaven and on earth. Close roads. Block Esther's eyes and ears. Let the devouring fire descend to annihilate all the milita grades she received from other witches. Destroy her airplane so that she can no longer fly aw Oh, heavenly fire. They say He is fire, and when Saul had the fire he fell down. Let us raise o arms in Jesus' name. You, who are a *mami wata*, go into the water and disappear in the wate Where do you hide like a queen with long hair resembling a siren's, and with long nails? T siren destroys and causes accidents and stirs up evil spirits in the middle of the water. Ho Spirit, take possession of her. Where are you? Grab her, take her with you. Victory is in Chris blood. So, out of the depths of our faith, because she is still a child, because of my faith a yours, raise your hands so that the blood of Christ may engulf this child and the powers of t night can no longer enter her body. Esther, repeat after me: I refuse the Satan, I refuse witc craft, I refuse *mami wata*, I refuse to live in the water. Save me so that I can become your hur ble servant. I refuse the works of Satan.

[In French] Oh Eternity, Almighty Father, Great God, I lift You up, You have given us t child, Eternal Father of Israel. Hallelujah! You deliver, You break the chains, You, my Etern King, have delivered this child from the powers of darkness and from the power of sirens. Jesu we ask for a sign. Let her grow! She is six years old now; we want to see how she will ha grown a month from now. Let her regain her health, let her grow normally.

God has told me: shave her hair; buy some new clothes; and throw the old ones away.

Children and the Geographies of Inclusion and Exclusion

As noted in the Introduction to this book (De Boeck and Honwana) the standa European and Northern American interpretations of children and youngsters usual view them as dependent, not fully grown and not yet ready to act in a responsible way. The social space to which children are relegated is that of the family and the school. This conceptualization is so pervasive that children who do not correspond to these definitions are immediately perceived as potential victims in need of help. Within the sub-Saharan African context, on the other hand, few children are familiar with the luxury of the protection afforded by parents, school and government in the West (Thomas, 2000). In the urban African context the local sociocultural construction of children is certainly radically different from the 'cultural politics of childhood' (Scheper-Hughes and Sargent, 1998) that applies in the realities of the West. Viewed from such a Western perspective, it is indeed not difficult to document how children are often reduced to victims requiring help because of the political, economic, sociocultural, psychological and sexual violence that pervades the African continent today (see Bruyère, 2001; Goodwin-Gill and Cohn, 1994; El-Kenz, 1996; Henderson, 1999; Kilbride et al., 2000; Marquez, 1999; Mickelson, 2000; Panter-Brick and Smith, 2000; Said and Last, 1991). Some even speak of a generalized African 'youth crisis' (Van Zyl Slabbert et al., 1994; see also Cohen, 1999; Richards, 1995).

To deny the realities that correspond to this general victimizing discourse with regard to children would be very shortsighted. Yet children, especially in the often extreme living conditions in which they grow up in Africa, are not only vulnerable and passive victims, *subjected* to, or 'made and broken' by, the socio-economic and political processes of the African reality, but also active *subjects*, 'makers and breakers' of that reality. Children in these worlds often have the capacity to act strongly on the world in which they live, both in positive as well as negative ways. In line with more local notions of agency, children and youngsters in such African contexts are often not regarded, nor do they regard themselves, as future or proto adults, but as social actors in the present, with a marked role and presence in the very heart of the societal context. As such, children and youngsters appear as janus-like figures and thereby embody a 'frontier' dynamics of mutation which has become one of the most essential qualities of the Central African postcolonial space (see De Boeck, 2000).

On the one hand, then, children in Kinshasa are increasingly relegated to sites of exclusion (chased on to the street, expelled from the kin group, secluded in the churches). On the other hand, however, children have never before been so prominently present in the urban public space. Firstly, there is the very real and violent power 'from the barrel of the gun' which child-soldiers (*kadogo*) have come to represent. In 1997, when these child-soldiers (some of whom were no more than ten years old) made their entry into Kinshasa as Kabila seized power, this was a totally new and quite shocking fact for most of the capital's inhabitants.

Economically as well, young adolescents occupy a more central position than ever. Throughout the 1990s, large numbers of Kinshasa's youth became 'children of Lunda' (*bana Lunda*) and trekked *en masse* to the Angolan province of Lunda Norte to gain access to dollars and diamonds. Upon their return these youngsters had often acquired a financial power that far exceeded that of their parents, and that allowed them to access versions of a 'modern' lifestyle from which their own elders were excluded. In Kinshasa today, it is said that the one who possesses *lard*,[6] money, is a *patron* or a *mwana ya kilo*, 'a child with weight,' regardless of his or her age. Thus, together with these youngsters' financial independence (and responsibility) came social power. This newly found power

---

[6] *Lard* derives from dol*lar*, which is commonly spelled as *dollard* in Congo, but it also makes reference to the French word for 'fat', as in *faire du lard*, 'to become fat'.

demonstrated itself most tangibly in the context of family and kin, and inevitably al
gave rise to intergenerational, diamond-related, witchcraft accusations triggered by di
putes over the redistribution of the newly accessed wealth. In relation to this diamor
witchcraft, rumours abound about 'witch children of Lunda' (*mukishi mwana Lunda*) wl
have sex with their mothers or kill and 'eat' their fathers and uncles in return for di
monds and dollars (see De Boeck, 1999a/b). In these contexts, the empowering witcl
craft idiom of eating, formerly the prerogative of elders, fully illustrates the nocturn
possibilities of immediate access to the fruits of modernity. As one twelve-year-old b(
explained to me in response to the question as to 'why he professed to like eating hum:
meat':

> In the human body, everything is useful. The blood is fuel, diesel, kerosene and red wine; t!
> water that may be found in the body is motor oil, brake oil, perfume, drinking water, medi(
> syrup, and other medicine like pomades to rub your body with. The backbone is a radio, a sat(
> lite telephone, a radio transmitter; the head is a cooking pot, the glass from which the patro
> drink, a swimming pool, a bucket which you can use to wash yourself in; the eyes are a mirr(
> a television, a telescope; the hair can be used to make a mattress from, or a sofa for the livin
> room. The skin serves many purposes: It can be used to make a patron's blanket, or to cover I
> couch; it may also be used to provide the carpet upon which the patron will sit. The bod
> slime is like Vicks pomade, or like shoe polish. Sperm is like the grease that one uses to mai
> tain motor and car parts. It can also be used to cure someone who is suffering from impoten(
> or who has broken his back. Other body liquids also have their use. They can be used in t!
> radiator of a car or an airplane.

Here the nocturnal consumption of one's elders gives direct access to, and is quite lite
ally an incorporation and ingestion of, modernity's spaces of consumption. In this sens
the space of the street and the time of the night form the time-space for the creation
multiple alternative or parallel modernities. One street etymology of the word *shege*
that it refers to Schengen, the town in Luxembourg where European Union Memb
States signed a treaty to abolish the internal frontiers and create a free and op(
European zone which can be accessed in its totality by means of a single visa. F(
Kinshasa's *bashege*, for whom travelling to Europe is not an option, the street is view(
as an alternative Schengen territory; it is the space where food, freedom, sex, drugs a)
money can be freely accessed. To them the world of the *cité*, which is referred to as *Bel(*
(derived from *Belgique*, Belgium, the name of one of Kinshasa's neighbourhoods duri)
colonial times), is a world of constraints, a backward world which belongs to the pa'
Significantly, the colonial modernist housing style was also referred to as *Belesi* becau
living in these durable brick houses with their corrugated iron roofs was perceived,)
doubt with some irony as well, as accessing the colonialist modernity as it was thoug
to exist in the metropole. In contrast to this, Kinshasa's street children now consider t!
street to be modern and exciting. The street and the night form the spatial and temp(
ral zones in which the young generate themselves in self-invented processes and narr
tives of globalization. Simultaneously, their material horizon, the singularity of th(
space, and the social geography of their lives, often extend only to the corner of the stre
or the borderline between one neighbourhood and the next.

Thirdly, in popular urban public culture as well, children and young adolescents ha'
again, often literally, started to appear before the footlights. In the lyrics of recent son
of the Congolese superstar Papa Wemba, the same street children (*shege*) who are sti,
matized as witches have been given a prominent place, while they are frequently invit(

onto the stage, in what is a bit of a public provocation, to sing along with Papa Wemba and his orchestra Viva La Musica.[7] The same Papa Wemba, in a 1999 record entitled *Fula Ngenge* launched the phenomenon of the *bafioti-fioti* (kiKongo) or *bakamoke* (Lingala), literally 'the little little ones', which celebrates little girls 'who love to dance' (*bafioti-fioti balingi babina*). On stage, twelve-year-old girls have indeed replaced female dancers in their late teens and twenties to entrance the audiences of Kinshasa's major orchestras with their dances and sexual radiation. By 2002 the *bafioti-fioti*, who by then were a couple of years older, were gradually replaced by the *nionio* (from Swahili 'small breasts' but in current Lingala slang also 'little grains of diamond'). In the process, the sexual attractions and dangers of little girls, the female counter-parts of the male child-soldiers, have developed into a widespread urban mythology in which the figure of the *kamoke sukali*, 'the little sugared one', appears as the ultimate *femme fatale* and man-eater. In weekly issues of locally produced comic strip serials, which are in many respects the printed equivalent of *radio trottoir*, the narrative figure of the *kamoke sukali* has become a central character.[8] As is attested by Esther's and other similar cases, the *kamoke sukali* is often related to the *mami wata* siren, a relationship that most fully embodies and realizes the linkages that exist between sexuality, gender, age, death, access to modernity's materiality, and the 'second world'.

Similarly, children have become central actors in the media. Not only do private, often religious, TV stations in Kinshasa stage regular shows during which individual children are produced and publicly denounced, but the new constellation of meaning that is being shaped around children and witchcraft is also modelled by more global media. Influential in this respect are the soap operas produced in Nigeria and Ghana, videos and audio adaptations of which circulate in Kinshasa. These films often contain narratives constructed around the adventures of 'spirit-children'.[9] They are frequently broadcast on popular religious TV and radio stations such as the RTMV (*Radio et Télévision Message de Vie*), which is owned by one of Kinshasa's most successful preachers, Fernando Kutino, founder of a church named the Army of Victory (*Armée de Victoire*).[10]

Nowhere, however, are children more centrally present on the public scene than in the space of the churches, and more precisely during the crucial moment of public confession and witnessing. As appears from the excerpts of the cases which I presented above, it is at moments like these that children are in a position to demonstrate the real power they possess, for in their testimony they in turn may implicate the adults who allegedly initiated them into the world of witchcraft: a market woman such as Losiya, who offered food to the child in order to link her to the nocturnal forces of evil; a father,

---

[7] See Viva La Musica and Papa Wemba on their 1995 hit record entitled *Pole Position*, in which the *atalaku* or shouting DJ of the band stirs up the audience with the slogan 'Shege chance eloko pamba' (street child, fortune, happiness is a small thing, that is, it is also within your reach).

[8] The best known in this genre are the comic strips of 'the enigmatic philosopher of the realm of the informal' ('l'enigmatique philosophe de l'informel'), Papa Mfumu 'Eto 1. His weekly issues of comic strips, extremely popular though of poor technical quality, are sold at crossroads and bus stops throughout Kinshasa. On urban gossip surrounding the sexual escapades of young girls (the so-called 'séries 8', those born in the 1980s), see also Nlandu-Tsasa (1997: 97ff).

[9] Compare with Ben Okri's acclaimed *The Famished Road* in which the leading protagonist, Azaro, is such a spirit-child.

[10] Other popular *pasteurs*, religious leaders and churches in Kinshasa today include 'Archbishop' Soni Kafuta 'Rockman' (of the *Armée de l'Eternel*, the Eternal Army), Soni Mukwenze (of *La Restoration*, Restoration), Mutombo (of *Ministère Amen*), Mama Olangi (of the church CFMCI), Tata Onda (of *Le Dieu des Africains*, 'The God of the Africans'), Pastor Kiziamina, Dieu Mukuna, and the church 'Hidden Manna' (*Manne Cachée*). On the appropriation of media technologies by charismatic and Pentecostal churches in Ghana and Nigeria, see also Hackett (1998).

mother or relative who offered a glass of water to the little friends of their son or daughter, but expected a nocturnal counter-gift of human meat in return. In many cases these public accusations have severe consequences for the adults whose names are mentioned in this way in the children's testimonies. Not infrequently they set in motion a violent reaction on the part of relatives or neighbours, and lead to the beating up, lynching or burning of the accused adults.[11] In this way children may also use their narratives and their status of 'witch' to settle certain scores with adult relatives or neighbours, or more generally, to remove themselves from parental or family control and thereby create their 'freedom'. As Barry (1998-9: 143) points out in an interesting article on street children in Ouagadougou, a prominent but scarcely debated motive for children to take to the streets is often also a longing for freedom. Paradoxically, the public space of the street is to some extent experienced as a space of quality time, of dream time (children use the word *rêvesser* to express the oneiric qualities of their nocturnal lifestyle: passing time in a nice way, dropping your defences and letting yourself go in your 'hidden life'). The public space of the street is thus experienced, at least to some extent, as a space that offers greater intimacy than the family household. It is not that many of these children have no family, home or relatives to turn to, or that they are no longer taken care of, but rather that they have made the decision wilfully to 'uninsert' themselves from their family context and from the responsibilities, expectations and futures that lie embedded within a normal family life. In Kinshasa, becoming a witch is certainly a way to attain such independence, to challenge parents, public authority and the established order, and to inscribe oneself into a specific temporality: the timeframe of the moment.[12]

Transformations in Kinship Models and Principles of Seniority? Adolescent Strategies of Self-realization

All of the above only becomes possible in a context of communal turmoil and complex societal shifts and changes. These are partly realized in and through the fundamental crisis *and* restructuring of common models of kinship. If, as Geschiere (1997) has stated witchcraft is the shadow side of kinship, then the generational shifts within the idiom of witchcraft, as well as the partial disconnection of witchcraft and kinship which occur especially in the urban context (and here the marketplace, for example, becomes a dangerously contaminating place where strangers such as Losiya skilfully intrude into one's life),[13] are indicative of profound transformations in the field of kinship and the ways in which it was structured until recently.

[11] Although it falls outside the scope of this essay, this issue also raises all kinds of legal and judicial problems. Often the adult thus accused turns to a justice of the peace, who can only state his incompetence in witchcraft-related matters. Contrary to some other African countries such as Cameroon (see Fisiy & Geschiere 1990), witchcraft is not included in the Congolese penal law. Judges are therefore forced to step out of the legal role to adopt a more informal mediating position in the conflict in question. In doing so, they adopt a role that comes much closer to that of the authoritative elder in the more familiar process of palaver and kin-based conflict negotiation.

[12] On the notion of freedom throughout childhood and adult life in a West African setting, see also Riesman's persuasive Fulani ethnography (Riesman, 1977). On temporality and marginality see Day et al. (1999).

[13] The dollarization of local economies in the rural diamond trade has produced very much the same change. Luunda villagers, for example, complain that 'the witchcraft of the elders' has been replaced by *ulaj chisakasak*, 'chaotic witchcraft', which can come from all directions, and no longer exclusively from your immediate kin-group.

Just as the unfolding urban dynamics in the West have contributed to the creation of a world of simultaneity in which the existence of time and chronicity is denied, so the ceaseless spread of modernity has led to frantic changes and ruptures in the collective memory work of the Congolese. These transformations are also reflected in a collectively shared sense of loss and irreversible change, which has become manifest, for example, in the crumbling of the patriarchal gerontocratic order that has always been so typical of the 'enduring time' of tradition and ancestrality. It is to this timeframe that the logic of kinship has always referred and through which it has realized and externalized itself. The transformations in this field, however, perhaps explain what Lambek calls 'the sometimes violent rejection of ancestral and parental figures in response to what is understood as their absence, their impotence, or their withdrawal of protection'(Lambek, 2000: 12).

At the micro level of the household, the family and the lineage, the pressures caused by the changing demands on the social environment in the urban context are most tangibly present in newly emerging relations of authority and respect between the sexes as well as between generations. These new shapes and attitudes are most clearly illustrated in the current transformation of divisions of labour. Whereas some youngsters have gained financial power and social status by means of revenues from the diamond trade, most family heads in Kinshasa are socially and economically reduced to the status of unemployed and inactive men today.[14] Also, many men are often absent from home. As elsewhere throughout Africa, Kinois men are caught up in processes of migratory labour and travel, such as in the diamond traffic or because of the war, or they have set up other households in different areas of the vast city that is Kinshasa.

As is well known, the *tontines, mozikis* and *likelembas*, the neighbourhood units of co-operation, the church support groups, and the small-scale production of goods for sale on the market, all of these social networks and daily strategies of survival are basically the work of women and mothers. To say that this goes hand in hand with an erosion of male authority is stating the obvious, but it is a factor that may help to explain why witch-children seem to accuse women and maternal figures more frequently than male elders. Where the socio-economic shifts are mediated by gender, the discourse of witchcraft seems to graft itself upon new, female, figures of authority in which old notions of power now concentrate themselves, rather than upon the male elder, who always embodied the ultimate personification of the witch. And when this occurs in a socio-cultural landscape of kin-based relations under strain, such shifts form an ideal ground for all kinds of further tensions and witchcraft accusations amongst adults, or between the adults and the children under their care.

For example, the realities of urban polygamy have called into existence a category of co-wives known as 'rivals' (*mbanda*). Unlike rural polygamous households, these co-wives usually do not live together in the same house or even in the same *quartier*, and frequently they do not even know of each other's existence. In many cases the relationships between these women are very tense. When a 'rival' dies or when she is absent for a long period because she left in search of a better life in the Diaspora or in the Angolan diamond trade, like Esther's mother, her children regularly end up in the recalcitrant care

---

[14] In Kinshasa only a tiny fraction of the active adult male population is employed in the formal sector and has a salaried job. Men do not easily find a niche in the 'informal' economy either, for this space seems to offer an advantage to youngsters, who are often more street-wise and therefore better equipped in terms of social skills to adapt to the flexibility that characterizes such an economic environment. Just as children rule in the second world of witchcraft, and just as this shadow world has taken over the first world, youngsters control the country's second economy which has become, in fact, the 'real economy' (MacGaffey, 1991).

of one of her husband's co-wives.[15] In Kinshasa, it is stated that 'to take care of the child of one's rival, is to take care of a dangerous monster' (*kobokola mwana ya mbanda obokoli elima*). Especially when these children's father dies as well, they often find themselves in a highly vulnerable and unprotected position. Such children end up very much marginalized in a family context in which they are merely viewed as a burden and an extra mouth to feed at a time when food is already too scarce to feed everyone. In many households in Kinshasa today people eat only once every two days: one day a meal is prepared for the children, and the next day for the adults. In such a context, children who occupy a structurally weak position in their kin group, or sometimes even end up with no family at all, are more likely to be singled out as witches.[16]

The same socio-economic changes have also contributed to a growing intergenerational rift. Certainly in a rural context children and youngsters are often no longer willing to lead the same life as their parents, to build a small house with a grass roof, and to till the fields. Despite its miserable conditions, the city often continues to be viewed by rural youngsters as a space of independence and freedom offering an escape from the social control (also in terms of witchcraft) exerted by the village elders. In Kinshasa and other urban settings in Congo, youngsters frequently create spaces of independence for themselves. They join, for example, a prayer group or a 'stable' (*écurie*), i.e. a small collaborative economic unit of (often male) age-mates who frequently, although not necessarily, share the same regional or ethnic background, and usually live in the same neighbourhood. Whereas the organization of a stable is often, in a gang-like fashion, characterized by a strict hierarchy between older and younger (*grands* and *petits*), or 'fathers' and 'sons' amongst its members, the prayer groups, which typically include both boys and girls, are much more structured around invented horizontal kinship ties within one generation rather than around vertical (intergenerational) relations. Thus, in these rapidly proliferating urban prayer groups, sometimes split-offs from or sub-groups of more established adult churches, all members call each other 'Brothers and Sisters in Christ'. Often such groups consist exclusively of children and youngsters. They usually meet several times a week, often during nocturnal prayer events that start at sunset and end early the next morning. They provide the ideal site for children and youngsters to remove themselves from parental control and other relations of seniority.

In spite of the crisis which structures of seniority are currently undergoing, age obviously remains an important marker to place and position individuals in the societal context, but with this difference: there seems to be an important shift from *absolute* age (via a periodization from child to adolescent, adult and elder, ritualized in different rites of passage that mark the transitions within the life-cycle) to *relative* age (in a social logic of *grand* and *petit*) in which normal hierarchies between 'absolute' age and gender categories become much vaguer. In this respect 40-year-old men can still be students, and thus belong to an 'adolescent' category, while 20-year-old *Bana Lunda* are *patrons* and act like elders.

It is important to underscore that the new, more relative, social hierarchies which emerge in the changing social world are still modelled on age, and that it continues to

---

[15] The term *mbanda* also applies to the relationship between the wives of two brothers. When one brother dies, the other brother will often be under the obligation to offer shelter and material support to the deceased's children and wife, who then becomes a 'rival' of his own wife.

[16] This applies even more strongly to children who already stand out in one way or another, because of their mental or physical handicap, for example, or their erratic or idiosyncratic behaviour. In this way, in one church I observed a witch-child who obviously suffered from Tourette's syndrome.

be the 'old' vocabulary of masculine gerontocracy that informs the transformed contexts and relations between the sexes and the generations. The principles of seniority and gerontocracy as such are not being dismantled, but have instead become the ground for a generational conflict, mediated by gender, in which the (urban) young claim for themselves the right to singularize and realize themselves as 'authoritative elders', and to use the syntax of gerontocracy before one's time, as it were. Thus the actual modes of adolescent self-realization in the contemporary urban context (the right to monopolize public space, the power to become the founder of a social network, the aspiration to become the pivotal point of mechanisms of redistribution within one's kin or peer group, that is, the power to position oneself, like an elder, as a good 'giver', with all the rights and duties this entails) do not really differ much from the old modalities of the established gerontocratic model. Girls and young women too will try to become more independent vis-à-vis the old hierarchical relations of authority that prevail in the context of lineage and household. Just like their male counterparts, they too will, in a certain way, replicate these structures, while reversing the gendered power relations between the generations. Young women such as Esther's mother, for example, who leave husband, family and children behind to search for material wealth in the context of the Angolan diamond trade, are called 'dogs which break the leash' (*bambwa bakata singa*): if successful, they gain independence thanks to their newly acquired financial power, but also because they have managed to become like successful hunters and older men. This, for example, becomes clear in the way in which, in the Angolan context, many of these women manage to monopolize and manipulate to their own advantage strategies of marriage and alliance, normally a prerogative of male elders (see De Boeck, 1999b).

In other words, what may be perceived as a crisis of long-standing models of gerontocracy and seniority is in reality a gender and generation conflict in which existing patterns of authority remain, in a sense, indelible, but are now being appropriated and accessed in new and flexible ways by different categories of social actors who were formerly excluded from these social sources and positions of power. The fact that this generational conflict does not unfold unproblematically is highlighted by the new discursive fields and practices of witchcraft which focus strongly on children, young people and women. The diabolization of children by adults may thus be understood as a dark allegory which tells us something about a deeply rooted anxiety that accompanies a broader societal transformation (which is itself linked to a generalized crisis of 'modernity', at least in the Central African postcolony). In this respect Africa does not differ from other places around the globe where the link between children and witchcraft (whether it is in terms of child abuse, child prostitution, Satanism and child sacrifice, paedophilia, organ trading or death squads hunting down street kids) expresses in similar ways a feeling of deep crisis (Comaroff, 1997; La Fontaine, 1997; Scheper-Hughes and Hoffman, 1998).

The Transformation of the Gift in the Urban World

The destructuring and transformations of existing patterns of kinship are accompanied by profound shifts in the structuring fields of gift, reciprocity and exchange, which have always underpinned social transactions, and especially with regard to marriage and alliance. However, in Congo today, many young men and their families find it impossible to observe and respect the gift obligations and transactions that make a marriage possible. As one vendor on Kinshasa's central market succinctly put it: *Tosalaka te, tobalaka te,*

'we don't work and we don't marry'. Therefore Kinshasa's youth has invented a n
kind of marriage, *yaka tovanda* ('come and let us live together'), that is, a *marriage racco*
or a 'short-cut' marriage in which youngsters *de facto* start living together, have a cl
and face both their families with a *fait accompli*, thereby shortcircuiting the gift-cycle
marriage and bridewealth transactions. Needless to say, this 'cheap marriage' or 'marri
without value' (*libala ya monyato*) in turn adds to the possible causes for conflict a
witchcraft accusations occurring in the urban family context.

The transformed nature of the circulation of women not only changes the whole p
tern of gift and reciprocity which underpins the total social field, and especially the re
tionships between agnates, uterines and allies, but also touches on the cultural status
the maternal figure. This may explain why women and mothers, more often than m
are implicated in the accusations which witch-children in turn direct against adu
Witch-children's stories exemplify a recurring pattern in which children beco
witches through a 'poisoned' gift offered by a man, as in Mamuya's account, but m
often still by a woman, a mother, grandmother, aunt, neighbour or market woman, a
Esther's case. In all of these stories something is being communicated about the statu
the gift and, more specifically, about the monetarization and commodification of
patterns in both kin- and non-kin-based relations.

As it is, there is nothing surprising in the linkage between witchcraft and gift, wh
are both ambivalent and dangerous 'total social facts' (see Latouche, 1998: 154
Bewitchment has always been defined in a context of inverted and perverted social re
tions, and witchcraft has always been transmitted by means of the gift (whether throu
food, sex or other interactions). The witch itself has always been a fundamental figure
exchange. Setting in motion a destructive internal mechanism of redistribution and 'e
ing', the witch, as a figure of crisis, has always defined negatively what extended so
reciprocity and 'eating together' or sharing mean positively. Therefore, the witch, as n
turnal shadow or double, had an non-alienated relationship with the diurnal subject,
as its reflection but as an integral part of this dual relationship, in which the gift op
ated as fulcrum. The gift positions itself at the heart of the oscillation which allows
nocturnal double to contribute to the institutionalization of its other half.

In older, rural discourses and practices related to witchcraft, ritual hindrance or wit
craft occurs only between relatives with whom one is most closely related in terms
consanguinity, commensality and other forms of sharing and reciprocity, corporeal in
macy or conjugality (see De Boeck, 1991). Whereas these practices thus ultima
strengthened kinship solidarity and acted as local forms of conflict prevention and re
lution, the newly emerging discursive formations surrounding witchcraft in the url
context contribute, on the contrary, to the weakening of kinship ties in quite drama
ways. In many of the new charismatic churches and prayer movements, the members
the extended family are almost invariably labelled as *bandoki*, witches. Although this
seems to tie in with the older notion of witchcraft as something coming from wit
one's own kin group, in reality it constitutes a major change in the ways in which
demarcating lines between kin and non-kin are drawn. Significantly, the church
attacks on extended family relations focus on the gift obligations which underpin th
larger kin-based solidarity networks. To underline their argument, the church lead
refer to the Bible passage in which it is stated that one should earn a living and work
the sweat of your brow', that is, through one's own effort. Those family members w
come to ask a relative for food, shelter, money and other forms of support, have alw
been fully entitled to do so in the open gift logic of kin-based solidarity and recipr

ity that is so characteristic of the social architecture throughout Central Africa. In these Central African worlds, also, the vocabulary of kinship has always been used in much more encompassing ways as a metaphor for opening up kin-based networks. By redefining strangers and outsiders as kin, for example, gift cycles were widened and new levels of trust summoned. In this way a political economy of gift exchange in the form of tributes between real, putative or fictive kin has always formed one of the most important organizational modes to create, enable, maintain and broaden the network of political relations. Tributary relations institutionalized the personal sphere and personalized the institutional level.

The new regimes of knowledge that are being installed in the urban context, and have started to penetrate the rural hinterland through the churches' expansion, introduce a radical break with these long-standing moralities of transmission and exchange. In these new religious arenas, the open social field of relations, which is constantly generated and renewed through the circulation and flow of gifts and transactions between its members, is increasingly becoming more closed. Basically, all those who fall outside the scope of the nuclear family are now being denied the right to insert themselves in such gift relations. What this means in practice is that they are not only being labelled as evil witches when they attempt to do so, but also that, as witches, they are redefined as non-kin.

Moreover, the new churches are contributing to a drastic redefinition of the gift itself. Referring themselves to Matthew 7:7, they have launched the phenomenon of *semence*, 'seed', under the motto: 'Give to God and he will give you back' (*pesa Nzambe, akopesa yo*). As such, all 'gifts' made to the church become short- or long-term investments: one sows in order to reap. As such, the gift has become a life insurance:

> Fieldnotes: Kinshasa, May 2001. In the 'Free Church of Africa' (Eglise Libre d'Afrique, ELDA, a church movement that broke away from the Kimbanguist Church) Mama Kalonji gives her testimony:
> My Brothers and Sisters, I died but I ressuscitated. When I died I went up to heaven. In Paradise [Lingala: Lola] I met the angels, but I did not see God. I can tell you this, however: All the gifts that we give in the church, I saw how these gifts are put to good use by God. God uses these gifts to build houses for us in Paradise. Those who do not contribute to God's work, and who refuse to give in the church, will find themselves in an unfinished house when they arrive in Heaven. Therefore, I beg you, give freely. To give is to prepare your house in Lola. In reality, the money, the Mercedes cars, the television sets that we give to the pastor are stored for us by God. I, Kalonji, who am speaking to you, I am still a young woman. When I will be old, God will listen to my prayers, and he will render manifold what I gave to him because I 'sowed' on time. To give is like sowing the seed. By giving to the pastor I will be able to harvest later. Giving is keeping.

The phenomenon of *semence* (in many respects, a religious counterpart of the money pyramids and games of chance, the 'Bindomanie', that became popular for a short while in Kinshasa in the early 1990s) has taken over daily reality in Kinshasa. Most 'miracle churches' draw ever larger crowds, while the gifts, the seeds that are sown by the 'believers' (*bandimi*), only continue to grow in importance. People 'sow' watches, jewelry, diamonds, money, cars and houses to obtain a miracle, a job, a marriage (*mpo bazwa mabala*), healing (*mpo babika*), children (*mpo babota*), prosperity (*mpo commerce e prosperer*). In the midst of all this, the 'free' and spontaneous character of the gift (even though a gift is always embedded in a structure of obligation) is being redefined as a calculated act. 'Giving', to quote Kalonji's words, 'has become keeping.'

In summary, Kinshasa thus witnesses a total breach with older concepts regarding both

the morality of gift exchange and the delineation of the relationships between kin
non-kin, inside and outside, endogamous and exogamous. First, witchcraft is no lon
something from within. Not only has the circle of kinship become much sma
through the restricting redefinition of lineage and clan relations imposed by
churches, but the outside world is also increasingly, and often in very brutal ways, pe
trating the intimate circle of the nuclear family. Contrary to older forms of witchc
the witchcraft 'new style' is wild, random and unpredictable, without clear direction
intention. This has also greatly affected local concepts of pathogenesis and has ope
up the older etiological and diagnostic grid. Because the possible sources of witch
are often disconnected from kinship relations, the danger may now come from a
where. One becomes bewitched in public places like markets and shops, and thro
relations with unrelated or anonymous people.

Secondly, what poses as gift in the social interaction is no longer what it appears to
Underneath the visible gift lurks another invisible pattern which corrupts regular patte
of exchange. Crucial with regard to the new patterns of witchcraft is the emergence
the notion that one can be tied by a gift which poses as such, but which in reality cre
a debt obligation. More important, the receiver of the gift does not even realize that
is actually contracting a debt and engaging in a relationship of a totally different natt
that of a nocturnal capitalism, with all that this entails – debts, unstable prices, inte
rates, and the laws of supply and demand. The gift of the witch who gives bread, biscu
fish or fruit to children pretends to be a free gift in the initial establishment of the r
tionship. But rather than being free, it turns into something else. In the accounts of wit
children, the witches' nocturnal village is described as a world of 'give-g
(*donnant-donnant*), of 'give and they will give you, receive and give back' (*pesa bapesa
bapesi yo, yo mpe pesa*). As such, not only are the rules changed because the logic of
and counter-gift is applied *a posteriori*, and hence turns what was a free gift into an o
gation to return, but also there no longer exists a balance between gift and counter-g
a human life is expected in return for a biscuit. Furthermore, there is no longer a rea
or cause, not even a provocation, to justify such a bewitching demand. Above all, this lo
of unequal reciprocity is applied erroneously. For one thing, not only are the exchan
gifts and counter-gifts of unequal status, but so are the exchange partners themselves
normal circumstances, the receivers would not even be expected or supposed to g
back, if only because they are children and have not yet attained the required social
tus to position themselves as givers and engage in relationships of reciprocity.

The stories of the children who are being pulled into the second world by unkn
ingly accepting a 'poisoned' gift mirror the mechanisms of debt creation that they ex
rience in the first world reality and that often force them to stay in the street. A comm
practice among street children is *confisquer*. This practice creates what is called 'fict
debts' through which a child is 'forced into a debt' (*kokotisa na nyongo*) and cannot le
the street until the debt is repaid to the street group of which he or she is a memb
The gang will, for example, send one of its members to the market to sell some goo
If after a whole day, the child was unable to sell the commodities, the group will nev
theless consider these goods as sold and will consequently claim from the child a sum
money equivalent to the goods' estimated selling price. Thus, both the market and
second world mirror each other. They force one into situations of social and econo
debt and dependency through which one is tied or knotted into an intimate but uneq
relationship with the claimant.

A final factor which has contributed to the transformation of the gift in the ur locale is the status of the mother. Mamuya's and most other children's accounts of how they were pulled into the second world often implicate women. The growing commodification of gift- and kin-based relations in the urban (and increasingly also the rural) world, combined with the fact that women have started to gain more economic, political and religious power than ever before and increasingly appear as the social actors who manipulate the gift, especially in relation to (their own) children, illustrates that even the most basic building-block of kin relations, namely, the relationship between mother and child, is touched by the profound transformations the urban context is currently undergoing. The image of the mother as witch goes radically against the deeply engrained cultural model which views women, in their role of genetrix, mother, cultivator and cook, as the ultimate figures of physical and social reproduction, and thus as the generative forces behind the socio-cultural weave. As such, women are those who generate social ties and 'knot' the links between the generations. In the contemporary urban context, however, it is precisely this 'knotting ahead' of the life-flow which has become problematic. Rumours and stories that have started to circulate in Kinshasa on a frequent basis comment upon this by making mention of mothers who give birth to witch-children or, even more dehumanizing, electric eels.

The changing status of women and mothers is indicative of the cracks and flaws that have started to appear in the urban gift logic, and so are the conceptualization and the collective experience of children in terms of witchcraft. In alliance transactions, children represent, even more so than 'wives', the supreme gift, or the ultimate binding agents, in the endless cycles of reciprocity and redistribution that underpin the societal field. As Lallemand has pointed out in a recent echo of Mauss, it is especially the circulation and the unremitting movement of children between various kinship units which allow the formation of the social architecture of kinship, alliance and residence in what she calls 'traditional' societies (Lallemand, 1993). Lévi-Strauss's reinterpretation of Mauss' classic *Essai sur le don*, however, is responsible for the fact that the role of children has disappeared from the analysis of the gift-cycle and that the role of women as ultimate gift has been stressed so strongly instead.[17] And yet, when rereading Mauss's essay, one is reminded of the fact that the exchange of *oloa* and *tonga* in Polynesia is not only set in motion by the birth of a child, but that the child itself also becomes a gift, a *tonga*, and as such becomes an integrative part of the gift-cycle itself.[18] Children thus appear both as media and as actors in the creation and extension of kin relations and alliance: without children, no gifts; and without gifts, no kin and allies. Therefore childless marriages in Congo usually end in the wife's return to and reintegration in her own family, together with the restitution of all the goods that were transferred during the marriage transactions from the side of the wife-takers to that of the wife-givers.

---

[17] It should be noted, however, that, contrary to exchange-based models of kinship and social organization which have ignored the role of children, descent-based models, beloved of English Africanists, have done so far less. Thus, while they have not always focused on children as such, they devoted much attention to issues of transmission between generations, as in the analysis of rites of passage and the like.

[18] 'Ainsi, l'enfant, que la soeur, et par conséquent le beau-frère, oncle utérin, reçoivent pour l'élever de leur frère et beau-frère, est lui-même appelé un *tonga*, un bien utérin [...]. Or, il est le canal par lequel les biens de nature indigène [...], les *tonga*, continuent à couler de la famille de l'enfant vers cette famille. D'autre part, l'enfant est le moyen pour ses parents d'obtenir des biens de nature étrangère (*oloa*) des parents qui l'ont adopté, et cela tout le temps que l'enfant vit. [...] En somme, l'enfant, bien utérin, est le moyen par lequel les biens de la famille utérine s'échangent contre ceux de la famille masculine.' (Mauss, 1985 [1950]: 155-6).

9.1 *Mothers exorcising a child in the church of Beth Shalom, Masina neighbourhood, Kinshasa, September 1999. (©Filip De Boeck)*

Conclusion: the Breach Between the Imaginary and the Symbolic, Structure and Experience

Much of the previous analysis embeds itself in what might be seen as a classic approach to witchcraft as an expression of social relations and processes. In such an approach to the witchcraft idiom, the social and structural tensions produced by intergenerational and cross-gender relations are usually interpreted as being amongst the strongest determinants of witchcraft accusations. Approaches of this nature have been criticized for their reductionism and instrumentalism, as well as their incapacity to reveal the autochtonous understandings and internal structures of symbolization (see Niehaus, 1997). Whereas such an approach does not indeed focus in depth on the inner meanings and ontological status of witchcraft and divination in the experiential reality of the Congolese subject (see, however, De Boeck & Devisch, 1994), I believe it does shed a light on the shifts that currently occur in the idiom of witchcraft itself. Furthermore, it also links these shifts to more profound societal alterations which touch more precisely on issues of ontology, local structures of symbolization, and the subjective experience of these realities.

While the emergence of witch-children is symptomatic of an underlying 'crisis' of the gift, this crisis is itself emblematic of what Barry (1998-9: 156) designates as the 'weakening of the cultural tools of symbolization' (*défaillance des outils culturels de symbolisation*), and what I have called a more generalized breach between the levels of the imaginary and the symbolic. The gift is the ultimate mediator between these two levels.

The classic interpretations of the gift by Lévi-Strauss, or Lacan for that matter, postulate the supremacy of the symbolic in relation to the imaginary (see also Nicolas, 1986). In this respect the signified is, to some extent, subordinated to the signifier: symbols are imbued with a larger reality value than that which they symbolize, that is, the levels of the imaginary and of what Lacan calls 'the real' (that which is neither imaginary nor symbolic). For Godelier, in his recent reinterpretation of Mauss's gift theory (1996), the levels of the symbolic and the real are materializations of the imaginary, which (re)creates and institutionalizes society. Here the symbolic is not a mental structure but encompasses an internalized social structure, constructed by a social logic that is unconscious but that constantly externalizes itself, as social essence, in the domains of sexuality, power and politics. It is the concentration of the three orders of the imaginary, the symbolic and the *réel* which makes social reality, the social life of people, but it is the register of the imaginary that offers the fixed points from which a society invents itself.

To return to the Congolese context: the first world of social reality is only formed in relation to a second world, a mirror image which is rooted in a collective imaginary. That is what the conceptualization of the witch as moment of inversion, shadow, or double means. The traditional figure of the witch works as an imaginary double, as imago and mirror. As figure of crisis, the witch thereby enables the realization of its opposite. However, the qualities of reality in Congo are no longer those of Lacan's *réel* (hence the importance of 'appearance' in the Congolese context, I would add). I hope to have illustrated that the processes of undoubling and mirroring between first and second world no longer find a comfortable place in the current Congolese context. The qualities of the structuring of symbolization have changed. Thus the linkages among the orders of imaginary, symbolic and real, have disappeared or weakened, and can no longer be trusted or taken for granted. Above, I argued that the gift, as the most central binding agent between these three levels, is itself undergoing a drastic transformation, which in turn is indicative of a more fundamental crisis of the possibilities of representation, or the capturing of relations in language.

Cross-culturally children are one of the most powerful points of reference on which socio-cultural imaginaries at the crossroads of sexuality and power graft themselves. In relation to the context of Congolese postcolonialism, the local collective imaginary is no longer symbolized, and (re)presented in the social reality of everyday life. Nor does it seem to underpin, institutionalize or legitimate other levels. Through a severing of the ties that operate the mechanisms of junction and disjunction, and the process of doubling and undoubling, it has become ontological instead. The imaginary as such has swallowed and replaced social reality. This also has enormous consequences for the meaning and the production of violence in the Congolese *societas*. The dynamics of witchcraft have always opened spaces of violence, but this violence contributed to and enabled the turning of the drama of social disorder into its opposite. It established (social and symbolic) consensus or institutionalized the breach. In the current context, however, an imaginary of violence does seem to represent social violence or offer a solution to it to a far lesser extent than it used to before; instead it has itself become the unmediated reality.

I contend that it is this fundamental change in the interplay between imaginary and symbolic, which is externalized and has crystallized in the figure of the child as witch. The witch-child is the terminus of a long process of disconnection, in which the non-alienated character of the relation with the double has gradually evolved to an alienated one. Here the relation with the double has ceased to be one of exchange and negotiation, and has turned from familiar to *mystique*. The shadow has become satanic and deadly, as an image also of all the dead that have been rejected and forgotten but do not agree to become meaningless for the living. Having said this, however, one should be careful with analytical models that suggest the dawning of new eras that require new means of understanding basic social processes, or models that imply total loss or evacuation of meaning. The difference between experience and structure is important here. Despite the experiential frame of urban Congolese life, it is difficult to understand how one can have a world (or an imaginative process) without symbolization. No doubt the question also centres on the changing, and thus historical, character of such symbolization: its stability, its collective power, its relation to 'realism', its imagic form, its capacity to fix ontology. Viewed in a more diachronic perspective, today's terminus might really turn out to be tomorrow's starting point for a further round of flexible transformations within continuing long-term historical trajectories.

References

Augé, M. 1999, *The War of Dreams. Studies in Ethno-Fiction*. London: Pluto Press.
Barry, A. 1998-9. 'Marginalité et errance juvéniles en milieu urbain. La place de l'aide psychologique dans les dispositifs de prise en charge des enfants de la rue', *Psychopathologie africaine* XXIX (2): 139-90.
Bayart J.-F. 1996. *L'illusion identitaire*. Paris: Fayard.
Baudrillard, J. 1976. *L'échange symbolique et la mort*. Paris: Gallimard.
Becker, G. 1997. *Disrupted Lives. How People Create Meaning in a Chaotic World*, Berkeley, CA: University of California Press.
Bruyère, J.M. (ed.) 2001. *L'envers du jour. Mondes réels et imaginaires des enfants errants de Dakar*. Paris: Editions Léo Scheer.
Cohen, P. 1999. *Rethinking the Youth Question*. Durham, NC: Duke University Press.

Comaroff, J. 1997. 'Consuming Passions: Child Abuse, Fetishism and "The New World Order"', *Culture* 17.

Comaroff, J. & J. Comaroff, 1999. 'Occult Economies and the Violence of Abstraction: Notes from the South African Postcolony', *American Ethnologist* 26 (2): 279-303.

Corten, A. and R. Marshall-Fratani (eds). 2001. *Between Babel and Pentecost. Transnational Pentecostalism in Africa and Latin America.* Bloomington/Indianapolis: Indiana University Press.

Day, S., E. Papataxiarchis and M. Stewart (eds). 1999. *Lilies of the Field. Marginal People Who Live for the Moment.* Boulder, CO: Westview Press.

De Boeck, F. 1991. 'Therapeutic Efficacy and Consensus among the Aluund of Southwest Zaire', *Africa* (Journal of the International African Institute) 61 (2): 159-85.

— 1998. 'Beyond the Grave: History, Memory and Death in Postcolonial Congo/Zaïre,' in *Memory and the Postcolony. African Anthropology and the Critique of Power.* ed. R. Werbner. London: Zed Books.

— 1999a. 'Domesticating Diamonds and Dollars: Identity, Expenditure and Sharing in Southwestern Zaire (1984-1997)', in *Globalization and Identity. Dialectics of Flow and Closure.* ed. B. Meyer & P. Geschiere. Oxford: Blackwell.

— 1999b. 'Dogs Breaking their Leash: Globalization and Shifting Gender Categories in the Diamond Traffic between Angola and D.R. Congo (1984-1997)', in *Changements au féminin en Afrique noire. Anthropologie et littérature. Vol. 1.* ed. D. De Lame & C. Zabus. Tervuren/Paris: Musée Royal de l'Afrique Central/L'Harmattan.

— 2000. 'Borderland Breccia: The Mutant Hero and the Historical Imagination of a Central-African Diamond Frontier', *Journal of Colonialism and Colonial History* 1 (2): [electronic journal].

— 2001. 'Dancing the Apocalypse in Congo: Time, Death and Double in the Realm of the Apocalyptic Interlude,' in: *Millennarian Movements in Africa and the Diaspora.* ed. J.-L. Grootaerts, Brussels: Royal Academy of Overseas Sciences.

— 2002. 'Kinshasa: Tales of the "Invisible City" and the Second World,' in *Under Siege. Four African Cities: Freetown, Johannesburg, Kinshasa, Lagos.* ed. O. Enwezor et al. *Documenta 11. Platform 4.* Kassel: Hatje Cantz.

— 2004. 'On Being *Shege* in Kinshasa: Children, the Occult and the Street', in *Reinventing Order in Kinshasa. How the People Respond to State Failure in Kinshasa.* ed. T. Trefon. London: Zed Books.

De Boeck, F. & R. Devisch, 1994. 'Ndembu, Luunda and Yaka Divination Compared: From Representation and Social Engineering to Embodiment and Worldmaking', *Journal of Religion in Africa* 24 (2): 98-133.

Devisch, R. 2001. 'Sorcery Forces of Life and Death among the Yaka of Congo,' in *Witchcraft Dialogues. Anthropological and Philosophical Exchanges.* ed. G.C. Bond & D.M. Ciekawy. Athens, OH: Ohio University Press.

Douglas, M. 1999. 'Sorcery Accusations Unleashed: The Lele Revisited', *Africa* 69 (2): 177–93.

El-Kenz, A. 1996. 'Youth and Violence,' in *Africa Now. People, Policies and Institutions.* ed. S. Ellis. The Hague/London/Portsmouth, NH: DGIS/James Currey/Heinemann.

Fisiy, C. & P. Geschiere, 1990. 'Judges and Witches, or How is the State to Deal with Witchcraft? Examples from Southeastern Cameroon', *Cahiers d'études africaines* 118: 135-56.

Geschiere, P. 1980. 'Child-Witches against the Authority of their Elders: Anthropology and History in the Analysis of Witchcraft Beliefs of the Maka (Southeast Cameroon),' in *Man, Meaning and Society. Essays in Honour of H.G. Schulte Nordholt.* ed. R. Schefold, J.W. Schoorl & J. Tennekes. The Hague: Martinus Nijhoff.

— 1997. *The Modernity of Witchcraft: Politics and the Occult in Postcolonial Africa,* Charlottesville, VA and London: University Press of Virginia.

Godelier, M. 1996. *L'énigme du don,* Paris: Fayard.

Goodwin-Gill, G.S. and I. Cohn. 1994. *Child Soldiers: The Role of Children in Armed Conflict.* Oxford: Clarendon Press.

Hackett, R.I.J. 1998. 'Charismatic/Pentecostal Appropriation of Media Technologies in Nigeria and Ghana', *Journal of Religion in Africa* XXVIII (3): 258-77.

Henderson, P. 1999. 'Living with Fragility: Children in New Crossroads'. Unpublished doctoral dissertation, University of Cape Town.

Kilbride, Ph., C. Suda and E. Njeru, 2000. *Street Children in Kenya. Voices of Children in Search of a Childhood.* Westport, CT/London: Bergin and Garvey.

La Fontaine, J. 1997. *Speak of the Devil: Allegations of Satanic Child Abuse in Contemporary England,* Cambridge: Cambridge University Press.

Lallemand, S. 1993. *La circulation des enfants en société traditionnelle. Prêt, don, échange.* Paris: L'Harmattan.

Lambek, M. 2000. 'Nuriaty, the Saint and the Sultan. Virtuous Subject and Subjective Virtuoso of the Post-Modern Colony', *Anthropology Today* 16 (2): 7-12.

Latouche, S. 1998. *L'autre Afrique. Entre don et marché,* Paris: Albin Michel.

Laurent, P.-J. 2003. *Les Pentecôtistes du Burkina Faso. Mariage, pouvoir et guérison.* Paris: Karthala.

Lutz, C. & D. Nonini, 1999. 'The Economies of Violence and the Violence of Economies,' in *Anthropological Theory Today.* ed. H.L. Moore. London: Pluto Press.

MacGaffey, J. (ed.) 1991. *The Real Economy of Zaire. The Contribution of Smuggling and Other Unofficial Activities* to National Wealth, London/Philadelphia: James Currey/University of Pennsylvania Press.

Marquez, P.C. 1999. *The Street is My Home. Youth and Violence in Caracas*. Stanford, CA: Stanford University Pre

Mauss, M. 1985 [1950]. 'Essai sur le don. Forme et raison de l' échange dans les sociétés archa"ques,' in ▮ Mauss, *Sociologie et anthropologie*. Paris: Quadrige/Presses Universitaires de France.

Mbembe A. 1997, *On the Postcolony*. Berkeley, CA: University of California Press.

Meyer B. 1999, *Translating the Devil: Religion and Modernity among the Ewe in Ghana*, Edinburgh: Edinbur▮ University Press.

Mickelson, R. A. (ed.) 2000, *Children on the Streets of the Americas. Globalization, Homelessness and Education the United States, Brazil and Cuba*. London: Routledge.

Midelfort, E. 1972. *Witch-Hunting in Southwestern Germany 1562-1684*, Stanford, CA: Stanford University Pre

Moore, H.L. and T. Sanders (eds) 2001, *Magical Interpretations, Material Realities. Modernity, Witchcraft and the Oc▮ in Postcolonial Africa*. London: Routledge.

Nicolas, G. 1986. *Don, rituel et échange marchand*. Paris: Institut d'Ethnologie, Musée de l'Homme.

Niehaus, I. 1997. 'A Witch Has No Horn: The Subjective Reality of Witchcraft in the South African Lowve▮ in *Culture and the Commonplace. Anthropological Essays in Honour of David Hammond-Tooke*, ed. P. McAllist Johannesburg: Witwatersrand University Press.

Nlandu-Tsasa, C. 1997. *La rumeur au Za"re de Mobutu. Radio-trottoir à Kinshasa*, Paris: L'Harmattan.

Panter-Brick, C. and M.T. Smith (eds) 2000, *Abandoned Children*. Cambridge: Cambridge University Press.

Richards, P. 1995. 'Rebellion in Liberia and Sierra Leone: A Crisis of Youth?' in *Conflict in Africa*. ed. O. Furl London: Tauris AcademicPress.

Riesman, P. 1977. *Freedom in Fulani Social Life: An Introspective Ethnography*. Chicago and London: University Chicago Press.

Said, H.I. & M. Last 1991. 'Youth and Health in Kano Today,' *Kano Studies* Special Issue.

Scheper-Hughes, N. & C. Sargent (eds) 1998a. *Small Wars: The Cultural Politics of Childhood*, Berkeley, C University of California Press.

— & D. Hoffman, 1998. 'Brazilian Apartheid: Street Kids and the Struggle for Urban Space,' in *Small Wars: 1 Cultural Politics of Childhood*. ed. N. Scheper-Hughes & C. Sargent. Berkeley, CA: University of Califor▮ Press.

Thomas, N. 2000. *Children, Family and the State. Decision-Making and Child Participation*. Basingstoke/New Yo▮ Macmillan/St Martin's Press.

Tonda, Joseph. 2002. *La guérison divine en Afrique Centrale (Congo, Gabon)*. Paris: Karthala.

Van Dijk R. 2000, *Christian Fundamentalism in Sub-Saharan Africa: The Case of Pentecostalism*, Occasional Pap▮ Centre of African Studies, University of Copenhagen.

Van Zyl Slabbert, P. C. Malan, H. Marais, J. Olivier & R. Riordan, 1994. *Youth in the New South Africa*. Pretor Human Science Research Commission.

10

TSHIKALA K. BIAYA
Youth & Street Culture in Urban Africa
Addis Ababa, Dakar & Kinshasa

Marked by violence, Africa's developing street culture establishes the role of 'youth' as political actors. In adopting a cultural aesthetic in sharp rupture with postcolonial logics, young people mingle 'globalized' images, attitudes and physical practices that sketch new popular figures of insurrection. In a veritable epistemological break, this juvenile street culture – one that can differ radically from one city to another – at the same time gives expression to novel forms of sociability and evokes the permanence of institutional violence.

Towards a Street Culture in Africa?

In urban Africa, the emergence of the notion of street culture is inseparable from that of the young person as a social actor. Even more recent studies on popular culture,[1] however, have tended to overlook this social category, which is nonetheless its principal producer. The primary reason for this is undoubtedly the confusion that reigns with regard to the status of the child and the young person. The fruit of a scientific academic syndrome emerging at the start of the twentieth century, the study of youth focused essentially on juridical issues and the body of prophylactic and therapeutic practices pertaining to delinquency. In addition, this subject had long been approached in an indirect manner via studies on the modernization process in African cities, the crisis of the urban system and urban management (Bertrand, 1998; Le Bris 2000; Simone, 1998).

Mention of these epistemological shortcomings inevitably reminds us of the treatment reserved for the question of women and the family before the discovery of these genres. The dynamic of scientific exclusion can be found as well in the analyses of marginality, a field long restricted to themes of violence, delinquency (drugs, prostitution) and the makeshift economy (*débrouille*). As a consequence, much of the early research carried out on youth, street culture and urban violence was directly inspired by colonial orientations. The international institutions themselves appeared to be locked into a brittle con-

My thanks go to Professors Berhane Abébé, a specialist in Ethiopian culture, for his insights on the notion of *shifta*, and Jean Omasambo, for having drawn my attention to the violence of the *shege*. I also wish to express my gratitude to Filip De Boeck and Alcinda Honwana for their criticisms of my first manuscript, and to Pierre Janin for his editorial work. I am nevertheless solely responsible for the analyses and comments made here. This article is translated from *Politique africaine* 80, 2000.

[1] See, in particular, Jewsiewicki, 1987 and Barber, 1997.

ceptualization and categorization of the young citizen, adopting a minimalist vision of the culture and a bourgeois conception of childhood (in which the child is nothing more than a fragile being to be protected) and youth (the future class of consumers. Empirical research (most notably that carried out by the IFRA at Ibadan) was, of cours. at times able to break out of these approaches, yet without fully succeeding in concep tualizing the main categories. That is why one still today encounters the refusal to rec ognize the real cultural dimension of street life in Africa. Such an analysis mu nonetheless be attempted, while taking into account its unique social dynamics and hi toricity and giving adequate attention to the most promising groups of actors (youth an women).

For perhaps the last two decades African societies have been undergoing an unprece dented multisectoral crisis, one that they struggle to overcome. Young people (constitu ing 40 to 50 per cent of the urban population, depending on the country) – the 'livin forces' of states obliged to submit to the draconian measures of structural adjustment have been particularly affected by the crisis of unemployment. They have at the sam time been confronted by the decline in the colonial model of education, the end to th ideal of a foregone access to the class of urban petty bourgeoisie, the disappearance the providential state and the increasingly extreme precariousness of living condition Many of them, whether native or recent immigrants, have therefore sought to explo new means of affirming their identities, asserting popular demands and developing th makeshift economy. In the urban milieu, this economic crisis has had equally significar repercussions for traditional, familial, clan or ethnic solidarities that have also favoure the formation of new groups and associative movements.

At the same time, we can observe a lively increase in street culture, which invariabl comprises factors such as a uniformity in the means of survival, the mechanisms respor sible for producing street children (extreme poverty, parental divorce, individualism an moral crisis) and violence, both visible and invisible (Hérault and Adesanmi, 1997). Ofte latent, this violence emerges as soon as the institutions and social regulations are weal ened, and corruption spreads through them like gangrene. Street culture can thus be see to develop in a particular context in which the various forms of violence complemer each other (social violence incites the counter-violence of the state), yet never reve more than a small part of the dialectic of violence. Brutal urban violence is hardly th sole and univocal means of expression available to young people; games, postures an attitudes of consumption and leisure serve their need to affirm their historical presenc as a social group and actors in each of their respective postcolonial societies.

The construction of street culture thus inscribes itself in the transformative dynam of the postcolony and its contradictions. It evolves in the course of several historic stages according to a double logic of rupture with the colonial society: being born in th postcolony and living on the margins of urban life. Inspired by this double horizon, th youth appropriate existing forms of leisure while transforming them for their own end Once spatialized in this manner, leisure becomes a founder of street culture; it express the violence of a reclamation and fabricates its own legitimacy in the public space. Th social practice is gradually enriched with successive borrowings and exchange promote by migration, transnationalism and globalization, thus outmoding all the dichotomo and diachronic perceptions that are usually bandied about: the local and the global, th rural and the urban, tradition and modernity, autochthon and allochton, native and for eign. It contributes to the formation of new urban identities, identities that demonstra the a-colonial character of the generation that produces and appropriates them. These i turn confirm the capacity of assimilation, autonomy, individualization and social recomposition possessed by today's urban youth.

Without always necessarily breaking with global society, or being relegated to its margins, street culture nevertheless clearly demarcates itself by its own forms of logic. These are, in fact, active modes of violent reclamation (whether symbolic, linguistic, restrained or effective violence) in opposition to any hegemonic project the state may put forward.

The present essay adopts a resolutely comparativist approach to the phenomenon in order the better to account for the vitality and the conditions for the emergence of these modes of popular expression among the urban young. It describes the processes of identity invention and the cultural aesthetic of leisure of the youth of Addis Ababa, Dakar and Kinshasa, and puts forward a socio-political analysis of these practices. It concludes with a rereading of the logics of rupture enjoined by the youth in the postcolony.

Popular Figures of Urban Culture

The postcolony, its episteme and its violence together constitute the model structuring life in contemporary Africa (Bayart et al., 1992). If the end of the Cold War allowed for a democratic renewal in Europe, in Africa many countries have apparently turned, during the past decade, in the direction of an economy of civil war (Ethiopia, the Congos, Sierra Leone, Liberia and Sudan). All things considered, these different warring episodes have been revealed as one of the principal means of 'corporealizing' youth, in which the last generation takes over from the rigid stratification of the single party, employment policies and civil service, the (de)structuring effects of which have had a significant impact on the living, consumption and speaking modes of the young urban population (Biaya, 2000; ILO, 1987). Each society has thus been able to develop its own typical figures of the young postcolonial citizen: the *shifta*, the *bul faale* and the *shege*.

The shifta *of Addis Ababa*
One of the most remarkable figures of Addis Ababa's urban youth is the *shifta*. It is organized around the chewing of tchat, the ceremonial consumption of coffee and a complex of pagan gestures linking private space to public space. This sociability of leisure has its equivalents in other countries, such as the preparation of tea (*ataya*) in Dakar or the consumption of beer (*kobenda kopo*) in Kinshasa. The *alter ego* of the Somali *mooryaan* (Marchal, 1993), the *shifta* may be considered a bandit, highwayman, plunderer and outlaw who finds in war an opportunity to win fame and glory (see Anon, 2000 and note 2).

Along with tea, tchat and coffee are stimulating plants that for centuries have been consumed in Ethiopia and even now constitute its major export products (Anon., 2000). Apart from its medicinal uses, tchat is principally chewed for its euphoric and excitant effects. In Addis Ababa, social consumption of tchat (*barkh'a*) – marginalized and even prohibited under the imperial regime as well as the socialist government – has since 1993 increased rapidly with the demobilization and return of young soldiers and militiamen. Formerly destined for export to Arabia, the consumption of coffee was similarly forbidden by the Orthodox Church which, at the beginning of the last century, went as far as excommunicating those who contravened the injunction. The coffee ceremony (*bunna mazagadjet*), appearing around 1930, is still considered a feminine practice full of sexual connotations; it is quite distinct from the commonplace drinking of coffee by the upper classes. A veritable ritual, the coffee ceremony has recently integrated the chewing of tchat so prized by the *shifta*.[2] This new social custom – constituting one of the most important night-time leisure activities of the young people – has reincorporated the fundamental elements of the *zar* ceremony, whose founder, Abba Tchanguaré, was himself a *shifta* (Rosset, 1997). The ceremony, in fact, begins with a short prayer addressed to the tchat, recalling the warrior and pagan identity of the *shifta* who for centuries contested and menaced the imperial Christian order.

In certain of its aspects, the familial ceremony of coffee and tchat serves to express the social dissent of the young. It often takes place in an atmosphere of domestic conviviality at the back of a bar and within a mixed group of boys and girls. The conversation is not boisterous, yet is very animated. Gradually, as the available tchat and coffee are used up, the young people, now in a second state close to trance, begin to invade certain public spaces (notably bars and nightclubs). While continuing to imbibe alcoholic drinks, they begin to dance frenetically in imitation of warring *shifta* on parade. One by one these gymnastic competitions depict the various ethnic groups from around the country now reconciled in the expression of a sort of postcolonial nationalism. This mood is encouraged by the hallucinogenic power of tchat. At the same instant, the dancer seems to communicate with the historic figure of the *shifta*, one that had become widespread in the troubled period of Ethiopian history prior to the coronation of the emperor and the restoration of the Empire (Zewde, 1996).

Today, this figure has a strong influence on the young person as an emerging citizen. Moreover, it affords young people the opportunity to root themselves in their own history, for the whole of the history of Ethiopia and Addis Ababa is written into the Amharic language through the semantics of the *shifta*. The *shifta* is the patriot who twice liberated the homeland from the Italian invader in the course of the nineteenth and twentieth centuries.[3] He is later reborn in the militiaman of the Mengistu era who sowed the red terror in Addis Ababa and fights in the struggles against Eritrea, Somalia and Sudan. The figure then extends after Mengistu to the young soldier who marches against Eritrea (1998-2000). Nonetheless, its present urban dimension fundamentally expresses the rejection of the post-imperial regimes that have regimented and militarized the youth in a long period of uninterrupted warfare (1974-2000).

My anthropological and historical reading of the phenomenon might be complemented with a psycho-sociological analysis. Would not the unbridled gestures of the young people,[4] founded on overlapping imaginaries and comprising leaps and howls, in fact express a symbolic struggle against the legal violence of the state? Do they not equally illustrate the pernicious effects of the overconsumption of tchat on the functioning of the society at large? Such scenes, more or less playful, certainly allow the dancers to reconcile harmoniously the body and the social imaginary, and to exorcize the enveloping social disorder. But if, in giving a corporeality to the culture of violence, the young people seek to denounce the quasi-permanent political censure, they are still not in any real position to liberate themselves: each young person always belongs to a

---

[2] The figure of the ancient *shifta*, a rebel warrior avid for power, such as Kessa Tewo, has evolved rapidly in the context of Addis Ababa. Today the *shifta* is more an individual in revolt; having committed some crime or carried out some act of protest against the social or political system, he takes refuge in the 'bush'.

[3] Apart from of a very short period of Italian occupation (1936-41), Ethiopia has never known real colonization and has struggled to preserve its millennia-long independence. On this, see Berhanou, 1998 and Zewde 1996. This heroic page in its history has transformed the *shifta*, warrior and robber, into an *arbagna*, a contemporary patriot.

[4] These dances are distinct from those executed by the same youth when they frequent nightclubs or other dance venues in the 'downtown' area where there is a perception of being policed.

marginalized social group that struggles to construct its own destiny. By remaining in the country, they sketch and integrate the national map of structural violence linked both to poverty and to the figure of the *shifta*. And it is only in the course of a real trip, not an imaginary one, to the outside world (most often to Italy or the United States) that they may be able to extract themselves from what would appear to be a 'carceral figure.'

The bul faale *of Dakar*

The syntagmatic expression *bul faale* – meaning 'never mind,' 'be indifferent' – first appeared in the region of Fass, in Senegal, before penetrating the densely populated quarters of Dakar, Pikine, where it was politicized and radicalized. This transformation came about on the occasion of a traditional wrestling contest (Senegal's national sport) in which Moustapha Guèye, a Sereer from Pikine nicknamed Tyson, triumphed over Moustapha Guèye, known as Tapha the Tiger, from Fass. In 1997 the expression *bul faale* still simply denoted an attitude among the young people affected by a serious economic crisis. *Ataya*, the tea ceremony, is one of the most emblematic manifestations of this attitude. The youth of Pikine rapidly gave it a more political signification, however, at once filling out its lexico-semantic content and engaging in a confrontation with the dominant classes. As a social movement, the *bul faale* rejects the political and religious traditions that the elites have imposed since independence on the youth of Dakar, in the process taking revenge for the ambiguous *set setal* movement that made its appearance in 1989.

Originally the *set setal* was a spontaneous movement whose aim was to beautify the city of Dakar, but it was quickly taken over by political interests. The practice of mural painting and the song that bears the same name marked an artistic renaissance among the unemployed young people who thereby rewrote their own urban history (Diouf, 1992). Thus, up until the appearance of the *Birima* song in 1996, the close alliance between the socialist party in power and the youth remained intact. Now this song, an extension of the youth movement, took exception to the Islamicized Senegalese culture and instead promoted a certain pre-Islamic and pagan hedonistic culture (*ceddo*). The lecherous character Birima was quickly equated with the political Senegalese bourgeoisie that had neglected public affairs, oppressed the people and enriched itself at the expense of the state. Yet it was not until the wrestler Tyson's victory that the *bul faale* movement reached maturity in a complex fusion of the physical expression afforded by *set setal* and the rhetoric of wrestling *à la Birima*. In turn, this semantic and philosophic mutation later took shape in the spread of interest in the martial arts that, in the period from 1997 to 1999, soon became the new national sport and the prime catalyst in many of the recent socio-political disturbances in Senegal.

The recent contest between Tyson and Tapha is, in fact, a perfect illustration of the nature of the tensions and power relations that permeate the social space of Dakar. Thus, in the popular imaginary, the expression 'Sérère stable' recalls the massive exodus of the rural Sereer since independence and symbolizes their recent and imperfect assimilation to the urban population of Dakar. Organized in clubs or 'stables', the champions would appear to be under the direct influence of the religious or political elites that support them. The permanent opposition between the generations, also thoroughly politicized, reinforces this phenomenon. The match facing off Manga II and Tyson – opposing two different generations and primed with CFAF 30 million in prize money – thus anticipated the mobilization of young voters in the presidential elections held in 2000. Prior to the contest it was widely believed that Tyson would lose, and his defeat was seen to prefigure the deathblow to the *bul faale* movement and to confirm the state of political paralysis, with the socialist party remaining in power. In the end, the impoverished urban population, and especially the youth, who had hoped for a radical change (*sopi*), perceived a sign of a more promising destiny in Tyson's ultimate victory. The *bul faale* movement rapidly became the symbol of protest against the state and of the struggle against Abdou Diouf's socialist party.[5] A cultural and libertarian expression (the cult of the unveiled body represents a total rupture with the virtue of modesty upheld within Islam) transformed into a way of life for the young people, the *bul faale* has equally become a form of political reclamation for the generations since independence. Today, the *bul faale* belongs neither to any political party nor to any particular clientele: he strives to be a citizen open to the world.

The shege *of Kinshasa*

In contrast with the terms used for the youth movements in Addis Ababa and Dakar, *shege* is a cultural loan word. Derived from Schengen,[6] in the urban Congolese imaginary it denotes the condition of the clandestine migrant in the West or in Congo itself (Biaya, 1998a). The trajectory of the social disaster connoted by the trope *shege* is in fact misleading inasmuch as the term is a cultural concept. This appellation – which in 1993 was used to denote *phaseur*, street children, drug addicts and unemployed or homeless persons – has been extended to refer to all Kinshasa youth born since independence. Alone, this trope sums up the urbanity of Kinshasa based on a particular ambience (music, alcohol and easy sexuality) and geographical mobility. Kinshasa, the real source from which this culture has spread, has, of course, always been a mosaic of 'sub-cultures' (Biaya, 2000), but the figure of the *shege* of Matonge (a borough of Kinshasa) – despite its multiple variations and evolution over time – may be considered a unifying type representing the crisis.

This term *shege* took root in the Democratic Republic of Congo in the figures of popular protest against the power of the rich and influential. An epicurean, the *shege* is a '*viveur*' who thrives in times of crisis and whose typical pastime ('*kobenda kopo*' – drinking, and '*s'ambiancer*' – living it up) nonetheless remains subordinated to making money, by hook or by crook. His leisure space is none other than the *Vata Vata* bar (literally, the village courtyard), thus giving an allegorical signification to the villagization of Kinshasa (Devisch, 1995) and the banalization of death (Grootaerts, 1998). This culture is in reality the opposite of that of the *ambianceur* (Biaya, 1996), the sort of Kinshasa big shot and socialite that Yoka described in the manner of La Fontaine (Yoka, 1995). Nevertheless, the *shege* has achieved some renown both in his country and elsewhere due to *ndombolo*.

Ndombolo is a complex dance performed to frenetic and staccato rumba rhythms that mimes, with graphic pelvic movements, the copulative acts of an ape in rut; the ape is not well-liked by Kinshasa residents who consider it a gross animal. Erotic hip movements are accompanied by an imaginary dialogue, conducted in Swahili, between a child-soldier (*kadogo*) and an impudent and vulgar Kinshasa socialite whom he is threatening. The musical sequence ends with the socialite being put to death, which provokes cries of satisfaction from the other soldiers and disgust on the part of the Kinshasa citizens. Then the dance of the ape in rut is resumed to signify the victory of brute force

---

[5] This party later attempted to recruit Tyson and involve him in A. Diouf's election campaign; this effort never succeeded in convincing the youngest members.
[6] Referring to the town of Schengen in Luxembourg, where EU leaders signed a treaty abolishing the EU's internal frontiers.

over civility. On a first level, this pleasure-seeking animal who threatens an *ambianceur* seems to be living in an unreal world. Yet this reading is far from exhausting the formal significance of *ndombolo*, perhaps better revealed by an investigation of the sociological process of its production. When he invents the *ndombolo*, the *shege*, whether a real or an imaginary migrant, already possesses a past replete with illegality and violent confrontation with the public authorities, an experience that authorizes his inordinate audacity. This lascivious dance is a satire on the presidency and on Kabila's regime in its attempt to force the Kinshasa citizenry to bend to its martial logic. The simian personality, an allegorical image of the savage – one barely stripped by city life of his grosser habits – equally stigmatizes the recent invasion of Kinshasa by the *mbokatier*, the child-soldiers from the bush who attempt to bring order to the city by violence and murder in the name of the state. Currently associated with the *diasadiasa*, those who belong to the Congolese diaspora, they will gradually form a new dominant and exploitative class.

In overthrowing Mobutu – who, with Omar Bongo and Sassou Nguesso, was one of the primary figures of the *Sape*[7] – in the war of 1998, Kabila achieved the transformation of the culture of ambience and the *Sape*. For his part, by subverting order, the *shege* contests the chaotic democratic transition and the arrogance of the immigrant political class. Prudently, Kabila's censure (once the deeper signification of the *ndombolo* became evident) was restricted to denouncing the erotic and indecent aspects of the dance and subjecting it to derision. The *shege* of Kinshasa vividly reacted by expressing a form of violence, both identificational and expiatory, over against the foreign *kadogo*. Furthermore, the month of August 1998 was marked by hunting out all the Tutsi residents of Kinshasa. By liberating itself from the grip of the Tutsi, who at the time were strongly represented in the government, the Congolese political class was able to recover some of the legitimacy that had eluded it. Its return to favour with the Kinshasa populace was nonetheless marked by a multiplication of victims who had been subjected to the barbarous rite of rubber necklacing. The numerous corpses abandoned in the streets made for a macabre scene. Without interrupting either dance or song, the Kinshasa youth performed a sort of collective catharsis that consisted of repeatedly burning the cadavers as if to reaffirm the victory of the population of Kinshasa over the foreigner. The passivity shown by adults at such events goes far beyond any form of cathartic participation, for, according to the dominant animist African culture, incinerating a corpse denotes killing its soul and denying it any vestige of humanity. In fact, this practice is believed to interrupt the cycle of reincarnation and therefore access to the status of ancestor in the hereafter (Erny, 1992). Such acts of bestial violence were nonetheless saluted by the national authorities as a 'radical medication against the vermin' in order to 'save the fatherland from danger'. These scenes demonstrate the extent to which, from this point on, political violence moved beyond the symbolic universe of the *ndombolo*, thus depriving itself of any order and regulation, and generated a new nationalist community – allying executioners and victims, holders of power and poverty-stricken citizens. This new alliance was consecrated on the altar of the 'fatherland in danger' precisely through the *ndombolo*, and old rivalries were forgotten. This process of reinvention of the nation, founding itself in street culture and finding expression in a sort of mortuary ritual, served to reconstruct the identity of the young as real *Kinois*, citizens of Kinshasa.

---

[7] 'La société des ambianceurs et des personnes élégantes,' roughly, 'Society of fun-loving and elegant persons'.

Popular Reclamation and Identity Construction

The production of street culture reveals the disastrous socio-economic conditions and the structural violence in which young people grow up. They belong to the sacrificed generation who have no promise of a future, and this is in total contradiction to the stated objectives and the discourse of those who govern. For it is often against the state and their own society that the youth must live, making their own the popular maxim: *yamba match, match eza te* (roughly: create and seize the opportunity, whether illegal or not, because the law no longer functions). Illegality has become the norm for young people and their territory for affronting the permanent counter-violence of the state. The African city, bent under the weight of the postcolony, nonetheless offers young people two perspectives for escaping the crisis and affirming their identity.

The first is that of the 'syntonic' identity. The behaviour of the young person is here determined by the weight of a religious framework and social regulations more than by the quest for an ideal. The Ethiopian Orthodox Church, the older and newer Congolese churches, as well as Sufism in Senegal, all intervene in order to temper the revolt of youth against their inhuman condition. In their different ritualized practices, all of these institutions are able to convey an ideology of forgiveness and submission. Their respective structures for taking in and guiding young people offer the most deserving individuals – good Orthodox, 'born agains', fervent Mourides, Talibès, or mystic *baye fall* – opportunities for rehabilitation. In daily life, the 'syntonic' identity may be expressed by behaviours of humility, sharing and poverty. However, this monastic model no longer incites the enthusiasm of contemporary urban youth.

The second perspective is that of a 'syncinesic' identity, which is increasingly attractive to an ever-growing number of young people desirous of self-realization. The 'syncinesic' identity may be assimilated with an artistic endeavour of self-creation. It is expressed by particular procedures and an aesthetic with which new forms of sociability and cultural expression are associated, and constitutes a complete rupture with the dominant urban culture and the identity of the postcolonial city-dweller.

The logics contributing to the rupture

In the three cities under review, the logic behind the 'syncinesic' identity attests to the similarity of the practices of rupture and the processes of identity construction among the young. The first rupture is linked to the production of a veritable urban street culture based on life at the margins. The street then ceases to be a simple space of administrative or religious control and becomes, rather, a place of creative and recreative activity. In this space young people can simultaneously develop a mode of territorial control, a culture of illegality and a political base from which their actions take on a signification of opposition to the state, its project of dominance and its practices. Mastery of a territory, which sometimes implies recourse to violence, begins with the demarcation of a space and the definition of its uses. In an extreme case, as occurred in Brazzaville, this course of action resulted in the total partition of the city by rival militias who in the process killed a number of unarmed citizens for the sole purpose of proving their masculinity and urbanity (Bazenguissa-Ganga, 2000).

The production of a global youth culture comprises a combination of local and global cultural traits. The staging of the *shifta*, the *bul faale* and the *shege* tends, for example, to validate forms of individual and state violence by invoking the martial experience of trained youth. Young people have interiorized, first at school and later in the youth movements and involvement in political parties (*l'école du parti*), a certain number of nationalistic behaviours (saluting the flag, wearing a school uniform and learning history lessons that glorify the anticolonial struggle). In Ethiopia, thirty years of war have produced some two and a half million young refugees, militia members or demobilized soldiers who, in 1992, were all registered in programmes of reintegration (World Bank, 1993). This is certainly an extreme case and one quite different from the partisan uprisings that took place in Dakar in 1989 or in Kinshasa (1991-3 and 1998). Violence, however, is not only apprehended by virtue of its physical intensity: urban violence may equally be symbolic, taking its inspiration from traditional wrestling that represents the opposition not so much of two men as of two neighbourhoods or two social groups. All forms of struggle associate a pagan with a political aesthetic, through the exposure of two denuded bodies, as occurs in the dancing bodies of the *shege* or the *shifta*. Each type of performance presents violated bodies, in a tortured eroticism and imaginary, that equally symbolize the poverty and suffering of the human body at work in the domestic, and lawless, 'sub-urban' spaces.

Paradoxically, it is the same body that progressively recovers its place in society at large and the public space by way of the youth leisure culture. Behavioural, dress and musical codes are not only the prerogative of a social group, of a marginalized category of persons: these signs are able to ensconce themselves in a referential space, for the moment a privileged territory, before moving on to the conquest of other life milieux or countries. In this process of progressive globalization of street culture, the young person – breaking with all cultural and political streams and heritages – believes himself to be a demiurge, the creator of his own destiny. In this conquest, the figures of the *bul faale* and the *shege*, profoundly inspired by the colonial and postcolonial experience, have had considerably greater success than that of the far more localized *shifta*. The dreamed imaginary is indubitably at the heart of this process. The young person manages to circumvent the moral codes imposed by the society or the religious authorities, either by turning his back on them or by making them the objects of derision. In this light, the public consumption of tchat, the exposure of the body in *bul faale* or the erotic *ndombolo* dance all possess an obvious power of subversion and political protest.

The 'message' remains ambivalent, however. In expressing a fundamental rejection of any political instrumentalization of his body or youth, the young person indirectly recognizes the weights and the historical success of national structures. His very language is only acquired in the revolt against these institutions and against the past. The expressions employed by the young radically question the culture of Dakar's *sassouman* or Kinshasa's *ambianceur*, for whom the French language, arts and letters constitute a goal in and of themselves, an attitude Birima is made to castigate, from 1996 on, in his parodial rhetoric. Youssou N'Dour, for his part, saluted the transformation of the 'country man' into a 'city boy', the mixing of cultures and styles that came to be one of the specific characteristics of street culture. Nonetheless, this culture is unable to achieve maturity or gain any notoriety without the emergence of an emblematic group or person. When this requirement is met, and only then, is it possible to believe in its ultimate victory over cultures inherited from a colonial or national project.

These acts of rupture clearly indicate that young people have had enough of the older social and political logics that bound the postcolonial urban culture to the yoke of the established religions, ethnicity, political parties, the state and urban African (post)colonial sociability. This process quite obviously does not occur without evoking resistance and difficulties in adjustment. And here, without a doubt, resides the challenge to this new youth culture itself: how to ensure its own reproduction (historical and social) and transmission. The former inevitably takes place in a permanent confrontation with the hegemonic system, now in a state of decomposition, under the combined effects of globalization and the politics of structural adjustment. Indeed, these factors guarantee street culture the conflictual instability necessary for its own survival.

The driving elements of street culture

Having only recently emerged, street culture has generated an epistemological rupture that every researcher must recognize: the end of decolonization and the appearance of 'localized globalization' (Meyer and Geschiere, 1998). Here the quest for gratification and diversion is not a goal in itself. On the contrary, young people seek to break with a weighty social historicity and escape from a postcolonial vision imposed from outside. In the cities studied here, the socialized customs (the tea and coffee ceremonies or the gesture of 'grabbing a beer') are thus remodelled in a fashion that has no resemblance to the sort of contemporary 'ethnographic' and exotic presentations that are often transmitted through the media (tourist brochures, for example). These are the aspects of street culture that create the rupture.

The appearance of new social forms among young people, inasmuch as they flirt with illegality and a certain marginality, clearly represents their rupture with the ethnographic, public and political logics. The more or less violent provocations and reclamations of the youth, far from restricting themselves to the domestic spaces, gradually invade the public space. In turn they invoke an insidious, and at times even violent, reaction on the part of the state apparatus. Mobutu, for example, would often invite his opponents to join him around a 'sweet' or a cup of tea before attacking them violently (Biaya, 1998). In Dakar, politicians have taken to buying off idle young people by inviting them to share in a 'tea ceremony' and join their political programme. Drinks, diverted from their first function, are thus discovered to be quite useful for the purposes of policing and politicizing the youth. Conscious of the risk of manipulation, the latter, of course, attempt to deflect the purposes of the 'drink' or postpone the encounter. The preparation of tea or coffee evidently provides a unique occasion for discussion, exchange and preparation for change.

In the city, the new images of the young person are clearly distinct from those of the 1960s and 1970s, which were most notably marked by the modernization of traditional African cultures. Beyond a certain physical similarity, beyond a certain political or cultural proximity, the *shifta*, for example, conveys a metaphor quite different from that of the Rasta or the Jamaican immigrant from Chacamane whose traits symbolically refer to the *nyabhinghi*, the lion-hunter or emperor's dancer. The Rasta, nourished in modern Ethiopian philosophy, is a domesticated *shifta* having broken with the ancient Ethiopian martial culture. His reclamatory political modernity is nonetheless indisputable. Inversely, the dress, hair style and musical tastes of young Ethiopians indicate a Western influence. With regard to music, for example, one finds that the *soukous* is easily accompanied by high life in passing through jive, rai, American hip-hop, rock, reggae, rap and Ethiopian music from the United States (Aster Awake or Gigi). The hair styles of the young *shifta* – close-cut, foamed or short dreadlocks – are quite distinct from Rasta styles. Where the 'Tyson cut' (shaved head) is quite popular in Dakar or Kinshasa, it is rarely seen in Addis Ababa (Biaya, 1998b). The Rasta style is clearly on the wane. The consumption of *ganja* is also much lower today than that of tchat, and is socially downgraded. In distinction to the *shifta*, Rasta is in fact perceived as a foreign element, deviant and dangerous.

In Dakar, the 'cool pose,' in Senegalese fashion – again distinct from the Afro-American version – is becoming quite the rage. This posture is rooted in the deaf violence of the religion and the democratic state, which are enveloped in a complicitous silence (*teranga*) that has now become established as a social rule; the renewal of traditional Muslim music is a good indicator of this state of affairs (McLaughlin, 1997). For certain young people, the tea ceremony is a pretext to take on new poses and attitudes inspired by the cultural models spread by the media and the *moddu moddu*, the transnational traders and fervent disciples of the Mouride marabouts. In contrast to these young adepts of rural origin, the *bul faale* abandon the *boubou* robe for trousers, shirt and the 'Tyson cut', and adopt a language permeated with Anglicisms. Here, one is far removed from preceding generations who were still proud of their primary-school graduate president who identified himself with his intellectual career, undertook his project for society and bowed to the edicts of Islam. Today, the enthusiasm of many of Dakar's youth is only raised with the prospect of erotic dances in the street (*sabar* and *arwatam*) that are just as quickly converted into *lembeul* in the nightclubs.

For their part, the fashionable youth of Kinshasa, or the *shege*, no longer play the dandy as did the real *sapeurs* who frequented the 'Boul'Miche' (the Boulevard Saint-Michel in Paris) or certain Italian or Japanese fashion designers. Impoverished, a young man in today's Kinshasa purchases his attire at the *tombola bwaka*, the second-hand clothing market. Next, with the help of a local tailor, he redesigns his own outfit and has a label copying that of a famed fashion designer affixed to it. Only then will he appear in public. Inspired by his peers in Dakar or Addis Ababa, he adopts a minimalist hair style dyed in vivid colours – yellow, called '*à la* Jospin' and red, '*à la* Rodman'[8] – that came to denote, in the Mobutu transition, the victory of the people over the dictator. The *shege* is therefore the bearer of an ideal of national transformation.

These three examples perfectly illustrate the importance of cultural loans and the capacity of the young people to reconstruct a popular culture and reappropriate their own destiny. One requires neither financial nor political means in order to amuse oneself and live freely; occupying the space of the street is sufficient. A simple presence and the cultural originality of their expressions guarantee an undeniable mediatic resonance. Their power of cultural expression constitutes the sole local power in a space left vacant by the dominant social categories. Their diverse figures of contestation, real or imaginary, siphon off an ever greater number of followers and serve as a founding pillar of a new identity for the city-dweller.

The second factor common to the three cities is the telling growth of urban violence and the legal counter-violence of the state. The violence perpetrated by the youth is undoubtedly in large measure linked to the crisis of educational models, implying a restructuring of the communitarian way of life. The young person is today brutally propelled into adulthood and is most often subordinated to and victimized by his elders and the reigning political powers. Street violence therefore serves him as an initiatory model, with all the risks that this implies for the society (El-Kenz, 1995). When a bankruptcy of pedagogical models is compounded by a 'corporalist' military framework, as is the case with certain sub-Saharan countries, street violence is further reinforced. In the hit parade of urban violence, the laurels go to Kinshasa, followed by Dakar, while Addis Ababa trails

---

[8] L. Jospin incarnated the opposition of the French Left against President Chirac, while D. Rodman represented the struggle against the moral order and American conformism (see Biaya, 1998).

far behind. On the other hand, Ethiopia has for decades practised an enforced recruitment of young people: in 1983 the Revolutionary Ethiopian Youth Association (REYA) counted 2.8 million youth organized in urban literacy brigades or in militias and military units having fought in Somalia, Sudan or Eritrea (ILO, 1987). Yet how does one explain the apparent passivity of the youth in Dakar or Addis that contrasts so sharply with the violence of Kinshasa? By a greater liberty of expression (greater consumption of alcohol, drugs and so on) or by what might be termed an attitude of psychological containment? The jury is still out on this question.

Escaping Postcolonial Logics

In Africa each age class bears its own identity, its particular forms of expression. A gap undoubtedly exists between groups of individuals who were born before or at the time when most of these countries gained their independence and those who may be called 'children of the crisis'. The very deficiencies of the global context have favoured the emergence of a 'syncinesic' identity prone to rupture. It won much terrain in almost all countries because it bore within it a new cultural aesthetic compiled of cultural loans, postures and games.

To begin with, in Africa, the notion of 'urban youth' itself deserves scrutiny inasmuch as it contains certain ambiguities. In the industrialized countries, the childhood phase quite logically precedes that of adolescence even if the boundaries are at times somewhat vague. In Africa, if the child can be said to occupy a privileged place, the situation and role of the young person are, in contrast, very poorly defined and highly relativized by culture and education. Adolescence begins very early and represents little more than a rapid transition between childhood and adulthood. This characteristic certainly plays a part in the crisis of identities and the violence to which the youngest are submitted, particularly outside the familial sphere. In the context of the far-reaching crisis affecting many African countries, the young person is often reduced to constructing his identity against communities and the group rather than being able to rely on them as a foundation on which he might build. However, it is only in the street that violence occurs in the absence of any form of mediation or regulation.

I shall not return here to the controversy regarding the concept of a 'street culture,'[9] one that has profoundly divided researchers, it must be said. Present methods of managing urban areas, forms of sociability and the permanence of institutional violence all allow us to conjecture that the concept possesses a real pertinence in Africa. The uncertain socio-political context and the precariousness of living conditions, far from weakening the desire for rupture or individualization among the youth, have tended rather to reinforce them. Imprisoned in the margins of society, a minority of young people have opted for a 'syntonic' identity, while all the others have preferred to embrace the 'syncinesic' identity, and sometimes violent protest. Street culture exists and no doubt possesses a future, since the conditions of its survival (poverty and oppression) are far from disappearing (UNDP, 1998).

Another specific aspect of the African city resides in the connections that may be established between different forms of violence – most notably that between urban petty

[9] This debate has only commenced in the reviews and publications of the research centres and institutions dealing with street children. See *Cahiers de Marjuvia* (EHESS); Enda Tiers-Monde (Dakar); IFRA, Ibadan; Unicef and so on. Also see Anon, 1996.

delinquency (Hérault and Adesanmi, 1997) and the armed violence of the militias (Reno, 1999; Richards, 1996). A budding 'syncinesic' identity among young people often feeds on these phenomena. Addis Ababa experienced this in the years of the red terror in 1976-7: thousands of youth and their parents or friends either killed or were killed at that time. Then it was Dakar's turn with the explosion of rage directed against immigrant Mauritanians resulting in many killings. Kinshasa also had its day during the failed invasion of the Uganda-Rwandan army (in August 1998), and that after having suffered through the terror of the 'owls' during the abortive democratic transition (1990-7) (De Villers and Omasombo, 1997). But the violence of Brazzaville in 1997 remains the most emblematic case of this composite brutality, there perpetrated by gangs of youths whose names reveal the grip of global culture (the Ninjas, Cobras or Cocoyes). In this case the youth exploited a multi-dimensional crisis and open violence in order to position themselves as political actors (Bazenguissa-Ganga, 2000) and thus harvest the fruits of a certain economic growth from which they had long been deprived by preceding generations. This form of urban predation also reflects the complex nature of geographical and sociological margins and the means available to young people for the appropriation of urban territories. Finally, it accounts for the decay of the state and the privatization of political resources (Mbembe, 1999). The mass mutilations perpetrated in Sierra Leone – rivalling the planned horror of Rwanda – demonstrate the extreme complexity of street culture and its intrinsic forms of violence.

In urban Africa, street culture appears to represent a struggle to transcend postcolonial and nationalist logics, and this is a struggle in which victory is hardly assured. Case studies have been devoted to showing how the formative process of street culture reproduces and extends, rather than throttling, the destructuring effects of the socio-economic and political contexts onto the city and the individual. The 'syncinesic' identity generated by this structural violence is evidently the product of transnationalism and globalization, which in turn legitimate the violence. In the three cities dealt with here, the choice of different cultural loans reveals a veritable rhetoric of violence at odds with each society. This violence fluctuates in the functioning of its modes of political, physical and cultural expression: the erotic production of the 'beautiful body desired and adorned' itself produces violence, but the exposed body is equally mutilating and sometimes mutilated. This over-valuation of the body justifies certain inhuman disciplinary practices in order to obtain and justify behaviours that are morally unacceptable (Honwana, 1999). At the limit, the body cannot attain beauty except by means of an aesthetic of dismemberment of the body of the other.

In many aspects, finally, street culture – a confirmation of the end of decolonization – prefigures what will be the new urban memory. The episteme of the commandment (Bayart et al., 1992; Mbembe, 2000) has in part vanished with the hoped-for end of the dictatorships, yet it has poured its venom on youth and on the street. Its disappearance has revealed what, for four decades, were the chimera that fed both the hopes and the conflicts of the continent: the struggles for independence, nationalism, developmentalist policies, the transfer of technology, globalization and structural adjustment programmes. A new episteme has yet to be identified and deliberated. Nonetheless, the logic of rupture and re-invention of identity has already produced new urban logics and new modes of expression and action. To be young and urban in Africa is a challenge that unquestionably deserves to be taken up.

References

Anon. 1996. 'Du côté de la rue', *Politique africaine* 63 (October).

Anon. 2000. 'Coffe, Tea and Tchat', *Ethiopia Seven Days Update* 7 (22): 1-2.

Barber, K. (ed.). 1997. *Readings in African Popular Culture*. Oxford/Bloomington, IN: James Currey/Indiana University Press.

Bayart, J.-F., A. Mbembe & C. Toulabor. 1992. *Le Politique par le bas en Afrique noire. Contributions à une problématique de la démocratie*. Paris: Karthala.

Bazenguisse-Ganga, R. 2000. 'The Popularization of Political Violence in the Congo', *Codesria Bulletin* 1: 55–9.

Bazenguissa-Ganga, R. & P. Yengo. 1999. 'La popularisation de la violence au Congo', *Politique africaine* 73 (May).

Berhanou, A. 1998. *Histoire de l'Ethiopie d'Axoum à la révolution* Paris: Maisonneuve et Larose/Centre français des études éthiopiennes.

Bertrand, M. 1998. 'Villes africaines, modernités en question', *Revue Tiers Monde* 39 (156): 885–904.

Biaya, T.K. 1996. 'La culture urbaine dans les arts populaires d'Afrique. Analyse de "l'ambiance" za"roise', *Revue canadienne des études africaines* 30 (2): 336–70.

— 1998a. 'Dynamique des performances et discours identitaires: espace d'énonciation dans la diaspora africaine', *Etude de la population africaine/African Population Studies*. 14 (2): 1–29.

— 1998b. 'Hair Statements in Urban Africa: the Beauty, the Mystic and the Madman', in *The African Art Fashion*, ed. van der Plas & Els. The Hague: The Prince Claus Funds.

— 2000. *Le Jeune, la rue et la violence à Kinshasa. Entendre, comprendre, décrire*. Dakar: Codesria.

De Villers, G. & J. Omasombo. 1997. 'Za"re: la transition manquée, 1990-1997', *Cahiers africains*: 27-9.

Devisch, R. 1995. 'Frenzy, Violence and Ethical Renewal', *Public Culture*.

Diouf, M. 1992. 'Fresques murales et écriture de l'histoire: le set/setal à Dakar', *Politique africaine* 46 (June).

El-Kenz, A. 1995. 'Les jeunes et la violence', in *L'Afrique maintenant*, ed. S. Ellis. Paris: Karthala.

Erny, P. 1992. *L'Enfant et son milieu en Afrique noire*. Paris: Payot.

Grootaers, J.-L. (ed.). 1998. 'Mort et maladie au Za"re', *Cahiers africains*: 31-2.

Hérault, G. & P. Adesanmi (eds) 1997. *Les Jeunes, la culture de la rue et la violence urbaine/Youth, Street Culture and Urban Violence*. Ibadan: IFRA.

Honwana, A. 1999. 'Negotiating Post-war Identity: Child Soldiers in Mozambique and Angola', *Bulletin du Codesria*. 1-2: 4–13.

International Labour Organization (ILO). 1987. *Youth Employment and Youth Employment Programmes in Africa. A Comparative Study*. Report on the Regional Workshop, 24-28 November 1986, Buea, Cameroon. Addis Ababa: JASPA.

Jewsiewicki, B. (ed). 1987. *Art populaire et politique en Afrique noire/Popular Art and Politics in Black Africa*. Québec: SAFI.

Le Bris, E. (co-ord.). 1999. 'Espaces publics municipaux ', *Politique africaine*, 74 (June).

Marchal, R. 1993. 'Les mooryaan de Mogadiscio. Formes de la violence dans un espace urbain en guerre', *Cahier d'études africaines* 32 (30).

Mbembe, A. 1999. *Du Gouvernement privé indirect*. Dakar: Codesria.

— 2000. *De la postcolonie*. Paris: Karthala.

McLaughlin, F. 1997. 'Islam and Popular Music in Senegal: the Emergence of a "New Tradition"', *Africa* 67 (4): 560–81.

Meyer, B. & P. Geschiere (eds). 1998. 'Globalisation and Identity. Dialectics of Flows and Closures', *Development and Change* 29 (4).

Reno, W. 1999. *Warlord Politics and African State*. Boulder, CO: Lynne Rienner.

Richards, P. 1996. *Fighting for the Rain Forest: Youth, War and Resources in Sierra Leone*, London/Portsmouth, NH: James Currey/Heinemann.

Rosset, G. 1997. *Michel Leiris à Gondar d'après 'L'Afrique fantôme'* (trad. Berhanou Abébé). Addis Ababa: Maison des études éthiopiennes, ambassade de France.

Simone, A. 1998. *Urban Change in Africa*. Dakar: Codesria.

UNDP. 1998. *Overcoming Human Poverty, UNDP Poverty Report*. New York: UNDP.

World Bank. 1993. *Ethiopia. Economy, Population, Health*. East Africa Office Report. Nairobi: World Bank.

Yoka, L.M. 1995. 'Lettres d'un Kinois à l'oncle du village', *Cahiers africains* 15.

Zewde, Bahru. 1996. *A History of Modern Ethiopia, 1855-1974*. London/Athens, OH/Addis Ababa: James Currey/Ohio University Press/Addis Ababa University Press.

Afterword

MAMADOU DIOUF

In the context of the contemporary African situation, young people find themselves taking a triple posture with regard to an environment marked by crises whose causes, forms and consequences are very diverse. They have in fact become the actors, resources and principal 'stakes' of social movements that have turned African societies back upon themselves.

The twisted itineraries they follow, in their behaviours or the means, whether licit or illicit, by which they seek to become a part of the given social structures, either formal or informal, serve to explore their own futures as well as to interrogate society at large. In both their violent interventions and artistic expression, musical, plastic or otherwise, African youth sketch their own economic inventiveness, communitarian engagement, religious appropriations and political allegiances. They achieve this by way of a grand and yet incomplete novel design for social geography that simultaneously struggles to conform itself to the contemporary world – that of globalization – and to extract itself, however brutally, from the vernacular orders of indigenous modernities.

African young people constitute 'stakes' in the sense that other groups seek to capture them and proclaim them as a particular measure of the success of a society, state or nation. They have seen themselves assigned the double role of fulfilling the project of the emancipation of the continent, of finally bringing it out of the colonial situation, and of placing African states within the orbit of economic development, political democracy and social justice. Thus, through education, youth were to become the instrument of modernization. Bearers of the double promise of national independence and social and economic development, they therefore bore the charge of cultural renewal at the same time as they were subjected to the injunctions of the ancestral African culture. This double concern for the modern state and the implacable tyranny of the ancestors seems to have been at the heart of the paradox of postcolonial African societies of the period between the 1960s and the 1980s. This was expressed in the wave of single-party governments as well as the strict logics of training and 'caporalization' or tight control of the youth and youth movements. These modes of organization were dominated by the quasi-systematic recourse to force and to violence.

Beginning with their organization as movements and the definition of their respective roles, those young people who demonstrated capabilities with regard to the enterprise of social and economic development became metamorphosed into political resources and leaders in the contemporary social, economic and political struggles.

As things turned out for the period indicated above, African youth became the primary victim of public and private violence in that they were largely marginalized as political forces in the public arena and completely bridled in the economic space, espe-

229

cially the young women. This is borne out by the testimony of the terrible repression of the student movements that peaked with the bloody settling of scores following the military *coup* in Ethiopia and the revolutionary movements beginning in 1974 – the silent violence imposed on the rural youth by the state and the traditional authorities and the manifestations of a patriarchal authoritarianism aimed at achieving greater control over girls and women just at the moment when, in most African countries, they were beginning to find their own feet in the marketplace of salaried labour.

The opinions held of youth that have been so carefully documented and analyzed in the excellent collection that Alcinda Honwana and Filip de Boeck have provided perfectly illustrate the relevance and richness of the approach maintained by the various authors of the essays to be found here. The very title of the work, emblematic as it is, reflects this admirably. Indeed, beyond the representations of youth made by adults and policy-makers, we must consider their physical pain and the suffering inscribed on their bodies. On the one hand, their very bodies were tested by their engagement and commitment to the causes held dear by the founding fathers of the new African nations whose ground-rules were the imposition of an authoritarian framework, an unquestioning conformity to party precepts, and an unreserved physical investment in the service of the nation, bringing them either reward or sanction. On the other hand, it seems that it was in their minds already configured by forms of traditional initiation for insertion into the family, the ethnic or religious community, or by modern forms for conformity to the State, the Nation, the Party, or the Father of independence that the imagined future of African societies was played out by those in positions of leadership.

As several of the essays demonstrate, the imperative and categorical character of such prescriptions directly led to the recourse to violence. The failure of the promise of independence, the dramatic vicissitudes of the economic crisis, political struggles, civil wars or simply the relentless harassment of the police and state security forces were signs of the extraordinary human and psychological cost paid by youth at each moment, whatever the cause of the conflict, whether they were the heroes, like the 'young lions' of South Africa in the face of the repressive machine of apartheid, or the delinquents and vagabonds, as one might find in the Sierra Leonean, Liberian, Congolese or Mozambican contexts (see Peters and Richards, 1998; Abdullah and Bangura, 1997; Honwana, 1999). Naturally there arose in the more painful manifestations, sometimes vain and often mortal, of youth dreams of a departure towards a hereafter, a somewhere beyond Africa, that affirmed the act of fleeing a continent without hope (*The Economist*, 2000). On these symptoms, which have been understood as an imperceptible return to a state of barbarity, are thus superimposed a fascination for the success of the West which, in most cases, proved to be an insane if not fatal option.

As a result, the Straits of Gibraltar has become a vast cemetery of sea-faring emigrants in search of receptive shores and the wheel compartments of airplanes the last refuge of candidates hoping to take off.

By losing the privileged place that was accorded them by the nationalist discourse, young people are able to escape the nationalist construct and its time, with all its attendant precepts and strict control over the distribution of rights and goods. Although they may be considered today's warriors and actors, constituting essential resources for the construction of the future and for the restoration of identities confiscated in the course of the colonial night, they have lost their place and function at the centre of society and now find themselves at the margins, feared, calumniated and avoided. In these marginal territories or in the clearings left by a state that finds itself obliged to loosen its totalitarian grip and political straitjacket because of economic bankruptcy, African youth have gone about piecing together their own geography and a narrative that attributes to them a new meaning and significance. The foundation of this narrative is precisely the radical questioning of the nationalist discourse, of its imaginary and the totality of its texts, whether economic, political or cultural.

In the face of their elders' pretensions to dictate the law and assure their domination of all the social registers, young people have elaborated dissident and dissonant cultures and civilities in the fissures of the social edifice. Socially and ideologically in the minority, yet forming the demographic majority, they fracture the public space or simply bypass it in creating alternative spaces that make African cities at times ungovernable or even taking outright control over some neighbourhoods.

Out of the whirlwind in which Africa finds itself and the diverse ways in which youth participate in the movement of globalization, with all its gaps and disjunctions, cultures and civilities are invented that rearticulate social organizations, the frameworks of life and death and new forms of socialization. These original creations put forward alternative proposals for the future of the continent that go beyond not only mere physical emigration but also the mental disarticulation and the erasure of the social imaginaries associated with Africa. These movements are combined with the adoption of new rules, the expression of new desires, the manifestation of new aspirations that adults could have conceived of only through violence. The voice of youth, however deformed, and the masks it takes – music, plastic arts, sport and fashions, for example – appear to have favoured the appearance of volatile and shady figures who consistently escape the gaze of the adults. At the same time, a common language and a profound malaise have been constructed which provide a source of creativity and innovation, while sparking off violent dissidence and destructive aberrations.

In a way one is witnessing the end of the representation of youth by adults. The prescriptions of the latter have given way to the self-assertion of young people, and the self-realization of their own desires and aspirations. In becoming the producers and writers of their own dramatic narratives, they have opened themselves up to the world and are overloading the national vernacular space with notions and customs from the outside. By thus widening the fissures of the social edifice, they position themselves doubly as both threat and promise, while definitively excluding the nationalist and pan-African narratives and with them their attributes, biographies and times. In the face of that cruel reality of the subjection of African economies to structural adjustment, they substitute for this an 'elsewhere,' either near or distant, and the illusions of economic globalization. Life such as this in a geographical 'in-between' between the African reality and the Euro-American dream has been admirably described by a young African novelist. Addressing the Congolese situation, he writes:

[France] was the distant country, inaccessible despite its fireworks that lit up the least of my dreams and, when I awoke, left me with a taste of honey in my mouth. True enough, I secretly cultivated, in the field of my reveries, the wish of crossing the Rubicon, of someday going there. It was an ordinary wish, hardly original, that everyone entertained. Who of my generation had not visited France 'by mouth', as it was so delicately put in my country? One single word, Paris, was sufficient to find ourselves, as if enchanted, gazing on the Eiffel Tower, the Arc de Triomphe or the Champs Elysées. Boys of my age tantalized the girls with the refrain: 'I'm going to Paris soon; I'll be living in the centre of Paris.' No one could prevent us from dreaming. It cost nothing. It required no visa, passport or plane ticket. Just to think of it, close one's eyes, fall asleep and snore away and one was there every night (Mabanckou, 1998: 36).

In this novel we encounter the ever-present variations on the theme of night in the repertory of images held of youth, of nightlife, of illicit activities and the desertion of the public space with its diurnal geography.

The geography of urban violence in its delinquent, sexist, political or military forms, as has been sketched by the contributions making up this volume, paints a brilliant portrait of a population caught in the vice of the patriarchal and gerontocratic authoritarianism of social and political indigenous traditions, on one side, and the imperatives of globalization, on the other. Their simultaneous decline, in an environment directed by institutional improvisation and the disintegration of the structures of socialization and education, on the one hand, and, on the other, the disordered and unstable redefinition of life stages, notably the passage from childhood to adulthood, opened up previously unknown opportunities to circumvent the given norms and prescriptions and to disregard the rites of passage and boundaries between childhood, adolescence and majority.

The ludicrous price attached to life and the right to mutilate, take lives or rape, combined with the apparition of a small minority of 'golden boys' of the 'dot com' generation, signalled the closure of the classic anthropological descriptions of elderhood and junior status, of the ordered and strategic circulation of women as reinforcement of the social institution, of a communitarian civility and the expert mastery of sorcery, or of African, Western or Eastern spiritualities as well. What one is thus witnessing is an explosive fusion of the visible and the invisible signalling the emergence of societies abandoned by God.[1]

Is it possible to account for African youth other than by calling on divine parables, the reprise and transcription of multiple registers that are often inaudible yet always raw and aggressive? Is it possible to escape the euphoria of their impossible dreams expressed in a lyric without borders, to resist the profound pain of their songs? Are we equipped not only to listen but also to understand and to propose solutions? One might define the complex challenge with which we are faced by adding yet another question to those already posed: how does one account for the pain and misery that present themselves as the most significant means of revealing the identities of youth in contemporary Africa? Must this analysis first address the places and connections that frame these identities in order to detect the points of social anchoring or loosening, or should it pose the question of the progressive inabilities of African societies totally overrun by their youth – youth who have embraced irregular ways and adopted dissident and unconventional practices that transport them toward worlds where Africa is either absent or ignored?

In such conditions, is it not illusory to interpret the condition of youth through the eyes of nations, states, governments and sometimes ethnic groups that now appear to have lost their dual functions as focal points of identity and purveyors of narratives serving to legitimate the social order?

The majority of texts presented in this collection that reconstitutes with a rare finesse for us the narratives of youth, summon us to ask precisely what it is that experiences of marginalization, violence, and social and economic exclusion reveal. Do these reconstitutions open up for us the plural worlds of youth? Can they offer us a key for identifying and tracing the tortured trajectories of youth? In sum, must one lend an ear to, or let oneself be persuaded to listen to, both the pain and the actions of actors who are often forgotten or labelled as immature? How, after all, can one be young in today's Africa? Is it possible, and at what price?

In the diversity of voices this collection makes heard and in the readings it proposes, the authors challenge us regarding the various imaginaries at work on the African continent. One can encounter such imaginaries as much among the producers, the images, the representations and the desires they give rise to as in the shock of the clashes between indigenous and cosmopolitan figures as they are lived out on a rickety stage.

---

[1] This is at least the ironic and tragic reading proposed by Amadou Kourouma in *Allah n'est pas obligé*. Paris Le Seuil, 2000.

This book spreads before us a series of arabesques that portray the presence of young Africans in the temporality of the world at large (*le temps du monde*). Active and passive at the same time, they trace the painful and costly, in terms of life and material, end to the age of colonization whose postcolonial moment disintegrates before our eyes in the din, the furore and the murderous and destructive violence of a generation that neither finds itself in the position of heir nor senses any vocation to realize the prophecies of national independence or development, and even less to restore the personality and historicity of African societies.

This volume tells us, undoubtedly in a contorted, almost inaudible and clandestine manner, and in words the authors struggle to capture, reveal and display, that what is at stake is the very 'future of tradition' (Diagne, 1922). To be sure, this is a tradition that invents and produces itself in the temporality of the world at large, in the multiplicity of its modernities, the apparent singularity of its space, and the power of its connections and networks. For young Africans, caught today between the acceleration and the disintegration of the African world and its dreams, images and histories that they re-enact on the screens of the world where a permanent dialogue with others is occurring, the corset of the continental geography, its history and its imaginary are giving way to the thrust of spaces whose territoriality and historicity transmute global centres into the periphery and vice versa. Paris and New York thus become suburbs of Dakar and Douala, Chicago of Lagos, Indianapolis of Kinshasa, Turin of Touba, and so on.

How is one able to follow these shifting conjunctures, the discourses of citizenship, of belonging, of commitment and of social and political morality, while the spaces of their development, like the places of life and death of the actors, have lost their magical qualities, whether ancestral, religious, communitarian, political, ethnic or otherwise?

What, if not the magic of words and practice, is left that would allow one to traverse the minefields, real or symbolic, to obtain a visa or successfully cross the Straits of Gibraltar that separate Africa from the Euro-American Eden? Or what drives another to take the clandestine path that leads to pillage in all its forms, appropriating to oneself the means to inflict pain, to murder or gamble one's life away, thus abolishing youth as a transitory stage in a long itinerary whose future is the sublime moment of achievement? Not a life to be lived in the future! Better a life to live, here and now, even if it means, simultaneously banishing the time to come, and a strong disdain for the past and the memories associated with it.

Thus chronology and genealogy are together placed in the balance. In any case, the jumble of the indigenous and global temporalities and trajectories that combine in subjecting African societies to unsuspected metamorphoses, under pressures emanating essentially from the youth, signal an opening for new opportunities whose nature and significations are as yet poorly legible.

This book takes on the task of decrypting these significations and indicates the new fields of work to be opened up and the new objects for study. To engage in this task, with a determination and lucidity equal to those of the authors of the different contributions making up this work, is to participate, I believe, in constructing the African side of the developing dialogue concerning youth within the social sciences. This book witnesses to the capacity of researchers engaged in African studies to take their place as significant actors in this field.

References

Abdullah, I. & Y. Bangura (eds). 1977. 'Lumpen Youth Culture and Political Violence: The Sierrea Leone Civil War, Special issue *African Development* 23 (3–4).

Diagne, Souleymane Bachir. 1922. 'L'Avenir de la Tradition', in *Sénégal. Trajectoires de l'Etat*. ed. M.C. Diop. Dakar: Codesria.

Economist, The. 2000. 'The Hopeless Continent', 13 May.

Honwana, A. 1999. 'Negotiating Post-war Identities: Child Soldiers in Mozambique and Angola', *CODESRIA Bulletin*, 1–2.

Kourouma, Amadou. 2000. *Allah n'est pas obligé*. Paris: Le Seuil.

Mabanckoou, Alain. 1998. *Bleu, Blanc, Rouge*. Paris: Présence Africaine.

Peters, K. & P. Richards. 1988. 'Jeunes combattants parlant de la guerre et de la paix en Sierra Leone', *Cahiers d'Etudes Africaines* 39: 150–2, 581–617.

Index

Lightning Source UK Ltd.
Milton Keynes UK
UKOW051538010213

205721UK00001B/7/P